Reth

Student Collection
Seven Day Loan

Return date

Since th·   r
politics   ·l
interest
  Japan   -
tion. Pe·   t
only tra·   e
book's f·   y
approach   e
and dipl   s
in recog   t
analytic·
  Addit   t
explores   ·o
date. Th   ·f
Japanes·

Peter J.   ·l
Studies ·

Books may be renewed online or telephone (01206 873187)
unless they have been recalled.

University of Essex

Security and Governance Series

Edited by Fiona B. Adamson, School of Oriental and African Studies, University of London
Roland Paris, University of Ottawa
Stefan Wolff, University of Nottingham

This series reflects the broadening conceptions of security and the growing nexus between the study of governance issues and security issues. The topics covered in the series range from issues relating to the management of terrorism and political violence, non-state actors, transnational security threats, migration, borders, and "homeland security" to questions surrounding weak and failing states, post-conflict reconstruction, the evolution of regional and international security institutions, energy and environmental security, and the proliferation of WMD. Particular emphasis is placed on publishing theoretically-informed scholarship that elucidates the governance mechanisms, actors and processes available for managing issues in the new security environment.

Rethinking Japanese Security
Internal and external dimensions
Peter J. Katzenstein

State building and International Intervention in Bosnia
Roberto Belloni

The UN Security Council and the Politics of International Authority
Edited by Bruce Cronin and Ian Hurd

Rethinking Japanese Security

Internal and external dimensions

Peter J. Katzenstein

Routledge
Taylor & Francis Group

LONDON AND NEW YORK

First published 2008
by Routledge
2 Park Square, Milton Park, Abingdon, Oxon OX14 4RN

Simultaneously published in the U.S.A and Canada
by Routledge
270 Madison Ave, New York, NY 10016

Routledge is an imprint of the Taylor & Francis Group, an informa business

© 2008 Peter J. Katzenstein

Typeset in Garamond by
RefineCatch Limited, Bungay, Suffolk
Printed and bound in Great Britain by
TJ International Ltd, Padstow, Cornwall

British Library Cataloguing in Publication Data
A catalogue record for this book is available from the British Library

Library of Congress Cataloging in Publication Data
Katzenstein, Peter J.
Rethinking Japanese security : internal and external dimensions /
Peter J. Katzenstein.
p. cm. – (Security and governance series)
Includes bibliographical references and index.
ISBN 978–0–415–77394–2 (hardback : alk. paper) –
ISBN 978–0–415–77395–9 (pbk. : alk. paper) –
ISBN 978–0–203–92874–5 (e-book : alk. paper)
1. National security–Japan. 2. Terrorism–Government policy–Japan.
I. Title.
UA845.K377 2008
355'.033052–dc22
2007042300

ISBN10: 0–415–77394–6 (hbk)
ISBN10: 0–415–77395–4 (pbk)
ISBN10: 0–203–92874–1 (ebk)

ISBN13: 978–0–415–77394–2 (hbk)
ISBN13: 978–0–415–77395–9 (pbk)
ISBN13: 978–0–203–92874–5 (ebk)

For Mary

Contents

List of contributors

H. Richard Friman is Eliot Fitch Chair for International Studies, Professsor of Political Science, Coordinator for the Interdisciplinary Major in International Affairs, and Director of the Institute for Transnational Justice at Marquette University.

Christopher Hemmer is an associate professor of International Security Studies at the Air War College and is the author of *Which Lessons Matter? American Foreign Policy Decision Making in the Middle East, 1979–1987* (State University of New York Press, 2000).

Peter J. Katzenstein is the Walter S. Carpenter, Jr, Professor of International Studies at Cornell University.

David Leheny is the Henry Wendt III '55 Professor of East Asian Studies at Princeton University. He is the author of *Think Global, Fear Local* and *The Rules of Play*, both published by Cornell University Press.

Nobuo Okawara is Professor of Political Studies, Faculty of Law and Graduate School of Social and Cultural Studies, Kyushu University.

Rudra Sil is Associate Professor of Political Science at the University of Pennsylvania. His publications include *Managing "Modernity:" Work, Community, and Authority in Late-Industrializing Japan and Russia* (2002) and *Reconfiguring Institutions across Time and Space* (2007, co-edited with Dennis Galvan).

Yutaka Tsujinaka is Vice-President, and Professor in the Graduate School of Humanities and Social Sciences, University of Tsukuba. He serves as the editor of the Civil Society and Interest Groups in Contemporary World Series (2 volumes published) from Bokutakusha Press.

Preface

The essays in this book were published between 1991 and 2004, and reflect the period in which they were written. They have had minor editing, but have not been updated to reflect more recent developments, and should be read and understood in their original context. They are the products of my research and writing on a subject for which, lacking the relevant language and area training, I needed an extraordinary amount of help from colleagues in Japan and in the United States, a number of whom became co-authors.

Most important among these has been Nobuo Okawara, co-author of no fewer than four of the following chapters. Nobuo is a fabulous scholar in the traditional sense of the word. He knows his subject extremely well. He is the most careful researcher I know. And he has exquisite judgment which I have learned to trust totally. I could not have had a better guide in learning about the broad contours and fine nuances of the politics of Japanese foreign policy. Yutaka Tsujinaka played a similar role in our extensive collaboration on Japan's counterterrorism policy. He was able to extract political meaning from many of the dry government reports on a subject that researchers had neglected for decades. Without his guidance I could not have mastered this policy domain. Collaboration with former students, I learned, is one of the great pleasures in the life of a teacher. Richard Friman and David Leheny decided to make Japan the center of their graduate studies at Cornell and of their professional careers. I have learned much more from them over the years about Japan than I ever managed to teach them. Another Cornellian, Christopher Hemmer, is a specialist of American foreign policy. Without his collaboration I would not have been able to enter a field of scholarship which American scholars of international relations, myself included, are exposed to on a daily basis, typically without grasping the deeper connections and implications that Chris helped me understand. Last but not least, Rudra Sil has become an intellectual companion in trying to articulate analytical eclecticism as a coherent stance in the analysis of politics. I had stumbled across the idea in my empirical work and sought to articulate it in my untutored ways. Rudy's writing on issues of the philosophy of the social sciences and research methods was focusing on related themes. We joined forces for the final essay in this collection and have the pleasure of looking forward to future collaborative writing on this subject. I thank all of my co-authors for their generous permission to allow me to reprint our co-authored work here.

Fiona Adamson first imagined this book. Her expert judgment on editorial matters both large and small proved to be indispensable in helping me conceptualize the project. The book appears in a series that she is co-editing with Stefan Wolff and Roland Paris. Heidi Bagtazo oversaw the editorial process at Routledge with great efficiency and tact. And Amelia McLaurin made sure that the cross-Atlantic wheels did not get stuck. I owe a great debt of gratitude to all three. Edward Leeson copy-edited this book with uncommon care, speed and grace. I am very grateful for his help as well.

Finally, Sandra Kisner was indispensable in preparing the manuscript for publication. The job was much bigger than we had imagined at the outset. The care and expertise with which Sandy does her work is extraordinary. Cutting corners is a concept I failed to introduce into her vocabulary. I am extremely grateful for her help.

In the interest of avoiding duplication, two sections in Chapters 2 and 6 have been deleted. Otherwise all these essays appear as they did originally, with a few minor editorial changes, but without any changes in evidence, interpretation or argument.

I dedicate this book to Mary. Our travel together, through *dick und dünn*, gives incomparably more meaning to my life than the many fascinating and enjoyable trips that I have taken to Japan while working on this book.

Ithaca, New York
August 2007

Acknowledgments

The author and publishers would like to thank the following copyright holders for granting permission to reproduce material in this work:

Chapter 2: Abridged from Peter J. Katzenstein and Nobuo Okawara, "Japan, Asian-Pacific Security, and the Case for Analytical Eclecticism," *International Security* 26, 3 (Winter 2001–2): 153–85, © 2001 by the President and Fellows of Harvard College and the Massachusetts Institute of Technology.

Chapter 3: Peter J. Katzenstein and Nobuo Okawara, "Japan's Security Policy: Political, Economic, and Military Dimensions," *The International Spectator* 26, 3 (1991): 103–18. Istituto Affari Internazionali grants permission to republish the article "Japan's Security Policy: Political, Economic and Military Dimensions" in slightly modified form.

Chapter 4: Peter J. Katzenstein and Yutaka Tsujinaka, "Nihon no Kokunai Anzen Hosho Seisaku: 1970, 80 nendainiokeru terorizumu to bouryokteki shakai kougi unndou heno seijiteki taiou" ["Japan's Internal Security Policy in Japan: Political Responses to the Terrorism and Violent Social Protest in the 1970s and 1980s"] (translated by Wakako Tsujinaka), *Leviathan* 9 (Spring 1991): 145–64.

Chapter 5: Nobuo Okawara and Peter J. Katzenstein, "Japan and Asian-Pacific Security: Regionalization, Entrenched Bilateralisms and Incipient Multilateralism," *The Pacific Review* 14, 2 (2001): 165–94. Taylor & Francis, reprinted by permission of the publisher.

Chapter 6: Abridged from Richard Friman, Peter J. Katzenstein, David Leheny, and Nobuo Okawara, "Immovable Object? Japan's Security Policy in East Asia," pp. 85–107 in *Beyond Japan: The Dynamics of East Asian Regionalism*, edited by Peter J. Katzenstein and Takashi Shiraishi. Copyright © 2006 by Cornell University. Used by permission of the publisher, Cornell University Press.

Chapter 7: Peter J. Katzenstein, "Coping with Terrorism: Norms and International Security in Germany and Japan," pp. 265–95 in *Ideas and Foreign Policy: Beliefs, Institutions, and Political Change*, edited by Judith Goldstein and Robert O. Keohane. Copyright © 1993 by Cornell University. Used by permission of the publisher, Cornell University Press.

Chapter 8: Christopher J. Hemmer and Peter J. Katzenstein, "Why Is There No NATO in Asia? Collective Identity, Regionalism, and the Origins of Multilateralism," *International Organization* 56, 3 (2002): 575–607. Copyright © 2002 The IO Foundation and the Massachusetts Institute of Technology.

Chapter 9: Peter J. Katzenstein, "Same War—Different Views: Germany, Japan and Counter-terrorism," *International Organization* 57, 4 (Fall 2003): 731–60. Copyright © 2003. Used by permission of the publisher, Cambridge University Press.

Chapter 10: Adapted from "Rethinking Asian Security: A Case for Analytical Eclecticism," pp. 1–33 in *Rethinking Security in East Asia: Identity, Power, and Efficiency*, edited by J. J. Suh, Peter J. Katzenstein, and Allen Carlson, © 2004 by the Board of Trustees of the Leland Stanford Jr University. By permission.

1 Japanese security in perspective

Peter J. Katzenstein (2007)[1]

Throughout the Cold War, the analysis of Japanese security was a topic largely overlooked by both American students of Japan and students of national security. Japan, after all, was the country that had adopted a Peace Constitution with its famous Article 9 interpreted as legally banning the use of armed force in the defense of national objectives. Its professional military had little public standing and was under the thumb of civilians. And its grand strategy aimed at gaining prestige as a civilian power. Japan sought to leverage its economic prowess to a position of regional and perhaps global leadership that would complement rather than rival that of the United States; at the same time Japan relied on continued protection by the U.S. military. To be sure, since the late 1970s the U.S. government had persistently pressed Japan to play a larger regional role in Asia and to spend more of its rapidly growing GDP on national defense. But Japan made no more than marginal concessions. On security issues it kept a low regional profile, and since the late 1980s Japanese defense spending had consistently stayed below 1 percent of GDP. Writing on problems of Japanese national security was thus left to policy specialists issuing regular conference reports on the ups and downs of the U.S.–Japan bilateral defense relationship. Theoretically informed scholarship was conspicuous by its absence.

Things have changed a great deal. The end of the Cold War, the collapse of the Soviet Union, and the 9/11 attacks have fundamentally transformed the international landscape. Having failed in understanding the political dynamics that led to the end of the Cold War, some specialists of national and international security turned their attention from the western to the eastern perimeter of the Euro-Asian land mass. Would not the rapid rise of Japan, South Korea and Taiwan, the newly industrializing economies in Southeast Asia, China and Vietnam yield fertile ground for the application of the timeless truths of realist theory? As peace was breaking out in Europe, was Asia not destined to get ready for war (Friedberg 1993/94)?

Yet war and ethnic cleansing returned to Europe in the 1990s, while Asia remained peaceful. Thought to be unstoppable in the 1980s, Japan's economic juggernaut foundered on more than a decade of economic stagnation. China's economy continued to grow annually by about 8–10 percent, creating new security dynamics in East Asia as well as between East Asia and the United States. The Asian financial crisis of 1997 illustrated how closely Asia's economic miracle had become linked to regional and global markets. It also showed how, with the exception of Indonesia's, Asian leaders skillfully maneuvered out of that crisis in a very short time. The attack of September 11 and the U.S. global war on terror increased regional concerns about the rise of al Qaeda (Chow 2005; Leheny 2005). More importantly, it elevated the political importance of North Korea as a member of what President Bush called "the axis of evil," comprising countries that were suspected of trading in the illicit international market for nuclear technology and thus enhancing the risk that weapons of mass destruction could end up in the hands of groups intent on large-scale violence.

The developments in Japan's and East Asia's security affairs are analyzed in this book from a perspective that is oriented toward theory development more than toward policy formation or historical clarification. In contrast to the analysis of many scholars of international relations who organize their writings along paradigmatic lines, such as realism or liberalism, this book opens and closes with two chapters which make a case for the fruitfulness of an eclectic approach, not as a substitute but as a complement to well-established styles of analysis. The book is also eclectic in a broader understanding of that term. Chapters 4, 6, 7, and 9 deal with counterterrorism, traditionally a neglected and unfashionable topic in the field of security studies—until the 9/11 attacks on New York and Washington, DC.

Specialists in national security had remained blind to the fact that state security could be threatened by non-state actors, and in many cases was. Since the late 1960s Japan had been a prime case for studying the volatile politics of terrorism and counterterrorism. For example, driven by a combustible mixture of millenarian religious politics, members of Aum Shinrikyo, a New Age religious movement, staged a massive attack on civilians in downtown Tokyo in 1995. For attacks they hoped to launch later, some members of Aum Shinrikyo even took lessons in Florida's flight schools. Briefly told in Chapter 9, this story is as sad as it is ironic. Al Qaeda's attack should not have come as a total surprise to scholars of national security. Japan's presumed marginality for an understanding of national security in the 1980s and 1990s turned out to be rooted in a wrong-headed conventional wisdom. With very few exceptions (Hughes 1998), an entire field of scholarship, and the torrent of policy advice it so freely offered, had missed the obvious. Eclecticism, broadly understood, this book suggests, may help in diminishing just a little the risks scholars and policymakers run of being totally blind-sided by events.

This introductory chapter reviews briefly some theoretical issues in the analysis of Japanese security (Part 1), places Japan in the broader context of the American imperium (Part 2), discusses Japan's relationship with China (Part 3), and concludes with a brief preview of the chapters included in this book (Part 4).

1 Japanese security and analytical eclecticism

Since the end of the Cold War, scholarship on Japan's security affairs has become theoretically more self-conscious. I credit three interrelated developments. First, the end of the Cold War compelled scholars of international relations to re-examine some basic assumptions that had informed the field of national and international security. That process of re-examination made it impossible to adopt standard realist arguments uncritically. Second, the economic rise of East Asia made compelling a definition of security that, besides traditional military concerns, encompassed also economic and social aspects of security. Students of national security no longer dismiss "comprehensive security" as a slogan behind which Japanese politicians seek cover for their reputedly meager defense efforts. Finally, the theoretical challenge that constructivist and sociological writings posed to the mainstream of both realist and liberal theorizing was particularly strong in the field of Japanese security affairs. For most students of international relations, concepts such as norms and identity were linked either to an outmoded tradition of area studies or to an unwelcome cultural turn in the social sciences. These students were not eager to rethink the premises on which they had based the analysis of national and international security. Yet, unexpectedly, the politics of Japanese security has reinforced the relevance of these concepts, which can enrich analyses that favor the traditional categories of interest and power politics.

In the analysis of Japanese security the initial resistance to the broadening of the theoretical spectrum was readily apparent. While some analysts were trying to break new ground by stressing the importance of norms and identities (Katzenstein 1996; Berger 1998), realist and liberal analyses of Japanese security policy and Asian security orders by and large chose to focus on other issues (Heginbotham and Samuels 1998; Mochizuki and O'Hanlon 1998). Although this is not the place to provide a detailed review, this evolution of the literature had a welcome benefit. Scholarship on Japanese security successfully sidestepped metatheoretical debates among adherents of different research traditions—a welcome contrast to many general studies of international relations (Green 1998). As a result, some writings on Japanese security may, in the future, be able to take a more eclectic turn, by incorporating elements drawn from three different styles of analysis—the testing of alternative explanations, the rendering of synthetic accounts, and historically informed narratives.

My own book on the subject (Katzenstein 1996), for example, illustrates the first of these three styles of analysis. It offers a sociologically informed analysis of the centrality of norms and identity in Japan's internal and external security policy, and evaluates it against two alternative accounts—a realist analysis of Japan's external security policy and a liberal analysis of Japan's internal security policy. Before 9/11, realism had no interest in internal security policy—one reason for the enormous gap that proponents of this approach have had to cover since 9/11. On questions of internal security, liberalism with its exclusive focus on "thin" regulatory norms and the norms-based explanation that I develop, which also encompasses "thick" constitutive norms, cannot be distinguished clearly. All the norms that operate in this case point toward a flexible policy. On questions of internal security the anti-Leftist bias in Japan's constitutive norm of collective identity was uncontested; social and legal norms were mutually reinforcing; and internationally Japan was passive, seeking to maximize tactical flexibility. Japan's policy of external security is largely shaped by factors that do not figure prominently in realist analysis with its focus on rational, unitary actors that compete in an anarchic international system through strategies of balancing or bandwagoning. Liberal analysis does take account of norms. But by focusing solely on thin regulatory norms and failing to analyze also thick constitutive norms it does not capture the striking difference in the economic and military dimensions of Japan's external security policy. In Japanese domestic politics norms operate to very different effect in economic and military domains. Uncontested norms of economic security are rooted in a shared collective identity of Japan as a highly vulnerable country; this produces enormous flexibility in policy. In sharp contrast, a conservative mainstream and a vigorous Leftist camp hotly contested the norms informing Japan's military security, and this accounts for a high degree of policy rigidity. While a liberal and a norms-based explanation are pointing in the same direction on questions of internal security, on questions of external security they point in opposite directions. And a norms-based explanation clearly has more explanatory power than a liberal one. In sum, for central aspects of Japan's security policy, realist and liberal styles of analysis leave central elements unexamined or fail to explain some of their most important aspects. Other authors have adopted this explanatory approach, some with more success (Twomey 2000) than others (Lind 2004).

The main intent in the testing of alternative explanations is to identify a concrete political problem and evaluate the explanatory strength of different perspectives or hypotheses. This move signals an important step away from both the metatheoretical clashes that consumed international-relations theorists in the 1990s, and the often unreflective realist or Marxist bias in much of the writing on Japanese security during the Cold War.

Yet this explanatory approach also has costs. It risks coding and interpreting data in a way that suits the epistemological and methodological presuppositions of a given perspective and thus offers no more than a partial snapshot. More importantly, especially in its problem specification, authors tend to set up the analysis in a way that favors their preferred approach over all others. The particular strength of distinctive analytical perspectives is, after all, to illuminate what puzzles us about the world. The way research questions are posed often emerges from the presumption of a given analytical perspective rather than from the world of politics. A smart researcher can frame the research question in a way that determines the answer.

Richard Samuels's (2007) magisterial account of Japanese security exemplifies a second, synthetic style of analysis. It shows none of the self-conscious deployment of analytical categories that characterizes attempts at developing and testing alternative explanations. Instead Samuels mixes freely a variety of different perspectives—international and domestic, realist and constructivist, discursive and coalitional. His narrative is well specified; it is deeply grounded in the analysis of Japanese domestic politics; it avoids conflation of categories; and it is highly nuanced. Yet, for all these admirable strengths, Samuels's analysis pays a price. In tracking the various strands of Japanese strategic doctrines over time, his analysis cannot help but leave unexamined a broad range of Japan's security challenges that these schools consider to be unimportant. In fairness to the author, his rather than the reader's interest should dictate what he chooses to study. And Samuels's historical analysis does illustrate how successful Japanese leaders have been in the past in adapting a limited number of ideas and strategic concepts in mastering a broad range of volatile international conditions. Yet it is striking how the discursive moves of the mainstream and anti-mainstream in various strategic traditions—Meiji Japan's "Rich Nation, Strong Army," Konoe's "New Order," and the Yoshida Doctrine of the cheap ride of democratic Japan after 1945—so carefully tracked in this book are remarkably narrow in what they have to say about the full range of Japan's contemporary security challenges. Terrorism, the environment and human security, for example, are not to be found in an analysis that distinguishes between contemporary Japan's normal nationalists, middle-power internationalists, new autonomists, neo-revisionists, realists, globalists, mercantilists, Asianists, and pacifists (Samuels 2007: 14). Noting these blind spots, and addressing their political causes and consequences, would have broadened the book's range. Considering the most important developments since the end of the Cold War in the international security environment, Samuels's rich account is a triumph of "old" security studies over "new" security issues.

While the book is superb in generalizing about Japanese security doctrine across time, it sidesteps an opportunity to place Japan in a comparative perspective. This is an important difference between synthetic analysis and analytical eclecticism. Since the book aims to give a definitive account of a particular slice of Japanese politics, for Samuels comparison is beside the point. Analytical eclecticism is more modest in its aspirations. It relies on comparison to discover new things about the world. Whatever the reason for this difference, the attentive reader is left with an analysis that makes Japan seem unique rather than distinctive—a view that, based on Samuels's other writings, is clearly not his own, even though, based on my own interviews with Japanese officials over the years, it is a view quite common among Japanese political and bureaucratic elites. The political consequence of this fact could be substantial. If Japan is unique, perhaps Japanese policymakers experience great crises with a special sense of loneliness that is spared elites in other countries who experience the rise and fall of national fortunes in a broader context.

Japan's self-defined sense of vulnerability is a subject that looms large in

Samuels's account. Yet this condition is hardly unique to Japan. Stubbs (1999, 2005), Zhu (2000, 2002), and Larsson (2007) have applied the same concept to explain a variety of outcomes in Asia, and I have tried to do the same for the small European states (Katzenstein 1985). Is there some distinctive quality to the experience of vulnerability that sets Japan apart from other states? Furthermore, in contrast to Germany, the other main Axis power suffering total defeat in its challenge to Anglo-American hegemony in the middle of the twentieth century, Japan has resisted firmly the internationalization of its state identity and security practices (Buruma 1994; Nabers 2006). Is there a relation between the experience of vulnerability and the resistance of internationalization? And if there is, what is its nature? Answers to such questions are important. Neglecting comparisons makes Samuels's core claim—that Japan is currently in the process of articulating a new grand strategy involving various forms of hedging—empirically indistinguishable from its main rival: that Japan is currently in the process of refurbishing its existing grand strategy. One of the great virtues of this book is the fact that repeatedly the author graciously concedes this central point (Samuels 2007: 64, 107–8, 209. See also Pyle 2007; Midford 2006; Mochizuki 2004).

A strong state that is embodied in different schools of strategic thought is grounded in the notion of Japan as a civilizational nation-state with an authenticity that is ancient, a product of deliberate political construction in the late nineteenth century, and subject of current debates over its problematic relation to the West (Eisenstadt 1996; Gow 2005). Samuels (2007: 202) quotes Ambassador Kitaoka Shinichi voicing the influential view that "the core of Japan's identity and attraction derives from its independence. Japan sits *outside* Western civilization and has never been overwhelmed by Western culture. This, he says, is 'the most important message Japan can send to other cultures.'"

Japan's deep and resilient identity is central to the domestic debates over its history, encompassing textbook controversies, prime ministerial visits to the Yasukuni shrine, the war-time involvement of the state in organizing a system of sexual slavery for the Japanese military, and appropriate levels of contrition for past atrocities. In this context it is noteworthy how little space Samuels's (2007: 113–14) richly contextualized and highly nuanced analysis allocates to the politics of memory. In Samuels's view memory, like ideology, is an instrument of the political elite wielded for achieving its political purposes, in Tokyo as much as in Beijing or Seoul.[2] It is surely that—and much more (Winter 2006). The astonishing degree of Japan's self-absorption that pervades Samuels's account invites a probing historical analysis—especially since, in a distrustful regional neighborhood, the politics of memory has a very direct effect on Japan's security.

An outstanding example of a third style of analysis, historical narrative, Ken Pyle's (2007) excellent book speaks to these urgent questions with great historical knowledge and sensibility. Pyle provides a detailed analysis that links changes in Japan's international context to different domestic political currents, many of them deeply grounded in history. Working as a historian rather than as a political scientist, Pyle displays an impressive yet economical mastery of historical material that links Japan's present political proclivities to its ancient historical moorings. Steeped in deep learning, the book's core arguments appeal to sweet common sense—about the nature of the competitive international system, the long-term consequences of geographic isolation, the realist mindset of Japan's conservative elite, and the paradoxical mixture of Japan's highly plastic and never-changing domestic institutions. Written in a lucid style for a broader public and policy community, Pyle's book betrays what I would call an unreflective realism that glosses over a number of indeterminate and contradictory arguments.

Pyle (2007: 3, 13, 18, 34, 43, 47) refers to Japan as a civilizational state inhabiting a set of islands, in strict isolation from the world.[3] Japanese civilization is marked by a value system that is based on the mundane rather than on the high-minded and is centered on human relationships rather than on transcendental ideas (Pyle 2007: 46). A civilizational identity, and the special sense of tradition, promise, and providence in which it is grounded, offers a compelling explanation for the depth and resilience of Japanese identity. The meaning of vulnerability may be more profound, and the experience of vulnerability may cut more deeply, in civilizations than in other types of social or political organizations; and the adoption of internationalized identities and security practices may be more difficult for civilizations than for other institutions.

The idea is powerful and carries Pyle's culturally inflected domestic analysis of Japan's foreign policy a considerable distance. But by no stretch of the imagination can the category of civilization be located in the universe of political realism. For realist theory's core assumption holds that states as the basic unit of analysis in the international system are fundamentally similar. Civilizational analysis of the kind that Pyle proposes is in fundamental disagreement with that key assumption. Furthermore, while he often agrees with the realist characterization of the international system as an unforgiving, highly competitive environment in which relative power position determines state strategy, Pyle (2007: 55) argues also that the Japanese see the outside world as a "single great unitary threat" to survival. That formulation contradicts the view of elites rationally calculating relative power imbalances and engaging pragmatically in the kind of *realpolitik* that Pyle sees operating in Japan's reactive state. It may, however, capture very well the perception of elites living in a civilizational state or polity.[4] This is a promising though unexplored perspective which opens up new ways of thinking about Japan.

Pyle's unreflective realism shows up also in his contradictory treatment of the role of geography and a number of other topics. In many passages Pyle (2007: 33–4, 50) is in full agreement with John Mearsheimer (2001) as he points to the critical importance of Japanese geographic isolation for the insular cultural dispositions with which Japan's conservative elites have met the country's international challenges. Most of the time geography offered powerful protection against foreign invasions, as Japan had been "wholly self-sufficient" until the arrival of the West (Pyle 2007: 25, 55). Yet in modern times geography had just the opposite effect. Because Japan depended on the import of virtually all of its raw materials, it increased rather than decreased vulnerability (Pyle 2007: 35, 49).

Other intellectual tensions recur in Pyle's analysis. In the realist pursuit of power and the opportunistic adaptations to changing power configurations in world politics, "concern with preserving the ideals of Japan's cultural heritage generally took second place" (Pyle 2007: 23). Yet civilizational isolation was an essential ingredient of Japan's cultural self-absorption and strong sense of identity when coping with the political challenges posed by its complicated relations with China in pre-modern and the United States in modern times (Pyle 2007: 36–8). Japan was able to stand apart from the Sinocentric world while also borrowing from it (Pyle 2007: 29, 35–6). Japan's feudal past was a training ground for the practice of *realpolitik* (Pyle 2007: 39–41) while also offering excellent preparation for "the logic of emulation" (Pyle 2007: 59). And, while Japan was beset by an insular mentality shaped by geography and more than a millennium of political practice, "the Japanese lacked the same barriers of cultural and religious self-absorption that in other countries impeded learning from other civilizations" (Pyle 2007: 59). In a chapter that develops at length the theme of Japan's capacity to surprise throughout the ages, at least in the contemporary period of its rise to great-power politics, Pyle characterizes Japan as changing in "quiet, almost imperceptible ways," "initiating a major restructuring of its domestic institutions, including revision of its constitution," and "moving cautiously" in the uncertainty of a regional interregnum (Pyle 2007: 8–13, 16, 29, 32).

Pyle (2007: 29, 62) refers explicitly to important strands in the writings of traditional realists like Carr and Morgenthau whose analyses recognize the importance of culture; these arguments have been acknowledged also by Robert Gilpin (1981: 14, 30–2), a major contemporary theorist of realism, who regards prestige as the everyday currency of international politics. Pyle's historical analysis is thus especially intriguing when read in the context of some major studies of international relations which also have combined realist and cultural reasoning (Nau 2002; Johnston 1995, 2008). His unexamined yet plausible assumption of Japan as a civilizational state may open fresh perspectives for the analysis of contemporary Japan. Furthermore, in his analysis of Japan's penchant for imitation and emulation, Pyle's analysis suggests possible connections to an institutional perspective that John Meyer and many of his students have developed into a major research program which enjoys considerable influence in the sociological and cultural turn in international relations.

Following Pyle's lead, one might find that Japan's experience illuminates that of another civilizational state: the United States. Woodrow Wilson's international liberalism and veto of the racial equality clause at Versailles, for example, had a very important effect on Japan (Samuels 2007: 21, 186; Pyle

2007: 143–7). Woodrow Wilson was not only a champion of internationalism and democratic values. He was also a man of the South, a racist who was opposed to the principle of racial equality and whose fear of communism undermined his respect for civil liberties. Rogers Smith's (1993) analysis of the multiple political traditions in America and Walter McDougall's (1997) analysis of the multiple traditions of American foreign policy resonate deeply with Samuels's detailed analysis of the discursive politics of Japan's different strategic traditions and Pyle's analysis of the coherence of a dominant elite view and its contestation by different societal actors. Contra Hartz (1955) and Huntington (1996), internal contestation is a central attribute of civilizational states (Collins 2000, 1998; Eisenstadt 2002, 2003). Japan and the United States are two such states, and in contrast, for example, to modern welfare states both may encounter greater difficulties in confronting the reprehensible acts they have committed in the name of their supposedly superior civilizational values.

Important and suggestive as Pyle's book is, its sweeping historical analysis encounters numerous contradictions and paradoxes. Unreflective realism does not serve well the purpose of identifying analytical modules or causal mechanisms that we might want to borrow from different approaches in the hope of posing new questions or exploring novel lines of argument.

The testing of alternative explanations, Samuels's synthetic scholarship, and Pyle's historical narrative provide scholars of Japanese security with important intellectual capital for an analytical eclecticism through which future scholarship might seek fresh insights—by incorporating different research traditions, different explanatory constructs, and different levels of analysis into problem-focused research. The analytical eclecticism that I advocate in Chapters 2 and 10 has some affinity with all three approaches. It, too, eschews metatheoretical debate in favor of a problem-focused analysis that is disciplined by evidence. But it advocates proceeding at a lower level of analytical aggregation than the evaluation of different types of explanations. It rejects the attempt, evident in Samuels's book, to create a synthetic explanation that subsumes all other accounts into one master narrative. And, in contrast to Pyle's intuitive realism, it is theoretically more self-reflective of a "middle-range" theorizing that encompasses multiple causal mechanisms. Analytical eclecticism aims to construct original causal modules that reflect the complexity and messiness of particular problems in international life. It does so by lifting analytical elements from multiple research traditions and allowing for the recognition of causal mechanisms not anticipated in the analytic frameworks of those traditions. Eclectic scholarship complements and utilizes, rather than replaces or subsumes, scholarship produced by existing research traditions, and it embraces existing, multiple accounts rather than seeking to integrate them into a single grand synthesis. Analytical eclecticism thus opens the door to the analysis of a host of questions and causal mechanisms that are often bypassed because they do not fit comfortably into the analytic categories of a given research tradition (Katzenstein and Sil forthcoming). In this way, analytic eclecticism, although distinct from the application of multi-method approaches, is responsive to recent calls for a less method-driven and a more problem-oriented approach to the study of politics writ large (Sil 2004). Its most important contribution is to recognize questions that have been overlooked, to open up new lines of inquiry, and thus to challenge us to think new thoughts. With specific reference to this book, for example, incorporating the analysis of counterterrorism into the mainstream of security analysis is an obvious example. The attacks of 9/11 have made the analysis of counterterrorism an obvious and acceptable subject of inquiry even though, in the 1980s and 1990s, inquiry into these questions was for virtually all academic specialists of security an eccentric indulgence that bordered on heresy.

2 Japan in the American imperium

The broader context in which Japanese and Asian security affairs play themselves out continues to be shaped heavily by the United States as the pre-eminent actor in the international system and in East Asia. For better and for worse, since the 1930s American policies have had an enormous impact on East Asia. The creation of a liberal international economic order after 1945 was an important precondition for the export-oriented economic miracles of East Asian states. And the permanent stationing of about 100,000 U.S. troops in Japan and South Korea guaranteed continued U.S. political involvement. The Korean and Vietnam wars killed millions and left divisive historical legacies, especially on the Korean peninsula. It would be a mistake, however, to equate the United States government solely with its economic, diplomatic, or military policies. The United States is both an actor in and a part of an American system of rule in world politics that has evolved over the last half century. The concept of imperium refers to both actor and system, to the conjoining of power that has both territorial and non-territorial dimensions (Katzenstein 2005).

American imperium [5]

The United States government deploys its power in a system of rule that merges the military, economic, political and cultural elements which constitute the foundations for the pre-eminence of the American imperium in world politics. Territorial power was the coinage of the old land and maritime empires that collapsed at the end of the three great wars of the twentieth century: World War I, World War II, and the Cold War. American bases circling the Soviet Union during the Cold War and springing up again after the 9/11 attacks underline the continued importance of the territorial dimensions of the American *empire*. The U.S. has a quarter of a million military personnel deployed on scores of large military bases scattered around the globe. The non-territorial dimension of American power is reflected in the American *Empire*, a constellation of flexible hierarchies, fluid identities, and multiple exchanges. It is defined by technologies which are shrinking time and space, the alluring power that inheres in the American pattern of mass consumption, and the attraction of the American dream in a land that, evidence to the contrary notwithstanding, is viewed by many millions around the world mainly as the promised land of unlimited possibilities.

Territorial empire and non-territorial Empire are ideal types. They merge in the political experience and practices of the American *imperium* and the formal and informal political systems of rule as well as in the combination of hierarchical and egalitarian political relations that it embodies. This imperium is both constraining and enabling. The relative importance of its territorial and non-territorial dimensions waxes and wanes over time, shaped by the domestic struggles in American politics that reflect the rise and fall of political coalitions with competing political constituencies, interests, and visions. Japanese and Asian security affairs are encompassed by an imperium which embodies both the material, territorial, and actor-centric dimensions of U.S. power on the one hand and the symbolic, non-territorial, and systemic dimensions of American power on the other.

Regional core states such as Japan and Germany play crucial roles in link-ing world regions such as Asia and Europe to the American imperium. Spe-cialists focusing on the politics of regional powers other than Japan and Germany—such as China, Korea, Britain, or France—may rightly object to the singling out of Germany and Japan as special core states. Yet core states play different roles: as supporter states in the case of Japan and Germany, and as regional pivots in the case of, for example, China and France (Chase *et al.* 1999). The distinction between pivot and supporter points to the difference between a structurally general and a historically specific argument. It identi-fies Japan and Germany as core states not because of their size and power but because of their specific historical experience and evolution in the Anglo-American imperium.

Because only Japan and Germany challenged the Anglo-American world order in the first half of the twentieth century, and experienced traumatic defeat and occupation, no other world region has evolved similarly situated core states. After its historic victory over the political alternative that fascism posed to Anglo-American hegemony in the middle of the twentieth century, U.S. foreign policies sought to anchor its Japanese and German clients firmly within America's emerging imperium (McCormack 2007a; Lake 1988).

Eventually, though, these two states rose to become regional powers in their own right and supporters of the United States, intent on exercising their economic and political power indirectly and thus extending the reach and durability of the American imperium (Katzenstein and Shiraishi 1997, 2006; Katzenstein 1997; "Roundtable" 2007). These two supporter states were of vital importance in keeping Asia and Europe porous rather than closed regions. Their attachment to the American imperium was steady, first in the name of anticommunism, and subsequently in the name of globalization and counterterrorism. Yet the difference in the geo-strategic context—as yet no politically viable East Asian community, no large immigrant Muslim population in Japan, a geographically proximate perceived national security threat in the form of North Korea, and a deep suspicion of an increasingly powerful China—has left Japan a more dependable supporter state of the United States than Germany. The bipartisan Armitage–Nye report of October 2000 illustrates how far American policy has come to recognize Japan's strategic importance for U.S. foreign policy in East Asia, and how far it has left behind policies that regarded Japan as a client (as in the 1950s) or the subject of external pressure politics (as in the 1980s) (Green 2007: 147).[6]

This is not to deny that, as history changes, so may the character and standing of these two supporter states. Japan and Germany are increasingly removed in time, although not necessarily in terms of memory, from their traumatic national defeats. Since 9/11 the Bush administration's sharp turn toward a militant and unilateralist policy has given rise to strong opposition among mass publics abroad (Katzenstein and Keohane 2007). For example, democratization in South Korean politics has given rise to an anti-Americanism that has been accentuated greatly by the abrasive political style of an unsuccessful U.S. diplomacy (Steinberg 2005). Anti-Americanism among the young in particular has risen to heights that had been inconceivable in the late 1990s. In China, American-inflected globalization is embraced while anti-hegemonism, especially its behavioral manifestations, continues to be a powerful oppositional ideology that resists American primacy. While it is not as virulent or racist as anti-Japanese sentiments, this anti-Americanism is a powerful latent force that is readily activated around many issues and most certainly around the volatile issue of Taiwan (Johnston and Stockmann 2007).

Japan is a notable exception to these changes in East Asian popular attitudes. In the mid- and late 1950s Japanese anti-Americanism ran so deep that President Eisenhower cancelled his visit in 1960, after the Japanese government informed the White House that a full mobilization of Japan's total police force could not guarantee the physical security of the presidential motorcade from Haneda airport to the Imperial Hotel in downtown Tokyo. Since the end of the Vietnam war anti-Americanism has virtually disappeared as Japan's party system has moved to center-right, and as a new national consciousness has taken hold of a younger generation psychologically no longer moved by the dominant concerns of the 1950s and 1960s and unnerved by North Korean bluster and China's rise. At a popular level the relationship between Japan and the United States is free from rancor. Despite sustained protests against American bases in Okinawa, public opinion polls typically show above 60 percent of the Japanese public favoring the United States, about twice as many as corresponding numbers for various European countries (Pew Global Attitudes Project 2007; Tanaka 2007).

Furthermore, as the character of the American imperium changes, its two supporter states are unavoidably repositioned in the matrix of Asian and European politics. Thus, there exists no reason why the role of these supporter states could not be filled by others. If Germany were to be submerged totally in a European polity (which seems very unlikely), and if Japan's GDP were surpassed, eventually, by China's (which seems very likely), together with other historical changes affecting Asia, Europe, and the United States, this might eventually transform the role played by traditional supporters and other regional pivots. In the case of France and China, for example, the magnitude of such changes would have to be very substantial. These two states are crucial pivots. But, for reasons of history, it is hard to imagine how they could replace Japan and Germany any time soon as Asia's and Europe's supporter states of the American imperium.

Japan

Japan's alliance with the United States has provided the political and strategic foundation for its economic rise in the American imperium (Ikenberry and Inoguchi 2003, 2007). To be sure, with the passing of time Asia has become more important as war and occupation have receded, and as Japan's reconstruction and economic clout have made it Asia's preeminent economic power. But it was Asia viewed from Tokyo through an American looking-glass. There was more than a whiff of the historical role that Japan sought after the Meiji restoration—casting itself in the role of interlocutor between Asia and the West.

Since 1945, Japan has experienced a phenomenal rise. Its economic fortunes were helped greatly by serving as the Asian armory in America's global struggle against communism, first in Korea in the 1950s and subsequently in Vietnam and Southeast Asia in the 1960s. The collapse of the Bretton Woods system, and the two oil shocks of the 1970s, set the stage for the economic rise of Japan in financial markets. The 1980s were the decade of Japan's global ascendance as an economic superpower, ending in a speculative bubble that collapsed into economic torpor lasting more than a decade. In manufacturing, Japan's technological prowess is no longer unchallenged in defining East Asia's economic frontiers. Japan has a mature economy that is trying to cope with an aging and thrifty population and with being one of the main sources of credit for the United States. This completed the transformation of Japan's strategic relationship with the United States from client to supporter state.

Japan has been important in supporting U.S. policies in a variety of ways (Krauss and Pempel 2004; McCormack 2007a; Pyle 2007; Hughes and Krauss 2007). It helped refurbish the institutional infrastructure of international financial institutions, led the way in seeking greater energy efficiency, became for a while the world's largest aid donor, and played a central role, especially in the mid-1980s, in intervening in financial markets to realign the values of the world's major currencies, thus setting the stage for an enormous outward shift of Japanese firms into South East Asia and beyond. Since the 1980s Japan has accommodated the United States on issues central to the functioning of the international economy, with evident reluctance in opening Japanese markets for goods, services and capital, and with an air of resignation in amassing close to a trillion dollars in reserves, thus helping to finance perennial U.S. budget and trade deficits.

As America's steady supporter in Asia, Japanese firms were to lead, Asian firms to follow. With governments deeply involved in shaping their nations' economic trajectories, Japan expected to lead Asia both directly, through aid, trade and advice, and indirectly by providing an attractive economic model. Japan could not develop and grow without Asia developing and growing. By focusing on the politics of productivity, Japan hoped to sidestep political quarrels and dispel historical animosities. It thus sought to create the political conditions in which its highly competitive industries could prosper through energetic export drives and smart foreign investments. Regional development and Japanese ascendance would thus be indelibly linked in a win–win situation which cloaked in liberal garments asymmetries in economic position and political power.

This strategy proved politically unworkable. In the 1960s different Japanese proposals for more formal regional integration schemes foundered on the deep suspicions that other Asian states harbored against Japan. Having been rebuffed, the Japanese government settled after the early 1970s on more informal and market-based approaches to Asian integration. After the dramatic appreciation of the yen in 1985, Japanese firms were quick to develop far-flung networks of subcontractors and affiliated firms. Foreign supplier chains of Japanese firms provided a new regional infrastructure for industries such as textiles, automobiles, and electronics. Thus, Japanese investment had a deep impact on specific economic sectors, on whole countries, and on the entire Asia-Pacific region. And the regionalization of Japan's economic power had the political benefit of diffusing much of the political conflict with the United States over bilateral trade imbalances. For Japanese enmeshment has helped create a more integrated regional economy in East Asia that is now fueled also by Korean, Taiwanese, Southeast Asian, and Chinese firms. The structural preconditions for this process of regionalization were the insatiable appetite of American consumers for inexpensive Asian products and the openness of American markets to imports from Asia. This outcome was fully compatible with the grand strategy of the United States which in the early 1970s normalized its relations with China to balance the Soviet Union during the Cold War, and which has consistently favored a far-reaching liberalization of markets. There would have been fewer and smaller Asian miracles and less Asian regionalism if the parking lots of American shopping malls had not been filled in America's irresistible emporium of consumption (DeGrazia 2005).

The role of supporter state was also evident in Japan's national security policies. Although it was constrained for decades by a pacifist public culture and, somewhat less, by Article 9 of its Peace Constitution, the Japanese government has consistently adhered to policies that supported the United States, especially in the 1980s and with increased intensity since 9/11. To be sure, there have been moments—such as in the mid-1970s and the mid-1990s—when American staying power in Asia appeared so uncertain as to suggest the need for possibly far-reaching changes in Japan's security strategy. But these moments of uncertainty passed quickly, and Japan remained a close ally of the United States—then and now.

The reasons for Japan's steadfast support have varied. The military, economic and political advantages of the American security umbrella were at the heart of the Yoshida doctrine and widely recognized in all political quarters. Expending less than 1 percent of Japan's GDP on national defense was feasible because American taxpayers spent a lot more. And, as Japan's standing in Asia-Pacific increased, so did the pressure of the U.S. government to have the Japanese government play a more expansive, and expensive, role in regional security affairs—as a reliable junior partner of the United States. Some of Japan's critics, both at home and abroad, detected in the 1980s a new tone of assertiveness and a new nationalism in Prime Minister Nakasone's Japan. Two decades later, under Prime Ministers Koizumi and Abe, the increase in an assertive Japanese nationalism was more prominently there for everybody to see. This was the political context in which the Japanese government, in February 2005, decided to raise its profile on one of the region's most vexing problems, by issuing a joint security declaration with the United States that identified the peaceful resolution of the Taiwan issue as a shared strategic objective.

Prime Minister Koizumi's strategy has been to attach Japan even more closely to the United States than in the past (Samuels 2007: 86–108; Hughes and Krauss 2007: 160–3), while toying with the idea of bringing about an opening toward North Korea. After the 9/11 attacks the Diet passed, in record time, legislation permitting the dispatch of the Japanese navy to the Indian Ocean to provide logistical support for the U.S.-led coalition forces in Afghanistan. After the U.S. invasion of Iraq the Diet enacted legislation permitting the deployment of the Japanese army to Iraq to aid in reconstruction and the stationing of the Japanese navy and air force in the Persian Gulf to provide logistical support for the American war. In 2003 the Japanese government agreed to acquire a ballistic missile defense system which should be fully operational by 2011. And legislation introduced in 2005 gives the prime minister and the military commanders the power to mobilize military force in response to missile attacks without cabinet deliberation or parliamentary oversight. Since Japan is buying the main components, the Patriot Advance Capability (PAC)-3 and the Aegis destroyers, from the United States, missile defense will further consolidate the U.S.–Japan alliance and tighten technological cooperation between the two militaries. In 2006 the U.S. and Japan completed a Defense Policy Review Initiative which strengthened the bilateral alliance to meet regional and global security threats. Toward that end, and overriding significant local objections, Prime Minister Koizumi agreed to a substantial and costly realignment of U.S. bases in Japan. The practical implication of this agreement was to make Japan a frontline command post in the projection of U.S. military power, not only in East Asia but also as far as the Middle East. Like previous agreements (Katzenstein 1996: 131–52), this was a further reinterpretation of the geographical scope of the U.S.–Japan security treaty and the mission of U.S. bases that went well beyond protecting the Japanese homeland and securing regional stability in East Asia. In fact, the Japanese and U.S. governments issued a joint statement stressing their shared global objectives: the eradication of terrorism and the prevention of the proliferation of weapons of mass destruction. These important changes in the U.S.–Japan alliance are clearly linked to changes in the character of Japan and the East Asian context. Yet it is easy to forget that, with the disintegration of the Japanese Left, strong opposition to Japan's playing a larger military role has changed as it has moved to other political parties; but opposition has not disappeared.

Japan has embraced what looks like a grand strategy of unquestioned security alignment with the United States. In an era in which the American imperium is under siege, Japan is deeply invested in enhancing its special relationship with the United States, imitating that other island nation, Great Britain. This policy change is surprising. The political fortunes of Prime Minister Tony Blair and Chancellor Gerhard Schröder during the Iraq war point to the wisdom of a strategy which is neither too supportive nor too critical of the United States when it indulges its deep urge for unilateral action (Hughes 2007).

The arrival of a new generation of more nationalist politicians at the center of Japan's political stage underlines the importance of political leadership (Samuels 2003). Prime Minister Koizumi's "fighting diplomacy" created an impasse in Japan's relation with South Korea and China over the issue of his controversial visits to the Yasukuni shrine (Pempel 2007). In the early weeks of his tenure, after entering office in September 2006, Prime Minister Abe surprised many with what the Japanese called his "soft mood" approach: a quick fence-mending trip to Beijing and Seoul, a calculated vagueness in declaring whether he would visit the Yasukuni shrine, and a go-slow approach to the issue of constitutional revision. Far from reflecting a betrayal of Abe's political beliefs, however, passing legislation revising the Fundamental Law of Education[7] and upgrading the political status of the Self-Defense Forces to full ministerial status, while also redefining their military mission, pointed to an ambitious political agenda that sought to accomplish much of Abe's program even if a full revision of the constitution proves to be unfeasible (Junkerman 2007; Pilling 2006b, 2006c). Most importantly, Japan's policy toward North Korea was harsher than that of the United States and Prime Minister Koizumi. Under Abe's leadership Japanese policy pushed the abductees issue at the expense of denuclearization. The reason was simple. Prime Minister Abe expressed a clear nationalist turn in Japanese politics and an increase in the salience of identity politics (McCormack 2007a: 6–28, 191–204; Samuels 2007: 72–81; Hughes and Krauss 2007).[8] Yet, at the very moment at which one faction of Japan's conservative camp was bent on reasserting more traditional notions of Japanese nationalism, Japanese society was beginning to accommodate a limited social heterogeneity that challenged the notion of Japan as a "family nation." The spectacular erosion of Abe's political support and his stunning resignation after only a year in office revealed both his failings as a leader and a deep tension in Japan's polity.

Beyond issues that motivate individual leaders, Japan is experiencing broader political changes. Social and generational turnover is remaking Japanese institutions from within; the atrophy of Japan's Left has remade Japan's political landscape; the prolonged experience of economic hard times at a level of historically unprecedented prosperity has robbed the Japanese of a fundamental sense of economic security; and a more contentious regional context, most notably "the rise of China," demands a rethinking of and experimenting with well-tested political formulas. Constitutional revision and the return of Japan as a "normal" country, on the one hand, and Japan's possible nuclearization to meet the perceived threat posed by North Korea and China's economic, political, and military ascent, on the other, define the endpoints on a spectrum stretching from political transformation to policy revolution. In between lies the stuff of more incremental political and policy changes reflecting the arrival of a generation of Japanese leaders that is seeking to raise the profile of Japan's security policy: the raising of the political status of the Japan Defense Agency to ministerial rank, numerous changes in the U.S.–Japan security relationship, growing military ties with Australia, a diplomacy that seeks to forge closer ties among Asian democracies, and a more explicit stance on Japan's interest in the peaceful resolution of the Taiwan issue.

Article 9 of the Japanese constitution renounces the use of force for settling international disputes and thus bars the possession of military force. A revision, the first in the sixty years since the constitution came into effect, would symbolize significant political change. A bill passed in May 2007 permitted the government to hold a referendum on the subject by 2010, following a two-thirds vote favoring such an amendment in both houses of the Diet (Onishi 2007a; Pilling 2006a; Martin 2007). For decades, Japanese pacifism and pragmatism were close cousins in the well-honed practice of constitutional reinterpretation (Boyd and Samuels 2005). They established Japan's right to individual self-defense and also, through Japan's close security cooperation with the U.S., a right to collective self-defense while prohibiting any exercise of it. The 1991 Gulf War, the lingering North Korean crisis, China's rise, and the redefinition of global security in the wake of the 9/11 attacks have created international and domestic pressures for reconsidering Japan's strict prohibition against participation in international peacekeeping operations involving use of military force. A flexible reinterpretation of Article 9 has facilitated the deployment of the Japan Self Defense Forces abroad. That process was assisted by the depolarization of Japanese politics with the Left and factions inside the Liberal Democratic Party (LDP) opposed to deployment and eventual revision fading in importance, with the strengthening of the position of the prime minister within the LDP and the policymaking process, and with the entry of the idea of constitutional revision into the political mainstream.

Yet in a democracy political winds are rarely steady. The political support of Prime Minister Abe collapsed with stunning speed, and shortly after suffering a crushing defeat in the Upper House election in July 2007 he resigned, signaling that nationalist issues mattered less to the electorate than government competence, honesty, and economic issues. By 2010, when the issue of constitutional revision can be put to a popular referendum, the LDP would need the support of its small coalition partner, the Komeito party. And it would need also the support of at least parts of the opposition, the Democratic Party of Japan (DPJ), which has a mixed stance on revision and sees as its main task to replace the LDP as the leading party rather than to help in a highly controversial political reform. And the LDP must deal with a public which is open to the idea of constitutional revision but remains deeply ambivalent about changing Article 9. This much is certain. The issue of constitutional revision is a crucial part of the deep-seated conflict about Japan's identity. It matters for Japan's democratic politics, for Japan's standing in East Asia, for Japan's aspiration to gain a permanent seat in the UN Security Council, and, arguably, for Japanese and Asian security.

North Korea's success in staring down the United States and crossing the nuclear threshold, one might think, should have had a strong effect on Japanese debates about nuclearization. North Korea's universally condemned nuclear test of October 2006 and the U.S. Congressional elections in November 2006, which shifted control of Congress from Republican to Democratic hands, prepared the ground for an agreement in February 2007 in the six-party talks in which the U.S. gave up most of its most cherished demands. Suddenly, Japan found itself isolated. While all other states were framing the issue in terms of national or regional security, Japan had given highest priority to resolving the abductions of Japanese citizens in the 1970s, the political issue that had greatly enhanced Abe's position inside the LDP and in national politics (Selden 2006; McCormack 2007b, 2007d).

A hard-line policy would have little public support if it aimed at a sharp escalation in Japan's military profile (L. Hughes 2007; McCormack 2007c). In contrast to American neo-conservatives (Lobe 2006), despite North Korea's nuclear program and missile tests threatening the Japanese homeland, most members of Japan's military elite and general public remain firmly opposed to the government's active exploration of its nuclear options. Japan's nuclear allergy was in plain sight once again when, only four weeks before the July 2007 Upper House elections, Japan's defense minister was forced to resign because one of his comments appeared to justify U.S. use of atomic weapons against Japan to end World War II (Onishi 2007b). Japan's extensive civilian nuclear energy program, including its large plutonium-reprocessing facilities, is not designed to hedge against American abandonment. Instead it is part of an energy policy designed to reduce dependence on external sources of energy. Government policy has consistently shied away from challenging directly the multilateral nonproliferation regime, while putting itself just as consistently into a position of being able to become a nuclear weapons state should changing circumstances dictate such a move because of a weakening in the American security guarantee. Japan's grand strategy is thus firmly rooted in investing in the extended deterrence provided by the United States. And that policy extends to maintaining ready access to high-tech non-nuclear weapons such as the F-22, which Japan is interested in buying to strengthen its hand against North Korea and China (Sevastopulo and Pilling 2007; Pilling 2007a). Llewelyn Hughes (2007: 70, 80–95) argues that domestic factors continue to be of much greater importance in accounting for Japan's lack of interest in a nuclear option than are changes in Japan's external conditions.

One of the most relevant domestic factors is public opinion, which continues to exercise a restraining influence on the conduct of Japanese security policy. Since the North Korean missile tests in 1998 the Japanese public has come to accept the fact that war is an ever-present possibility even for a civilian power. And that awareness provides the ground on which the issue of constitutional revision and nuclearization is debated. With China, Japan is one of East Asia's two leading military powers. Yet, since 1994, Japanese defense expenditures have declined in both nominal and real terms, and Japan's defense budget has been reduced for five straight years between 2003 and 2007 (Samuels 2007: 195). The public's realist recognition is thus tempered by a democratic politics that continues to prefer butter to guns. Furthermore, as Paul Midford (2006) argues, public opinion is defensive in recognizing the usefulness of military power *only* for homeland defense and not for the pursuit of any other political objective such as democracy promotion, the defense of human rights, or the suppression of weapons of mass destruction—all declared objectives of the United States. Instead, and very much in line with Japan's doctrine of comprehensive security, Japan's public continues to support strongly nonmilitary instruments of foreign policy. This support is reflected in the shape of Japan's overseas military missions: rear-area logistical support in the Indian Ocean for U.S. ships, humanitarian relief operations for refugees in Pakistan, and, until recently, reconstruction and relief efforts in southern Iraq protected by the militaries of other coalition members. It thus seems highly improbable that Japanese security policy will jettison its characteristic caution any time soon and start playing the role of "Britain in Asia," eager to project military force in support of the United States and its at times expansive political objectives (Hughes 2007). Indeed, the catastrophic failures of American foreign policy in Iraq and the growing political pressure in American domestic politics to end the war are likely to temper the ambitions of any successor to the current administration and thus reduce U.S. interest in pushing Japan to play a more assertive role in regional and global affairs.

3 Japan and China: two tigers on one mountain?

Since the collapse of the Soviet Union, China's entrance into global markets and its gradual socialization into the role of a responsible regional power have been the two most important developments affecting Japan and East Asia. This is not to argue that China has already replaced Japan as the pre-eminent economic power in Asia. Far from it. In 2002, Japan accounted for 13.5 percent of global GDP—almost four times China's figure. In terms of market exchanges, a better measure of regional and global power dynamics than pur-chasing-power parity measures of GDP, Japan was leading China by a ratio of 4:1 and about 40:1 on a per-capita basis.[9] After a decade of economic stagna-tion Japan's share of the combined regional GDP of Northeast and Southeast Asia had slipped from 72 to 65 percent. And during the same period of explosive economic growth China's GDP as a proportion of Japan's had increased from 13 to 23 percent (Katzenstein 2006: 2).[10] And, even though the situation is changing from year to year, it is good to remember that, until 2005, China was still lagging behind Germany as the world's leading exporter. Current Chinese plans call for increasing the country's GDP to $4.4 trillion by 2020, quadrupling the figure for the year 2000. If successful, China is likely to top Japan by that time in terms of market size measured at current exchange rates. Although these facts deflate a bit the breathless adulation with which some journalists and politicians are greeting the Chinese juggernaut, just as they greeted Japan's in the 1980s, it is beyond doubt that very significant changes in China are having a profound effect on Asian and Japanese security.

China's rise

The political rise of China as a responsible regional power is an important political development (Johnston 2008, 2004; Kang 2007; Economy and Oksenberg 1999; Johnston and Ross 1999; Selden 1997). In the 1970s and 1980s China exchanged the role of a revolutionary for that of a realist power. China's *raison d'état* had a hard edge of *realpolitik* that reminded some obser-vers of Imperial Germany in the decades leading up to World War I. After more than a century of humiliation and isolation, was not China finally entitled to its rightful place in the sun? The international politics of sports, energy, xenophobic nationalism, and economic mercantilism all seemed to point in that direction. Indeed, some realist theorists who had been baffled by the end of the Cold War and the disintegration of the Soviet Union in Europe saw in Asia a region "ripe for rivalry" (Friedberg 1993/94).

China's diplomacy, however, is not only hardcore realist. On many issues China has adopted a multilateral and accommodating stance. It has recog-nized the long-term advantages that accrue from its growing economic power and that dictate a diplomatic strategy supporting what has come to be known as China's "peaceful rise." This change is visible in comparison to both the United States and Japan. A shift in its national security doctrine in September

2002 established the United States as a revisionist power, in contrast to China playing the role of a status-quo power in the international system. In its war against terror the U.S. government sought far-reaching changes. Most importantly, it has claimed the right to pre-emptive attack, even under circumstances in which there would be time and opportunity to seek approval from the United Nations. In sharp contrast China joined many other states in insisting on the importance of the legitimacy that international approval confers, as the U.S. had in the era of multilateralism that it had ushered in at the end of World War II. Antihegemonism became once again the watchword in Beijing as it balanced carefully a strong interest in China's territorial sovereignty with growing demands of multilateral diplomacy, including on hot-button issues such as North Korea's nuclear weapons program. In East Asia in particular, instead of running the risks of Eurocentric balance-of-power politics China is seeking to return to a Sinocentric bandwagoning politics, thus creating political space for the cautious hedging strategies of a number of East Asian states. And Chinese diplomacy has shifted to include multilateral regional arrangements as an explicit tool to supplement its bilateral approach to regional and global issues.

In contrast to Japan with its more inward and nationalist orientation, the distinctiveness of China's ascendance lies in an economic might and a political clout that are structurally predisposed to reinforce rather than challenge East Asia's openness in a world of regions. Central to that structural predisposition is the realignment, rather than (re)unification, of a vibrant Chinese diaspora in Taiwan and Southeast Asia with the Chinese state (Gomez and Hsiao 2004, 2001; Callahan 2003; Naughton 1997; Weidenbaum and Hughes 1996; *Dædalus* 1991).[11] Millions of overseas Chinese had left the southern coast of China in the nineteenth century for destinations throughout Southeast Asia. Over time they became the economic elites in various countries. As successive waves of Asian states experienced their economic miracle, often with the help of developmental states, throughout East Asia networks of overseas Chinese were ready as important intermediaries connecting national political elites with foreign firms. While the core of Chinese business has remained family-controlled, surrounding layers of equity-holding and political control were gradually taken over by members of the indigenous political elites. In the 1990s, in terms of its sheer economic size, the overseas Chinese economy in Southeast Asia reportedly ranked fourth in the world.

The category of "overseas Chinese" is ambiguous. In the nineteenth century the Chinese diaspora lacked a homogenous identity as it was divided by—among other things—dialect, hometown, blood relationships, and guild associations. As mainland China was engulfed in civil war, revolutionary upheaval, and Maoist rule, a thin veneer of common expatriate experience grew, but not enough to conceal the enormous variability in the political experience and standing of the overseas Chinese in different parts of Southeast Asia. Thus, the cultural trait that helps define the overseas Chinese is an almost infinite flexibility in their approach to business.

The overseas Chinese presented the Chinese state with a formidable problem after the Communist Party seized power in 1949. The 1953 census listed the overseas Chinese as part of China's population. And the 1954 Constitution of the People's Republic of China provided for representation of all overseas Chinese in the National People's Congress (Suryadinata 1978: 9–10, 26, 29). However, conflict with Indonesia and the other Southeast Asian states forced a change in policy. All of these states were wary of the political allegiance of their ethnic Chinese populations. After 1957, Chinese foreign policy encouraged the overseas Chinese to seek local citizenship and local education. And, since 1975, China's Constitutions have stripped overseas Chinese of membership in the National People's Congress. During the last generation an overwhelming number of overseas Chinese have accepted citizenship in new homelands. The term "overseas Chinese" now denotes ethnic Chinese of Southeast Asian birth and nationality.

In China both provincial and central governments have sought to strengthen the relationship between China's surging economy and the overseas Chinese, and especially Taiwan, through an active encouragement of foreign investment, remittances, and tourism. What Barry Naughton (1997) calls the "China Circle" connects Hong Kong, Taiwan, and the overseas Chinese throughout Southeast Asia. Upward of 1 million Taiwanese businessmen now live in China, undercutting ineffective attempts of the Taiwanese government to resist the strong pull of China's surging economy. And it is easy to forget that outside this China Circle the overseas Chinese constitute also a North American and indeed a global diaspora.

Since the late 1970s China has attracted half a trillion dollars in foreign investment, about ten times the total foreign investment that has flown into Japan since 1945. Between 1985 and 1995 about two-thirds of realized foreign investment in China is estimated to have come from domestic Chinese sources which used Hong Kong to circumvent domestic taxes, and one-third from foreign investors. Since 1995 this proportion is widely believed to have reversed itself. Of the $250 billion of total foreign investments, perhaps as much as half has come from Taiwan, and additional undetected funds have flown in from Southeast Asia.[12] Whatever the precise figures, which are unknown, in the coming years even closer tie-ups between overseas and mainland Chinese business are the next phase in the global spread of Asian business networks. It is these market- and state-driven tie-ups, not formal political institutions, which are the defining characteristic of the rise of China and the role of Asia in world politics. Thus, the evolution of Chinese capitalism is not only a domestic but also a regional phenomenon. Across a broad range of issues, uniquely in Asia, China is linked inextricably to the Asia-Pacific. And, as a rapidly emerging creditor of the United States and a looming military rival at least in the eyes of important segments of the American defense establishment, China is also linked intimately to the American imperium.

Japan and China

Japan must come to terms with a China that is both a vital economic partner and a political rival in East Asia (Lam 2006; Dreyer 2006; Cohen, 2005; Abramowitz *et al.* 2002; Friedman 2000; Wang 2000; Zhao 1997; Taylor 1996; Iriye 1992). Japan adheres to an increasingly international economic and a fully internationalized security strategy. In sharp contrast, China follows a fully international economic and a decidedly national security strategy. Both reinforce the porosity of East Asia. In the latter stages of the Koizumi administration the deterioration in Sino-Japanese relations was striking. Between May 2004 and October 2005, for example, the relations between these two regional powers were affected negatively by a series of high-profile political events, on average once a month (Pei and Swaine 2005: 5). By the end of Koizumi's prime ministership, Japan's relations with China had reached rock-bottom. In 2005 just under 10 percent of the Japanese and Chinese public held favorable views of the other country (Sato 2007: 3; Tanaka 2007). Perceptions of imagined slights and hurt pride have played themselves out on both sides against very different interpretations of the past. They are illustrated by the strong opposition of the Chinese public to any historical revision in the interpretation in Japanese textbooks of Japan's role as the aggressor in the East Asian war. Japanese fear and envy feed anti-Chinese sentiments as Chinese rates of growth since the early 1990s have outstripped Japanese rates by margins of 13:1 in per-capita GDP and ownership of personal computers, 12:1 in patent applications, 11:1 in total trade, and 9:1 in research and development expenditures (Pei and Swaine 2005: 6). Domestic politics creates political incentives in both countries to magnify and exploit popular sentiments, driven by factional infighting in China and electoral strategizing in Japan. China and Japan thus risk being trapped in a political relationship of deepening suspicion and enmity that runs counter to their growing economic interdependence and the prospect of joint gains.

Prime Minister Abe's visit to Beijing in October 2006, right after he took over from Koizumi, and the return visit of Chinese Premier Wen Jiabao in April 2007, helped improve the political climate between the two countries. Both governments saw the change in Japanese leadership as a chance for bringing about an improvement in bilateral relations. Furthermore, there existed concrete plans for resumption of more frequent meetings between the political leadership of the two countries (Pilling 2006c; Dickie and Pilling 2007). But many contentious issues persisted under the surface. Most importantly, Prime Minister Abe was deliberately ambiguous in his talks with the Chinese government and Japanese journalists about a possible visit to the Yakukuni shrine, thus cleverly sidestepping the need to tell the Chinese that he was not going and domestic supporters that he was going to make such a visit. Furthermore, Japan opposed a lifting of the EU's arms embargo against China, openly criticized in its 2007 Defense White Paper China's military modernization program (Pilling 2007b), and favored a "value-based" foreign policy that created an "arc of freedom and prosperity across the democracies in Pacific Asia," that is, excluding China. For its part, China was critical of Japan's reinvigorated security alliance with the United States, the refashioning of Japan's national security apparatus, and plans to revise the Constitution (Pei 2007). Chinese exploitation of natural gas reserves in the middle of disputed waters in the East China Sea, and Japan's hope for Chinese backing for its permanent seat on the UN Security Council, provided additional roadblocks for improvement in political relations between the two governments.

The domestic, regional and global contours of politics suggest that the evolution of Sino-Japanese relations will be shaped by a mixture of engagement and deterrence in their bilateral relations, by their competitive and complementary region-building practices in an East Asia that will resist domination by either country (Katzenstein 2006), and by the cultivation of their different strategic and economic links to the American imperium. As a traditional supporter, Japan has developed a deep strategic partnership with the United States that has lasted for more than half a century. In the case of China, those links are rooted in a developmental trajectory that prizes economic openness. Through Japan and China a porous Asia is tethered in both its security and economic relations to the American imperium. The U.S. presence in East Asia can help stabilize Sino-Japanese relations at least in the near and medium term while political efforts at East Asian region-building proceed. Despite the political turbulence and rapid changes in Sino-Japanese relations, for some years to come the American imperium and a porous East Asia may remain politically compatible. And, because their political strategies are so different, the two tigers may learn how to live on the same mountain.

4 Conclusion

This chapter has developed three arguments. First, since the end of the Cold War some analyses of Japanese security affairs have become theoretically more self-conscious in how they deploy alternative explanations, synthetic accounts, or historical narratives. These styles of analysis help scholars sidestep the temptation to engage in fruitless metatheoretical debates and may create some intellectual space in the future to pursue eclectic styles of analysis. Second, Japan, China, and East Asia are placed firmly in the American imperium. And it is Japan's specific role as a supporter rather than as a client or a pivot state that defines its place in East Asia. Third, Japan's military dependence on the United States and China's economic dependence on international markets continue to keep East Asia porous. Even though the balance of power between Japan and China is shifting, this political constellation keeps East Asia anchored in the American imperium.

The chapters in this book span two important periods during the last fifteen years. The four chapters in Part I focus on domestic and regional aspects of Japan's internal and external security policies in the early 1990s and after 2001. These chapters convey one strong message. What amounted to a seismic shift in Europe after 1989–91 and in the United States after 9/11 turned out to be much less momentous for Japan's security stance. In the era of globalization, domestic and regional forces continue to be of very great importance. Hence, despite the rise in tensions between Japan and China, the rise of North Korea as a nuclear-weapon state, the possibility of abandonment by a more erratic United States, and the relative decline of the Japanese economy, the implications of these chapters for Japan and its ever-changing security environment point to marginal policy change and adaptation rather than to dramatic breaks from past practices. Furthermore, at a regional level we can detect the emergence of an embryonic regionalism that complements rather than replaces a still deeply entrenched bilateralism in Asian security affairs.

The three chapters in Part II place Japan's and Asia's internal and external security policy in an explicitly comparative perspective. Chapters 7 and 9 analyze Japanese and German counterterrorism policies, respectively, in the 1970s and 1980s and after 9/11, and show in which ways they differ both from each other and from American policies. Although strong versions of globalization theory expect a flattening of the world and convergence in best state practices when confronting global threats, the observed differences are not surprising to students of the Japanese and German state and Japanese and German security practices. Chapter 8 examines a foundational moment in the late 1940s when American diplomacy, for a variety of reasons, helped lay down different tracks that were to shape Asian bilateralism and European multilateralism for the next half century.

The two framing chapters, 2 and 10, rely on the analysis of Japanese and Asian security to illustrate the advantages of analytical eclecticism over the paradigmatic approaches that mark much of the scholarship on international relations. The 1990s witnessed a strong turn toward sociological styles of analysis that highlight the importance of norms and identity. Like the other chapters in this book, both partly incorporate this sociological (or constructivist) turn, in the hope that it will enrich and engage rather than replace or subsume rationalist styles of analysis.

Fifteen years ago, only area specialists were thinking about the questions of Japanese security, and those questions were narrowly framed. A more fully theorized approach to Japanese security has become more widely accepted. It has opened new analytical vistas that may encourage an exploration of new political possibilities at the very time that a more assertive and less certain Japan is seeking to recalibrate its policies in a changing world.

Notes

1 For their their numerous and insightful criticisms, comments and suggestions, I would like to thank Amitav Acharya, Fiona Adamson, Richard Friman,

Christopher Hemmer, Mary Katzenstein, Paul Kowert, Ellis Krauss, David Leheny, Paul Midford, Nobuo Okawara, T. J. Pempel, Richard Samuels, Mark Selden, Rudra Sil, and Stefan Wolff. All remaining errors of omission and commission are due to my stubbornness rather than to their good counsel.

2 Personal communications, June 14, 2007.

3 In the light of some recent scholarship Pyle is probably taking insufficient account of the many ways in which Japan was connected to the outside world. See Hamashita (forthcoming).

4 Here I am passing over the issue of whether Japan should be called a civilizational state or polity (*kokutai*) with a very high degree of stateness compared to Islamic civilization.

5 This section summarizes some of the major arguments in Katzenstein (2005). See also "Roundtable" (2007).

6 My interpretation on this key point thus disagrees with McCormack's (2007a: 79–80): "it is hard to escape the feeling that they [U.S. officials] functioned rather as proconsuls, advising and instructing, while seeing Japan still as an imperial dependency, rather like General MacArthur a half-century earlier, who was acclaimed a benevolent liberator even while treating the Japanese people as children." In private conversation (October 25, 2007) Professor McCormack concedes that for reasons yet unspecified the label of "client state" is not appropriate for characterizing Britain's position in world politics.

7 The revision of this law shifts power from local school boards to the central government and thus affects the perennial conflicts over the content of historical instruction and the mandatory singing of the national anthem at school ceremonies.

8 Twenty-two of the twenty-five Diet members in Abe's cabinet, the cabinet secretariat, and his core advisory staff were members of nationalist alliances, the Shinto Association of Spiritual Leadership, and the Japan Conference. The Shinto Association is dedicated to promoting Japanese traits, reverence for the imperial family, and worship at the Yasukuni shrine. The Japan Conference is committed to the staple of nationalist causes: historical revisionism, revising the constitution and education laws, Yasukuni, and upgrading the position of the Self-Defense Forces. Before becoming prime minister, Abe had served as secretary-general of both of these Diet organizations, as well as of the History Education Alliance, a lobby in the Diet seeking to purge Japanese history textbooks of the discussion of Japanese war crimes and what it regards as excessively critical views of Japan (Junkerman 2007: 3; Morris-Suzuki 2007). However, the most recent and authoritative World Bank calculations of China's GDP, in terms of purchasing power parity, lowers its 2005 figure by 40 percent from $8.9 trillion to $5.3 trillion, compared with $2.2 trillion using market rate exchange rates. See *The Economist* (December 22, 2007), p. 68.

9 In terms of purchasing-power parity, according to some estimates China's economy surpassed Japan's as early as 1994 (Shiraishi 2006: 10).

10 According to the IMF, by 2006 Japan's GDP was $4.367 trillion compared to China's figure of $2.630 trillion, a ratio of 1.66:1 <http://www.imf.org/external/pubs/ft/weo/2007/01/data/index.aspx> (accessed August 4, 2007).

11 The material in the next four paragraphs draws on Katzenstein (2005: 63–7).

12 Interviews, Tianjin and Beijing, March–April 2006.

References

Abramowitz, Morton I., Yoichi, Funabashi, and Jisi, Wang (2002) *China–Japan–U.S. Relations: Meeting New Challenges*, Tokyo/New York: Japan Center for International Exchange.

Berger, Thomas (1998) *Cultures of Anti-Militarism: National Security in Germany and Japan*, Baltimore, Md.: Johns Hopkins University Press.

Boyd, J. Patrick and Samuels, Richard J. (2005) *Nine Lives? The Politics of Constitutional Reform in Japan*, Policy Studies No. 19, Washington, DC: East–West Center.

Buruma, Ian (1994) *The Wages of Guilt: Memories of War in Germany and Japan*, New York: Farrar, Straus & Giroux.

Callahan, William (2003) "Beyond Cosmopolitanism and Nationalism: Diasporic Chinese and Neo-Nationalism in China and Thailand," *International Organization*, 57 (Summer): 481–517.

Chase, Robert, Hill, Emily, and Kennedy, Paul (eds) (1999) *The Pivotal States: A New Framework for U.S. Policy in the Developing World*, New York: W. W. Norton.

Chow, Jonathan T. (2005) "ASEAN Counterterrorism Cooperation since 9/11," *Asian Survey*, 45, 2: 302–21.

Cohen, Danielle F. S. (2005) *Retracing the Triangle: China's Strategic Perceptions of Japan in the Post-Cold War Era*, Maryland Series in Contemporary Asian Studies Number 2–2005 (181).

Collins, Randall (1998) *The Sociology of Philosophies: A Global Theory of Intellectual Change*, Cambridge, Mass.: Harvard University Press.

Collins, Randall (2000) "The Sociology of Philosophies: A Précis," *Philosophy of the Social Sciences*, 30: 157–201.

Dædalus (1991) *The Living Tree: The Changing Meanings of Being Chinese Today* (Spring).

DeGrazia, Victoria (2005) *Irresistible Empire: The American Conquest of Europe*, Cambridge, Mass.: Harvard University Press.

Dickie, Mure and Pilling, David (2007) "Warm Words, Old Wounds: How China and Japan Are Starting to March in Step," *Financial Times*, April 9, p. 9.

Dreyer, June Teufel (2006) "Sino-Japanese Rivalry and Its Implications for Developing Nations," *Asian Survey*, 46, 4 (July/August): 538–57.

Economy, Elizabeth and Oksenberg, Michael (eds) (1999) *China Joins the World: Progress and Prospects*, New York: Council on Foreign Relations Press.

Eisenstadt, S. N. (1996) *Japanese Civilization: A Comparative View*, Chicago, Ill.: University of Chicago Press.

Eisenstadt, S. N. (2002) "Multiple Modernities," *Dædalus*, 129, 1 (Winter): 1–29.

Eisenstadt, S. N. (2003) *Comparative Civilizations and Multiple Modernities*, 2 vols, Leiden: Brill.

Friedberg, Aaron (1993/94) "Ripe for Rivalry: Prospects for Peace in a Multipolar Asia," *International Security*, 18, 3 (Winter): 5–33.

Friedman, Edward (2000) "Preventing War between China and Japan," pp. 99–128 in Edward Friedman and Barrett L. McCormick (eds) *What If China Doesn't Democratize: Implications for War and Peace*, Armonk, NY: M. E. Sharpe.

Gilpin, Robert (1981) *War and Change in World Politics*, New York: Cambridge University Press.

Gomez, Edmund Terence and Hsiao, Hsin-Huang Michael (eds) (2001) *Chinese Business in Southeast Asia: Contesting Cultural Explanations, Researching Entrepreneurship*, Richmond, Surrey: Curzon.

Gomez, Edmund Terence and Hsiao, Hsin-Huang Michael (eds) (2004) *Chinese Enterprise, Transnationalism, and Identity*, London: RoutledgeCurzon.

Gow, James (2005) *Defending the West*, Malden, Mass.: Polity.

Green, Michael J. (1998) "State of the Field Report: Research on Japanese Security Policy," *Access Asia Review*, 2, 1 (September): 5–39.

Green, Michael J. (2007) "Japan Is Back: Why Tokyo's New Assertiveness Is Good for Washington," *Foreign Affairs*, 86, 2 (March/April): 142–7.

Hamashita, Takeshi (forthcoming) *China, East Asia and the Global Economy: Regional and Historical Perspectives*, ed. Linda Grove and Mark Selden, London: Routledge.

Hartz, Louis (1955) *The Liberal Tradition in America*, New York: Harcourt, Brace.

Heginbotham, Eric and Samuels, Richard J. (1998) "Mercantile Realism and Japanese Foreign Policy," *International Security*, 22, 4: 171–203.

Hughes, Christopher W. (1998) "Japan's Aum Shinrikyo, the Changing Nature of Terrorism, and the Post-Cold War Security Agenda," *Pacifica Review*, 10, 1 (February): 39–60.

Hughes, Christopher W. (2007) "Not Quite the 'Great Britain of the Far East': Japan's Security, the U.S.–Japan Alliance and the 'War on Terror' in East Asia," *Cambridge Review of International Affairs* 20, 2 (June): 325–38.

Hughes, Christopher W. and Krauss, Ellis S. (2007) "Japan's New Security Agenda," *Survival*, 49, 2 (Summer): 157–76.

Hughes, Llewelyn (2007) "Why Japan Will Not Go Nuclear (Yet)," *International Security*, 31, 4 (Spring): 67–96.

Huntington, Samuel P. (1996) *The Clash of Civilizations and the Remaking of the World Order*, New York: Simon & Schuster.

Ikenberry, G. John and Inoguchi, Takashi (eds) (2003) *Reinventing the Alliance: U.S.–Japan Security Partnership in an Era of Change*, New York: Palgrave Macmillan.

Ikenberry, G. John and Inoguchi, Takashi (eds) (2007) *The Uses of Institutions: The U.S., Japan and Governance in East Asia*, New York: Palgrave Macmillan.

Iriye, Akira (1992) *China and Japan in the Global Setting*, Cambridge, Mass.: Harvard University Press.

Johnston, Alastair Iain (1995) *Cultural Realism: Strategic Culture and Grand Strategy in Chinese History*, Princeton, NJ: Princeton University Press.

Johnston, Alastair Iain (2004) "Beijing's Security Behavior in the Asia-Pacific: Is China a Dissatisfied Power?," pp. 34–96 in J. J. Suh, Peter J. Katzenstein and Allen Carlson (eds) *Rethinking Security in East Asia: Identity, Power, and Efficiency*, Stanford, Calif.: Stanford University Press.

Johnston, Alastair Iain (2008) *Social States: China in International Institutions, 1980–2000*, Princeton, NJ: Princeton University Press.

Johnston, Alastair Iain and Ross, Robert S. (eds) (1999) *Engaging China: The Management of an Emerging Power*, London: Routledge.

Johnston, Alastair Iain and Stockmann, Danie (2007) "Chinese Attitudes toward the United States and Americans," pp. 157–95 in Peter J. Katzenstein and Robert O. Keohane (eds) *Anti-Americanisms in World Politics*, Ithaca, NY: Cornell University Press.

Junkerman, John (2007) "Japan's Neonationalist Offensive and the Military," <http://japanfocus.org/products/details/2302> (accessed January 2, 2007).

Kang, David C. (2007) *China Rising: Peace, Power, and Order in East Asia*, New York: Columbia University Press.

Katzenstein, Peter J. (1985) *Small States in World Markets: Industrial Policy in Europe*, Ithaca, NY: Cornell University Press.

Katzenstein, Peter J. (1996) *Cultural Norms and National Security: Police and Military in Postwar Japan*, Ithaca, NY: Cornell University Press.

Katzenstein, Peter J. (ed.) (1997) *Tamed Power: Germany in Europe*, Ithaca, NY: Cornell University Press.

Katzenstein, Peter J. (2005) *A World of Regions: Asia and Europe in the American Imperium*, Ithaca, NY: Cornell University Press.

Katzenstein, Peter J. (2006) "East Asia—Beyond Japan," pp. 1–33 in Peter J. Katzenstein and Takashi Shiraishi (eds) *Beyond Japan: The Dynamics of East Asian Regionalism*, Ithaca, NY: Cornell University Press.

Katzenstein, Peter J. and Keohane, Robert O. (eds) (2007) *Anti-Americanisms in World Politics*, Ithaca, NY: Cornell University Press.

Katzenstein, Peter J. and Shiraishi, Takashi (eds) (1997) *Network Power: Japan and Asia*, Ithaca, NY: Cornell University Press.

Katzenstein, Peter J. and Shiraishi, Takashi (eds) (2006) *Beyond Japan: The Dynamics of East Asian Regionalism*, Ithaca, NY: Cornell University Press.

Katzenstein, Peter J. and Sil, Rudra (forthcoming) "The Contributions of Eclectic Theorizing to the Study and Practice of International Relations," in Chris Reus-Smit and Duncan Snidal (eds) *Oxford Handbook of International Relations*.

Krauss, Ellis S. and Pempel, T. J. (eds) (2004) *Beyond Bilateralism: U.S.–Japan Relations in the New Asia-Pacific*, Stanford, Calif.: Stanford University Press.

Lake, David (1988) *Power, Protection, and Free Trade: International Sources of U.S. Commercial Strategy, 1987–1939*, Ithaca, NY: Cornell University Press.

Lam, Peng Er (ed.) (2006) *Japan's Relations with China—Facing a Rising Power*, London: Routledge.

Larsson, Tomas Henrik (2007) "Capitalizing Thailand: Colonialism, Communism, and the Political Economy of Rural Rights," PhD dissertation, Government Department, Cornell University.

Leheny, David (2005) "Terrorism, Social Movements, and International Security: How Al Qaeda Affects Southeast Asia," *Japanese Journal of Political Science*, 6, 1: 87–109.

Lind, Jennifer (2004) "Pacifism or Passing the Buck," *International Security*, 29, 1 (Summer): 92–121.

Lobe, Jim (2006) "U.S. Neo-Conservatives Call for Japanese Nukes, Regime Change in North Korea," *Japan Focus*, <http://japanfocus.org/products/details/2249> (accessed June 9, 2007).

McCormack, Gavan (2007a) *Client State: Japan in the American Embrace*, London: Verso.

McCormack, Gavan (2007b) "A Denuclearized Deal in Beijing: The Prospect of Ending the 20th Century in East Asia," *Japan Focus*, <http://japanfocus.org/products/topdf/2354> (accessed February 19, 2007).

McCormack, Gavan (2007c) "Japan as a Nuclear State," *Japan Focus*. Available at <http://japanfocus.org/products/details/2488> (accessed August 6, 2007).

McCormack, Gavan (2007d) "North Korea and the Birth Pangs of a New Northeast Asian Order," *Japan Focus*, <http://japanfocus.org/products/topdf/25557 (accessed November 4, 2007).

McDougall, Walter A. (1997) *Promised Land, Crusader State*, New York: Houghton Mifflin.

Martin, Craig (2007) "The Case Against 'Revising Interpretations' of the Japanese Constitution," *Japan Focus*, <http://japanfocus.org/products/topdf/2434> (accessed June 8, 2007).

Mearsheimer, John (2001) *The Tragedy of Great Power Politics*, New York: W. W. Norton.

Midford, Paul (2006) *Japanese Public Opinion and the War on Terrorism: Implications for Japan's Security Strategy*, Washington, DC: East–West Center.

Mochizuki, Mike M. (2004) "Japan: Between Alliance and Autonomy," pp. 103–38 in Ashley J. Tellis and Michael Willis (eds) *Confronting Terrorism in the Pursuit of Power: Strategic Asia, 2004–2005*, Seattle, Wash.: National Bureau of Asian Research.

Mochizuki, Mike M. and O'Hanlon, Michael (1998) "A Liberal Vision for the U.S.–Japan Alliance," *Survival*, 40, 2 (Summer): 127–34.

Morris-Suzuki, Tessa (2007) "Who Is Responsible? The Yomiuri Project and the Enduring Legacy of the Asia-Pacific War," *Japan Focus*, <http://japanfocus.org/products/topdf/2455> (accessed June 25, 2007).

Nabers, Dirk (2006) "Culture and Collective Action: Japan, Germany and the United States after September 11, 2001," *Cooperation and Conflict*, 41, 3 (September): 305–26.

Nau, Henry (2002) *At Home Abroad: Identity and Power in American Foreign Policy*, Ithaca, NY: Cornell University Press.

Naughton, Barry (ed.) (1997) *The China Circle: Economics and Technology in the PRC, Taiwan, and Hong Kong*, Policy Studies 27, Washington, DC: Brookings Institution.

Onishi, Norimitsu (2007a) "Japan to Vote on Modifying Pacifist Charter Written by U.S.," *New York Times*, May 15, p. A3.

Onishi, Norimitsu (2007b) "Japan Defense Chief Resigns over Bomb Remark," *New York Times*, July 4, p. A3.

Pei, Mixin (2007) "Ways to End the Sino-Japanese Chill," *Financial Times*, April 10, p. 13.

Pei, Mixin and Swaine, Michael (2005) "Simmering Fire in Asia: Averting Sino-Japanese Strategic Conflict," *Policy Brief 44* (November), Carnegie Endowment for International Peace.

Pempel, T. J. (2007) "Japanese Strategy under Koizumi," pp. 109–33 in Gilbert Rozman, Kazuhiko Togo and Joseph P. Ferguson (eds) *Japanese Strategic Thought toward Asia*, New York: Palgrave Macmillan.

Pew Global Attitudes Project (2007) "Global Unease with Major World Powers: Rising Environmental Concern in 47-Nation Survey" (June 27). <http://pew-global.org/reports/display.php?ReportID=256> (accessed July 13, 2007).

Pilling, David (2006a) "Abe Vows to Review Japan's Pacifist Principles," *Financial Times*, November 1, p. 2.

Pilling, David (2006b) "The Son also Rises," *Financial Times*, September 16–17, pp. W1–W2.

Pilling, David (2006c) " 'To Befit the Reality': How Abe Aims to Secure Japan Its Desired World Status," *Financial Times*, November 1, p. 11.

Pilling, David (2007a) "Japan's Military Prepares for a More Assertive Foreign Role," *Financial Times*, March 29, p. 5.

Pilling, David (2007b) "Japan Feels Threat of China's Military," *Financial Times*, July 7/8, p. 4.

Pyle, Kenneth B. (2007) *Japan Rising: The Resurgence of Japanese Power and Purpose*, New York: Public Affairs.

"Roundtable: Peter J. Katzenstein's Contributions to the Study of East Asian Regionalism," (2007) *Journal of East Asian Studies*, 7: 359–412.

Samuels, Richard J. (2003) *Machiavelli's Children: Leaders and Their Legacies in Italy and Japan*, Ithaca, NY: Cornell University Press.

Samuels, Richard J. (2007) *Securing Japan: Tokyo's Grand Strategy and the Future of East Asia*, Ithaca, NY: Cornell University Press.

Sato, Peter (2007) "The View from Tokyo: Melting Ice and Building Bridges," *China Brief*, 7, 9 (May 2): 2–4.

Selden, Mark (1997) "China, Japan and the Regional Political Economy of East Asia, 1945–1995," pp. 306–40 in Peter J. Katzenstein and Takashi Shiraishi (eds) *Beyond Japan: The Dynamics of East Asian Regionalism*, Ithaca, NY: Cornell University Press.

Selden, Mark (2006) "The Future of Korea: An Asia-Pacific Perspective," *Japan Focus*, <http://japanfocus.org/products/topdf/2190> (accessed September 1, 2006).

Sevastopulo, Demetri and Pilling, David (2007) "Abe to Explore U.S. Stealth Jet Option," *Financial Times*, April 23, p. 4.

Shiraishi, Takashi (2006) "An Asia Strategy for Koizumi's Successor," *Japan Echo*, 33, 6 (December): 7–11.

Sil, Rudra (2004) "Problems Chasing Methods or Methods Chasing Problems? Research Communities, Constrained Pluralism, and the Role of Eclecticism," pp. 307–31 in Ian Shapiro, Rogers M. Smith and Tarek E. Masoud (eds) *Problems and Methods in the Study of Politics*, New York: Cambridge University Press.

Smith, Rogers M. (1993) "Beyond Tocqueville, Myrdal, and Hartz: The Multiple Traditions in America," *American Political Science Review*, 87, 3 (September): 549–65.

Steinberg, David I. (ed.) (2005) *Korean Attitudes toward the United States: Changing Dynamics*, Armonk, NY: M. E. Sharpe.

Stubbs, Richard (1999) "War and Economic Development: Export-Oriented Industrialization in East and Southeast Asia," *Comparative Politics*, 31, 3: 337–55.

Stubbs, Richard (2005) *Rethinking Asia's Economic Miracle*, Basingstoke: Palgrave Macmillan.

Suryadinata, Leo (1978) *"Overseas Chinese" in Southeast Asia and China's Foreign Policy: An Interpretive Essay*, Singapore, Institute of Southeast Asian Studies, Research Notes and Discussion Papers No. 11.

Tanaka, Akihiko (2007) "Asian Opinions: A Mixed Bag for Japan," *Japan Echo* (June): 31–4.

Taylor, Robert (1996) *Greater China and Japan: Prospects for an Economic Partnership in East Asia*, London: Routledge.

Twomey, Christopher P. (2000) "Japan, a 'Circumscribed Balancer:' Building on Defensive Realism to Make Predictions about East Asian Security," *Security Studies*, 9, 4 (Summer): 167–205.

Wang, Qingxin Ken (2000) *Hegemonic Cooperation and Conflict: Postwar Japan's China Policy and the United States*, Westport, Conn.: Praeger.

Weidenbaum, Murray and Hughes, Samuel (1996) *The Bamboo Network: How Expatriate Chinese Entrepreneurs Are Creating a New Economic Superpower in Asia*, New York: Free Press.

Winter, Jay (2006) *Remembering War: The Great War between Memory and History in the Twentieth Century*, New Haven, Conn.: Yale University Press.

Zhao, Suisheng (1997) *Power Competition in East Asia*, New York: St Martin's Press.

Zhu, Tianbiao (2000) "Consistent Threat, Political–Economic Institutions, and Northeast Asian Developmentalism," PhD dissertation, Government Department, Cornell University.

Zhu, Tianbiao (2002) "Developmental States and Threat Perceptions in Northeast Asia," *Journal of Conflict, Security and Development*, 2, 1: 6–29.

2 Japan, Asian-Pacific security, and the case for analytical eclecticism

Peter J. Katzenstein and
Nobuo Okawara (2001)[1]

Extolling, in the abstract, the virtues of a specific analytical perspective to the exclusion of others is intellectually less important than making sense of empirical anomalies and stripping notions of what is "natural" of their intuitive plausibility. With specific reference to Japanese and Asian-Pacific security affairs, this article argues against the privileging of parsimony that has become the hallmark of paradigmatic debates. The complex links between power, interest, and norms defy analytical capture by any one paradigm. They are made more intelligible by drawing selectively on different paradigms—that is, by analytical eclecticism, not parsimony.

We illustrate this general point with specific reference to Asia-Pacific, an area central to security affairs since the end of the Cold War. In the first section, we question briefly what is supposedly "natural" or "normal" about Japan. Next we argue that styles of analysis that focus exclusively on either material capabilities, institutional efficiencies, or norms and identities overlook key aspects of the evidence. We conclude with some general reflections on the advantages and disadvantages of analytical eclecticism for understanding Japanese and Asian-Pacific security affairs.

What is a "natural" or "normal" Japan?

To many observers, U.S.–Japan security arrangements and Japan's passive stance on issues of defense are unnatural, to be superseded sooner or later by an Asia freed from the shackles of U.S. primacy and a Japan no longer restrained by pacifism.[2] We disagree on both empirical and analytical grounds. Based on the evidence, we argue that an eclectic theoretical approach finds that there is nothing "natural" about a multipolar world with U.S. primacy and nothing "normal" about a Japan without the institutional legacy of Hiroshima and defeat in World War II.

According to one group of Asia experts, the ongoing presence of U.S. forces in South Korea and Japan prohibits the restoration of a regional balance of power as the "natural" course of events in Asia-Pacific. Chalmers Johnson, for example, argues that U.S. policy has a stranglehold over Japan and regional actors that carries an exorbitant cost to both the United States and its regional partners (Johnson 2000a; 2000b: 4). Far better, Johnson argues, to recall the U.S. military and let Asians be in charge of Asia. With the end of the Cold War and the disintegration of the Soviet Union, the United States no longer needs its far-flung empire, military or otherwise. China's high-growth economy, the eventual reunification of North and South Korea, and a Japan that overcomes its self-willed form of political paralysis are all natural developments that U.S. policymakers need to recognize. According to Johnson, only by bending to the natural course of history will the United States escape from the mounting cost of empire blowback at home that he suggests threatens the very fabric of American society.

Our main empirical finding points to a different conclusion: The continued U.S. presence in Asia appears to be beyond doubt for the short to medium term; that is, for the next three to ten years. Formal and informal bilateralism is thriving in Asia-Pacific, while an incipient multilateralism is beginning to take shape.[3] Whether this incipient multilateralism will become sufficiently strong and durable to offer a partial complement to traditional balance-of-power politics, as evidently has happened in Western Europe, remains an open question. But in the short to medium term most of the governments in Asia-Pacific will continue to welcome the U.S. presence. As has been true in Europe since 1989, in Asia-Pacific the United States is seen as more distant and more benign than other regional powers, such as Japan and China. The period of U.S. security reassurance, to be sure, may well be limited to a few decades. But in Asia-Pacific there is nothing natural about incipient multi-lateralism or the tendency to balance power. History is not a series of devia-tions from a "natural" state of stable or unstable affairs. Rather it is an open-ended process in which the accumulation of events and experience from one period alters the contours of the next. Nothing about this process is "natural" unless we permit our analytical perspectives to make it so.

Another group of Asia-Pacific analysts takes a different, more threatening view of Japan that also cuts against this article's analytical and empirical grain. According to this view, Japan is once again becoming a "natural" major power. It is spending more money on developing its military prowess and power projection capabilities. Japan's military is beginning to equip itself with both shield and spear. By passing the International Peace Cooperation Law (which authorized the Japanese military to participate in United Nations peace-keeping operations); purchasing modern fighter planes such as the F-2; and moving to acquire airborne refueling capabilities, develop spy satellites, and adopt a theater missile defense system, the Japanese are signaling their intention to play a more active role in regional security.

Also according to this view, Japan's domestic politics is increasingly revealing traits that mark the return to a "normal," right-wing nationalism. The Japanese military is no longer viewed as a pariah and is evidently experi-encing a process of normalization (Frühstück 2000).[4] In both houses of the Diet, panels were set up in 2000 to debate a possible revision of the 1947 Constitution, with the war-renouncing Article 9 likely to be at the center of the debate. In 1999 the Diet enacted legislation to implement new defense guidelines giving the Japanese military broader missions. Moreover, the Diet passed an anti-organized crime law that allows wiretapping of citizens' telephones and electronic mail, and it curtailed the civil liberties of members of Aum Shinrikyo, the religious cult that organized the 1995 sarin nerve gas attack in the Tokyo subway, bypassing a law that allows law enforcement to monitor the cult's activities. In addition, in 1999 the Diet officially recognized the sun flag as Japan's national flag and a song that celebrates the emperor's reign as its national anthem. In October 1999 a newly appointed parliamentary vice-minister of defense, Shingo Nishimura, claimed that the Diet ought to consider arming the country with nuclear weapons. This and his subsequent resignation created a furor that, in the words of Howard French, "laid bare deep fault lines in the new and politically shaky coalition government" (French 2000: A6). And former Prime Minister Yoshiro Mori has made a number of public statements evoking the spirit of Japanese nationalism in the 1930s. Most recently, in April 2001 controversial junior high-school history and social studies textbooks that downplay Japanese aggression in Asia and are tinged with nationalistic sentiments passed screening by the Ministry of Education. In sum, this more threatening view seems to suggest that there is ample reason to bemoan the stubborn ignorance with which U.S. policymakers and media continue to deny obvious historical parallels between contemporary Japan and Japan of the 1930s.[5]

The above news items are like dots that we can connect to create an image of a Japan readying itself to strike militarily once again. But these dots can be connected in many other ways. How we go about drawing connections depends largely on the implicit analytical lenses that we use to interpret Japanese politics. Because it regards as "natural" the displacement of a 1960s-style liberal pacifism by a 1930s-style militant nationalism, a pessimistic interpretation of the evidence neglects many facets of Japanese politics and society that may be worth consideration. But none of the political movements on the left or the right is "natural." Instead they influence one another in a process of historical evolution that is likely to be combinatorial in creating unforeseen outcomes. The kind of nationalism that will shape Japanese politics remains largely unknown. Falling back on past events to make sense of snippets of current news is a mistake. Instead our analysis should focus on the institutional norms and practices that Japan's political and other public leaders use to evolve novel forms of politics and policy (Katzenstein and Okawara 1993; Katzenstein 1996).

No polity remains frozen in time, and none returns to its "natural," historical origin. Obviously, it would be wrong to rule out the emergence of a new kind of nationalist politics in Japan. Here and elsewhere in Asia-Pacific, historical animosities and suspicions run deep. Thomas Berger may therefore be correct in looking to ethnic and racial hatreds as the most likely source of future military clashes in Asia-Pacific (Berger 2000). But the combined legacies of Japanese nationalism and pacifism are likely to produce new political constellations and policies that will resist analytical capture by ahistorical conceptions of a "normal" Japan. Real life is likely to be both more complicated and more interesting.

Analytical eclecticism in the analysis of Japanese and Asian-Pacific security

A robust bilateralism and incipient multilateralism in Japanese and Asian-Pacific security affairs are typically not well explained by the exclusive reliance on any single analytical perspective—be it realist, liberal, or constructivist. Japan's and Asia-Pacific's security policies are not shaped solely by power, interest, or identity but by their combination. Adequate understanding requires analytical eclecticism, not parsimony.

Disadvantages of parsimonious explanations

Strict formulations of realism, liberalism, and constructivism sacrifice explanatory power in the interest of analytical purity. Yet in understanding political problems we typically need to weigh the causal importance of different types of factors; for example, material and ideal, international and domestic. Eclectic theorizing, not the insistence on received paradigms, helps us understand inherently complex social and political processes.

Realism

Realist theory has various guises. Drawing on an increasingly rich literature, Robert Jervis (Jervis 1999), for example, operates with a twofold distinction (between offensive and defensive realism). Alastair Johnston (1999a) favors a more complex fourfold categorization (balance of power, power maximization, balance of threat, and identity realism). Although they formulate their analyses somewhat differently, they and other realists share many insights— the most important being the effects of the security dilemma on state behavior. Realists such as Kenneth Waltz underline the brevity of the unipolar moment that the United States has enjoyed since the end of the Cold War and the disintegration of the Soviet Union (Waltz 1998). For them, however, the magnitude of current U.S. capabilities is less important than the policy follies—such as interventions in areas of the world not directly tied to the national interests of the United States—that squander it. Hence "the all-but-inevitable movement from unipolarity to multipolarity is taking place not in Europe but in Asia. . . . Theory enables one to say that a new balance of power will form but not to say how long it will take" (Waltz 1998: 30, 19). Though distinctively his own in style of argumentation, Waltz's analysis is in broad agreement with other types of realist analysis that consider factors besides the international distribution of capabilities, such as absolute security needs and threats. Japan and China are rising great powers in Asia-Pacific. In view of a large number of potential military flashpoints, the security dilemma confronting Asian-Pacific states is serious. Between 1950 and 1990, one study reports 129 territorial disputes worldwide, with Asia accounting for the largest number. Of the fifty-four borders disputed in 1990, the highest ratio of unresolved disputes as a fraction of total contested borders was located in East and Southeast Asia (Huth 1996: 32). In this view, Asia-Pacific may well be "ripe for rivalry" (Friedberg 1993/4; Betts 1993/4). For realists, balancing against the United States as the only superpower, currently by China and in the near future by Japan, is the most important prediction that the theory generates (Mochizuki 1997).

Realist theory, however, is indeterminate. It cannot say whether Japan will balance with China against the United States as the preeminent threat or whether it will balance with the United States against China as the rising regional power in East Asia.[6] Balance-of-power theory predicts that a withdrawal of U.S. forces from East Asia would leave Japan no choice but to rearm. Alternatively, balancing theory can also support a very different line of reasoning in which Japan, though wary of China, might recognize China's central position in Asia-Pacific and stop far short of adopting a policy of full-fledged remilitarization.[7] To infer anything about the direction of balancing requires auxiliary assumptions that typically invoke interest, threat, or prestige—all variables that require liberal or constructivist styles of analysis. Moreover, it is unclear whether a united Korea will balance against Japan (with its powerful navy that might ultimately control the sea-lanes on which Korean trade depends so heavily) or against China (with the strongest ground forces in Asia and with which Korea shares a common border) (Cha 2000). Thus realist theory points to omnipresent balancing behavior but tells us little about the direction of that balancing.

Nor do military expenditures alone yield a clear picture of the geostrategic situation in Asia-Pacific. Asia's 1997 financial crisis slowed Asian-Pacific arms rivalries and lowered military spending.[8] Thus, instead of worrying about escalating arms rivalries, some defense experts began to express greater concern over potential risks created by possible imbalances in military modernization and financial strength. After 1997 countries less affected by the financial crisis—such as China, Japan, Korea, Singapore, and Taiwan—appeared to be much better positioned to harness sophisticated technologies to enhance their military strength (Richardson 2000).

Liberalism

On its own, liberal theory also encounters serious difficulties. Some analysts have suggested that the U.S.–Japan alliance can last only if it articulates common values. Mike Mochizuki and Michael O'Hanlon, for example, have advocated that the alliance should become as "close, balanced and principle-based as the U.S.–UK special relationship." Not a common military threat but common interests derived from shared democratic values, Mochizuki and

O'Hanlon argue, are the best guarantor for sustaining the U.S.–Japan alliance (Mochizuki and O'Hanlon 1998: 127).

What would happen, however, if the United States or Japan were no longer a member of the "free world"? Liberal analysis is hindered by the theory's underlying assumption that identities are unchanging. Do liberal values really constitute both the United States and Japan as actors? This is implausible. The promotion of democracy as a positive value, for example, is handled very differently by the U.S. and Japanese governments. The philosophical assumption informing U.S. policy is that democracy and human rights should proceed hand in hand with economic development. In contrast, Japanese policy assumes that economic development is conducive to the building of democratic institutions. This difference in philosophy leads to an equally noticeable difference in method. The United States operates with legal briefs, economic sanctions, and "sticks." Japan prefers constructive engagement through dialogue, economic assistance, and "carrots" (Takeda 1997). Such systematic differences in approach undercut a liberal redefinition of the U.S.–Japan alliance. To Japan they make the United States appear high-handed and evangelical, while to the United States Japan seems opportunistic and parochial. These differences point to the importance of collective identities not shared rather than of democratic institutions that are shared.

An alternative neoliberal analysis of the U.S.–Japan alliance focuses not on shared values but on efficiency (Kahler 1995; Inoguchi and Stillman 1997). For example, after the 1993–4 missile crisis on the Korean peninsula, policymakers in Japan and the United States became convinced that their bilateral defense guidelines needed to be revised to enhance the efficiency of defense cooperation. The 1960 Mutual Cooperation and Security Treaty and the 1978 Guidelines for Japan–U.S. Defense Cooperation had left unclear the role to be played by Japan in regional crises. Specifically, they left undefined both the extent to which Japan would provide logistical support and whether the U.S. military would have access to Japan's Self-Defense Forces and civilian facilities. The 1997 revised defense guidelines reduce these ambiguities and thus help to prepare Japan for potential participation in both possible U.S. and UN operations undertaken, in the eyes of the proponents of the revised guidelines, in the interest of regional peace and security. This is an instance of government policies seeking to lower transaction costs and enhance efficiencies through institutionalized cooperation (Council on Foreign Relations Independent Study Group 1998).

The revision of the defense guidelines was, however, a central feature of Japanese security policy in the last decade that eludes neoliberal explanations. It extends the scope of the U.S.–Japan security arrangement under the provisions of the treaty for the maintenance of peace and security in "the Far East" to include "situations in areas surrounding Japan." The operative understanding of "the Far East" in Article 6 of the security treaty was geographically defined by the Japanese government in 1960 as "primarily the region north of the Philippines, as well as Japan and its surrounding area," including South

Korea and Taiwan. The revised guidelines explicitly state that the phrase "situations in areas surrounding Japan" (short for "situations in areas surrounding Japan that will have an important influence on Japan's peace and security") is conceptual and has no geographic connotations. In situations when rear-area support may be required, these areas are not necessarily limited to East Asia.[9]

This ambiguity has given rise to much debate in Japan and beyond. Under the revised guidelines, U.S.–Japanese cooperation in combat is obligatory only in situations involving the defense of Japan's home islands. In the view of revision advocates, problems may emerge in a crisis not involving an attack on Japan—including any that arise in the Asia-Pacific region—but that would require general defense cooperation with the United States in the interest of regional stability and security. For some the revised defense guidelines free Japan to provide logistical and other forms of support to the United States, falling short of military combat, as long as the crisis is politically construed as constituting a serious security threat to Japan.[10] Adopting a less flexible approach, the Ministry of Foreign Affairs director of the North American Affairs Bureau stated in May 1998, before the Lower House Foreign Affairs Committee, that "situations in areas surrounding Japan" were restricted to those occurring in the Far East and its surrounding areas.[11]

In the future, the clash between more or less flexible interpretations of the scope of U.S.–Japan defense cooperation will be shaped by changing international and domestic political conditions. The ambiguity that lurks behind conflicting viewpoints and temporary victories of one side or the other is central to how Japanese officials adapt security policy to change. According to the government's official interpretation, it is the specific security threat at a specific time that in the judgment of the Cabinet and the Diet will determine whether that threat will be covered by the ambiguous wording of the revised guidelines. Thus, the scope of the areas surrounding Japan is variable and depends on a functional and conceptual, rather than a geographic and objective, construction of Japan's changing security environment.

Neoliberal explanations of the U.S.–Japan alliance cannot explain the deliberate ambiguity in the definition of the term "surrounding area" in the revised defense guidelines. This ambiguity undercuts efficiency because it leaves unspecified the contingencies under which the Japanese government might choose to participate in regional security cooperation measures. Yet, for the guidelines' advocates, ambiguity, by deflecting criticism in Japan, may well increase U.S.–Japanese defense cooperation. In seeking to create flexibility in policy through a politics of interpretation and reinterpretation of text, ambiguity is a defining characteristic of Japan's security policy (Katzenstein 1996).

Constructivism

Parsimonious constructivist analysis of Japanese and Asian-Pacific security also lacks plausibility. Contrary to claims by neoliberals, multilateral institutions do more than facilitate the exchange of information. ASEAN (Association of Southeast Asian Nations) processes of trust building, for example, appear to be well under way (Simon 1998; Acharya 2000a, 2000b, 1999a, 1998, 1995, 1991; Khong 1998, 1997). The ASEAN Regional Forum (ARF) is more than an intraorganizational balancing of threats and capabilities. Yuen Foong Khong writes that it is the only "mechanism for defusing the conflictual by-products of power balancing practices" in Asia-Pacific (Khong 1997: 296). It is thus understandable why governments are eager to adjust regional security institutions to new conditions rather than to abandon them altogether. Exclusive reliance on balancing strategies of the kind favored by realists appears to Asian-Pacific governments to be fraught with risk (Acharya 1999a).

In three carefully researched case studies dealing with relations between Malaysia and the Philippines between the 1960s and 1990s, ASEAN's policies after Vietnam's 1978 invasion of Cambodia, and the period of strategic uncertainty after the end of the Cold War, Nikolas Busse has shown that ASEAN norms have noticeably influenced government policy (Busse 2000, 1999). In the 1990s, specifically, ASEAN members did not balance against the destabilizing possibilities of U.S. disengagement, Japanese reassertion, and Chinese expansion. Instead member states sought to export the ASEAN way of intensive consultation to East Asia through the ARF and the Workshops on Managing Potential Conflicts in the South China Sea that Indonesia has convened since 1990. More recently, the ASEAN Plus Three meetings have provided a forum for discussion of security issues involving ASEAN members, Japan, South Korea, and China.[12] And in 2000 the ARF officially accepted North Korea as a member. Busse's research points to the importance of the legitimacy, success, and prominence of norms of informal consultations; consensus building; and nonintervention for Asian-Pacific security. In brief, ASEAN's strategy made China, the United States, and Japan part of ongoing security dialogues that replicate three important ASEAN norms: informal diplomacy, personal contacts, and respect for the principle of nonintervention.

The redefinition of collective identities, however, is a process measured in decades, not years. The accomplishments of various track-one and track-two security dialogues in Asia-Pacific remain limited. Bilateralism and multilateralism, as Acharya has pointed out, are less threat- and more uncertainty-oriented (Acharya 2000b). Collective identity is therefore less directly at stake than are trust and reputation. Skeptics have joked that the bark of the ARF is worse than its bite. The ARF has sidestepped the most pressing security issues in Asia: conflicts on the Korean peninsula, across the Taiwan Strait, and in the South China Sea. North Korea's nuclear and missile programs have become a major source of instability in Asia-Pacific (Hughes 1996). Hoping to defuse this crisis, the United States, Japan, China, and South Korea are all engaged in complicated, interlinked diplomatic initiatives that exclude both ASEAN and the ARF. The same is true of the smoldering Taiwan Strait crisis. With China declaring the status of Taiwan a domestic matter, the ASEAN norm of nonintervention has prevented the ARF from playing a mediating role in this crisis.[13] Finally, in the South China Sea the ARF has been slightly more engaged while still falling well short of seeking the role of active mediator between clashing state interests.[14]

The restricted scope of ARF activity is reflected in its minuscule organizational resources. Since its first meeting in 1994, the ARF has modeled itself after ASEAN. It has "participants" rather than "members," thus signaling the premium that it places on a lack of permanency and formality. The ARF has no headquarters or secretariat, and it is unlikely that either will be established.[15] Although there are a number of intersessional working groups, the ARF itself meets annually for one day only.[16]

The ARF has been weakened further by three developments in the late 1990s. First, Asia's financial crisis has put new strains on relations among several ASEAN members (including Malaysia and Singapore) and has illustrated, in the words of former Prime Minister of Singapore Lee Kuan Yew, that "we can't help each other" (*Economist* 1998: 44; Acharya 1999a; Rüland 2000: 439). Second, the ARF was unable to act in a politically meaningful way in the 1999 crisis in East Timor. The United Nations, not the ARF, was the central international arena and actor to which Indonesia turned. Third, there are some indications that, according to Michael Leifer, the accession of Cambodia, Laos, and Vietnam to ASEAN is leading to "revisionary fragmentation," with the three governments meeting separately at times from the older ASEAN members (Leifer 2000: 4). In addition, the United States is putting increasing emphasis on bilateral diplomatic and military relationships. Since 1996, for example, it has strengthened its links with Japan and Australia, and has expanded its military access to ASEAN members such as Singapore, Malaysia, Indonesia, Thailand, and the Philippines (Acharya 1999a: 2).

The Taiwan problem has imported the ARF's track-one problems into track-two talks. The ARF has not admitted Taiwan as a participant. After China joined CSCAP (the Council for Security Cooperation in the Asia Pacific) in 1996, Taiwanese participation in working group discussions occurred only by special invitation that had to be vetted informally by China (Fukushima 1999a; Hoshino 1999: 181; Terada 1998: 361).[17] Procedural and political controversies thus lurk just below the surface and tend to hamper progress in CSCAP. Its working groups are typically staffed by relatively young researchers given to a relatively free and informal style of exchanging views. The Chinese representative, however, is often unwilling to participate in these discussions except to stop them whenever they veer toward the politically sensitive issues of Taiwan's status or sovereignty disputes in the South China

Sea. In the context of the working group discussions, some Japanese participants interpret China's role as bordering on systematic obstructionism of the track-two process.[18]

The self-blocking tendencies of security multilateralism require much patience and reinforce, in the eyes of Japanese policymakers, the advantages of bilateral approaches to security issues.[19] The Japan Institute of International Affairs (JIIA) is the undisputed center for Japan's active involvement in a broad range of track-two activities.[20] Founded in the late 1950s and well connected in Japan, Asia-Pacific, and throughout the advanced industrial world, the JIIA has acted as the coordinator and secretarial office in Japan not only for CSCAP (since 1994) but also for the Pacific Economic Cooperation Council (since 1980), and for the Northeast Asia Cooperation Dialogue (since 1998).[21] Bilateralism marks the activities of JIIA. Based on a decade-long tradition of bilateral meetings with think-tanks, universities, and international affairs institutes in North America and Western Europe, regular bilateral exchanges with Asian-Pacific countries have increased sharply only since the mid-1980s—for example, with the China Institute of International Studies (since 1985), the South Korean Institute of Foreign Affairs and National Security (since 1986), the North Korean Institute for Disarmament and Peace (since 1990), the Vietnamese Institute for International Relations (since 1992), and the Indian Institute for Defense Studies and Analysis (since 1995).[22]

Advantages of eclectic explanations

Compelling analyses of empirical puzzles can be built through combining realist, liberal, and constructivist modes of explanation. Realism and liberalism together, for example, can generate powerful insights into the mixture of balance-of-power and multilateral politics. A soft form of balance-of-power theorizing, for example, informs the 1995 Nye report that provides a rationale for continued U.S. military engagement in East Asia (Bandow 1999; Council on Foreign Relations Independent Study Group 1998; Nye 2001). At one level the report is about increasing trust, communication, transparency, and reliability in a U.S.–Japan relationship marked by complex interdependence, thus seeking to stabilize the alliance and enhance predictability and stability in the region. But it is also about maintaining U.S. primacy. The 1997 Revised Guidelines for Japan–U.S. Defense Cooperation spell out the operations that Japan would be expected to carry out in a regional crisis, and thus ensure that in such a crisis potentially hostile states could not drive a wedge between the United States and Japan; Japan's support of U.S. forces would be sufficiently robust to prevent a backlash in the U.S. Congress against either the alliance or the forward deployment of U.S. forces in Asia-Pacific; Japan's defense posture would continue to be guided by alliance planning; and, finally, the United States would be able to win decisively in a possible military conflict with North Korea without shouldering excessive costs.[23]

In this realist–liberal perspective, the United States remains militarily and economically fully engaged in Asia-Pacific, thus reassuring Asian-Pacific states against the threat posed by Japan's present economic preponderance and potential military rearmament. Japan emerges as a potential economic and political leader contained within well-defined political boundaries. This double-barreled U.S. approach is rounded out by hopes for a unified and peaceful Korea and an economically prospering China increasingly engaged with the West, Japan, and the rest of Asia-Pacific (Auer 1998).

Japan's China policy also reflects a mixture of realist and liberal elements.[24] Just as Germany avoids at all cost having to choose between the United States and France, Japan avoids having to choose between the United States and China. Without risking its primary security relationship with the United States, Japan since the 1970s has consistently sought to engage China diplomatically. This entails an element of balancing as Japan seeks to constrain China, a potential opponent, through a policy of engagement. From Japan's perspective, countering China is possible only through alignment with the United States. Because China's military does not currently pose a serious threat to the region, and because military modernization is a costly and prolonged process measured in decades rather than years, the military aspects of the Japan–China relationship are relatively unimportant. Instead Japan's diplomacy aims at a slow, steady, and prolonged process of encouraging China to contribute more to regional stability and prosperity. On several issues— such as China's growing involvement in the ARF, an officially unacknowledged but nonetheless evident policy of seeking to enhance stability on the Korean peninsula, and the somewhat greater flexibility with which the leadership in Beijing has addressed encroachments on China's sovereignty on issues of political authority and economic independence (as opposed to those involving territorial integrity and jurisdictional monopoly)—Japanese patience is being rewarded.[25] See also the cautious notes of optimism in Christensen (1999). The settlement of virtually all of China's border conflicts, its acceptance into the World Trade Organization (WTO), and its far-reaching domestic reforms all point to a general political climate conducive to Japan's policy of engagement.[26]

A combination of realist and constructivist styles of analysis also has considerable heuristic power, as David Spiro and Alastair Johnston have argued (Spiro 1999; Johnston 1995). The volatile issue of Taiwan, potentially the most serious troublespot in Asia-Pacific, illustrates this analytical possibility (Christensen 1999: 62–9). The use of the term "surrounding areas" rather than "Far East" in the revised guidelines creates ambiguities, but they have been acceptable to both U.S. and Japanese defense officials for instrumental reasons. The United States has an interest in enhancing the deterrent effect of its alliance with Japan against China; Japanese officials have an interest in leaving undefined Japan's response to a possible crisis over Taiwan. The advantages of ambiguity on Taiwan are widely acknowledged inside the Japanese government,[27] as are the risks.[28] In the 1979 Taiwan Relations Act, the United States combined its diplomatic recognition of the People's Republic of China with a commitment to Taiwan's military defense. Japan, however, has kept its stance on Taiwan as ambiguous as possible. Japanese insistence on the domestic nature of the conflict between Beijing and Taipei, however, may not suffice in future crises. More than any other issue, Taiwan's status potentially confronts Japan and the United States with serious difficulties in defense cooperation should China seek to resolve this issue through military means.[29]

A combination of constructivism and realism also offers historical insights. John Fairbank, for example, has offered a broad interpretation of East Asian international relations (Fairbank 1968). For many centuries, Asian international relations were institutionalized as a suzerain, rather than as a sovereign, system of states in which the central power did not seek to subordinate or intervene unduly in the affairs of lesser powers within its ambit (Kang 2003: 174–6; Feske 1997: 18–19). China was the center of a system of tributary trade in which polities emulated and aligned with the central power. Focusing on systems with a preponderant source of power, Randall Schweller speaks of "bandwagoning for profit" (Schweller 1994). Less material objects than profits narrowly construed were involved, however. In Asia tribute was not only trade. It was also an institutional transmission belt for collective norms and identities in Chinese culture. Power, trade, and culture were central in defining the political relationships between the Middle Kingdom and its neighbors.

The Sinocentric world order was anarchic and organized around the principle of self-help. Power and geographic location mattered, just as realism leads us to expect. Yet Chinese diplomatic practices also facilitated cultural emulation, thus yielding a system with a distinctive mixture of hierarchy and equality. In this Sinocentric world, discrepancies between norms and practice were common, as is true of the Westphalian system of sovereign states. But, as Michel Oksenberg has observed, the nature of the misfit was different, so that certain ambiguous solutions of the past concerning territorial disputes over Taiwan, Tibet, and Hong Kong are today rendered more intractable.[30] Amending his own published work, Robert Jervis usefully underlines a theoretical point that many realists and neoliberals discount unduly: the dynamic and unanticipated consequences that institutions can have for preferences over outcomes, especially by effecting through domestic politics "deeper changes in what the actors want and how they conceive of their interests" (Jervis 1999: 61–2).

Liberalism and constructivism can also be combined to good effect. The years since the end of the Cold War, for example, have witnessed the growth of formal and informal multilateral security arrangements in Asia-Pacific. "Cooperative" approaches focus on military and nonmilitary dimensions of security, seek to prevent the emergence of manifest security threats, and are inclusive in their membership. Dialogues and various confidence-building measures are crucial to the creation of mutual trust (Kamiya 1997). These seek to lower the costs of making political contacts, facilitate the exchange of information, enhance transparency, and strengthen trust between governments.[31]

Multilateral security institutions can enhance efficiencies and over time alter underlying preferences and thus redefine interests (Gourevitch 1999: 137; Jervis 1999). The analytical difference between these two effects is mirrored in the attitudes of Japanese officials between a more skeptical and "realistic" stance on Asian security institutions on the one hand and a more enthusiastic and "pacifist" one on the other.[32]

Over longer periods, multilateral security institutions can do more than create efficiencies in the relations between governments. They can redefine identities and acceptable standards of behavior, and thus reduce or enhance fear and hostility or the collective pursuit of economic prosperity and political cooperation. Scholars who have written on the ARF, for example, have made a strong case for the importance of informal and formal dialogues as ways of creating not only more transparency but also arenas of persuasion and a partial change in preferences and interests (Acharya 1999a, 1999b, 1998, 1995; Busse 2000, 1999; Cheng n.d.; Johnston 1999b; Khong 1998; Simon 1998).

Analytical eclecticism offers distinct advantages. Whether they stress materialist or ideational factors, rationalist analytical perspectives such as realism and liberalism are enriched when employed in tandem. They are also enriched by the incorporation of constructivist elements. When realists and liberals in their empirically informed theoretical and policy writings slight norms and identities, they undermine the contribution to knowledge and policy advice they seek to make.[33]

Conclusion

The paradigmatic clashes in international relations theory and the field of security studies are part of a broader set of disagreements in political science and the social sciences. Theoretical debates between proponents of rationalist, culturalist, and historical–institutional approaches appear these days in various guises and combinations in virtually all fields of social inquiry. These debates reveal differences in problem focus, acceptable analytic methods, and substantive hypotheses. More important, they point to deep divides about unverifiable underlying assumptions concerning the possibilities, character, and purpose of social knowledge; the different routes we take to gain that knowledge; and the ontological status and epistemological significance of the relations between agents and structures and of the material and ideal aspects of social life (Sil 2000).

Many scholars offer reasonable and seemingly convergent postulates on every side of these debates that stress the need to build bridges between multiple analytical perspectives. Yet paradigmatic debates rarely succeed in moving us closer to a better integrated or more unified perspective in the social sciences—and for good reason. According to Rudra Sil, standard rhetoric in the field of comparative politics, for example, emphasizes "not a unified synthetic approach, but rather the greater flexibility of a particular research tradition vis-à-vis the others; the objective is not to encourage theoretical integration but to ward off the standard criticisms each approach typically faces from proponents of competing approaches." In this genre of academic writing, smart rhetorical posturing dictates pragmatic flexibility, not cultish monism, in the effort to subsume the particularistic and myopic concerns of competing perspectives without relaxing any of the original foundational assumptions of one's own preferred perspective (Sil 2000).

Instead of approach-driven analysis, we advocate problem-driven research. The insistence on parsimony clashes with the complexity of social processes occurring within specific contexts of both time and space (Jervis 1997). As this chapter has illustrated, and with no claim to originality, international relations analysis can build on the identification of empirical anomalies for any one analytical perspective. A problem-driven approach to research has one big advantage. It sidesteps often bitter, repetitive, and inherently inconclusive paradigmatic debates. Such debates distract scholars and graduate students from the primary task at hand: recognizing interesting questions and testing alternative explanations.

A glance at examples from other fields is instructive. A world of complex processes can be captured by thinking about what Arthur Koestler dubbed "holonic principles of architecture," that is, the relation between the whole and its parts, in two different ways (Mathews 1996; Koestler 1967). First, following Herbert Simon, we can think of the social world as a set of nearly decomposable systems with tight causal linkages among subsystems of factors that form a loosely coupled, broader ensemble (Simon 1981). In developing his point, Simon used the parable of two Swiss watchmakers, Tempus and Horus. Tempus assembled his watches from separate parts. When interrupted, he had to put the unfinished watch down on the table, where it fell apart, forcing him to start again. Tempus produced few watches. Horus, on the other hand, built his watches by assembling the individual pieces into modules that he subsequently put together. Horus produced many watches. The recent history of watchmaking illustrates a second point about the whole and its parts. Seiko watchmakers revolutionized miniaturization by splitting the motor into three components and inserting them into tiny spaces between the watch's gears. Rather than thinking, as did the Swiss, of motor and gear as natural components that help in the production of the watch, Seiko engineers thought of the total product and the purpose and role of each component in relation to the whole (Mathews 1996).

In contemporary social theory, the variable relation between the whole and its parts is the core insight of structuration theory. Thinking of political reality as a sequence or co-occurrence of structure and agency opens up the possibilities for an agnostic epistemological stance in which empirical puzzles drive the analysis within a broader perspective that is not committed a priori to the primacy of either agency or structure, materialism or idealism (Sil 2000; Daase 1999). Choosing such an agnostic position has the advantage of being in agreement with much extant research practice: the implicit relaxation of strong a priori epistemological and ontological commitments in the process of relating substantive findings to analytical perspectives. In the analysis of international relations, too, epistemological flexibility that supports a problem-driven, eclectic analytical stance in both scholarship and teaching suits the needs of individual scholars.

This is not to argue that analytical eclecticism is cost-free. This approach may be too flexible to define by itself a research program capable of mobilizing strong political preferences and enduring professional ties. The advantages of eclecticism, however, may well outweigh these costs. Scholars and policymakers try to gain analytical leverage over multilayered and complex connections between power, interest, and norms. Analytical eclecticism highlights different layers and connections that parsimonious explanations conceal. And it is attuned to empirical anomalies that analytical parsimony slights. Eclecticism protects us from taking as natural paradigmatic assumptions about the world. It regards with discomfort the certainties that derive from relying solely on a single paradigm. And it protects us, imperfectly to be sure, from the inevitable failings of any one paradigm, unfounded expectations of what is natural, and the adoption of flawed policies that embody those very expectations. Theory and policy are both served better by eclecticism, not parsimony.

Notes

1   Without blaming them for any of the remaining errors of omission or commission, we would like to thank for their criticisms, comments, and suggestions on earlier drafts of this article: Amitav Acharya, Thomas Berger, Robert Bullock, Thomas Christensen, Susanne Feske, Michael Green, Walter Hatch, Brian Job, Chalmers Johnson, Alastair Iain Johnston, Kozo Kato, Robert Keohane, Stephen Krasner, Ellis Krauss, David Leheny, T. J. Pempel, Richard Samuels, Keiichi Tsunekawa, and Robert Uriu, as well as members of seminars at the University of California, San Diego, Cornell University, and Aoyama Gakuin University. We are also very much indebted to two anonymous reviewers for their criticisms and suggestions, and to a large number of Japanese and Chinese government officials and policy advisors for generously sharing their time with us.
2   The precise meaning and geographic scope of "Asia" and "Asia-Pacific" are highly controversial. Geography is a subject-matter of both material reality and political construction. For the purposes of this article, we have chosen Asia-Pacific as the most general concept that encompasses U.S. relations with Asia and that also describes security affairs in East and Southeast Asia (Hemmer and Katzenstein 2000; Lewis and Wigen 1997).
3   The parallel to economic developments is striking. After the débâcle of the 1999 World Trade Organization Ministerial Conference in Seattle, the Japanese government, seeking to forestall isolation, wasted little time in beginning to negotiate bilateral free-trade arrangements with Singapore, South Korea, and Mexico, with the intent of eventually building a free-trade area in Asia-Pacific that would supplement the WTO (Scollay and Gilbert 2001: 14).
4   Interview 10-00, Tokyo, January 14, 2000.
5   Official reactions in Beijing to recent developments in Japan have been

remarkably restrained considering that some of China's harshest critics of Japan hold powerful positions, especially in the Chinese military (Shambaugh 1999/2000; Christensen 1999; Interviews 01-98, 04-98, 03-00, 04-00, Beijing, June 15 and 16, 1998, and June 13, 2000).

6 This limitation is not restricted to realist analysis of Asian-Pacific security affairs. In strict analogy, realism was unable to specify whether, at the end of the Cold War, European states would balance with Germany against the United States as the remaining superpower or with the United States against a united Germany as a potential regional hegemon.

7 The astonishing reticence on, and lack of contact with, Taiwan that characterizes the Japanese bureaucracy provides some evidence for this view (Interview 04-00, Tokyo, January 12, 2000).

8 Taking account of weakening currency values, defense spending (measured in U.S. dollars, 1997 prices) was cut in 1998 by 39 percent in Thailand, 35 percent in South Korea, 32 percent in the Philippines, 26 percent in Vietnam, and 10 percent in Japan—if measured in yen, this represents the first reduction since 1955 (Asagumo Shimbun-sha 1998; Huxley and Willett 1999). Many analysts expect that these reductions will continue for several years (Richardson 1998; National Institute for Defense Studies 1999). Only China, Taiwan, and Indonesia have avoided cuts in military expenditures (Huxley and Willett 1999: 16; Umbach 2000; Ball 2000). Since the end of the Cold War, Japanese defense expenditures show rates of increase that are much smaller than those of China. Between 1990 and 1997, while China's defense spending increased 45 percent from $25.1 billion to $36.5 billion, Japan's defense budget increased only 18 percent from $34.3 billion to $40.8 billion (1997 exchange rates) (Asagumo Shimbun-sha 1998: 267; Bessho 1999: 35). Differences in China's and Japan's inflation rates overstate, however, the real increases in Chinese expenditures in the first half of the 1990s.

9 The political leadership has denied, however, that "situations in areas surrounding Japan" involve no geographic element whatsoever. Prime Minister Keizo Obuchi claimed before the lower house budget committee that the "Middle East, the Indian Ocean, and the other side of the globe" cannot be conceived of as being covered by the new guidelines. According to this interpretation, even though an interruption of oil supplies from the Middle East would constitute a potentially serious threat to Japan, that threat, insofar as it is located in the Middle East or the Indian Ocean, would not be covered by the guidelines (*Asahi Shimbun*, January 27, 1999; Interview 01-99, January 11, 1999).

10 Interview 03-99, Tokyo, January 12, 1999.

11 (*Asahi Shimbun*, May 23, 1998). Because the statement ran afoul of the government's wariness of Chinese criticism of the revised guidelines, the official was removed from his post (*Asahi Shimbun*, July 7, 1998; *Asahi Shimbun*, July 8, 1998).

12 Interview 01-00, Singapore, June 7, 2000. South Korea used to be wary of ASEAN-led multilateral consultations, which it saw as being focused primarily on South China Sea issues (Kurata 1996).

13 This is not an exception. All Asian states either voted against or abstained from voting on the September 27, 1999, United Nations High Commissioner for Refugees resolution calling on the UN secretary-general to establish an international commission of inquiry into violations of international law in East Timor (Foot 2000: 20).

14 Interviews 08-98, 01-00, and 07-00, Beijing, June 21, 1998, June 13, 2000, and June 15, 2000.

15 Interview 07-00, Tokyo, January 13, 2000.

16 In 1996, for example, Japan co-chaired the ARF working group on confidence-and security-building measures (Boeicho 1999: 187; Gaimusho 1998: 31; Masaki 1998).

17 Interviews 01-98 and 02-98, Beijing, June 12, 1998; Brian Job, personal communication, July 1, 2000.

18 Interviews 01-98, 02-98, and 07-00, Beijing, June 15, 1998 and June 15, 2000; Interview 04-00, Tokyo, January 12, 2000. The dynamics in CSCAP's working groups differ, however (Interview 09-00, Tokyo, January 13, 2000). With its twenty to thirty participants, the working group on transnational crime, for example, meets semi-annually to deal with more specific issues. It is staffed by equal numbers of police professionals, policy experts, and scholars (mostly criminologists), who are more interested in exchanging information than in discussing solutions to policy problems. The working group has recently added the issue of illegal trafficking in people, migrants, and women and children to its traditional topics of illegal trade in narcotics and small firearms. The nature of the subject-matter and the group's diversity yield a different style of discussion and group dynamic. Chinese representatives balk when infrequent policy discussions even suggest ways to cooperate that might be seen as infringing on state sovereignty. Although they do not tend to participate actively, the Chinese typically do not object to discussion of the problems that organized crime in China creates for other countries and the region as a whole. In meetings of this working group, China thus looks less obstructionist to its Asian-Pacific neighbors than it does in discussions of traditional national security issues in other working groups; but Chinese officials are clearly less forthcoming in a multilateral setting than in bilateral police discussions and joint operations.

19 Interview 04-00, Tokyo, January 12, 2000.

20 Interview 04-00, Tokyo, January 12, 2000.

21 Although JIIA is important and has particularly close relations with the Ministry of Foreign Affairs, both in terms of finance and personnel, other research organizations—including the Research Institute for Peace and Security and the Institute for International Policy Studies—are routinely engaged in similar kinds of meetings and exchanges that are designed to strengthen Asian-Pacific networks. The National Institute for Defense Studies, for example, has hosted since 1994 an annual security seminar focusing on the development of confidence-building measures. The seminar is attended by professional military personnel; in November 1998 participants from nineteen countries attended (Boeicho 1999; Fukushima 1999b: 31; Interviews 02-99 and 04-99, Tokyo, January 11–12, 1999).

22 Such bilateral meetings and exchanges are also characteristic of other Japanese research organizations. The National Institute for Defense Studies, for example, runs a series of annual bilateral meetings with representatives from China, Russia, and South Korea. It hosted eight researchers from ASEAN in 1999 (Interview 04-99, Tokyo, January 12, 1999).

23 We would like to thank Michael Green for clarifying this point for us.

24 Interview 03-00, Tokyo, January 11, 1999.

25 Interviews 01-98, 04-98, 05-98, 07-98, and 09-98, Beijing, June 15, 16, 19, 20, and 22, 1998; Carlson 2000.

26 A mixture of realist and liberal categories is also better than either alone to capture the combination of balancing and engagement characteristic of the diplomatic strategies of many Asian-Pacific states (Interview 02-00, Tokyo, January 11, 1999). Even though some Southeast Asian states (such as Indonesia, the Philippines, and Vietnam) are wary of China because of past or current territorial disputes, they nevertheless seek to engage it in multilateral institutions such as the ARF. And, even though Japan is the overwhelming power in Southeast Asia,

its relations with states in the region have been good and are getting better in the wake of the Asian financial crisis.
27 Interviews 02-99, 05-99, 11-99, and 13-99, Tokyo, January 11–12 and 14, 1999.
28 Interview 03-99, Tokyo, January 12, 1999.
29 Interviews 02-99 and 13-99, Tokyo, January 11 and 14, 1999.
30 (Oksenberg 2001; Krasner 2001). Fairbank has been criticized often for taking the self-interested descriptions of Chinese court literati as unproblematic data describing how the system of tributary trade was actually working. For follow-up research that investigates how this system of trade may have operated in practice, see Rossabi (1983); Wills, Jr (1984); Hevia (1995). Fairbank's failing is not uncommon. It is shared by realists who rely on Thucydides as an unquestioned historical source for the Peloponnesian War.
31 Interview 13-99, Tokyo, January 14, 1999.
32 Interview 04-00, Tokyo, January 12, 2000.
33 To the extent that recent analyses of Japanese and Asian-Pacific security have chosen to simply ignore or misinterpret sociology or constructivism, they have unnecessarily weakened the contribution they make by misconstruing socio-logical analyses as inherently optimistic (Uriu 1998a) and ahistorical (Uriu 1998b); failing to address explicitly the relevance of collective identities, while appealing obliquely to regional security communities that presuppose the existence of such identities (Mochizuki and O'Hanlon 1998); offering a misleadingly partial analysis of mercantilism that both neglects the ideological component of that intriguing concept and misinterprets a sociological explanation of Japanese foreign policy as dealing merely with an exceptional case in a realist world (Heginbotham and Samuels 1998), in sharp contrast to the much richer and more compelling argument proposed by Richard J. Samuels in his book *Rich Nation, Strong Army* (Samuels 1994); wavering between a cultural and a material-ist presentation of realist theory (Green 1998); neglecting that, in the case of Japanese security, sociological analyses focus their attention not on specific vari-ants of realism but on rationalist explanations more generally, and that they explain not merely national security narrowly construed but also internal and economic security more broadly understood, issues that elude realist theorizing (Kawasaki 1999); and by overlooking how norms that constitute Japan's collec-tive identity as a "non-threatening, peace-loving, state" are nested in underlying and more fundamental norms of Japan as a nonmajoritarian political community (Okimoto 1998).

References

Acharya, Amitav (1991) "The Association of Southeast Asian Nations: 'Security Community' or 'Defense Community'?" *Pacific Affairs*, 64, 2 (Summer): 159–77.
Acharya, Amitav (1995) "A Regional Security Community in Southeast Asia?" *Journal of Strategic Studies*, 18, 3 (September): 175–200.
Acharya, Amitav (1998) "Collective Identity and Conflict Management in Southeast Asia," pp. 198–227 in Emanuel Adler and Michael Barnett (eds) *Security Communities*, Cambridge: Cambridge University Press.
Acharya, Amitav (1999a) "Institutionalism and Balancing in the Asia Pacific Region: ASEAN, U.S. Strategic Frameworks, and the ASEAN Regional Forum," Toronto: Department of Political Science, York University; and Singapore: Institute of Defense and Strategic Studies, Nanyang Technological University.
Acharya, Amitav (1999b) "Regionalism and the Emerging (Intrusive) World Order:

Sovereignty, Autonomy, Identity," paper presented at the CSGR (Centre for the Study of Globalisation and Regionalisation) Third Annual Conference, After the Global Crisis What Next for Regionalism? Scarman House, University of Warwick, September 16–18.

Acharya, Amitav (2000a) *Constructing a Security Community: ASEAN and the Problem of Regional Order*, London: Routledge.

Acharya, Amitav (2000b) "Regional Institutions and Security Order in Asia," paper prepared for the second workshop, Security Order in the Asia-Pacific, Bali, Indonesia, May 29–June 2.

Asagumo Shimbun-sha (1998) *Bōei Hando Bukku* [Defense Handbook], Tokyo: Asagumo Shimbun-sha, pp. 263–7.

Asahi Shimbun (1998) "Shuhen Jitai no Chiriteki Han'i; Kyokuto to sono Shuhen" [Geographical scope of situation in areas surrounding Japan is Far East and its surrounding areas], May 23, 1998, 14th edn.

Asahi Shimbun (1998) "Seifu Hokubei Kyokucho wo Kotetsu" [Government removes director of North American Affairs Bureau from post], July 7, evening, 4th edn.

Asahi Shimbun (1998) "Shuhen Jitai ni Aimaisa" [Situation in areas surrounding Japan is ambiguous], July 8, 14th edn.

Asahi Shimbun (1999) "Shuhen Jitai; Chiriteki Yoso Fukumu" [Situation in areas surrounding Japan includes geographical factor], January 27, 14th edn.

Auer, James E. (1998) "A Win–Win Alliance for Asia," *Japan Times*, August 8.

Ball, Desmond (2000) "Military Balance in the Asia Pacific: Trends and Implications," paper prepared for the Fourteenth Asia-Pacific Roundtable, Kuala Lumpur, Malaysia, June 3–7.

Bandow, Doug (1999) "Old Wine in New Bottles: The Pentagon's East Asia Security Strategy Report," *Policy Analysis*, no. 344, CATO Institute, May 18.

Berger, Thomas (2000) "Set for Stability? Prospects for Conflict and Cooperation in East Asia," *Review of International Studies*, 26: 405–28.

Bessho, Koro (1999) *Identities and Security in East Asia*, Adelphi Paper 325, Oxford: International Institute for Strategic Studies.

Betts, Richard K. (1993/4) "Wealth, Power, and Instability: East Asia and the United States after the Cold War," *International Security*, 18, 3 (Winter): 34–77.

Boeicho (Defense Agency) (1999) *Boei Hakusho* [Defense White Paper], Tokyo: Okurasho Insatsu-kyoku.

Bueno de Mesquita, Bruce and Morrow, James D. (1999) "Sorting through the Wealth of Notions," *International Security*, 24, 2 (Fall): 56–73.

Busse, Nikolas (1999) "Constructivism and Southeast Asian Security," *Pacific Review*, 12, 1: 39–60.

Busse, Nikolas (2000) *Die Entstehung von Kollektiven Identitäten: Das Beispiel der ASEAN-Staaten* [The Rise of Collective Identity: The Example of the ASEAN States], Baden-Baden: Nomos.

Carlson, Allen M. (2000) "The Lock on China's Door: Chinese Foreign Policy and the Sovereignty Norm," PhD dissertation, Yale University.

Cha, Victor D. (2000) "Abandonment, Entrapment, and Neoclassical Realism in Asia: The United States, Japan, and Korea," *International Studies Quarterly*, 44, 2 (June): 261–91.

Cheng, Joseph Y. S. (n.d.) "China's ASEAN Policy in the 1990s: Pushing for Multipolarity in the Regional Context," Contemporary China Centre, City University of Hong Kong.

Christensen, Thomas J. (1999) "China, the U.S.–Japan Alliance, and the Security Dilemma in East Asia," *International Security*, 23, 4 (Spring): 49–80.

Council on Foreign Relations Independent Study Group (1998) *The Tests of War and the Strains of Peace: The U.S.–Japan Security Relationship*, New York: Council on Foreign Relations.

Daase, Christopher (1999) *Kleine Kriege—Grosse Wirkung: Wie Unkonventionelle Kriegführung die Internationale Politik Verändert* [Small Wars—Big Effects: How Unconventional Warfare Alters International Politics], Baden-Baden: Nomos.

Desch, Michael C. (1998) "Culture Clash: Assessing the Importance of Ideas in Security Studies," *International Security*, 23, 1 (Summer): 141–70.

Duffield, John S., Farrell, Theo, Price, Richard, and Desch, Michael C. (1999) "Correspondence: Isms and Schisms: Culturalism versus Realism in Security Studies," *International Security*, 24, 1 (Summer): 156–80.

Economist, The (1998) "ASEAN's Failure: The Limits of Politeness," February 28, pp. 43–4.

Fairbank, John King (ed.) (1968) *The Chinese World Order: Traditional China's Foreign Relations*, Cambridge, Mass.: Harvard University Press.

Feaver, Peter D., Hellmann, Gunther, Schweller, Randall L., Taliaferro, Jeffrey W. Wohlforth, William C., Legro, Jeffrey W., and Moravcsik, Andrew (2000) "Correspondence: Brother, Can You Spare a Paradigm? (Or Was Anybody Ever a Realist?)," *International Security*, 25, 1 (Summer): 165–93.

Feske, Susanne (1997) "Japan und die U.S.A: Zivilmächte im asiatisch-pazifischen Raum?" [Japan and the U.S.A: Civilian Powers in Asia-Pacific?] Trier Arbeitspapiere zum DFG-Forschungsprojekt "Zivilmächte in der internationalen Politik" [Trier working papers for the DFG research project "Civilian Powers in International Politics"], Trier, Germany, July.

Foot, Rosemary (2000) "Global Institutions and the Management of Regional Security in the Asia Pacific," paper prepared for the Second Workshop on Security Order in the Asia-Pacific, Bali, Indonesia, May 30–June 2.

French, Howard W. (2000) "U.S. Copters? No, No, No. Not in Their Backyard," *The New York Times*, January 20, p. A6.

Friedberg, Aaron L. (1993/4) "Ripe for Rivalry: Prospects for Peace in a Multipolar Asia," *International Security*, 18, 3 (Winter): 5–33.

Frühstück, Sabine (2000) "Normalization and the Management of Violence in Japan's Armed Forces," Department of East Asian Languages and Cultural Studies, University of California, Santa Barbara.

Fukushima, Akiko (1999a) *Japanese Foreign Policy: The Emerging Logic of Multilateralism*, Basingstoke: Macmillan.

Fukushima, Akiko (1999b) "Japan's Emerging View of Security Multilateralism in Asia," University of California Institute on Global Conflict and Cooperation, Policy Paper 51 (June).

Gaimusho (1998) *Gaiko Seisho 1998* [Foreign Affairs Blue Book 1998]. Tokyo: Okurasho Insatsu-kyoku.

Gourevitch, Peter Alexis (1999) "The Governance Problem in International Relations," pp. 137–64 in David A. Lake and Robert Powell (eds) *Strategic Choice and International Relations*, Princeton, NJ: Princeton University Press.

Green, Michael J. (1998) "State of the Field Report: Research on Japanese Security Policy," *Access Asia Review*, 2, 1 (September).

Heginbotham, Eric and Samuels, Richard J. (1998) "Mercantile Realism and Japanese Foreign Policy," *International Security*, 22, 4 (Spring): 171–203.

Hemmer, Christopher and Katzenstein, Peter J. (2000) "Collective Identities and the Origins of Multilateralism in Europe but Not in Asia in the Early Cold War," paper presented at the annual meeting of the American Political Science Association, Washington, DC, August 31–September 3.

Hevia, James L. (1995) *Cherishing Men from Afar: Qing Guest Ritual and the Macartney Embassy of 1793*, Durham, NC: Duke University Press.

Hopf, Ted (1998) "The Promise of Constructivism in International Relations Theory," *International Security*, 23, 1 (Summer): 171–200.

Hoshino, Toshiya (1999) "Nichi-bei Domei to Asia Taiheiyo no Takoku-kan Anzen Hosho: Nihon no Shiten" [Japan–U.S. Alliance and Multilateral Security in the Asia-Pacific: A Japanese Perspective], pp. 166–85 in Hideki Kan, Glenn D. Hook, and Stephanie A. Weston (eds) *Asia Taiheiyo no Chiiki Chitsujo to Anzen Hosho* [Regional Order and Security in the Asia-Pacific], Kyoto: Minerva Shobo.

Hughes, Christopher W. (1996) "The North Korean Nuclear Crisis and Japanese Security," *Survival*, 38, 2 (Summer): 79–103.

Huth, Paul K. (1996) *Standing Your Ground: Territorial Disputes and International Conflict*, Ann Arbor, Mich.: University of Michigan Press.

Huxley, Tim and Willett, Susan (1999) *Arming East Asia*, Adelphi Paper 329, Oxford: International Institute for Strategic Studies.

Inoguchi, Takashi and Stillman, Grant B. (eds) (1997) *North-East Asian Regional Security: The Role of International Institutions*, Tokyo: United Nations University Press.

Jervis, Robert (1997) *System Effects: Complexity in Political and Social Life*, Princeton, NJ: Princeton University Press.

Jervis, Robert (1999) "Realism, Neoliberalism, and Cooperation: Understanding the Debate," *International Security*, 24, 1 (Summer): 42–63.

Johnson, Chalmers (2000a) *Blowback: The Costs and Consequences of American Empire*, New York: Henry Holt.

Johnson, Chalmers (ed.) (2000b) "Dysfunctional Japan: At Home and in the World," special issue of *Asian Perspective*, 24.

Johnston, Alastair Iain (1995) *Cultural Realism: Strategic Culture and Grand Strategy in Chinese History*, Princeton, NJ: Princeton University Press.

Johnston, Alastair Iain (1999a) "Realism(s) and Chinese Security Policy in the Post-Cold War Period," pp. 261–318 in Ethan B. Kapstein and Michael Mastanduno (eds) *Unipolar Politics: Realism and State Strategies after the Cold War*, New York: Columbia University Press.

Johnston, Alastair Iain (1999b) "The Myth of the ASEAN Way? Explaining the Evolution of the ASEAN Regional Forum," pp. 287–324 in Helga Haftendorn, Robert O. Keohane, and Celeste A. Wallander (eds) *Imperfect Unions: Security Institutions over Time and Space*, Oxford: Oxford University Press.

Kahler, Miles (1995) *International Institutions and the Political Economy of Integration*, Washington, DC: Brookings.

Kamiya, Matake (1997) "The U.S.–Japan Alliance and Regional Security Cooperation: Toward a Double-Layered Security System," in Ralph A. Cossa (ed.) *Restructuring the U.S.–Japan Alliance: Toward a More Equal Partnership*, Washington, DC: Center for Strategic and International Studies Press.

Kang, David C. (2003) "Hierarchy and Stability in Asian International Relations," pp. 163–90 in Michael Mastanduno and John Ikenberry (eds) *International Relations Theory and the Asia-Pacific*, New York: Columbia University Press.

Katzenstein, Peter J. (1996) *Cultural Norms and National Security: Police and Military in Postwar Japan*, Ithaca, NY: Cornell University Press.

Katzenstein, Peter J. and Okawara, Nobuo (1993) *Japan's National Security: Structures, Norms, and Policy Responses in a Changing World*, Ithaca, NY: East Asia Program, Cornell University.

Kawasaki, Tsuyoshi (1999) "Postclassical Realism and Japanese Security Policy," paper prepared for the annual meeting of the American Political Science Association, Atlanta, Georgia, September 2–5.

Keohane, Robert O. and Martin, Lisa L. (1995) "The Promise of Institutionalist Theory," *International Security*, 20, 1 (Summer): 39–51.

Khong, Yuen Foong (1997) "Making Bricks without Straw in the Asia Pacific?," *Pacific Review*, 10, 2: 289–300.

Khong, Yuen Foong (1998) "ASEAN's Collective Identity: Sources, Shifts, and Security Consequences," paper prepared for the annual meeting of the American Political Science Association, Boston, Massachusetts, September 3–6.

Koestler, Arthur (1967) *The Ghost in the Machine*, London: Hutchinson.

Krasner, Stephen D. (2001) "Organized Hypocrisy in 19th Century East Asia," *International Relations of the Asia-Pacific*, 1, 2: 173–97.

Kupchan, Charles A. and Kupchan, Clifford A. (1995) "The Promise of Collective Security," *International Security*, 20, 1 (Summer): 52–61.

Kurata, Hideya (1996) "Multilateralism and the Korean Problem with Respect to the Asia-Pacific Region," *Journal of Pacific Asia*, 3: 129–47.

Legro, Jeffrey W. and Moravcsik, Andrew (1999) "Is Anybody Still a Realist?," *International Security*, 24, 2 (Fall): 5–55.

Leifer, Michael (2000) "Regionalism Compared: The Perils and Benefits of Expansion," paper prepared for the Fourteenth Asia-Pacific Roundtable, Kuala Lumpur, Malaysia, June 3–7.

Lewis, Martin W. and Wigen, Karen E. (1997) *The Myth of Continents: A Critique of Metageography*, Berkeley, Calif.: University of California Press.

Martin, Lisa L. (1999) "The Contributions of Rational Choice: A Defense of Pluralism," *International Security*, 24, 2 (Fall): 74–83.

Masaki, Hisane (1998) "Japan to Co-chair Peacekeeping Group," *Japan Times*, July 17.

Mathews, John (1996) "Holonic Organisational Architectures," *Human Systems Management*, 15: 27–54.

Mearsheimer, John J. (1994/5) "The False Promise of International Institutions," *International Security*, 19, 3 (Winter): 5–49.

Mearsheimer, John J. (1995) "A Realist Reply," *International Security*, 20, 1 (Summer): 82–93.

Mochizuki, Mike M. (1997) "American and Japanese Strategic Debates: The Need for a New Synthesis," pp. 43–82 in Mike M. Mochizuki (ed.) *Toward a True Alliance: Restructuring U.S.–Japan Security Relations*, Washington, DC: Brookings.

Mochizuki, Mike M. and O'Hanlon, Michael (1998) "A Liberal Vision for the U.S.–Japan Alliance," *Survival*, 40, 2 (Summer): 127–34.

National Institute for Defense Studies (1999) *East Asian Strategic Review, 1998–1999*, Tokyo: National Institute for Defense Studies, 1999.

Niou, Emerson M. S. and Ordeshook, Peter C. (1999) "Return of the Luddites," *International Security*, 24, 2 (Fall): 84–96.

Nye, Joseph S. (2001) "The 'Nye Report': Six Years Later," *International Relations of the Asia-Pacific*, 1, 1: 95–104.

Okimoto, Daniel (1998) "The Japan–America Security Alliance: Prospects for the Twenty-First Century," Stanford University, Institute for International Studies, Asia/Pacific Research Center.

Oksenberg, Michel (2001) "The Issue of Sovereignty in the Asian Historical Context," pp. 83–104 in Stephen D. Krasner (ed.) *Problematic Sovereignty: Contested Rules and Political Possibilities*, New York: Columbia University Press.

Powell, Robert (1999) "The Modeling Enterprise and Security Studies," *International Security*, 24, 2 (Fall): 97–106.

Richardson, Michael (1998) "Asian Crisis Stills Appetite for Arms," *International Herald Tribune*, April 23.

Richardson, Michael (2000) "Asia's Widening Arms Gap: Uneven Spread of New Weapons Systems May Jeopardize Balance of Power in East," *International Herald Tribune*, January 7.

Rossabi, Morris (ed.) (1983) *China among Equals: The Middle Kingdom and Its Neighbors, 10th–14th Centuries*, Berkeley, Calif.: University of California Press.

Ruggie, John Gerard (1995) "The False Premise of Realism," *International Security* 20, 1 (Summer): 62–70.

Rüland, Jürgen (2000) "ASEAN and the Asian Crisis: Theoretical Implications and Practical Consequences for Southeast Asian Regionalism," *Pacific Review*, 13, 3: 421–51.

Samuels, Richard J. (1994) *Rich Nation, Strong Army: National Security and the Technological Transformation of Japan*, Ithaca, NY: Cornell University Press.

Schweller, Randall L. (1994) "Bandwagoning for Profit: Bringing the Revisionist State Back In," *International Security*, 19, 1 (Summer): 72–107.

Scollay, Robert and Gilbert, John P. (2001) *New Regional Trading Arrangements in the Asia Pacific?* Washington, DC: Institute for International Economics.

Shambaugh, David (1999/2000) "China's Military Views the World: Ambivalent Security," *International Security*, 24, 3 (Winter): 52–79.

Sil, Rudra (2000) "The Foundations of Eclecticism: The Epistemological Status of Agency, Culture, and Structure in Social Theory," *Journal of Theoretical Politics*, 12, 3: 353–87.

Simon, Herbert A. (1981) *The Sciences of the Artificial*, 2nd edn, Cambridge, Mass.: MIT Press.

Simon, Sheldon W. (1998) "Security Prospects in Southeast Asia: Collaborative Efforts and the ASEAN Regional Forum," *Pacific Review*, 11, 2: 195–212.

Spiro, David E. (1999) *The Hidden Hand of American Hegemony: Petrodollar Recycling and International Markets*, Ithaca, NY: Cornell University Press.

Takeda, Yasuhiro (1997) "Democracy Promotion Policies: Overcoming Japan–U.S. Discord," pp. 50–62 in Ralph A. Cossa (ed.) *Restructuring the U.S.–Japan Alliance: Toward a More Equal Partnership*, Washington, DC: Center for Strategic and International Studies Press.

Terada, Takashi (1998) "The Origins of Japan's APEC Policy: Foreign Minister Takeo Miki's Asia-Pacific Policy and Current Implications," *Pacific Review*, 11, 3: 337–63.

Umbach, Frank (2000) "Military Balance in the Asia Pacific: Trends and Implications," paper prepared for the Fourteenth Asia-Pacific Roundtable, Kuala Lumpur, Malaysia, June 3–7.

Uriu, Robert M. (1998a) "Domestic–International Interactions and Japanese Security Studies," *Journal of Asian and African Studies*, 33, 1: 76–93.

Uriu, Robert M. (1998b) "Domestic–International Interactions and Japanese Security Studies," pp. 76–93 in James Sperling, Yogendra Malik, and David Louscher (eds) *Zones of Amity, Zones of Enmity: The Prospects for Economic and Military Security in Asia*, Leiden: Brill.

Walt, Stephen M. (1999a) "Rigor or Rigor Mortis? Rational Choice and Security Studies," *International Security*, 23, 4 (Spring): 5–48.

Walt, Stephen M. (1999b) "A Model Disagreement," *International Security*, 24, 2 (Fall): 115–30.

Waltz, Kenneth N. (1998) "Realism after the Cold War," Institute of War and Peace Studies, Columbia University, December.

Wendt, Alexander (1995) "Constructing International Politics," *International Security* 20, 1 (Summer): 71–81.

Wills, John E., Jr (1984) *Embassies and Illusions: Dutch and Portuguese Envoys to K'ang-hsi, 1666–1687*, Cambridge, Mass.: Harvard University Press.

Zagare, Frank C. (1999) "All Mortis, No Rigor," *International Security*, 24, 2 (Fall): 107–14.

Part I

Japan's internal and external security policies

3 Japan's security policy: political, economic, and military dimensions

Peter J. Katzenstein and Nobuo Okawara (1991)

In order to understand the logic behind Japanese choices, a central argument of political realism must be abandoned. International structures that are in rapid flux give ambiguous cues to policymakers on how to define the purposes of policy. The international state system is thus becoming a less important determinant of the interests that underlie Japanese security policy. The view put forth here is that these interests are shaped primarily by two other sets of factors: Japan's domestic structure and the normative context that informs the definition of security interests. In contrast to the dramatic change in international politics, Japan's domestic structures and norms have been changing only gradually.

Domestic structures

Japan's security policy is formulated within an institutional structure that biases policy strongly against a forceful articulation of military security objectives. It is no accident that the ministry that is formally in charge of some aspects of Japan's military security is the Ministry of International Trade and Industry (MITI). Its jurisdiction extends not only over questions of trade and investment but also over the military security field, especially on questions of military procurement. The Defense Agency is run by civilians who are in full control of the three branches of Japan's Self-Defense Forces (SDF). The Ministry of Finance plays a central role in defense as it does in all other issues. Finally, the Ministry of Foreign Affairs is in charge of providing the "comprehensive coordination" of the activities of all ministries and agencies, including the Defense Agency, that are involved in Japan's external relations.

MITI is deeply enmeshed in security issues for the simple reason that it has jurisdiction over Japan's defense industries. Operational control over defense industry-related issues rests with the Aircraft and Ordnance Division in the Machinery and Information Industry Bureau of MITI. In the early 1950s the Security Agency, which in 1954 would become the Defense Agency, challenged MITI's control over Japan's small defense industry by proposing the nationalization of specific industries for national security reasons. MITI, on the other hand, insisted until the mid-1950s that its mission was to develop an export industry in defense which would have technological spin-off effects advantageous for civilian industries. The Defense Agency's attempt was defeated in part also because of the opposition of a fiscally conservative Finance Ministry. One important consequence of this political defeat was that the Agency lost much of its interest in developing an indigenous defense industry and remained instead content with a substantial degree of import dependence, especially on the American armaments industry (Otake 1984: 31–3). A second consequence was to affirm pride of place to MITI's economic orientation in decisions involving Japan's defense industries. Thus, MITI still reviews the Defense Agency's procurement plans with an eye to what its impact might be on Japan's industrial development (Kataoka and Myers 1989: 66).

Despite its links to Japan's defense industries, MITI's policy perspective is characterized by the lack of a military security perspective. The Toshiba incident is one example. In response to what the United States government felt was a deplorable lapse of policy judgment, MITI imposed greater controls over the export of high-technology products. Personnel was transferred from the Defense Agency and the National Police Agency to MITI's Trade Bureau Export Division to implement stronger controls. MITI has also set up the Strategic Technology Trade Information Center which was to engage in intelligence activities concerning high technologies. It is staffed by former officials of the Defense Agency and the National Police Agency as well as by experts from the industries which are militarily most sensitive (Asahi Shimbun Keizai-bu 1989: 112–17). It is too early to tell the extent to which this institutional innovation will shape the ministry's perspective in a period of declining global tension.

Because of its interest in balancing the government's budget, the Ministry of Finance has been a very important brake on the unrestrained growth of the Self-Defense Forces and the defense industries. But the ministry's influence extends only over those issues which involve substantial outlays of government funds. The ministry has been largely excluded from other questions of considerable military significance, such as the development of joint operational planning between the United States and the Self-Defense Forces since the mid-1970s (Otake 1983: 142).

Throughout the postwar era the Ministry of Foreign Affairs has suffered from a chronic budget and personnel shortage. West Germany's Foreign Ministry, for example, in 1984–5 had a budget that was twice as large and a staff that was one and a half times as large as that of the Japanese Foreign Ministry (Drifte 1990: 22). But the ministry derives considerable strength from its close political relations with the United States, forged during the Occupation, under the political leadership of former diplomats like Ashida and Yoshida. The widespread perception, especially among members of the political elite, that Japan's military security is dependent on a stable relationship with the United States, as well as on the subordinate position of the

Defense Agency in the bureaucracy, has contributed much to the important position of the Foreign Ministry on questions of military security. Indeed, the ministry's North American Affairs Bureau includes the Security Division, a key unit in the Japanese government dealing with defense policy. Despite occasional encroachments of the Defense Agency, it has been the Ministry of Foreign Affairs that has been in charge of applying the Security Treaty with the United States (Otake 1983: 143, 226, 277–8, 306).

Although the relationship with the United States is politically central, it is less important on questions of economy than on military security. Nevertheless, the Ministry of Foreign Affairs tries to modify any economic policy that is likely to have harmful effects on the U.S.–Japanese relationship, as demonstrated by the well-known example of Japan's energy policy. While MITI is interested in maintaining good relations with the Middle East oil-producing states, the Ministry of Foreign Affairs works hard to avoid an Arab tilt in foreign policy that might damage Japan's political relations with the United States. This was the pattern during the two oil crises in the 1970s and again in the decision to impose sanctions against Iraq in August 1990. After the invasion of Kuwait on August 1, the Ministry of Foreign Affairs argued that the request of the United States for Japan's participation in the sanctions against Iraq be honored, especially since Japan had adequate oil reserves. The ministry wanted to avoid at all costs a repetition of the unseemly scramble of Japanese trading firms for scarce supplies on the spot market that occurred in 1979 to the consternation of Japan's Western allies. MITI, on the other hand, focused on the issue of energy supply. About 12 percent of Japan's oil imports come from Kuwait and Iraq. The Prime Minister was caught between these opposing sides and was planning to defer a decision until after the UN Security Council had passed its resolution on sanctions. But, when the European Community decided in favor of sanctions on August 4, 1990, Prime Minister Kaifu, fearing "international isolation," decided in favor of the Ministry of Foreign Affairs' position the following day (*Asahi Shimbun*, August 4, 5, 6, 1990, evening editions).

Japanese security policy is formulated and implemented largely by these three major ministries operating along two axes. On questions of economic security, MITI, the Ministry of Finance and the Ministry of Foreign Affairs are the core in which Japanese policy is articulated. On questions of military security the central bureaucratic organizations are the Ministry of Finance, the Ministry of Foreign Affairs and the Defense Agency. While an informal interministerial coordination routinely takes place between both areas of security policy, distinctive institutional arrangements affecting issues of military security assure that political and economic perspectives retain paramount importance in national security policymaking.

Major defense decisions requiring the approval of the Cabinet need to be cleared first by the Security Council, known until 1986 as the National Defense Council. This Council advises the Prime Minister. It is composed of the Prime Minister, Vice Prime Minister, Foreign Minister, Finance Minister,

Chief Cabinet Secretary, Chairman of the National Public Safety Commission, and the Directors of the Defense Agency and the Economic Planning Agency. Other ministers are invited to meetings of the Security Council on an ad hoc basis. Significantly, MITI was excluded from formal membership when the National Defense Council was originally established in 1956, on the grounds that the inclusion of MITI would necessitate the incorporation of other economic ministries, such as the Ministry of Agriculture, Forestry, and Fisheries or the Ministry of Transportation (Ishiguro 1978: 287). The MITI minister became a formal member in 1972 but was again excluded when the Council was reconstituted in 1986 (Hirose 1989: 54).

The Security Office of the Cabinet Secretariat functions as the staff for the Council. Officials from various ministries serve in the Office, which consists of eleven councilors. Six of them—among others, for example, the Defense Agency's Defense Planning Division Chief, the Finance Ministry's Budget Examiner in charge of defense, MITI's Aircraft and Ordnance Division Chief—serve concurrently in their respective parent ministries. The Security Council and the Security Office are institutional expressions of the notion that any important defense policy proposal must go through an especially cautious consensus-building process, in which all relevant ministries participate. The Defense Agency is thus firmly embedded in a framework of interministerial coordination.

Certain ministries have in fact placed their officials within the Defense Agency, thus colonizing the process of defense policymaking at its inner core. Officials "detached" from a number of important ministries constitute a significant part of the Agency's personnel. For example, the Agency has eleven top bureaucratic posts: the Administrative Vice-Minister, Chief Secretary, five Bureau Chiefs and four Councilors. (Since the Chief Secretary and the Bureau Chiefs serve concurrently as Councilors, the organizational chart of the Defense Agency shows ten Councilors.) Of these eleven positions a minimum of four are always reserved for officials from other ministries. One Bureau Chief position (Equipment) is always held by a MITI official; another one (Finance) is almost always occupied by an official from the Finance Ministry. Two Councilor posts (one in charge of international relations, the other in charge of health) are reserved for the Ministry of Foreign Affairs and that of Health and Welfare. In addition to these four positions the Finance Ministry as well as the National Police Agency frequently place their officials in the posts of Administrative Vice-Minister, Chief Secretary, and Bureau Chief. For example, from the 1950s to the 1970s, nine of the twelve Administrative Vice-Ministers came from the National Police Agency. Five of them first entered the Defense Agency at the Bureau Chief level and went on to become the top bureaucratic official of the Agency. In the 1980s, four of the six Administrative Vice-Ministers came from the Finance Ministry; two of them were first sent to the Defense Agency at the Bureau Chief level. In such cases, officials have typically had no prior working experience in the Agency. Thus, with only one exception, all of the Bureau Chiefs recruited from MITI, the

Ministry of Foreign Affairs, and the Ministry of Health and Welfare who have occupied the positions, respectively, of Equipment Bureau Chief, Councilor in charge of International Relations, and Councilor in charge of Health joined the Agency for the first time at a senior stage of their careers. Such late rotation makes it virtually impossible for them to be inculcated with the perspectives of a professional military (Hirose 1989: 85–9, appendixes 1, 2).

In the lower echelons of the Agency this pattern of outside penetration recurs. Several additional positions are also staffed by officials from other ministries who serve in the Agency for the first time in their careers. Among the about twenty-five division chiefs of the Defense Agency, for example, at least four are always recruited from outside the Agency: the Finance Division Chief in the Finance Bureau (Finance Ministry), the Health and Medical Division Chief in the Education and Training Bureau (Ministry of Health and Welfare), the Coordination Division Chief in the Equipment Bureau (MITI), and the First Defense Intelligence Division Chief in the Defense Policy Bureau (National Police Agency) (Hirose 1989: 89, Appendix 3). Outside appointments also occur among some of the remaining twenty-one division chiefs. It took those who started their careers in the Agency between 1955 and 1968 sixteen to twenty-one years to reach the position of division chief. The average number of officials entering the Agency in this period was only 3.4. But, with the gradual increase in the number of officials who have made their career in the Agency, several ministries and agencies, in addition to the four mentioned above, have had to relinquish division posts that used to be staffed from the outside (Hirose 1989: 89–95, appendix 3). Despite this change, the Defense Agency remains deeply penetrated by other economic and political ministries in top- and middle-level appointments.

And it is chiefly through this layer of civilian personnel that the uniformed officers of the SDF interact with the outside world, including other ministries, the Diet and the mass media. The chain of command is very clear. The administrative hierarchy for military operation is subordinate to that for military administration, which in turn answers to the Director of the Agency, an elected official with cabinet rank, who is accountable to the Diet (Hirose 1989: 60–72; Kataoka and Myers 1989: 72). Because several of the opposition parties have regarded the Self-Defense Forces as unconstitutional, the Diet's exercise of "civilian control" has been weak. These parties have simply refused to create institutional mechanisms for controlling the Defense Agency. Doing so, they argued, would amount to nothing less than a tacit assent to the constitutionality of the Self-Defense Forces. Although a special committee on defense was created in the Lower House in 1979 and in the Upper House in 1981, the Diet still has no standing committees specializing in defense issues. Instead, parliamentary debates on defense issues take place primarily in the Budget Committees and in the Cabinet Committees which have jurisdiction over the laws that established the Defense Agency and the Self-Defense Forces (Hirose 1989: 44–5, 48–9, 248–9).

In the absence of an effective system of parliamentary oversight, the tight control which the civilian staff of the Defense Agency exercises over the professional military in Japan is called "civilian control." This system of strict supervision of the professional military by a civilian bureaucracy that lacks a military ethos and perspective was introduced by the Occupation. It has been wholeheartedly endorsed by Japan's postwar political and economic elites, which on the basis of prewar experiences have a profound distrust of the professional military. The military professionals have chafed under this system of civilian control, without being able to dislodge or seriously undermine it. In the eyes of the professional military, the principle of "civilian control" implies that it is the exclusive responsibility of the professional military to advise the Prime Minister on matters requiring professional military expertise (Hirose 1989: 5). But neither the Chairman of the Joint Staff Council nor the Chiefs of Staff of the three Services brief the Prime Minister on military issues (Otake 1983: 189–91; Kataoka and Myers 1989: 75). And uniformed officials do not take part in the deliberations of the Diet (Hirose 1989: 48). It is even considered a challenge to the principle of "civilian control" for top officers of the Self-Defense Forces to speak to the general public on important defense issues. In June 1978, for example, Hiroomi Kurisu, then Chairman of the Joint Staff Council, spoke on television about the Soviet military exercises on one of the Kuril Islands and was subsequently subjected to public criticism by the Defense Agency's civilian officials. In the following month, Kurisu was summarily dismissed after he had ventured to discuss in a press conference what he regarded as defects in the Self-Defense Forces Law and the possibilities of the Forces' "extra-legal" operations in an emergency (Otake 1983: 184–7).

At times the two policymaking axes intersect. For example, in the early 1980s, one of the contentious issues was whether Japan should make an exception to the 1967 ban on exporting arms or armament-related technologies. The proponents of granting such an exception, the Ministry of Foreign Affairs and the Defense Agency, argued that basing the export of militarily sensitive technology on the Mutual Defense Assistance Agreement of 1954 would sidestep possible problems with other countries, for example in the Middle East as MITI feared, because in contrast to the United States these states did not have a defensive alliance with Japan (Gotoda 1989: 30–5).

But more normal is the separation of the two dimensions and of economic and military security issues. This separation rests on the premise that the use or threat of military force to ensure economic security is simply no longer a viable political option for Japan. This premise was not shaken by the Persian Gulf crisis of 1987 when the United States requested Japanese military contributions to the Western effort to ensure the safe passage of Kuwait's tankers in the Gulf. According to the memoirs of the then Cabinet Secretary, the Prime Minister and the staff of the Ministry of Foreign Affairs initially favored a military deployment. They eventually changed their minds. First, Japanese ships might have become entangled in belligerent acts, thus violating Japan's basic principle of the non-use of military force in all cases other than a direct attack on Japan. Secondly, the deployment of Japanese ships was in open contradiction with Japan's policy of maintaining friendly relations with all states in the area. Since Cabinet Secretary Gotoda, as a member of the Cabinet, refused to sign a cabinet decision to deploy military force, Prime Minister Nakasone would have had to dismiss Gotoda—an act for which the government would have paid a heavy political price. Because it became clear that the United States would accept nonmilitary contributions to a joint defense effort, the opposition of the Cabinet Secretariat to the proposal for deploying military force was unyielding and in the end successful (Gotoda 1989: 104–8).

The Gulf crisis is not likely to have the effect of undermining Japan's basic policy of shunning military force. In response to American requests for military cooperation, the government prepared legislation that would establish a "Peace Cooperation Corps" to be deployed as part of UN-sponsored peacekeeping operations. The legislation provides for the participation of units of the Self-Defense Forces in such a corps. The Ministry of Foreign Affairs and the Defense Agency are in disagreement over points such as the carrying of light arms by SDF personnel for personal protection and whether those forces will be on leave from the SDF while on such international assignments. The Defense Agency, in particular, advocates letting members of the forces serve concurrently in the proposed corps and the forces so that, for instance, they may be able to use SDF equipment. The Ministry of Foreign Affairs, on the other hand, is concerned about the negative reactions of Asian countries about any deployment of SDF forces outside of Japan. While these issues have been the subject of open and acrimonious debate inside and outside of government, there is a widespread consensus that the proposed corps will not be allowed to exercise military force (*Asahi Shimbun*, September 27, 28, 1990, evening editions). If or when, some time in the future, the use of military force in defense of Japan's economic security were to become accepted policy, the two distinct axes of Japan's domestic structure of security policy would merge.

Despite the growth in its bureaucratic power, the Defense Agency remains politically colonized by other ministries. In contrast to its uniformed personnel, the civilian staff of the Agency are characterized by a lack of strong organizational identity and its tendency is to subordinate the military to the economic and political aspects of security policy (Hirose 1989: 116–18). And the principle of "civilian control" within the executive branch of government reinforces the bias against any attempt to introduce a military definition of security.

In sum, Japanese security policy is shaped by distinctive political arrangements that revolve around two axes within the government that connect the ministries of Finance and Foreign Affairs with the Defense Agency, on the one hand, and with MITI on the other. But the ministries of Finance and Foreign Affairs are not the only institutions by which Japanese politics integrates the economic and military requirements of security policy into an all-encompassing political strategy carried by a broad consensus. The Defense

Agency is staffed to a substantial degree by the political appointees of other ministries. This reinforces the economic and political bias against a military interpretation of Japan's national security requirements. These political arrangements in the structure of the Japanese government are deeply entrenched and make it highly unlikely that dramatic changes in the international state system will lead in the foreseeable future to an ascendance of the military dimension of Japanese security policy.

This conclusion could be supported further by an analysis of the effects of state–society and transnational relations on Japanese security policy. The Defense Agency is small and isolated from Japanese society. It has no allies commanding large resources and prestige. And it lacks a mission with which to build a political constituency in the foreseeable future. Japan's small defense economy and its far-reaching ban on weapons exports, unique in the major industrial states, are two telling examples that contrast sharply, for example, with the role of the German chemicals industry in the Middle East. The links between Japan's domestic and transnational structures create similar effects. The security treaty with the United States provides for various links with the U.S. military and imposes a number of limitations on the growth of Japan's military organizations—in terms of procurement, personnel training, and the development of strategic doctrine. Furthermore, these restraints in the military field must be seen within a broader context of transnational relations. There has been a sharp increase in the importance of American bureaucratic organizations and political interests in the formulation of Japanese economic policy. And in the United States a powerful Japanese lobby has emerged that seeks to shape the general climate of opinion and thus, in the long run, a public policy favorable to Japanese interests. In other words, the transnational links of Japan's domestic political structures add further constraints to the independent role of the military and enhance the influence of economic and political actors. The subordination of military to economic and political considerations in Japan's policy of comprehensive security is thus no surprise and should not be affected greatly in the foreseeable future by the dramatic changes in the international state system.

Normative contexts

Japan's national security policy is not simply a matter of domestic structures shaping the international pursuit of wealth and power. It is also a matter of the different principles and practices on which Japanese politics is based and which are, in the case of this powerful state, projected into the arena of international politics. National security policy is a hollow and dangerous symbol if it undermines the norms of a society. "The realist view does not go far enough when it defines interest (i.e., wealth and power) and ignores identity (i.e., whose wealth and power), and the Wilsonian view goes too far when it assumes a common political identity (i.e., all nations express similar political values) and considers relative power and wealth to be irrelevant" (Nau 1990a: 8, 1990b).

David Bobrow has taken stock of a voluminous literature on Japanese public opinion on international affairs (Bobrow 1989). His findings are in broad agreement with established findings and assumptions about the Japanese public. Public attitudes favor a passive over an active stance, alignment with the United States over a policy of equidistance between the United States and the Soviet Union, political dependence over autonomy, and minimal over extensive military spending. Furthermore, generational effects have been relatively small in the last two decades. The overwhelming majority of the Japanese are skeptical about any departure from the status quo. Among the major industrial states, "Japanese public opinion on basic security policy," concludes Thomas Risse-Kappen, "has been the most stable" (Risse-Kappen 1990: 39). On questions of national security, public opinion favors economic strength, peaceful diplomacy, and a low-key consensus approach; it does not feel threatened by the Soviet Union and does not think much of the Self-Defense Forces; it overwhelmingly supports Article 9 of the Constitution; and it opposes nuclear weapons probably more strongly than the public in any other Western state (Risse-Kappen 1990). In short, the military is viewed as marginal, and the public shows a marked lack of willingness to resort to armed defense even if Japan should be attacked. "Fewer than one in five respondents would resort to force to resist invasion" (Bobrow 1989: 571–604).

These public attitudes reflect the depth of social learning which came with the disastrous loss of World War II and the American occupation. Many, although by no means all, studies of Japanese foreign policy credit public opinion with a substantial impact on national security policy. This is the result of the combined weight of the left-wing opposition in the Diet, the possibility of popular demonstrations in the streets, and the critical attitude of the mass media toward any attempt to enhance the status of the military and to develop a more active defense policy.

But public opinion does not dictate Japan's security policy. If it did, what would account for the substantial changes in Japan's defense policy (for example, a decline in defense spending after the early 1950s and an increase in the 1980s) that have occurred since the early 1950s? Public opinion, as Risse-Kappen argues, sets limits that are fairly broad and unspecified and that leave substantial room for different factions of the Liberal Democratic Party (LDP) to fight internal battles and to mobilize public opinion in an unending struggle for power in the party as well as over government policy. Such conflicts were very much in evidence when the Mutual Security Treaty was renewed in 1960, and when the Japanese government negotiated with the United States the return of Okinawa in 1969. In the 1970s and 1980s, such conflicts were not prominent. But the intense discussions over the modalities of Japan's possible participation in an international military force in the Middle East in September 1990 once again revealed the complex interaction between factional politics and public opinion in Japan (Sanger 1990).

The norms that are expressed by Japanese public opinion are informed by the constitutional and anti-militaristic principles that have distinguished Japanese security policy over two decades. But in the 1980s these norms permitted important changes in policy—a substantial increase in defense spending and the buildup of Japan's military capabilities, an active rather than a passive integration of the Self-Defense Forces in the military defense planning of the United States for the Asia-Pacific region, and a partial relaxation of the ban on the export of weapons and defense-related technologies for the Strategic Defense Initiative (SDI) of the United States (Hook 1988). The normative context of Japan's security policy is thus both firmly anchored in public opinion and at the same time remarkably open to incremental modification and change.

This pattern of norms that are both firmly fixed and at the same time open to a process of informal and incremental change is also evident in the way the Japanese government has dealt with the explicit restraints that Article 9 of the Constitution has imposed on the conduct of Japan's security policy. Since the LDP could never muster the two-thirds majority in the Diet required to revise Article 9, the government has chosen the principle of constitutional interpretation rather than revision to make its policy conform to explicitly stated norms. "In other words, the LDP does not admit to abrogating constitutional principles; rather, it claims to observe them, as in the case of the Self-Defense Forces—these are not 'land, sea and air forces' as prohibited by Article 9, but forces for 'self-defense' " (Hook 1988: 388). In the 1980s, the practice of constitutional interpretation was, for example, evident in the expansion of the boundaries of the term "self-defense" to include collective defense activities—including convoying U.S. ships, patrolling sea lanes of communication up to one thousand miles and participating in the SDI program (Hook 1988: 386). In an internationalizing world, Japanese leaders have apparently been willing to reconceive of the "Japanese self" in broader terms, at least in the area of security policy. And they have done so in a manner that acknowledges the existence of important norms that constrain the way Japanese security interests are defined, while at the same time modifying some of these norms.

But the interests underlying Japan's security policy are not just shaped by domestic norms that express the lessons of Japan's historical experiences and the dynamics of its domestic politics. Security interests are also shaped by the redefinition of Japanese interests that emanate from the international system. The most important norm that has helped define the interests informing Japanese foreign policy since 1945 is Japan's relationship with the United States. Questions of Latin American debt, political unrest in the Middle East, the end of the Cold War in Europe, as well as many political issues in Japanese domestic politics are interpreted not so much on their merits as on their likely effects on Japan's relations with the United States—its most important trading partner and the main guarantor of its military security.

The redefinition of interests is clearly evident in the external pressures that have increasingly affected Japanese policymaking (*gaiatsu*). The coalition politics between the "nationalist" and the "internationalist" camp that increasingly characterized Japanese policymaking in the 1980s is significant not only because it, as is frequently noted, brings foreign actors either directly or indirectly into the domestic policy coalitions (Campbell 1989; Weatherford and Fukui 1986; Yamaguchi 1988); it is also important because it incorporates in the policy process new norms—for example, full reciprocity, open market access, burden sharing in the defense sector, and the responsibilities that attend the role of a financial superpower—that affect the way Japanese policymakers reconceive their policy interests from short term to long term. These new norms affect the way Japanese policymakers conceive of the policy interests that they wish to pursue.

Much of the literature on Japanese politics and the policy of liberalization in trade, finance, and services can be read from this perspective. This literature is too voluminous to be reviewed here, but it supports the general conclusion that a secular shift in norms and interests that is likely to be irreversible in the economic and social realms is underway. Not generally considered a proponent of arguments celebrating the early convergence between Japan's developmental state and other forms of capitalism, Chalmers Johnson nonetheless concludes that

> young and middle-aged Japanese born in the 1950s and 1960s, are just now achieving responsible positions in government and private industry. They differ from all other Japanese born in this century in their ready familiarity with peace and prosperity. . . . They can be expected to persist with the internationalization of the economy since it has become fundamental to Japan's continued prosperity.
>
> (Johnson 1983: 24)

A reallocation of political and military responsibilities reflecting the shifting balance of economic strength between the United States and Japan is for Chalmers Johnson an essential part of bringing the postwar era to a satisfactory end. Such a reallocation depends on the norms and interests that motivate different sectors of the Japanese political class. Susan Pharr argues that traditionally strong sectors speaking for nationalism and neutralism are now distinctive minorities compared to the forces speaking for neomercantilism and internationalism. Neomercantilists have a narrow and short-term conception of interest, favor domestic economic growth and social stability, and seek to limit costly responsibilities abroad. Japan's postwar successes, Pharr argues, carried with them long-term costs that Japan struggles with today: the development of an extremely narrow, economics-centered definition of national self-interest rather than a major global view that takes into account political, economic and strategic factors simultaneously, a passivity in the political and strategic (as opposed to economic) dimensions of foreign policy, and a national political leadership chosen almost exclusively on the basis of their ability to manage the economy and domestic concerns.

(Pharr 1988: 35)

And neomercantilists view Japan either as an "Eastern" power or as a country which is unique, neither "Eastern" nor "Western." This, according to Pharr, is still the majority view among the Japanese public and in the LDP.

But this view is now increasingly challenged by the internationalist camp, which argues for a break with past policies and the need for a new stance in global affairs. In pushing for economic, social, and political change across a broad array of issues, proponents of internationalization (*kokusaika*) make this Japan's *perestroika*. They view Japan as a "Western" power, which is subscribing to the tenets of the Anglo-Saxon liberalism that has left such a deep mark on the modern world over the last three centuries. "This perception of themselves as 'Western' colors how internationalists think and the reasoning they bring to their foreign policy choices, even when they back policies that also enjoy the support of neo-mercantilists" (Pharr 1988: 36).

Internationalists renounce a strong military buildup and favor a more active international stance on other issues such as economic aid and international debt relief. But internationalists are more likely to consider Japan's actual strategic needs rather than judge military issues in terms of the necessity of maintaining good political relations with the United States, as neo-mercantilists do. Although the internationalists are still, according to Pharr, a minority, their influence has increased greatly during the last two decades. And internationalists, aided by the structural changes in the international system, certainly occupy the center stage in the policy discussions on many of the important policy choices that Japan is facing today. Pharr's conclusion echoes those of Johnson:

In the future, the internationalist line may well come to predominate in the debate, but I see this shift coming rather slowly. The fact that the debate is where it is, though, reflects a profound change in Japan. Twenty years ago, the tension and debate in Japanese society was not between the internationalists and neo-mercantilists, but between a powerful majority and a neutralist position that, especially in the 1950s and the early 1960s, carried strong moral authority.

(Pharr 1988: 38)

In sum, the normative consensus for Japanese security policy is shaped by the historical lessons of World War II and the re-emergence of Japan as a peaceful and prosperous major actor in world politics since 1945. Characteristic of Japan's political culture is the fact that the deeply ingrained pacifism is not rooted primarily in the constitutional mandate imposed by Article 9. What counts more heavily is the weight of public opinion. The Constitution has been reinterpreted in the past to fit an evolving public consensus on the requirements of Japanese security policy in a changing world. This process of reinterpretation is grounded in a deep public resentment and fear of any experimentation with a policy that might rely on the threat or use of military force. Japan's consensus culture facilitates gradual and incremental policy change that might be more difficult in a legal culture requiring that a redefinition of Japan's interest be codified in law. The future evolution of Japan's security policy will be shaped to a substantial degree by a gradual adjustment and change in the normative restraints that inform domestic public opinion rather than dramatic changes in global structures.

Backed by broad political consensus, the Japanese elite views the relationship with the United States as the only prism through which all major events in world politics must be viewed. The collapse of communism in Eastern Europe, the possible disintegration of the Soviet Union, a thawing of the Cold War in Asia or the threat of war in the Middle East, all of the momentous events of 1990 are viewed, as all major developments in international politics during the last three decades have been, primarily in terms of the effect they have on the alliance between Japan and the United States. The primacy of the United States in Japan's foreign relations has greatly accelerated the process of a redefinition of Japan's security interest from short-term to long-term interests and from a restrictive to a broader conception of self. Internationalization in the 1980s brought about this remarkable change in Japan, thus strengthening the relationship.

The domestic norms underlying policy are probably more firmly established in the institutions and political practices of Japanese democracy than is the more recent redefinition—from short term into long term—of interests that have affected Japan's security policy so substantially in the past decade. Until there is a better understanding of the process by which long-term interests are eventually internalized as norms affecting behavior, conclusions about the normative constraints that act on Japan's security policy can only be very tentative. But it is safe to conclude this much: the gradualism that marks Japanese security policy in a world of rapid flux is rooted in both domestic norms and a conception of self-interest that has increasingly taken on a long-term perspective during the last two decades.

Conclusion

The evolution of Japanese security policy is often interpreted in broad analytical categories that highlight the effect of different international structures on Japan's policy options, typically with reference to a recalibration of power and purpose in the U.S.–Japanese relation: *Pax Nipponica*, the reassertion of

American leadership, the continuation of Japan as a supporter state, or the establishment of a new "bigemony" uniting Japan and the United States around the Pacific as the nucleus of future growth and vitality in the global economy (Inoguchi 1986, 1989).

The view put forth here is that the recent, dramatic changes in the structure of international politics will not lead to radical changes in Japan's security policy. Both its domestic structures and the normative context in which security interests are defined appear to be evolving only very gradually. And it is these domestic features rather than the rapidly changing and dimly perceived determinants in the international system that contribute to the analysis of Japanese security policy.

A comparison with Japan's policy of internal security offers some suggestive insights into why Japan's external security policy is likely to evolve only gradually in a time of dramatic international change (Katzenstein and Tsujinaka 1990). The penetration by bureaucratic and political organizations is markedly greater in the Japanese military than it is in the powerful police force. And, while the military is less closely linked to Japanese society, transnational military ties, especially with the United States, are probably stronger on questions of external than of internal security. The low degree of Japanese vulnerability to any serious threat to its internal security has favored an autonomous policy stance in contrast to the country's reliance on the American political guarantee of its external security. Japan's domestic structure thus makes an independent policy more likely for questions of internal than of external security.

On both internal and external security issues social rather than legal norms help define and redefine Japanese policy interests. In the case of internal security, this has facilitated the gradual expansion of police power in state and society, while impeding international policies by underlining, until very recently, the importance of Japanese uniqueness. On questions of external security, in contrast, informalism has facilitated a gradual redefinition of Japan's international role by providing the margin of political flexibility needed to make some of the important policy changes that have broadened Japan's policy profile on important economic and security issues in the 1980s. The normative context in which the interests of Japanese security policy are defined and redefined thus increasingly favors international over national policy solutions. In contrast to questions of internal security, Japan's domestic structures and norms thus tend to favor approaches that emphasize international interdependence over national autonomy on external security policy issues.

Japanese security policy will be focused on the U.S.–Japan relationship in the foreseeable future. This alliance is of such cardinal importance in economic, political, and military terms that Japan's government may well seek to intensify mutual vulnerabilities to create stronger political bonds between the two countries. A European comparison may be helpful here. The unexpected turn of French foreign policy on questions of European integration appears to be motivated primarily by the objective of tying down in a European framework a Germany that otherwise might be too strong and threatening to French interests. France appears to be prepared to move ahead with monetary integration while continuing to regard questions of defense policy as a matter of exclusively national control.

Tying down a potentially volatile and unpredictable ally is a daunting task not only for the French but also for the Japanese. Within a changing context of norms and interests it is quite conceivable that a Japanese government may be prepared to accept, especially in the sphere of military security, a structural integration of defense and defense-related high-technology industries across the Pacific.

Such integration would contradict not only the relentless push of Japanese corporations for a position of leadership in world markets, but also the American preference for national autonomy and political unilateralism, especially on questions of national defense. But it would be congruent with the Japanese notion of sovereignty as permitting for inequalities of rank and cultural significance. Accepting the position of junior partner in the provision of military security fits the Japanese ethic of mutual hostage-taking, which creates a system of self-deterrence with the effect of keeping fears of repeating past crimes firmly in check. Acceptance of the norm of vulnerability-interdependence does not clash with the Japanese concept of sovereignty as the juridical equality of actors differentiated by status and cultural legacies. Since it vitiates the existence of any one decisive source of political power and influence, such an international system of asymmetric vulnerabilities may not agree with American notions of autonomy. Instead, it acknowledges the existence of multiple nodes of power that require a skillful game of politics. This is the kind of politics that the Japanese have cultivated so successfully at home in the last fifty years, and that they now seek to project abroad.

Japan's domestic structures and the norms that help define Japanese security interests make possible a second choice that is not necessarily antithetical to a contentious deepening of the structural relations between Japan and the United States. Within the established political–economic framework for interpreting Japanese security in broadly international terms, Japan appears to be prepared to pursue a more activist policy in Asia, supported by a continued close alliance with the United States. This outcome would conform to the emergence of a new regionalism in Europe centering around the EU and a united Germany, but also involving the United States as a participant in a regionwide collective security agreement and as both a partner and a competitor in the European single market. Compared to Germany, the structural integration of Japan with its neighbors as well as with the United States is much smaller. But, as in Germany, the domestic and normative determinants of Japan's security policy point to the continuation of a policy that favors international cooperation with the United States and the Western Alliance. The political pluralism of the new postwar order may, however, require the exercise of new political leadership qualities in a world of soft regions managed by a political process of trilateral policy coordination that is both tested and sustained by self-imposed integration between some of the central powers of world politics during the next decade or two.

References

Asahi Shimbun Keizai-bu (1989) *Mili-tech Power: Kyukyoku no Nichibei Masatsu* [Mili-tech Power: The Ultimate Japan–U.S. Conflict], Tokyo: Asahi Shimbun-sha.

Bobrow, D. B. (1989) "Japan in the World: Opinion from Defeat to Success," *Journal of Conflict Resolution*, 33, 4: 571–604.

Campbell, J. C. (1989) "The Functions of Nichibeigata Sesshho," submitted to *Chuo Koran* (October).

Drifte, R. (1990) *Japan's Foreign Policy*, London: Routledge.

Gotoda, M. (1989) *Naikaku Kanbo Chokan* [Cabinet Chief Secretary], Tokyo: Kodansha.

Hirose, K. (1989) *Kanryo to Gunjin: Bunmin Tosei no Genkai* [Bureaucrats and Military Officers: The Limits of Civilian Control], Tokyo: Iwanami Shoten.

Hook, G. D. (1988) "The Erosion of Anti-Militaristic Principles in Contemporary Japan," *Journal of Peace Research*, 25, 4: 381–94.

Inoguchi, T. (1986) "Japan's Images and Options: Not a Challenger but a Supporter," *Journal of Japanese Studies*, 12, 1: 95–119.

Inoguchi, T. (1989) "Four Japanese Scenarios for the Future," *International Affairs*, 5, 1: 15–28.

Ishiguro, T. (1978) "Jieitai Sosoki no Civilian Control: Kokkai Rongi o Chushin ni" [Civilian Control in the Early Years of the Self-Defense Forces: Based on Debates in the Diet], in E. Sato (ed.) *Seiji to Gunji: Sono Hikakushiteki Kenkyu* [Politics and Military Affairs: A Comparative Historical Study], pp. 259–95, Tokyo: Nihon Kokusai Mondai Kenkyujo.

Johnson, C. (1983) "The 'Internationalization' of the Japanese Economy," *California Management Review*, 25, 3: 5–26.

Kataoka, T. and Myers, R. H. (1989) *Defending an Economic Superpower: Reassessing the U.S.–Japan Security Alliance*, Boulder, Colo.: Westview Press.

Katzenstein, P. J. and Tsujinaka, Y. (1990) "Japan's Internal Security Policy: Political Responses to Terrorism and Violent Social Protest in the 1970s and 1980s" (unpublished manuscript, Cornell University, Ithaca, NY).

Nau, H. R. (1990a) "Rethinking Economics and Security in Europe," paper presented at the conference on Europe held by the American Enterprise Institute for Public Policy Research, March.

Nau, H. R. (1990b) *The Myth of America's Decline: Leading the World Economy into the 1990s*, New York: Oxford University Press.

Otake, H. (1983) *Nihon no Boei to Kokunai Seiji: Detente kara Gunkaku e* [Japan's Defense and Domestic Politics: From Détente to Military Buildup], Tokyo: Sanichi Shobo.

Otake, H. (1984) "Nihon ni okeru 'Gunsakan Fukugotai Keisei no Zasetsu'" [The Failure of the Attempt at Forming a 'Military–Industrial–Bureaucratic Complex' in Japan], in Hideo Otake (ed.) *Nihon Seiji no Soten* [Issues in Japanese Politics], pp. 13–69, Tokyo: Sanichi Shobo.

Pharr, S. J. (1988) "Japan and the World: The Debate in Japan," *International Review*, 10, 4.

Risse-Kappen, T. (1990) "Public Opinion, Domestic Structure, and Security Policy in Liberal Democracies," unpublished manuscript, Cornell University, Ithaca, NY.

Sanger, D. (1990) "After Silence, Japan's Army Pushes for Armed Gulf Role," *New York Times* (September 24).

Weatherford, S. M. and Fukui, H. (1986) "The International Economy as a Constraint on Domestic Economic Policymaking: Comparing the United States and Japan," paper prepared for presentation at the 1986 Annual Meeting of the American Political Science Association, Washington, DC, 28–31 August.

Yamaguchi, J. (1988) "External Pressure and Policy Making in Japan," unpublished paper, Cornell University, Ithaca, NY.

4 Japan's internal security policy

Peter J. Katzenstein and Yutaka
Tsujinaka (1991)

This chapter examines how Japan has reacted to the rise of terrorism and violent social protest that has affected its internal security (Apter and Sawa 1984; Steinhoff 1988, 1989a, 1989b, n.d.; Farrell 1990). Japanese terrorism has centered around the Japan Red Army (JRA). After a brief period of operation in Japan in the late 1960s and early 1970s the police forced the JRA to relocate to the Mideast which became the base for its operation during the next two decades (Steinhoff 1988, 1989a). Internal security was also challenged by social movements in the 1970s and 1980s that opposed, for example, the construction and subsequent enlargement of Tokyo's Narita Airport and that embraced a host of other left-wing causes (Apter and Sawa 1984). Although the JRA and violence-prone social movements have been largely unconnected, they are typically discussed by police officials and the media under the same label of the "radical Left." Police estimates of the strength of violence-prone groups on the Left vary widely between about 18,000 and 36,000 members in the 1980s; but everyone agrees that the JRA enjoys virtually no active support inside Japan (National Police Agency 1982: 89; *Advanced Course* 1989: 421; Clifford 1976: 25).

Japan's internal security policy has responded during the last four decades to new forms of social protest. In a very short time in the early 1970s the police succeeded in forcing Japan's terrorists offshore. The Japanese, it seemed, were good at exporting TV sets, automobiles, and terrorists. This joke could not conceal the grim reality of the "embarrassingly violent and defiant activities of Japanese Red Army political radicals abroad in the service of other causes . . . one might be excusably tempted to observe facetiously that Japan is able to control its crime at home simply because it exports its violence and terrorism abroad" (Clifford 1976: 3, 23).

Political concern over the activities of the JRA continue both in Japan and abroad. In May 1988, Yasuhiro Shibata was arrested in Japan. He had entered illegally from North Korea to where he and a group of the JRA had hijacked a plane in March 1970. In November 1987 the Japanese police arrested the number two man of the JRA, Osamu Maruoka, in Tokyo after he had traveled throughout Asia for several months. After Maruoka's arrest, traces of two other members of the JRA were found in the Philippines. Two other JRA members, Junzo Okudaira and Tsutomu Shirosaki, have been linked to a series of bombing and rocket attacks in Asia and Europe. The female leader of the JRA, Fusako Shigenobu, was reportedly in a powerful bomb attack at a U.S. facility in Naples which killed five people and injured seventeen others in April 1988. And only a few days earlier another member of the Red Army, Yu Kikumura, was arrested on the New Jersey turnpike with three pipe bombs in his car, apparently planning an attack in New York City or on a meeting of international finance ministers in Washington, DC (Steinhoff 1988: 1; National Police Agency 1989b: 68).

Violent social protest inside Japan also has remained a staple of domestic politics. Protest around Narita Airport, though less frequent, has not abated. In December 1989 about 6,500 policemen used large steel cages and an armored box suspended from several cranes to dislodge about a dozen protesters, armed with firebombs and slingshots as well as arrows and bows, who were opposing the expansion of Narita Airport (Sterngold 1989). The protestors occupied a shack and four steel towers built on a newly proposed runway. The police sprayed the protestors incessantly with powerful water cannons and lowered two huge steel cages from cranes which deflected firebombs and stones hurled at them from the towers. And the police used a steel gondola, also suspended from a crane, from which five crouching policemen eventually leaped to take one of the towers. After a day of fighting, the police had arrested three protestors. There were no injuries.

Terrorism and violent social protest have triggered policy responses in Japan that have been remarkably consistent. These responses derive from the historical evolution in the organizational structure of Japan's police, the growing role the police has played in politics, its osmotic relation with society, and its weak transnational links. The organizational structure of the Japanese police is a blend of centralization and decentralization. Its operative mission is no longer informed exclusively by the notion of state service through social surveillance aiming, as it did in the 1930s and 1940s, at the eradication of political dissent. Instead since 1945 Japan's police has been revamped. While it retains a largely centralized structure for protecting Japan's internal security and, over time, has moved closer to the center of Japan's policy network, its mission has been redefined to respond to broader social needs. The societal orientation of Japan's police is effective. It blends traditional community service with modern police technologies. "The police have not been molded in a vacuum. Rather, they fit Japanese society like a glove fits the hand, and the societal hand has determined the form of the glove" (Ames 1981: 1). And when that hand forms a fist, as is true of some aspects of Japan's internal security policy, so does the glove. Its transnational links with the law enforcement agencies of other states, on the other hand, until the late 1980s have remained remarkably weak.

This chapter summarizes some of the findings of a longer monograph (Katzenstein and Tsujinaka 1991). It analyzes both the domestic and the international politics of Japan's internal security policy. It describes the organizational structure of the police with particular emphasis on the security police in the first section, analyzes the position the police holds in Japanese politics in the second, examines its relation to domestic and international society in the third, details the domestic and international aspects of Japan's internal security policy in the fourth section, and ends with a brief summary.

The structure of the Japanese police

Although a substantial number of organizations seek to protect Japan's internal security—including the Ministry of Justice (MOJ), the Prosecutor's Office, the Public Security Investigation Agency (PSIA) and even the Defense Agency and the armed forces—the police is clearly the center of a network of relations that are both institutional and political. Bayley, for example, describes Japan as having a multiple, coordinated police system which delegates central enforcement to subordinate levels of government (Bayley 1985: 58–9). Political and institutional relations link different government bureaucracies; they establish connections between government bureaucracies and a variety of societal institutions and actors; and they join government bureaucracies with a variety of transnational structures and actors. Japan's internal security policy is shaped in part by the constraints that these organizational structures and relationships impose as well as the opportunities that they provide for the exercise of power.

During the past three decades the total number of policemen has almost doubled from 118,700 in 1955 to 220,900 in 1988. And the total police budget has increased by a factor of 40 between 1955 and 1988 from 61,393 million to 2,443,970 million yen (Keisatsucho 1977: 492–506, 551–6; 1989: 331, 336). In the early 1970s Japan spent 0.90 percent of its GNP on policing, considerably more than the 0.52 percent figure for the United States (Bayley 1978: 190).

These aggregate figures tell us little about the size of the security police. The government's penchant for secrecy makes it difficult to give reliable data about the size of Japan's security police. But the best estimates available put the size of the Metropolitan Police Department (MPD) at about 10,000 in the 1960s. This figure includes 5,700 members of the Riot Police, 1,800 to 2,500 of whom were thought to be serving in the Metropolitan Riot Police, as well as 1,200 members of the security police, with 700 serving in the Metropolitan Security Police (Tsuji 1966: 319; *Asahi Nenkan* 1961: 245; Hironaka 1973: 223–4, 308–9). In the early 1960s the security police was reported to account for about 7–8 percent of Japan's total police manpower. By 1988 estimates for the size of the security police had increased threefold to 30,000–40,000 men, including 4,000 members of the Metropolitan Riot Police, 1,500 riot policemen permanently stationed at Narita Airport, 9,500 other riot police officers, 2,000 members of the Metropolitan Security Police, 1,000 other members of the security police, 4,000 members of the regional riot police and 15,000 members of a standby riot police force. By 1988 the share of the security police had risen to approximately 13–18 percent of the total police force (*Asahi*, June 29, 1978; Mizutani 1987: 117; Jiyuhosodan 1986: 203). Other sources provide similar estimates. One such estimate for the year 1972, for example, reports that the security and riot police together accounted for about 16 percent of Japan's total police force (*Asahi Nenkan* 1973: 284). And the early 1970s probably saw the security police at its peak strength.

Japan's police is characterized by a combination of institutional stability combined with a great flexibility and secrecy in the practical work of the police. These traits are defining characteristics of the political arrangements that typify postwar Japan. In 1954 the Police Law was totally rewritten in line with a more conservative political climate and the policy of the "reverse course" (Hironaka 1973: 147–8; Hoshino 1974: 346–7; Sugai 1957: 11–12; Rinalducci 1972: 1–17). One result of this important reform was that the national government assumed full control over questions of internal security through its control of the security police, personnel affairs, and budgets. Although they continue to pay for most of the police budget, prefectural governments lost much authority, especially in the area of internal security policy. "Centralization is much more conspicuous than in the prewar system" (Sugai 1957: 12; Arai 1979: 21). In the words of Tamaki Uemura, the Public Safety Commission exercises no more than nominal control and in the new atmosphere soon became a mere "agent for transmitting government policy" (*Asahi*, October 30, 1958 cited in Hatakeyama 1984: 97). Despite the social upheavals which mass protest and terrorist violence caused in the 1960s, 1970s, and 1980s, no major institutional changes have occurred in the structure of the police since the reforms of the mid-1950s.

With the revision of the Police Law in 1954, the National Police Agency (NPA) was formally established, and Tokyo's MPD was reorganized in the same year. In 1954 the NPA had four bureaus and a secretariat; in 1988 it had five bureaus, one department, and a secretariat. It employs about 1,000–1,100 police officials, 900 members of the Imperial Palace guards, as well as 5,000–6,000 civilians. In 1988 two-thirds of the NPA officials were serving in seven Regional Police Bureaus and two Communication Divisions. Over 15 percent of the personnel are assigned to three affiliated organizations: the Imperial Guard Headquarters, the National Research Institute, and the National Police Academy. Of the 1,304 officials working in NPA's inner bureaus, 254 are placed in the Security Bureau, second largest after the Criminal Investigation Bureau (Somucho 1988). Compared to the total police force of Japan, the NPA has decreased from 0.76 percent in 1962 to 0.54 percent in 1988; corresponding budget figures are 18.2 percent in 1955 and 7.4 percent in 1988. Evidently, the burden of an increasingly expensive police system is falling more heavily on the prefectures than on the national government (Keisatsucho 1977, 1989).

Within the structure of the NPA the security police plays an important role. It has been noted, for example, that the security police has dominated the criminal police since the late 1960s. After Yutaka Arai (1965–9) none of the NPA's eight Commissioner Generals have come from the criminal police except the present Commissioner, Akio Kanazawa, whose appointment may well have been a symbolic gesture to placate criminal police officials (Tawara 1986a: 96–7; 1990). The influence of the security police inside the NPA became particularly noticeable with the conclusion of the Asanuma Commission (1974–8) (*Yomiuri* 1986: 184–94).

Although the NPA rarely investigates crimes, it has taken measures to counter the threat by political extremists especially since the mid-1960s. In 1965 a division to counter right-wing extremism was spun off from NPA's domestic division, and in 1972 an independent division for dealing with left-wing extremism was established. Since 1978 the NPA has taken special measures against the JRA, and a special antiterrorist division was set up in 1988. It seeks to integrate the scattered work on international terrorism and the JRA done in different divisions of the NPA. Its specific purpose is to stop the return or immigration of international terrorists, to locate and arrest terrorists living in Japan, and to eradicate organizations supportive of the JRA. But this division does not investigate terrorists who have their basis exclusively inside Japan like, for example, the Chukaku (Kokusai Tero Mondai Kenkyukai 1989: 56).

Besides the NPA, the Metropolitan Police Department (MPD) is Japan's second major police organization. The MPD is proud of "being the only organization that can provide protection against terrorist attacks."[1] Through the rotation of personnel, MPD and NPA are closely linked, and it appears that over time the traditional independence of the MPD from the NPA has become weaker.[2] While the MPD is legally and financially one of the prefectural police forces, organizationally it resembles the NPA and in particular its security section (Kubo 1984: 93–102).

With respect to the organizational development of the security police, the MPD has been a driving force. Although the 1947 Police Law separated the MPD from the national police, it has behaved like a national security police. The organizational structure of the MPD is more complex than that of the other prefectural police forces and of the NPA. Two bureaus among seven, the Security Bureau and the Public Security Bureau, are in charge of the security police. Both bureaus can be traced back to 1952 just after the passage of the Subversive Activity Prevention Law. The Security Bureau has grown from two divisions in 1952 to five today. Their primary responsibility is to provide physical security and manage the riot police. The Public Security Division supervises the surveillance, investigation, and arrest of political radicals. It has become progressively more complex.

Since 1969 the work of the Public Security Bureau of the MPD has become more and more secret. Within the existing organization sharp increases in manpower occurred. After the terrorist attacks at the time of the 1986 Tokyo Summit, for example, the MPD decided to double its force against the New Left from 250 to 450 according to one source (*Mainichi*, June 19, 1986) and from 290 to 600 according to another (*Yomiuri*, June 19, 1986). Chukaku is the specific target of this enlarged police force.[3]

Since information about the police forces assigned to intelligence and police work against radicals is classified as top secret, such estimates must be taken with a grain of salt. We do know, however, that the Special Investigation Corps in Public Security, established in July 1969, is used to investigate incidents covered by the Subversive Activity Prevention and Crime of Riot Article in the Penal Law. According to two reports several antiterrorist emergency squads have been set up at the prefectural level since the early 1970s. The existence of one or several combat teams with a total of 105 men was reported in 1976. They were well trained and maintained at a high state of readiness to swing into action at times of crisis (*Asahi*, May 29, 1976 and June 28, 1978; Nishio 1984: 26). According to a second source, special antiguerilla squads, armed with automatic rifles and belonging to the Sixth Riot Corps of the MPD, were set up in Tokyo and Osaka on January 10, 1978 (*Mainichi*, May 11, 1982). These units were established because of an NPA order to the MPD and the Osaka prefectural police in response to an international agreement Prime Minister Fukuda reached at the Bonn summit in 1977. The members of this unit are selected and trained secretly as ordinary riot police (*Mainichi*, May 11, 1982; Nishio 1984: 26).

Like the NPA the MPD has traditionally strongly opposed being held accountable under the terms of the Public Information Ordinance. It insists, for example, on its special status and a role that is qualitatively different from that of other prefectural police forces, among other reasons because it is the source of much sensitive information (*Yomiuri* 1986: 192–3). The MPD sees itself as the center of Japan's internal security policy and does not want that position put at risk either by political interference, as in the 1970s, from elected government officials or by unwanted public attention and information. In contrast to many of the other prefectural police forces which operate at the periphery of Japanese politics and are less intimately tied to the NPA, the MPD offers its security police a powerful base for operation (Kubo 1984).

A discussion of the position of the security police in the NPA, the MPD, and the other prefectural police forces conceals the de facto integration of these different branches of the security police. The security police in Japan apparently works like one organization (*Yomiuri* 1986: 192–3).[4] Apart from the regular round of meetings before, during or after important incidents touching on Japan's internal security, national meetings of directors or director generals in charge of security and public security affairs in the prefectural police forces are held on an ad hoc basis. Such meetings, for example, have reportedly been held on January 9, 1987 and April 4, 1986, as well as earlier on March 28, 1978, and July 17, 1963 (*Sankei*, January 9, 1987; *Nikkei*, April 4, 1986; *Nikkei*, March 29, 1978; *Asahi*, July 17, 1963). The coordination of the work of different intelligence and security organizations dates back to the late 1960s and accelerated with the series of terrorist attacks in the 1970s. As part of the reform of the Cabinet Secretariat in 1987 coordination was institutionalized in the form of the Joint Information Exchange Meeting. This de facto integration on a national basis offers a sharp contrast to the criminal police where competition between different prefectural police forces is often quite intense.

The political position of the police

The informal integration of the security police forces throughout Japan is one instance of a more general structural feature of Japanese politics. The sectionalism and bureaucratic pluralism of Japanese bureaucracies has often been noted (Inoguchi 1983; Yamaguchi 1989). It is partly overcome by the exchanges, loans, and transfers of personnel between different bureaucratic organizations.

The rotation of NPA personnel shows a distinctive pattern. The NPA sends between seventy and ninety officials to other ministries and agencies while receiving only about twenty officials from other ministries, most of them at the prefectural police offices. Furthermore, very few officials from other agencies reach senior office positions inside the NPA. In 1980, for example, there was only one senior official from the Ministry of Home Affairs (MOHA) working at the NPA. And in 1984 only four chiefs of prefectural police headquarters were held by officials from other ministries, including the Ministry of Foreign Affairs (MOFA), Construction, Defence, and National Railway (*Mainichi*, June 29, 1984). In contrast, the NPA has been very successful in reaching senior positions in the Cabinet Secretariat. In 1986 the NPA placed fourteen officials in the Cabinet Secretariat, three in the Defense Agency, and two in the Imperial Palace Agency. And the NPA sends many of its promising junior officers to the major ministries. Twenty-six junior NPA officials worked for the Cabinet Secretariat in 1989, sixteen for MOFA, six for the Defense Agency, five for the Administrative Management and Coordination Agency, four for Justice, and three for the Imperial Palace. It thus appears that the security police in particular has succeeded in carving out for itself a powerful position not only within the police but also within the security-related government ministries and agencies. After Masaharu Gotoda became the Deputy Secretary General in the Tanaka Cabinet in 1972, several former NPA bureaucrats became politicians, in the 1970s and 1980s: Hatano, Kamei, Gotoda, Shimoinaba, Watanabe, and Suzuki, among others, are prominent names that illustrate this trend.

Over time the bureaucratic balance of power has changed in favor of the police. At the local and prefectural level, police bureaucracies have gained at the expense of politicians. The NPA, and possibly the MOHA, have arguably increased their power compared to such economic ministries as Finance (MOF) and the Ministry of International Trade and Industry (MITI), and also in comparison to left-wing, progressive prefectural governments. Since the late 1970s many governors of major metropolitan areas have been defeated and have been replaced by office-holders many of whom had held important bureaucratic positions in the MOHA. Under Prime Minister Nakasone, himself originally an Inspector in the MPD, many former police bureaucrats who entered politics have been given important offices. From this vantage point the 1970s and 1980s appear to some as "the age of police bureaucrats or new *Naimu* (Ministry of Imperial Home Affairs, MIHA) bureaucrats" (Tawara 1986b). Over time it thus has been the police rather than a revived MIHA that has created a link between the Cabinet and politics.

This link is not evident in the formal organizational structure of the Japanese government. At the national level the growing power of the police in the structure of Japanese politics is less evident on the surface. The Cabinet in postwar Japan, for example, has no analogue to the powerful MIHA in charge of police and other matters in prewar Japan. None of the government agencies dealing with questions of security have any direct representatives in the Cabinet.

In contrast to its relatively weak formal position, the NPA has succeeded in gaining substantial power in the Cabinet Secretariat, normally the center of power of Japanese politics. High-ranking police officers have traditionally held one of the Prime Minister's four secretary positions as well as one of the three Secretary General's secretary of the Cabinet positions (Nikkan Keisatsu Shimbunsha 1989; *Nikkei*, February 4, 1990; Nishio 1984: 164; Toyokeizai 1986–90). In other words the police made up for its weak representation in the Cabinet through its direct presence at two of the most important centers of Japanese politics.

Among those following Japanese politics closely, the reorganization of the Cabinet was widely interpreted as a sign of increasing police power and a check on the power of the Ministry of Finance in the Cabinet (Sentaku 1986; Tawara 1986b: 107–9). The reorganization of the Cabinet Secretariat in July 1986 resulted in an increase of the original four offices to six. But the new organizational setup includes not only the addition of two offices and the granting of greater autonomy to a third office, with the Foreign Office, the Domestic Office and the Cabinet Safety Security Office, which previously had been part of the National Security Council, employing, respectively, nineteen, forty-six and twenty-four new staff members. This reorganization further increased the political power of the NPA. In addition to retaining the power of staffing two of the most important positions in the Cabinet Secretariat, the NPA now also staffs the position of the Chief of the Security Office (Sentaku 1986; Toyokeizai 1986–90). Furthermore, in the Cabinet Information Research Office that integrates different sources of information for the Cabinet, the NPA holds a prominent position. In 1987, fifteen of the twenty-eight senior research officials of the Cabinet Information Research Office came from the NPA: eight from the Security Bureau, four from the Police Affairs Bureau, and three from other NPA bureaus (Japan Communist Party 1988: 132).

The National Security Council and the Committee for Information Exchange are the only standing committees in the Cabinet that can review issues of internal security. Other committees hold meetings on an ad hoc basis, such as the Headquarter for the Prevention of Hijacking and Other Inhumane Violence. But, since the meetings of these groups are ad hoc to cope with particular emergency situations, the Cabinet plays a relatively unimportant role in the evolution of Japan's internal security policy.[5] And, despite the creation of new offices and standing committees in the Cabinet, some observers might agree with the opinion of one official that "there are no intelligence agencies in Japan."[6]

This fact makes doubly important the central positions that the NPA in particular has succeeded in habitually staffing in the Cabinet Secretariat. Although internal security questions do not figure importantly at the Cabinet level, the NPA has succeeded particularly in the 1980s in increasing its political power substantially in the Cabinet Secretariat. The ranking of different ministries and agencies among the graduates of Tokyo University, an annual contest of the status and power of organizations as well as of the abilities of individuals, confirms this assessment. The NPA was not able to recruit a career staff on its own until 1965. At that time it was ranked lowest among all ministries and agencies. But in the 1980s it was ranked among the top three ministries together with the traditionally powerful MOF and MITI (*Yomiuri* 1986: 83–90; Inoguchi 1989: 108–9). This is telling testimony to the growing political importance of the police in Japanese politics.

The police in its domestic and international setting

The growing political prominence of the Japanese police must be viewed within a context that is provided by its links to the domestic as well as the international society.

Domestic society

Japan's relatively centralized system of police administration operates with a remarkable degree of openness toward Japanese society. The presence of the police in society is pervasive, unofficial and low-key (Bayley 1978: 46–7). "Police penetration of the community in Japan is more routine and personal than in the United States and it is more active in ways unrelated to law enforcement. . . . In Japan private persons are mobilized in explicit ways to assist policemen in the performance of their duties, creating a cooperative relationship between police and public that is unknown, if not unthinkable, in the United States" (Bayley 1978: 91). For all members of the police, contacts with individual citizens, civic associations, and reporters are very important (Taikakai 1971: vol.1, 680–91; 1970: vol. 2, 260–1, 273–4; Tawara 1986b: 56; Inoguchi 1989: 108–9; Kaneko *et al.* 1987). Furthermore, the importance of police contacts with the public has increased over time (Sassa 1984: 52–3).

The link between the police and Japanese society is the local police box, which is called *koban* in urban areas and *chuzaisho* in rural communities

(Bayley 1978: 13–32, 1984; Ames 1981: 17–55; Parker 1984: 44–98; Clifford 1976: 79–80; Kühne and Miyazawa 1979: 125–31; Mizumachi 1982). In his sympathetic treatment David Bayley dubs the police as "the most pervasive government agency in society" (Bayley 1978: 87). Karel Van Wolferen in a more critical vein calls the *koban* system "the friendly neighborhood police state" (Van Wolferen 1989: 184). Japanese policemen draw on the information gathered through the extensive personal knowledge of their districts. Masayuki Murayama's research on the Tokyo patrol police has underlined the changes that have occurred in the work of the local patrol police since about 1970 (Murayama 1980, 1989a, 1989b, 1990). Some of his data point to the continuing social service role of the police. For example, between 1960 and 1985 emergency phone calls to the police increased by almost six times, while the number of crimes committed remained quite stable. The patrol police obviously serves as a primary contact point for citizens concerned about the maintaining of public order and in need of social services. In fact little more than 10 percent of all calls concern crimes (Murayama 1989a: 21–2).

The police establishes its presence in the community also by regular house-calls. In fact a substantial amount of a policeman's day is taken up by the semi-annual visits (*Junkai Renraku*) that each officer is expected to pay to each household and business in his area (Ames 1981: 38–40; Bayley 1978: 26–7, 84–7; Parker 1984: 55–8). In contrast to the prewar household survey, individuals do not have to provide the information which the police requests. But most do so willingly anyhow. "The police say that 'only Communists' refuse to answer" (Ames 1981: 38). The *koban* thus contains a wealth of additional information that is relevant for police investigations, including data on left- and right-wing political groups active in the area (Ames 1981: 39–40). The security police is a major beneficiary of what can be viewed as a decentralized memory bank that can be activated when needed (Murayama 1989a: 12; Bayley 1978: 85). Murayama goes as far as to conclude on the basis of his data that "if the police have suppressed crime efficiently, it is because police have developed an efficient surveillance system based on residential survey [sic] and have emphasized law enforcement in their routine work" (Murayama 1989b: 2).

This surveillance system has many facets (Katzenstein and Tsujinaka 1991: 110–16). Programs such as "community relations" and institutions such as the elaborate system of crime prevention associations represent only the tip of an iceberg of an extensive network of cooperative institutions linking police with society. "Japanese society is honeycombed with committees made up of private citizens and officials that consult on matters of public safety. . . . There are hundreds of private organizations representing almost any role a person can play in society that petition the police about matters affecting their members" (Bayley 1978: 98–9). In most instances it remains true that the police is willing to cooperate with virtually any social group in order to defend public order. Community relations is a tool "to induce public cooperation with the police for the purpose of crime control . . . community organizations were organized and controlled from 'above' " (Murayama 1980: 16, 87–8).

The ties that link the Japanese police to various social sectors are not concentrated but extend broadly throughout society. By 1989 a total of 525 retired police officers had been placed, through the system of *amakudari*, in private-sector jobs after retirement. A broad range of companies—public and private, large and small, industrial and service-oriented—employs retired police officers. During as well as after their active careers Japanese police officers have access to the most important social sectors. In sum there exist a large variety of exceptionally close institutional links between the police and Japanese society.

International society

The links between the Japanese police and international society are very weak. In contrast, for example, to the extensive connections between different European police forces that have intensified greatly since the mid-1970s, Japan's police still operates in virtual isolation from the police forces of other states. This is in part just a matter of the geographic isolation of an island nation. The Netherlands, with a population of about 15 million, registered more than 200 million border crossings in 1987 (Birch 1989: 11). The Federal Republic of Germany, with a population of 62 million, counted about 1 billion border crossings in the same year (Katzenstein 1990: 5). This compares with 10.8 million border crossings for Japan in 1988, a sharp increase from 5.2 million in 1980, 1.7 million in 1970 and 0.3 million in 1960 (Somucho 1989). And in relative terms the number of foreigners living in Japan was less than one-sixth of that of Germany in the late 1970s (Kühne and Miyazawa 1979: 69). Japan simply lacks participation in the broad range of transnational police structures that have sprung up in Western Europe during the last three decades (Katzenstein 1990: 34–8).

Limited transnational links also characterize Japan's relations with the International Criminal Police Organization, commonly called Interpol (Anderson 1989; National Police Agency 1987a: 36–7). Interpol links designated national police organizations such as the NPA in an international network designed to facilitate and strengthen international police cooperation. In 1975 the NPA established an International Criminal Affairs Division in its Criminal Investigation Bureau which handles the routine exchange of information with Interpol (National Police Agency 1987b: 36). The NPA has delegated three officers to serve with Interpol. Since 1985, Akira Kawada has served as head of the Police Division. Two lower-ranking Japanese police officers serve in the sections for criminal affairs and for communication (Anderson 1989: 52).[7]

Interpol's activity concentrates overwhelmingly on the investigation of crimes other than terrorism. In the mid-1980s about 50,000 of its 2 million files were searched actively each year (Katzenstein 1990: 33). About 80 percent of the requests for information originate from Western Europe and the United States. Japan's role in Interpol is by comparison minor. It accounts for only a very small share of Interpol's total number of messages. Between 1977 and 1988, Japan's total annual number of international messages concerning international crimes increased from about 4,500 to more than 7,800, with the NPA receiving in 1988 more than three times as many messages from abroad (5,509) as it was sending out (1,751). And in 1988 only 366 of these were direct requests acted upon under the provisions of the International Criminal Investigation Assistance Law (National Police Agency 1987a: 35; National Police Agency 1989a: 49–50). The volume of the NPA's international messages is by European standards extremely small. West Germany, for example, sends or receives each year more than 200,000 international messages concerning international crime (Katzenstein 1990: 33).

But in recent years Japan's growing internationalization has generated increasing contacts between its law enforcement officials and those of other countries. The Justice Ministry, for example, instituted in the 1980s a variety of programs to afford especially junior officials the opportunity of traveling and learning abroad. A study program sends each year two bureaucrats abroad for a leave lasting up to two years; about seven officials are sent as interns to foreign governments for about five months each; another half dozen officials travel each year for a month on study tours that the ministry organizes for them. The Prosecutor's Office sends eight of its officials to serve at the Japanese embassies in the major Western countries, the People's Republic of China and the United Nations Crime Prevention Bureau. And in 1990 it set up a new program which sends forty young prosecutors abroad for two-week periods.[8] The Public Security Agency has six of its officers stationed abroad, temporarily on loan to the MOFA, presumably involved in the gathering of intelligence. This provides at least some release from the strong opposition of the domestically oriented MOJ to the gathering of foreign intelligence.[9]

The NPA and the prefectural police forces also delegate about twenty officers each to the MOFA to be stationed at Japanese embassies abroad. Although precise figures are not available, about half of them serve as liaison officers with foreign police forces and deal primarily with the physical security of Japanese embassies, while the other half is involved in intelligence work. The number of embassies with at least one staff member from the NPA has increased from about ten in the 1970s to twelve in 1984. By 1989, nineteen NPA officials were serving with sixteen Japanese embassies around the world.[10] The overseas training program of the NPA sends each year about seventy policemen, grouped into several teams, abroad for about a month both to observe foreign police systems and to receive practical training. Between 1973 and 1986 a total of 923 young police officers, about 1 percent of the relevant age cohort, were admitted into this program (National Police Agency 1987a: 34). Between twenty and thirty of the 500 career officers of the NPA are serving abroad at any given period.[11] According to one informed, rough estimate, the total number of Japanese police officials annually traveling abroad on business has increased from about 120 in 1970, to 250 in 1980, and about 600 in 1990.[12]

In addition some Japanese ministries seek to gather information relevant for Japan's internal security. MITI's Institute for Middle East Economies does mainly economic research, some of which has strategic implications; but, according to one source, the institute also does some military–strategic work which it does not publish in its journal. A sizeable staff in Cairo receives assistance and briefings from Japan's diplomatic missions in the area, and its staff makes annual visits to the countries in the region. Other ministries, including the MOJ, have their own personnel stationed abroad for the purpose of gathering intelligence, including on the JRA. Compared to the early 1970s when only one person in the Japanese embassy in Beirut was collecting intelligence information, the situation has probably changed quite dramatically, including the growing contacts between Japan and foreign intelligence services.[13] But whatever intelligence is gathered is hoarded rather than systematically pooled in Tokyo. The Japanese bureaucracy is a system that creates information redundancies.

Ad hoc coordination of policy with the United States confirms this impression of limited internationalization. A small number of Japanese police officers attend joint training programs held at the National Academy of the FBI. Since 1962 the FBI has admitted foreign police officials for training into its National Academy. By 1986 a total of thirty-three Japanese police officials, or less than two a year, had participated (National Police Agency 1987a: 35). NPA officials also attend the annual Far East Training Program for Senior Drug Investigators that is organized each year by the Drug Enforcement Agency of the U.S. Department of Justice. And since 1980 the NPA has organized, together with the United States, U.S.–Japanese conferences on countermeasures against organized crime. In 1986 the NPA sent for the first time some representatives to the Conference on Asian Organized Crimes, a meeting of American law enforcement officials dealing with the activities of Japanese and Asian organized crime in the United States. The extent and depth of transnational links existing between Japan and different national police forces is evidently growing; but these links still remain quite weak.

The NPA has also accepted two or three high-ranking foreign police officials for training in its general courses for new police inspectors. And with the assistance of the Japan International Cooperation Agency (JICA) the NPA has organized regular short-term seminars for foreign police officials dealing with such issues as drugs, crime investigation, and traffic. In 1988 the NPA took additional steps toward forging stronger international links through organizing additional conferences and providing technological assistance.

By the late 1980s the growing international contacts of the Japanese police and law enforcement system had led to a number of changes in organizational structure. A special research office dealing exclusively with the JRA was established in April 1978 with a staff of about twenty. The NPA set up two additional research units for international terrorism in 1981 and 1984.

Finally, on May 29, 1988, some of the most important agencies and ministries dealing with terrorism established new divisions for international crime
control, focusing primarily on JRA's international terrorist activities. A
full eighteen years after JRA's first hijacking, the NPA established the 2nd
Foreign Affairs Division in its Security Bureau, with a staff of thirty-two. The
new division integrated two former subsections in the 3rd Public Security
Division and the Foreign Affairs Division. The work of the new division
covers all practical measures against the JRA and international terrorism more
generally: gathering and analyzing information, maintaining international
contacts, attending international meetings, overseeing domestic measures
such as the prevention of terrorists infiltrating the country, and locating JRA
suspects and JRA support groups (Kokusai Tero Mondai Kenkyukai 1989;
Mainichi, June 29, 1989; Keisatsucho 1979, 1982, 1985).

A new division in the MOFA, the Division for the Prevention of Terrorism,
also targets the JRA and international terrorism directly. Its purpose places
more emphasis on information retrieval and analysis to prepare the Prime
Minister at the summit meetings and to support foreign ministers at other
international meetings. It also exchanges relevant information with the
Japanese Overseas Enterprise Association.[14]

Finally, a new division of the MOJ, the International Division in the
Criminal Investigation Bureau, formerly called the International Criminal
Affairs Section, with a staff of four, is in charge not only of international judicial cooperation, including extradition, but also of international treaties and
agreements. Questions of international terrorism are evidently not unimportant; the first director of the new division was recruited from the Division of
Public Security. Although there are no reliable data to evaluate the trend, the
gradual internationalization of the Japanese police is probably slowly affecting also the organizational structure and capacities of Japan's prefectural
police, which does most of the practical police work.

In sum, despite clear changes in recent years, the transnational links
between Japan's police system and foreign police forces are weak. In the era of
Japan's internationalization the functional imperatives for the international
coordination of police activities seeking to combat border-crossing crimes
such as terrorism are growing. But the past isolation of Japan's police system,
especially noticeable in comparison with the deep entanglement of the police
with Japan's domestic society, is changing only very gradually.

Japan's policy of internal security

Japan's internal security policy has had a domestic and an international component. Challenged by mass protests at home that in the 1970s and 1980s
often turned violent, the police has continued to perfect tactics of crowd
control and selective intimidation which it learned in the 1960s. This continuity contrasts with two embryonic changes in the international aspects of
Japan's policy of internal security. Confronted with the JRA operating largely

outside Japanese territory, Japan's policy has changed from substantial indifference to international concerns about terrorism to a hesitant involvement with the police forces and law enforcement officials of other countries. Furthermore, although it remains to be tested in real life, at least in principle Japanese policy in dealing with terrorists has changed from being "soft" to being "hard." Ever since the Bonn summit of 1978, the Japanese government has been committed, at least on paper, to a policy which refuses, even at the risk of human life, to cave in to terrorist blackmail.

Domestic policies of internal security

The leadership of the police chose an informal extension of its power (*unyo*) as a viable midway point between the constitutional revision that looked increasingly unlikely after 1958 and the existing laws and regulations that in the eyes of the police made it difficult to implement an effective policy of internal security. In a general context of legal passivity the police developed informal techniques for conducting security investigations. The police favored two types of informal investigation techniques: a systematic application of minor, miscellaneous laws, ordinances, and rules to cover the deficit created by the absence of proper legal instruments, and a systematic expansion in the interpretation of the small number of security laws that did exist, particularly the Police Duty Execution Law.

Japan's pretrial detention system is a case in point. It is focused on over 1,200 centers run by the police, eight times as many as those run by the MOJ. It permits keeping arrested suspects in police cells, separate from regular prisons, for up to twenty-three days. After three, ten and twenty days a judge must authorize continued detention for additional questioning, usually a routine formality. The procedures of the judicial system are therefore organized in a way that in some instances has permitted keeping political radicals isolated for up to a decade in pretrial detention. Suspects are kept in the police centers primarily for extracting confessions, under conditions that according to a 1983 report can only be described as shocking (Kühne 1973: 1083–4; Murayama 1980: 89, note 24; Van Wolferen 1989: 188–90). "In effect, the leaders of the most extreme protest groups have been treated within the letter of the law, but legal maneuvers have been contrived to keep them out of society for long enough to destroy the effectiveness of their leadership. The limits of acceptable dissent have been set primarily by bureaucrats trained in the law, who are clever enough to uphold it and still accomplish their aims" (Steinhoff 1989b: 190).

Before major public events, house searches with or without warrants have been reported frequently (Hosaka 1986: 186–209; Nishio 1984: 162).[15] For example, in preparation for the funeral of Emperor Showa the police searched illegally, that is without a warrant, 200,000 apartments three times during the week before the funeral procession. Compared to the precautions taken at the Tokyo summit of 1986, this was a vast increase in numbers.[16] A knock at the door, a polite request, a quick search of the apartment and virtually universal compliance were the norm. Citizens who were hesitant or opposed to the police, by opening their doors, still afforded the police the opportunity of at least a quick scan of their typically small quarters. In any case no lawsuit was filed protesting the search method the police was employing even though this "Apartment Roller Operation" which utilizes door-to-door questioning of residents is in clear violation of Article 35 of the Constitution. This particular police tactic is not new. At the height of the student movement it netted 36,500 arrests between October 1967 and December 1971; and between 1971 and 1978 the police arrested more than 1,000 suspects each year using the same method. But the massive reliance on this particular tactic illustrates dramatically how the police strategy of informalism, operating with public support, has drastically enlarged the scope of Japan's policy of internal security.

The public's tolerance of and cooperation with the police remains a key ingredient in Japan's policy of internal security. It is true that some of the major security risks during the late 1980s have been managed largely by the police alone. For example, before and during the Olympic Games held in Seoul in 1988, the police protected Korean targets throughout Japan. And it is now standard operating procedure of the police that in preparation for a major event thousands of manholes in Tokyo are searched for explosives and then sealed. More important, though, is the fact that the police actively seeks and promotes public support, among others through well-orchestrated media campaigns. In many instances the massive security checks that the police has run, especially in Tokyo, since 1985 work only with the active cooperation of the public. Roadblocks manned by the police to protect the foreign dignitaries attending the funeral of the Emperor, for example, were effective because the public heeded the urgent pleas of the police and left its cars at home. And it did not object, either, to the fact that many subway exits were closed so that a larger than usual crowd could, through a smaller than usual number of subway exits, pass by police officers inspecting their bags.[17]

An internationalizing Japan not only hosted two economic summit meetings in 1979 and 1986 but also welcomed President Reagan in 1983 and President Chun in 1984, and also celebrated the sixtieth anniversary of the Showa Emperor's reign in 1986, planned the Emperor's visit to Okinawa in 1987 as well as his funeral in 1989, and staged the new Emperor's coronation in 1990.

Mobilization for these events has increased sharply over the years. In the 1960s a maximum of about 5,000–10,000 policemen were estimated to have been mobilized by the MPD for protection of events such as the Tokyo Olympics in 1964 or USSR Vice-Prime Minister Mikoyan's visits in 1961 and 1964. However, on the occasion of President Ford's visit in 1974 the MPD mobilized 23,000 policemen on a daily basis. This number increased to 26,000 at the Tokyo summit in 1979, and 30,000 at the 1986 summit and the Emperor's anniversary; and it increased still further to 32,000 in 1989 at the time of the Emperor's funeral. Indicating a sharp increase in the extent of police precautions taken, the total number of policemen mobilized during these events increased from 16,000 during President Ford's visit, to 412,000 at the first summit in 1979, and 810,000 at the second summit (*Asahi Nenkan* 1962, 1965, 1975, 1980, 1987; Keisatsucho 1975, 1980, 1987). These figures illustrate that when it is necessary the police mobilizes on a scale and with a thoroughness that reminds us how important internal security is considered in Japan.

These large-scale public events as well as the Narita struggle provided the police with the opportunity to develop the new key concept of a "comprehensive security policing" in domestic politics that soon thereafter found also a programmatic expression in Japanese foreign policy. According to this concept a comprehensive policy of internal security must involve not only the various departments of the police but also other public bureaucracies, such as public corporations and related organizations, in supporting the police (Tawara 1986b: 164–70). By the late 1980s this emphasis on a comprehensive security policy had become unmistakable. Commissioner Yamada's official notice of May 7, 1986, following the second Tokyo summit, stressed that the police had acquired comprehensive powers that had permitted a substantial strengthening of its surveillance of radicals and the monitoring of particular localities without losing public support. It was thus only natural that the MPD and other prefecture police forces doubled their manpower dealing with radicals.

The close ties which the police has to the public and the great weight that it attaches to public opinion explain why the imperative of Japan's internal security policy has been to avoid bloodshed at almost all cost. This has been evident in the police's restrained reaction to many of the pitched battles which a coalition of groups and social movements have waged against the construction, operation and enlargement of Narita Airport, the symbol for many of the violent demonstrations in the 1970s and 1980s (Smith 1983: 131). But the imperative was perhaps most clearly displayed in February 1972 when the police, having pushed into rural Japan student radicals who had been responsible for a rash of deadly bombings, cornered five of them and one hostage in an expensive villa in central Japan. Thus began an extraordinary ten-day drama: the siege of Asama-Sanso. The last ten hours of the siege were carried live by all major TV channels and watched by 95 percent of the Japanese viewing public (Steinhoff n.d.: 112; Ames 1981: 159–60; Bayley 1978: 160–2; Kühne and Miyazawa 1979: 121–2).[18] Eventually the radicals surrendered and the hostage was found unharmed. Two policemen and one TV cameraman were killed, and twenty-three policemen were injured. Although it was confronted by a group armed with several rifles and 2,000 rounds of ammunition, during the entire drama the police had fired only fifteen rounds from their pistols (Steinhoff n.d.: 112).

Since an additional fourteen members of the JRA were still at large, the police was intent on avoiding at all cost making the JRA in the eyes of the public a group of martyrs. Soon afterwards one of the captured members of the JRA took the police to the grave of one of twelve JRA members that had been tortured and killed in a brutal process of self-criticism and purges within the group (Steinhoff n.d.). Revelations of these facts signaled the end of the JRA's operations in Japan, as a horrified public turned against it. The police strategy of patient nonviolence had scored an impressive triumph.

The restraint which the Japanese riot police has shown in the use of violence is, by international standards, also remarkable. The principle of avoiding bloodshed at almost all costs explains why the police adamantly opposed the demands of politicians in 1960 and 1970 that the Self-Defense Forces be used as a backup force to defend Japan's internal security at the height of mass protest against the renewal of the Security Treaty and the Vietnam war. And it makes intelligible why even at the height of the protest movement in the 1960s the police never seriously demanded a force of 200,000 (consisting in equal parts of the normal and the riot police) which had been part of some police statements in the 1960s (Suzuki 1980: 250). In fact, the largest concentration of police in the last two decades has never exceeded 35,000. At the height of what came to be known as the 990 days of mass protest—between October 8, 1967 and June 23, 1970—there occurred not a single death among the protestors, while the police made 15,000 arrests and suffered itself 12,000 injuries.[19]

Speaking generally, Japan's policy of internal security has led not to large-scale structural changes in police or society as much as to a set of incremental adjustments over time. In opting for the politically compelling path of constitutional "revision by interpretation" relying on *unyo* the police has been able to gradually change its political practices in ways that would have been deemed impossible two or three decades ago. Without any conspicuous organizational changes or great political debates, the police has enhanced greatly its capacities to deal with violence-prone social movements, guerilla attacks and acts of terrorism. And it has done so largely shielded from the public eye and without endangering its legitimacy.

International policies and international security

In contrast to its domestic side the international dimension of Japan's internal security policy has shown greater changes. The imperative of avoiding bloodshed governed Japan's policy until 1978 and explains why the government was blackmailed by the JRA after each of a series of spectacular hijacking operations in the mid-1970s. A change in policy occasioned by the Bonn summit of 1978 committed the Japanese government to stand fast in the face of terrorist blackmail, a change that until the summer of 1990 had not yet been tested in reality.[20] A second change was the government's hesitant but nonetheless growing involvement in the international coordination of antiterrorist policy.

Compared to Israel, the United States, Britain, and West Germany, the

Japanese government was accommodating to terrorist blackmail in the 1970s (Miller 1986: 409–10). The government's accommodating stance was very much in evidence when Palestinian terrorists seized the Japanese ambassador in Kuwait in 1974 to effect the release of Japanese and Palestinian terrorists trapped on a ferry in Singapore harbor after bungling an attempt at setting fire to an oil refinery. And it was also evident when a JRA team of terrorists hijacked a Japanese airplane to Dacca in 1977; the Japanese government quickly acceded to the demand to release six prisoners and to provide a $6 million ransom as well as a supply of blank passports.

In the initial attacks the government showed little interest in the fact that some of the terrorists were Japanese, and it misjudged the significance of that fact. "When the Government learned that two of the four guerillas who struck in Singapore on January 31 were Japanese youths, the Foreign Ministry's reaction was one of disinterest. It remained cool and aloof to guerilla demands for an aircraft, arguing that settlement of the incident was within the competence and authority of the Singapore Government" (Nakamura 1974: 22). Similarly, at the time of an attack on the diplomatic offices of the United States and Sweden in Kuala Lumpur in August 1975, Japanese government and security officials were reportedly caught by complete surprise. "They had been under the impression that the estimated 30 members of the JRA who were reportedly based abroad had been forced to remain quietly underground, having been integrated into larger groups in which their presence was said to have been 'rather insignificant' "; the link between the Popular Front for the Liberation of Palestine (PFLP) and the prominent role of the JRA was, according to police officials in Tokyo, "more than we have ever expected" (Nakamura 1975).

But by 1977–8 opposition in Tokyo against the government's accommodating stance had grown significantly. As early as 1974 top police officials let it be known in public that they thought the government's policy unwise in that it would encourage further attacks leading to the release of additional members of the Red Army who were being held in jail (*Economist* 1974). In 1977 the Minister of Justice, Hajime Fukuda, was strongly opposed to acceding to the demands of the terrorists, refused to be involved in the release of jailed members of the JRA, and resigned together with his deputy at the end of the crisis (*Economist* 1977; Hielscher 1977).

The incipient changes in Japanese policy received a major boost from an agreement reached by the heads of state of the major democratic states at the Bonn summit of 1978. It provided the Japanese government with an opportunity to back some of its general rhetoric favoring international cooperation with a more specific commitment. In response to the wave of terrorist attacks that Japan experienced in the early 1970s the NPA, for example, had stressed in its annual report as early as 1974 the need for international cooperation to deal with the internationalization of crime (Clifford 1976: 27). In the evolution of Japan's policy the Bonn declaration on terrorism was an important historical accident. Since no prior staff work had been done on the issue,

Prime Minister Fukuda found himself in the uncomfortable position of having to respond to an idea which emerged literally over lunch. The occasion demanded a show of international solidarity, a political opportunity which the Ministry of Foreign Affairs seized in order to reshape Japanese policy.[21] In accord with the resolution passed at Bonn, a Cabinet decree issued in September 1978 committed the Japanese government to stand firm in the face of future terrorist blackmail.

The implementation of this policy was, however, slow and tortuous. The Tokyo summit of 1986, held at a time of heightened threats from Libyan and Syrian terrorism, found the Japanese government only a hesitant supporter of the activist stance of the United States and several European countries. But as host and chair of the meeting the Japanese government was forced to coordinate the different national viewpoints and thus to support a policy which a narrow conception of Japan's foreign policy interest might have rejected. But in part because of the continued emphasis on the importance of a coordinated antiterrorist policy, the 1987 Venice summit finally translated the broad principles of the Bonn declaration into more operational measures.[22]

Difficulties of implementation were also evident on the domestic side. In September 1978 the Cabinet allocated the necessary resources to equip and train a 53-member-strong special antiterrorist unit (*Asahi Nenkan* 1979: 286; Suzuki 1980: 131). Staffed equally by the police (28) and by the Self-Defense Forces (SDF) (25), it was to be deployed at selected Japanese diplomatic missions abroad. In fact no such unit was ever created, possibly because of the precedent it would have set for involving the SDF on questions of internal security. Instead special antiterrorist squads have been training in each of the prefectural police forces as well as in the MPD.

Translating the internationalization of Japan's policy of internal security into policy terms thus has been a slow and difficult process. It seems, for example, entirely plausible to assume that through a variety of channels the Japanese government may have used its foreign aid policy to influence Syria to restrict the movement of the JRA at certain times, for example around the time Emperor Hirohito was planning foreign travels. We do know that the Emperor traveled in Europe in the fall of 1971 and in the United States in the fall of 1975. Unfortunately there is no conclusive proof one way or the other that the sharp increases in Japanese aid to Syria in 1972 and 1975 were related to these trips (Organization for Economic Cooperation and Development 1978: 222).

But advances in internationalization are readily apparent in the 1980s. A symbol of this process of internationalization was the convening, under the auspices of the National Police Agency, in June 1988 of the Ministerial Conference on Security Matters for the Asia-Pacific Region. It was the first such high-level meeting that the NPA had convened since 1945. The meeting dealt with a broad array of law enforcement issues but focused among others also on questions of terrorism and some pressing security questions of the 1988 Olympic Games in Seoul, South Korea (Nagamatsu 1988).[23] This kind of international police cooperation is organized by NPA's antiterrorist division. An internal study group explained in a recent report that "anti-terrorist equipment should be deployed internationally because it would not be effective if only Japan owned such equipment. In line with this change in policy Japan now provides equipment free of charge, as part of its develop-ment aid budget for international technological cooperation, to areas where terrorists concentrate like the Mid-East countries" (Kokusai Tero Mondai Kenkyukai 1989: 72). Between Japan and South Korea practical police cooperation on questions of terrorism has also increased in recent years. Such cooperation had ceased since 1973–4. But because the 1988 Olympic Games posed great security risks for both South Korea and Japan both countries began again to actively cooperate in 1986, especially in the areas of immigra-tion and surveillance (National Police Agency 1989a: 125–6).[24]

Japan is slowly but inevitably drawn into international society. In 1989, for example, the Japanese police chose to no longer request the General Secretariat of Interpol to issue blue international inquiry notices but asked instead for the international red wanted notices as a step preceding extradi-tion requests. The change in policy occurred because the Japanese government had become convinced that strict reciprocity was no longer the norm in the international coordination of antiterrorism policy. Although under Japanese law red notices are insufficient ground for the detention of a suspect, Japan's police started to request red notices on fugitives from Japan and in particular for members of the JRA (National Police Agency 1989a: 49, 127).[25]

Interpol is from the Japanese perspective very useful for disseminating information and for receiving backup information on suspected terrorists. But Japan relies on bilateral contacts rather than multilateral cooperation to deal with any sensitive issue such as terrorism. For the Japanese govern-ment, police cooperation may be strengthened by occasional conferences held between government officials; but it is best left uninstitutionalized. In prac-tice this means that Japanese police officers will occasionally travel abroad since virtually no foreign police officials come to Japan for conducting serious business.[26]

As is true of other aspects of internal security policy extradition policy reflects Japan's relatively high degree of isolation from the international system (*Advanced Course* 1989: 82–91). Between 1945 and 1985, Japan responded to five formal and four de facto requests for extraditing fugitives. In the same forty-year span Japan made six formal and twenty-four de facto requests to other states (Nishimura n.d.: 4, ii–v). This adds up to a total of thirty-nine requests in forty years, or about one a year; but in recent years the numbers have increased significantly.[27] Corresponding figures for the Federal Republic of Germany are several magnitudes larger. Between 1980 and 1985 the annual figure was about 750 (Katzenstein 1990: 93).

Japan's policy of internal security has been marked by continuity in its domestic component and embryonic, though still untested since the Bonn summit of 1978, change in its international dimension. Most significantly there appears to be underway a gradual process of internationalizing Japan's policy approach to questions of internal security. It is important, however, to put this process in perspective. Its undeniable importance lies in the fact that it signifies a victory of the internationalist factions in what must arguably be counted among the least international political institutions in contemporary Japan: the police and the judiciary. But, important as it is, the kind of internationalism that is emerging in policy and politics is restricted to the level of exchanging liaison officers with other countries and organizing study tours. In contrast to the European industrial states, we do not find any significant instances of an institutionalized operational cooperation with the police of other countries.[28] The depth of Japan's internationalization remains relatively shallow. In fact, the Japanese police was utterly surprised and confounded by the attacks which the JRA has staged in Asia since the mid-1980s. Its intelligence in Europe and the Mideast was much stronger than in Indonesia and the Philippines.[29] In light of the heterogeneity of Southeast and Northeast Asia, the legacy of Japanese imperialism and Japan's overwhelming relative influence in these two regions, it is unlikely that Japan's internationalization will deepen quickly in the coming years.

Conclusion

For Japanese ears, the concept of strategy has unwelcome military and authoritarian connotations, painful reminders of the 1930s and 1940s. According to virtually all police officers, Japan's internal security policy is not based on a sense of strategic mission but emerged instead by trial and error in reaction to social developments.[30] To the outside observer, though, there exists a discernible pattern in the policy response during the last two decades. In the initial phase in the late 1960s and early 1970s the Japanese police succeeded in infiltrating the JRA and, within a short period of time, pushing it outside the country. In the hope of gradually strangling the organization of the JRA, a patient and long-term policy has sought to narrow its operational base and resources abroad and at home; since the mid-1980s that strategy has been rewarded by the arrest of several key suspects. Such a long-term approach also informs the police approach to radical groups operating inside Japan. After their failure to mobilize the Japanese public for mass protests, various radical groups have moved underground since the late 1970s. Since Chukaku and other radical groups lack new recruits and face a general decline of support in urban areas, the police tries to contain their operations rather than to eliminate them altogether. By most accounts, the MPD is so effective in protecting important events in Tokyo that radicals move outside of the city for their duration; but the MPD lacks the information and resources to seriously curtail the operations of radical groups in normal times.[31] While the police is, by comparative standards, extraordinarily restrained in its reliance on violent tactics, it would be wrong to underestimate its pressure through surveillance and the extension of the informal powers it has succeeded in acquiring.

Japan's policy of internal security reflects the structure and political importance of Japan's police forces and the relationships that link it to domestic and international society. The Japanese police has adopted a strategy aspired to also, if less successfully, by urban guerillas in Latin America: to swim like little fishes in the warm sea of the people. The police are one of the few reminders that a state exists in Japan. And they "have turned the habit of leniency into a kind of second nature. But a condition is attached: the recipient must in turn acknowledge the goodness of the established social order; political heterodoxy elicits tough measures" (Van Wolferen 1989: 182–3). The police is able to mobilize totally, often working unpaid overtime shifts, to make the security arrangements for the major events that since the mid-1980s have occurred at least once a year in Tokyo. It does so relying on a cooperative public. But it lacks the support of the political parties for a resumption of a sustained campaign against terrorist organizations or violent social movements, as the National Police Agency has at times demanded.[32] The police thus has adopted a long-term strategy of attrition that aims at reducing the scope of operation and the resources available to the radical movements operating both inside and outside Japan. Meanwhile it waits patiently for the aging of radicals and the lack of new recruitment to gradually sap the strength of radical movements.[33]

Culture and geography explain why internationalization has come later and more haltingly to Japan than to other industrial states. Internal security policy is no exception to this generalization. Japanese terrorists have not operated in proximate areas of Japan. After moving to the Mideast in the early 1970s it took the JRA more than a decade to set up the logistical infrastructure in Asia to permit its members to operate at closer range to Japan. In doing so the JRA has underlined the fact that even Japan's NPA can no longer neglect the international dimensions of its internal security policy. With the rise of Japan's international position Japanese embassies, corporations and nationals will become more attractive targets for international terrorists. And as Japanese terrorists are beginning to move closer to Japan other Asian states from whose territory these terrorists are now operating are likely to develop a stronger interest in cooperating with the Japanese police. Japan's greatest political challenge thus will lie in learning how to manage the unavoidable tensions between the resilience of adapting institutions, norms, and practices which contain violent crimes at home and the fragility of evolving institutions, norms, and practices in an international society that Japan can no longer escape.

Notes

1   Interview no. 16, Tokyo, May 17, 1990.
2   Interview no. 3, Tokyo, May 14, 1990.
3   Interviews, no. 8, May 15, 1990 and no. 12, May 16, 1990.
4   Interview no. 16, Tokyo, May 17, 1990.

5 Interviews nos 12, 15, and 18, Tokyo, May 16, 17, and 18, 1990.
6 Interview no. 12, Tokyo, May 16, 1990.
7 Interview no. 6, Tokyo, May 15, 1990.
8 Interview no. 18, Tokyo, May 18, 1990.
9 Interview no. 14, Tokyo, May 16, 1990.
10 Interview no. 1, Tokyo, December 6, 1988; Interviews nos 3, 15 and 16, Tokyo, May 14 and 17, 1990.
11 Interview no. 16, Tokyo, May 17, 1990.
12 Interview no. 3, Tokyo, May 14, 1990.
13 Interview no. 11, Tokyo, May 15, 1990.
14 Interview no. 9, Tokyo, May 15, 1990.
15 Interview no. 15, May 17, 1990.
16 And it was double the 300,000 targeted apartments that the police was planning to search in February 1972 when it was looking for 200 student radicals (Steinhoff n.d.: 228).
17 Interview no. 16, Tokyo, May 17, 1990.
18 Interview no. 15, Tokyo, May 17, 1990.
19 Interviews nos 15 and 17, Tokyo, May 17, 1990.
20 Interview no. 4, Tokyo, December 7, 1988; Interviews nos 1 and 15, Tokyo, May 14 and 17, 1990.
21 Interview no. 9, Tokyo, May 15, 1990.
22 Interview no. 9, Tokyo, May 15, 1990.
23 Interview no. 1, Tokyo, December 6, 1988; Interview no. 6, Tokyo, May 15, 1990.
24 Interview no. 15, Tokyo, May 17, 1990.
25 Interview no. 6, Tokyo, May 15, 1990.
26 Interview no. 1, Tokyo, December 6, 1988.
27 Interview no. 18, Tokyo, May 18, 1990.
28 Interviews nos 11, 14 and 20, Tokyo, May 15, 16 and 19, 1990.
29 Interview no. 11, Tokyo, May 15, 1990.
30 Interview no. 1, Tokyo, December 6, 1988; Interviews nos 1 and 17, Tokyo, May 14 and 17, 1990.
31 Interviews nos 1 and 12, Tokyo, May 14 and 16, 1990.
32 Interviews nos 13, 14, 19, Tokyo, May 16 and 18, 1990.
33 Interviews nos 1 and 15, Tokyo, May 14 and 17, 1990.

References

Advanced Course for Senior Police Administrators (1989) Tokyo: Japan International Cooperation Agency and National Police Agency.

Ames, Walter L. (1981) *Police and Community in Japan*, Berkeley, Calif.: University of California Press.

Anderson, Malcolm (1989) *Policing the World: Interpol and the Politics of International Police Co-operation*, Oxford: Clarendon Press.

Apter, David E. and Sawa, Nagayo (1984) *Against the State: Politics and Social Protest in Japan*, Cambridge, Mass.: Harvard University Press.

Arai, Yutaka (1979) "80 nendai no Keisatsu" [Police in the 1980s], *Keisatsu Kenkyu* [Police Studies], 589 (January): 28–36.

Asahi Nenkan [Asahi Almanac] (1961) Tokyo: Asahi Shimbun.

Asahi Nenkan [Asahi Almanac] (1962) Tokyo: Asahi Shimbun.

Asahi Nenkan [Asahi Almanac] (1965) Tokyo: Asahi Shimbun.

Asahi Nenkan [Asahi Almanac] (1973) Tokyo: Asahi Shimbun.

Asahi Nenkan [Asahi Almanac] (1975) Tokyo: Asahi Shimbun.
Asahi Nenkan [Asahi Almanac] (1979) Tokyo: Asahi Shimbun.
Asahi Nenkan [Asahi Almanac] (1980) Tokyo: Asahi Shimbun.
Asahi Nenkan [Asahi Almanac] (1987) Tokyo: Asahi Shimbun.
Bayley, David H. (1978) *Forces of Order: Police Behavior in Japan and the United States*, Berkeley, Calif.: University of California Press.
Bayley, David H. (1984) "Police, Crime and the Community in Japan," pp.177–98 in George DeVos (ed.) *Institutions for Change in Japanese Society*, Berkeley, Calif.: Institute of East Asian Studies, University of California.
Bayley, David H. (1985) *Patterns of Policing: A Comparative International Analysis*, New Brunswick, NJ: Rutgers University Press.
Birch, Roger (1989) "Policing Europe in 1992," London: Royal Institute of International Affairs, April 19.
Clifford, William (1976) *Crime Control in Japan*, Lexington, Mass.: Lexington Books.
Economist, The (1974) "Very Low Profile" (August 16): 44.
Economist, The (1977) "Bitter Aftermath" (October 15): 76.
Farrell, William (1990) *Blood and Rage: The Story of the Japanese Red Army*, Lexington, Mass.: D. C. Heath Lexington Books.
Hatakeyama, Hirofumi (1984) "Keishokuho Kaisei to Seijiteki Leadership" [The Revision of the Police Duty Execution Law and Political Leadership], pp. 71–126 in Hideo Otake (ed.) *Nippon Seiji no Soten* [Political Issues in Japan], Tokyo: Sanichi-shobo.
Hielscher, Gebhard (1977) " 'Ein Leben wiegt schwerer als der Erdball' ," *Süddeutsche Zeitung* (September 30).
Hironaka, Toshio (1973) *Keibikoan Keisatsu no Kenkyu* [A Study of the Security Police and the Public Security Police], Tokyo: Iwanami-shoten.
Hosaka, Kunio (1986) *Shin Keisatsu Kokka Nippon* [The New Police State, Japan], Tokyo: Shakai Hyoronsha.
Hoshino, Yasusaburo (1974) "Keisatsu Seido no Kaikaku" [Reform of the Police System], pp. 287–350 in Tokyo Daigaku Shakai Kaguku Kenkyusho (ed.) *Sengo kaikaku* [The Postwar Reforms], Tokyo: Iwanami-shoten.
Inoguchi, Takashi (1983) *Gendai Nippon Seiji Keizai no Kozu* [Contemporary Political Economy in Japan], Tokyo: Toyokeizai-shimpo-sha.
Inoguchi, Takashi (1989) "Kokusaika Jidai no Kanryosei" [The State Bureaucracy in the Era of Internationalization], *Leviathan*, 4: 100–14.
Japan Communist Party (1988) *Seiji Keizai Soran 1988* [Political Economy Annals 1988], Tokyo: Japan Communist Party.
Jiyuhosodan (1986) *Shimin no Seikatsu to Keisatsu* [Citizens' Lives and the Police], Tokyo: Equality Mizuchi-shobo.
Kaneko, Jinyo *et al.* (1987) "Keisatsu no Genzai" [The Present Situation of the Japanese Police: A Roundtable Discussion], pp. 2–26 in *Hogaku Semina: Sogo Tokushu 36 Keisatsu no Genzai*, Tokyo: Nihon Hyoronsha.
Katzenstein, Peter J. (1990) *West Germany's Internal Security Policy: State and Terrorism in the 1970s and 1980s*, Ithaca, NY, Cornell University, Center for International Studies, Western Societies Program, Occasional Paper No. 28.
Katzenstein, Peter J. and Tsujinaka, Yutaka (1991) *Defending the Japanese State: Structures, Norms and the Political Responses to Terrorism and Violent Social Protest in the 1970s and 1980s*, Ithaca, NY: Cornell University, East Asia Program, Cornell East Asia Series.

Keisatsucho (1975) *KeisatsuHakusho* [White Papers on Police], Tokyo: National Police Agency.

Keisatsucho (1977) *KeisatsuHakusho* [White Papers on Police], Tokyo: National Police Agency.

Keisatsucho (1979) *KeisatsuHakusho* [White Papers on Police], Tokyo: National Police Agency.

Keisatsucho (1980) *KeisatsuHakusho* [White Papers on Police], Tokyo: National Police Agency.

Keisatsucho (1982) *KeisatsuHakusho* [White Papers on Police], Tokyo: National Police Agency.

Keisatsucho (1985) *KeisatsuHakusho* [White Papers on Police], Tokyo: National Police Agency.

Keisatsucho (1987) *KeisatsuHakusho* [White Papers on Police], Tokyo: National Police Agency.

Keisatsucho (1989) *KeisatsuHakusho* [White Papers on Police], Tokyo: National Police Agency.

Kokusai Tero Mondai Kenkyukai (1989) "Kokusai Tero no Genjo to Taisaku" [International Terrorism: Present Situation and Counter-Measures], *Keisatsuhaku Ronshu* [Police Theory], 24, 9: 56–77.

Kubo, Hiroshi (1984) *Nippon no Keisatsu: Keishicho vs. Osaka-fukei* [The Police in Japan: MPD vs. the Osaka Prefectural Police], Tokyo: Kodansha.

Kühne, Hans-Heiner (1973) "Opportunität und quasi-richterliche Tätigkeit des japanischen Staatsanwalts," *Zeitschrift für die Gesamte Strafrechtswissenschaft*, 85: 1079–81.

Kühne, Hans-Heiner and Miyazawa, Koichi (1979) *Kriminalität und Kriminalitätsbekämpfung in Japan*, Wiesbaden: Bundeskriminalamt.

Miller, Reuben (1986) "Acts of International Terrorism: Governments' Responses and Policies," *Comparative Political Studies*, 19, 3 (October): 385–414.

Mizumachi, Osamu (1982) "Patrol Police in Japan," *International Criminal Police Review*, 37, 359: 150–5.

Mizutani, Kiyoshi (1987) "Keisatsu Chusu no Anbu o miru" [A Look at the Dark Spots at the Center of the Police], pp. 114–19 in *Hogaku Semina: Sogo Tokushu 36 Keisatsu no Genzai*, Tokyo: Nihon Hyoronsha.

Murayama, Masayuki (1980) "A Comparative Study of Police Accountability: A Preliminary Work," unpublished paper, Berkeley, University of California.

Murayama, Masayuki (1989a) "Patrol Police Activities in Changing Urban Conditions: The Case of the Tokyo Police," unpublished paper, Chiba University (January).

Murayama, Masayuki (1989b) "Intra-Organizational Control of Patrol Activities in Tokyo," paper presented at the Annual Meeting of the American Society of Criminology in Reno, Nevada, November 8.

Murayama, Masayuki (1990) *Hoan Keisatsu no Kenkyu* [A Study of Safety Police in Tokyo], Tokyo: Seibundo.

Nagamatsu, Yoshisato (1988) "Ajia-Taiheiyo Chiiki Chian Tanto Kakuryo Kaigi Kaisai" [A Report on the Ministerial Conference on Security Matters for the Asia-Pacific Region], *Keisatsukoron* (September): 45–53.

Nakamura, Koji (1974) "The 'Effective Pawns'," *Far Eastern Economic Review* (February 18): 22–3.

Nakamura, Koji (1975) "Japan: A Feeling of Helpless Anxiety," *Far Eastern Economic Review* (August 15): 10.

National Police Agency (1982) *White Paper on Police 1982 (Excerpt)*, Tokyo: National Police Agency.

National Police Agency (1987a) *White Paper on Police 1987 (Excerpt)*, Tokyo: National Police Agency.

National Police Agency (1987b) *The Police of Japan 1987*, Tokyo: National Police Agency.

National Police Agency (1989a) *White Paper on Police 1989 (Excerpt)*, Tokyo: National Police Agency.

National Police Agency (1989b) *The Police of Japan 1989*, Tokyo: National Police Agency.

Nikkan Keisatsu Shimbunsha (1989) *Zenkoku Keisatsu Kanbu Shokuinroku* [National Directory of Senior Police Officials], Tokyo: Nikkan Keisatsu Shimbunsha.

Nishimura, Itsuo (n.d.) "Extradition: Theory and Practice in Japan and the United States," unpublished manuscript, Cambridge, Mass., Harvard University Law School.

Nishio, Baku (1984) *Nippon no Keisatsu* [The Japanese Police], Tokyo: Gendaishokan.

Organization for Economic Cooperation and Development (1978) *Geographical Distribution of Financial Flows to Developing Countries: Data on Disbursements 1971 to 1977*, Paris: Organization for Economic Cooperation and Development.

Parker, L. Craig, Jr (1984) *The Japanese Police System Today: An American Perspective*, Tokyo: Kodansha International.

Rinalducci, Ralph J. (1972) *The Japanese Police Establishment*, Tokyo: Obun Intereurope.

Sassa, Atsuyuki (1984) (Original edition, 1979–80). *Kikikanri no Nouhau* [Crisis Management], Volumes 1–3, Kyoto: PHP Kenkyusho.

Sentaku (1986) "Naikaku-kanbo" [Cabinet Secretariat], *Sentaku* (August): 126–9.

Smith, Robert J. (1983) *Japanese Society: Tradition, Self and the Social Order*, Cambridge: Cambridge University Press.

Somucho (Gyosei-kanri-kyoku) (1988) *Gyosei Kiko-zu* [Public Administration Almanac of Japan], Tokyo: Somucho Gyosei-kanri-kyoku.

Somucho (Tokei-kyoku) (1989) *Nihon Tokei Nenkan* [Statistical Almanac of Japan], Tokyo: Somucho Tokei-kyoku.

Steinhoff, Patricia G. (1988) "What Will the Japanese Red Army Do Next?," unpublished paper, Honolulu, University of Hawaii.

Steinhoff, Patricia G. (1989a) "Hijackers, Bombers, and Bank Robbers: Managerial Style in the Japanese Red Army," *The Journal of Asian Studies*, 48, 4 (November): 724–40.

Steinhoff, Patricia G. (1989b) "Protest and Democracy," pp. 171–98 in Takeshi Ishida and Ellis S. Krauss (eds) *Democracy in Japan*, Pittsburgh, Pa.: University of Pittsburgh Press.

Steinhoff, Patricia G. (n.d.) "Deadly Ideology: The Lod Airport Massacre and the Rengo Sekigun Purge," unpublished manuscript, Honolulu, University of Hawaii.

Sterngold, James (1989) "Japan's Police Use Steel Cages to Subdue Foes of Airport Expansion," *New York Times* (December 6): A9.

Sugai, Shuichi (1957) "The Japanese Police System," pp. 1–14 in Robert E. Ward (ed.) *Five Studies in Japanese Politics*, Ann Arbor, Mich.: University of Michigan Press.

Suzuki, Takuro (1980) *Nippon Keisatsu no Himitsu* [The Secret of the Japanese Police], Tokyo: Chobunsha.

Taikakai (1970) *Naimusho-shi* [The History of the Ministry of Imperial Home Affairs], Volumes 1–4, Tokyo: Taikakai, Harashobo.

Taikakai (1971) *Naimusho-shi* [The History of the Ministry of Imperial Home Affairs], Volumes 1–4, Tokyo: Taikakai, Harashobo.

Tawara, Soichiro (1986a) *Nippon Dai-Kaizo* [Reconstructing Japan: New Japanese Bureaucrats in the Heisei Era], Tokyo: Bungeishunjyu.

Tawara, Soichiro (1986b) *Keisatsu Kanryo no Jidai* [The Age of Police Bureaucrats], Tokyo: Kodansha.

Tawara, Soichiro (1990) *Heisei Nippon no Kanryo* [Japanese Bureaucrats in the Heisei Era], Tokyo: Bungei shunjyu.

Toyokeizai (1986) *Seikai Kankai Jinjiroku* [Directory of Politics and Bureaucracy], Tokyo: Toyokeizai Shinpo-Sha.

Toyokeizai (1987) *Seikai Kankai Jinjiroku* [Directory of Politics and Bureaucracy], Tokyo: Toyokeizai Shinpo-Sha.

Toyokeizai (1988) *Seikai Kankai Jinjiroku* [Directory of Politics and Bureaucracy], Tokyo: Toyokeizai Shinpo-Sha.

Toyokeizai (1989) *Seikai Kankai Jinjiroku* [Directory of Politics and Bureaucracy], Tokyo: Toyokeizai Shinpo-Sha.

Toyokeizai (1990) *Seikai Kankai Jinjiroku* [Directory of Politics and Bureaucracy], Tokyo: Toyokeizai Shinpo-Sha.

Tsuji, Kiyoaki (ed.) (1966) *Shiryo Sengo 20 nen-shi: Seiji* [Sourcebook of the Twenty-Year History of Postwar Japan: Politics], Tokyo: Nihon Hyoronsha.

Van Wolferen, Karel (1989) *The Enigma of Japanese Power: People and Politics in a Stateless Nation*, New York: Knopf.

Yamaguchi, Yasushi (1989) *Seiji Taisei* [Political Regimes], Tokyo: Tokyo-daigaku Shuppan-kai.

Yomiuri (Shimbun Shakaibu) (1986) *Nippon Keisatsu* [The Japanese Police], Tokyo: Yomuiri Shimbun-sha.

5 Japan and Asian-Pacific security: regionalization, entrenched bilateralism, and incipient multilateralism

Nobuo Okawara and Peter J. Katzenstein (2001)[1]

Regionalization is becoming an increasingly important aspect of Japan's and the Asia-Pacific's security affairs. We support this claim by showing the existence of a variety of formal and informal bilateral arrangements in Japan's security policy that in turn help generate different forms of incipient multi-lateralism in the Asia-Pacific. The chapter concludes that Asian-Pacific multilateralism is traditional, in contrast to the "new" types more readily apparent in Europe and the subjects of critical security studies.

The precise meanings of the terms "region" and "security" are, however, far from clear. Regions are combinations of physical, psychological, and behavioral traits (Mansfield and Milner 1997: 3–4; Lake and Morgan 1997: 11–12; Fawcett 1995: 10–11; Morgan 1997: 20; Daase 1993: 77–9; Thompson 1973; Cantori and Spiegel 1970; Russett 1967). While geographical proximity is important, regions cannot be reduced to spatial dimensions. Jeffrey Frankel (1997: 37, 118, 124–5), for example, has demonstrated the powerful effects that political borders have. But he also finds that "the effect of sharing a common language, even for far-removed countries, is very similar in magni-tude to the effect of sharing a common border" (Frankel 1997: 75). Regions are thus not only geographically given but also politically made.

A world of regions is shaped by economic and social processes of regional-ization and by structures of regionalism (Grugel and Hout 1999; Fishlow and Haggard 1992; Fawcett and Hurrell 1995). Regionalization describes geo-graphic manifestations of political, military, economic or social processes at the international level. As we argue in this chapter, regionalization can be both societal and governmental. We argue below that it occurs in the area of social phenomena, such as crime, and in the area of national security policies that governments adopt.

The concept of "comprehensive" security was initially championed by Japan in the late 1970s (Alagappa 1998; Inoguchi 2002). It was developed further by ASEAN in the 1980s. When in the 1990s China made increasing use of the concept, it gained even wider currency throughout the Asia-Pacific. Throughout most of the Asia-Pacific region, the Asian financial crisis of 1997 has reinforced further the belief that security must be understood in "comprehensive" terms that go beyond traditional military connotations.

In the case of Japan the concept of comprehensive security includes both external ("international") and internal dimensions. Both are bringing Japan's Defense Agency (JDA), the Maritime Safety Agency (MSA) which is a part of the Ministry of Transportation, and the National Police Agency (NPA) closer together. By exchanging information and developing new forms of cooperation the Ground Self-Defense Forces (GSDF), the Maritime Self-Defense Forces (MSDF), and the police are attempting to meet what to the government looks like novel threats to Japan's national security including incursions into Japan's coastal waters, acts of terrorism and guerilla attacks on airports, nuclear power plants and harbors (*Japan Times*, June 17, 1999).[2]

This chapter traces the formal and informal aspects of Japan's robust bilateralism on issues of external security in the first section and internal security in the second section, and discusses a variety of embryonic multilateral arrangements that have sprung up in the 1990s in the third section. The Conclusion argues briefly that Asian-Pacific multilateralism differs in kind from the multilateralism that has become the object of attention of students of globalization.

Formal bilateralism and changes in the U.S.–Japan security arrangements

The political consolidation of the formal U.S.–Japan security arrangements since the mid-1990s has regionalized their scope in the Asia-Pacific's evolving security orders. In the early years of the Clinton administration growing bilateral trade conflicts, Japanese uncertainty about U.S. strategy in the Asia-Pacific, and a growing emphasis on the Asia-Pacific in Japanese policy pointed to the possibility of a loosening of bilateral ties. But the actual parameters of change in Japan's security policy were outlined in the August 1994 Higuchi report to the Prime Minister. Even more important, they were shaped by the February 1995 Nye Report.[3] Subsequently, Japan's first revision of the National Defense Program Outline (NDPO) since its adoption in 1976 (November 1995) culminated in the Japan–U.S. Joint Declaration on Security of April 1996 and a review of the 1978 Guidelines for U.S.–Japan Defense Cooperation in September 1997. This review spells out concretely the roles of the U.S. military and the GSDF in the eventuality of a crisis. Based on the review, a new Acquisition and Cross Servicing Agreement (ACSA) was signed by the two governments in April 1998 (*Asahi Shimbun*, April 28, 1998, evening 4th edn).[4] The new agreement referred specifically to "situations in areas surrounding Japan that will have an important influence on Japan's peace and security" as the context in which the two governments could provide supplies and services to each other (*Gaiko Forum* 1999: 139).[5]

The negotiation of the guidelines was deadlocked until low-level staff from the Japan Defense Agency (JDA) interviewed U.S. military personnel about the practical planning issues that, from the perspective of the U.S., needed to be addressed. The list those interviews generated was eventually passed on to the higher echelons inside the JDA. Negotiations that eventually resulted in forty specific measures were affected by the 1994 crisis over North Korea's nuclear program. That crisis convinced the Japanese government of the need for a legal framework that covers emergency situations not involving direct attacks on Japan (Ina 1997: 30; *Asahi Shimbun*, May 21, 1998, 13th edn; February 10, 1999, 14th edn; April 27, 1999, 14th edn).[6]

Political implementation of the revised guidelines in the form of Japanese legislation proved to be controversial. The original bill was approved by the Cabinet in April 1998, but leaders of the LDP and the government admitted that, because it was so controversial, the bill would not be able to pass during that year's Diet session (Jo 1998a; *Asahi Shimbun*, April 26 and May 3, 1998, 14th edn). Eventually, several changes were made to the bill to assure its passage, among them the dropping of controversial clauses on ship inspections.[7] The defense guideline bills eventually passed the Lower House in April 1999 and the Upper House one month later.

The new guidelines pose formidable challenges for a redefinition of the mission and operations of Japan's military, specifically of the MSDF. Military and bureaucratic experts now pay great attention to having their voices heard as the government attempts to clarify the operational implications of the new guidelines.[8] In the context of modern warfare the new defense cooperation arrangements have diluted somewhat the traditional postwar policy of prohibiting any use of force in the absence of a direct attack on Japan. They have done so in part because of the extension in the scope of the U.S.–Japan security arrangements. For one simple reason regionalization is likely to complicate matters in a future crisis. For the GSDF it is easier to draw a line in the sand than it would be for the MSDF to draw a line in the water.[9]

The Japan–U.S. Treaty of Mutual Cooperation and Security has always performed an important regional function owing to (1) "an implicit contribution to regional security through Article 5 of the Treaty (the defence of Japan)" (Green and Self 1996: 42) and (2) the placing of U.S. bases in Japan under Article 6 (the maintenance of international peace and stability in the Far East) (Watanabe and Ina 1998: 20). But the growing importance of regional considerations has linked the regional scope of the treaty with authorization of SDF operations in crisis situations that do not involve any direct attack on Japan. In its effects the security arrangement between the two countries has been more thoroughly regionalized than before. SDF operations will no longer focus solely on the defense of the Japanese home islands.[10] A key provision of the revised NDPO underlines this regional dimension:

> Should a situation arise in the areas surrounding Japan which will have an important influence on national peace and security, [Japan will] take appropriate response in accordance with the Constitution and relevant laws and regulations, for example, by properly supporting the United

Nations activities when needed, and by ensuring the smooth and effective implementation of the Japan–U.S. security arrangements.

(Boeicho n.d.: 38)

Put differently, the scope of the NDPO and the Defense Cooperation Guidelines has broadened, in the eyes of the proponents of such development, from having the SDF defend Japan against direct attack, and thus securing Japan's position in a global anticommunist alliance, to having the SDF enhance through various measures stability in the Asia-Pacific region, and thus Japan's own security. In the 1997 Defense Cooperation Guidelines a new type of "mutual cooperation planning" complements traditional "bilateral defense planning" (Igarashi and Watanabe 1997: 35).

The Security Treaty itself has been left untouched. Attention has been drawn inside Japan to a provision in the new guidelines stating that the "rights and obligations" under the treaty remain unchanged. And according to the Japanese government, which sees a revising of the treaty as too controversial to be politically feasible, the implementing of measures included in the new guidelines is not required by the treaty. Thus, in the context of Japanese domestic politics, an extension in the scope of the security arrangements between the two countries is sharply differentiated from any broadening of the scope of the treaty itself.

The redefinition in the scope of future U.S.–Japan defense cooperation raises concerns in many quarters: among those, mostly in Japan, fearing the risk that Japan might be dragged into global conflicts; among those, mostly in the U.S., doubting Japan's commitment to a more equal partnership in securing, through collective defense measures, regional peace and stability in the Asia-Pacific; and among those, in the Asia-Pacific, worrying about the possible application of the revised guidelines to the Korean peninsula and Taiwan.

The fear of a globalization of Japan's defense cooperation with the U.S. had existed throughout the Cold War, especially among members of the Japanese Left. It was therefore no surprise that, in the Diet, Social Democratic and Communist parties opposed the Cabinet bill implementing the new guidelines. With roughly a third of its Diet members former Socialists, the largest opposition party, the Democratic Party, also voted against the bill (*Asahi Shimbun*, April 21, 28, and May 25, 1999, 14th edn).[11] The fear of getting entangled in international military conflicts remains widespread in Japan.

With such a fear in view, the new guidelines attempt in various ways to reassure a skeptical audience in Japan. According to the guidelines, "[w]hen the two governments reach a common assessment of the state of each situation, they will effectively coordinate their activities" (V); and the two governments' taking of appropriate measures in response to crises will be "based on their respective decisions" (V-2). The revised guidelines also say that "Japan will conduct all its actions within the limitations of its Constitution and in accordance with such basic positions as the maintenance of its exclusively defense-oriented policy and its three non-nuclear principles" (II-2); and they limit contingencies in which the SDF will provide rear-area support to the U.S. forces to "situations in areas surrounding Japan that will have an important influence on Japan's peace and security" (V). Furthermore, the 1999 law implementing the guidelines offers, as a typical example of such "situations," a "situation that, if allowed to stand as it is, is in danger of developing into a direct armed attack on Japan." Thus the new guidelines, in face of strong opposition, have been presented to the public as both securing independent decisionmaking by Japan, and sustaining postwar Japan's low-profile security policy.

The fear in the U.S. defense establishment runs in the opposite direction. In the mid-1990s there was a pervasive sense that the alliance was eroding from within. Japan's growing interest in regional multilateral arrangements and its renewed attention to the United Nations were seen as a hedging strategy against a possible weakening of the U.S. presence in East Asia (Cronin and Green 1994: 2). Since 1995/6 such sentiments, though weaker, persist. Whether it is justified or not, the perception of Japan's "tepid" and "cautious" response to many U.S. requests for closer defense cooperation in the past makes ambiguity in the scope of future defense cooperation worrisome. When the chips are down, ask members of the U.S. defense establishment, can U.S. policy really count on the active support of the Japanese SDF?

The volatile issue of Okinawa is a case in point (Mochizuki 1997: 24–8; Cossa 1997: 43–7; Shimada 1997; Yamaguchi 1997; Johnson 1997; Institute of Social Science 1998). In a bloody battle in the waning months of the Pacific War, a quarter (by one estimate) of the citizens of Okinawa were killed. Ever since, U.S. policy has been one of occupation rather than reform. Many Okinawans regard themselves as different from and having been treated in less than an equitable way by the rest of Japan, a sentiment increasingly recognized by non-Okinawan Japanese. The issue of American bases has brought these powerful emotions into the open in the 1990s. The smoldering conflict erupted when three U.S. servicemen raped a 12-year-old Okinawan schoolgirl on September 4, 1995. Okinawa was the prefecture in Japan which had the lowest per capita income in 1997. It was saddled with the costs of hosting more than half of the U.S. military presence in Japan. American bases occupy about 20 percent of the main island. In terms of land area about 75 percent of all U.S. military facilities in Japan are situated in Okinawa, about a third of which are located on private property (*Asahi Shimbun*, February 16, 2000, 14th edn; Johnson 1997: 5). A staging area for the U.S. military in the Asia-Pacific, Okinawa suffers from a variety of social ills and from economic opportunities forgone.

Under the leadership of a popular governor, Masahide Ota, about 53 percent of the total Okinawan electorate voted in the first-ever prefectural plebiscite held in Japan, on September 8, 1996, for both consolidation and reduction of the U.S. military presence and a reform of the U.S.–Japan Status of Forces Agreement. At present the situation is at a stalemate, between the U.S. and Japan as well as between the central government and the citizens of Nago who on December 21, 1997 voted by a slight majority, despite heavy political pressure, against the relocation of the Futenma Marine Corps Air Station to their community. The Japanese central government is trying to buy the assent of the 55,000 citizens of Nago, with approximately $1 billion in subsidies to be invested during the coming decade. For the time being the operational side of U.S.–Japan security relations exists on a politically fragile basis of support (French 2000).[12]

The application of the revised guidelines to potential instabilities on the Korean peninsula is also a source of political controversy (Hughes 1996). In March 1999, Japanese destroyers fired warning shots at intruding North Korean vessels. This was the first time since its creation in 1954 that the Maritime Self-Defense Forces (MSDF) engaged in such operations. Ignoring several warnings by the destroyers as well as gunfire from the Japanese coast-guard (MSA) patrol boats, the North Korean vessels were apparently permitted to escape after they went beyond Japan's air defense identification zone (Kristof 1999a; Defense Agency 2000: 210). North Korea's nuclear and missile programs as well as its faltering economy have raised the specter of another Korean War that could enmesh Japan and affect it directly if weapons of mass destruction were to be deployed or if large-scale refugee movements were to occur.[13] After expressing initially strong reservations, South Korea has come to appreciate the considerations that have pushed Japan to acquiesce in U.S. pressure to revise the defense guidelines, especially since the historic visit of President Kim Dae Jung to Tokyo in October 1998 has improved diplomatic relations between the two states.[14]

Military toughness is not a recipe for Japan's approach to China. For historical, political, and military reasons, China is a central challenge for Japan and Asian-Pacific regional security and in the long run probably more important than Korea (Green 1999; Christensen 1999). The change in the U.S.–Japan security relationship was met with mixed emotions by Beijing's policy elites. Condemnation of the new security guidelines adopted in September 1997 was swift. The changes were interpreted as inherently more aggressive, in particular with respect to Japan's ambiguous stance in case of an outbreak of hostilities between Taiwan and the PRC (Kynge 1999a). At the same time many members of China's political and military leadership are fully aware of the stabilizing effects of the U.S.–Japan security alliance (Christensen 1999: 58–9; Wang and Wu 1998; Ross 1999; Garrett and Glaser 1997).[15] Before 1995, Chinese policy elites were alarmed by the prospect that a fraying of the U.S.–Japan relationship might remove the "bottle cap" that had contained a possibly unilateral remilitarization of Japan. After 1995 they were equally concerned by the consolidation of the U.S.–Japan relationship and the creation of an "egg shell" which eventually would hatch, under U.S. tutelage, a militarist and expansionary Japan in the Asia-Pacific (Christensen 1999: 59–62).

The issue that has Chinese officials concerned more than the possibility of Japan's nuclearization is the development of weapon systems that are tailored to Japan's proven strength in dual-use technologies such as Theater Missile

Defense (TMD) systems (Hildreth and Pagliano 1995; Cambone 1997; Green 1997; Crowell and Usui 1997).[16] In the view of Japanese policymakers the joint research project with the U.S. government on TMD is useful politically both in the short and medium term. In accommodating requests that the U.S. government has made since 1993, TMD strengthens cooperative security arrangements with Japan's most important partner, and it responds to the strong sense of worry of the Japanese public over the 1998 North Korean missile test. But this policy also affects political developments in the Asia-Pacific even without Japan altering its traditional policy of barring the export of military technologies to all countries except the United States.[17] Specifically, TMD further complicates Japan's relations with the PRC, which have already been clouded by the new guidelines. It will also strain Japan's defense budgets with R&D expenditures over five years expected to run in the range of 20–30 billion yen (*Mainichi Daily News*, August 14, 1999). Considering the system's uncertain technical prospects, a decision on deployment will most likely be delayed for at least a decade (Sims 1999).[18]

For various reasons, Japan's decision to participate in TMD research has aroused strong Chinese opposition.[19] The fact that TMD is perceived to be linked to an intense discussion in Washington and a likely U.S. decision on the building of a National Missile Defense (NMD) system makes it unpalatable to China, as well as Russia, France and most other European states. China in particular objects to the TMD on political–military grounds and also because of possible technological spillover effects from one program to the other.[20] From the Chinese perspective the notion that weapons, such as TMD, are inherently defensive rings hollow. TMD would strengthen the hand of the Taiwanese government in its quest for sovereign statehood, an inherently aggressive act from the perspective of the PRC. Introduced into a specific political and historical context, a jointly developed and produced U.S.–Japanese TMD system, from the perspective of Beijing, thus is a factor seriously destabilizing Asian-Pacific security. To be sure, TMD had been on the agenda of the U.S. and Japan since 1993, long before the Nye Report; Japan had been reluctant to commit itself to the project; and Japanese policy changed only after a North Korean missile test across Japanese territory on August 31, 1998. These facts are recognized in Beijing. But they are judged to be much less consequential than the fact that TMD might counter missiles as the preeminent military asset the PRC possesses in its relations with Taiwan (Christensen 1999: 64–9; Dickie and Fidler 1999; Walker and Fidler 1999; Kynge 1999b; Wiltse 1997).

The importance of bilateral relations with the U.S. fits a broader pattern of Japan's security policy. Senior JDA officials have met annually between 1993 and 1997, and again in 1999, with their Chinese counterparts, with the 1998 hiatus most likely occasioned by the adoption of the New Guidelines.[21] Besides China, Japan has initiated also regular bilateral security talks with Australia (since 1996), Singapore (since 1997), Indonesia (since 1997), Thailand (since 1998) and Malaysia (since 1999).[22] Japan's JDA is increasingly engaging the

Asia-Pacific in a broad range of bilateral security contacts.[23] In sum in the 1990s regionalization has increased in Japan's external security affairs.

Informal bilateralism and Japan's internal security policies

Compared to formal bilateralism on issues of external security, on questions affecting Japan's internal security the government has responded through informal bilateral arrangements to the actual or perceived growth of transnational organized crime. In the Asia-Pacific, problems such as illegal immigration, organized crime, money laundering, narcotics and terrorism remain almost without exception under the exclusive prerogative of national governments. But the Japanese police has begun to cultivate systematically its contacts with foreign law enforcement agencies on a bilateral basis. Japanese policy aims at increasing trust among police professionals throughout the region, thus creating a general climate in which Japan's police can cooperate more easily with foreign police forces on an ad hoc basis. Put briefly, on a case-by-case basis Japanese police organizations are attempting to share more freely information with other police forces in the Asia-Pacific.[24]

Japan's crime syndicates, or *yakuza*, make most of their money inside Japan, traditionally in gambling, prostitution, racketeering and extortion, especially in the entertainment and construction industries. With the advent of the bubble economy in the late 1980s the syndicates entered Japan's corporate world on a large scale. David Kaplan estimates that, despite Japan's prolonged recession in the 1990s, the net worth of the syndicates doubled between the mid-1980s and mid-1990s. Easy loans, especially in real estate and the securities industry, created a new type of economic gangster in Japan. Some estimates put the direct and indirect share of uncollectable bank loans to the *yakuza* at 40 percent of the estimated total of about $1 trillion of bad loans held by Japanese banks. In the views of several observers Japan was experiencing in the 1990s an economic recession prolonged not only by the blunders of party politicians and the mismanagement of Ministry of Finance bureaucrats but also by the hesitation of bankers, intimidated by the occasional murder, to push the mob to pay up. This delayed further the banks' interest in beginning the process of writing off bad loans (Kaplan 1996: 3, 6; Friman 1999: 6; Takayama 1995; Fulford 1995).[25]

Japan's crime syndicates have important international connections throughout the Asia-Pacific that net annually large amounts of revenues (Flynn 1998: 25–6). Links to the Chinese triads, for example, date back to the Pacific War and the Japanese occupation of China. Recruiting among Japan's heavily discriminated Korean minority, Japanese crime syndicates also have close ties to Korea where *yakuza*-financed laboratories used to supply most of the world's market for crystal methamphetamine. In Taiwan, Thailand, and the Philippines, Japan's crime syndicates have organized a burgeoning sex tourism. And Hawaii's real-estate market became a convenient place for laundering illegal funds in the 1980s and early 1990s.

Japan's NPA seeks to cooperate with the law enforcement agencies of other countries primarily by cultivating a systematic exchange of information.[26] The NPA is most satisfied with the good working relations it has established with Hong Kong, Singapore, and Taiwan; it is very eager to build up its contacts with police officials from Fujian province;[27] and it funds projects that bring Japanese researchers to provinces in northeast China, relying on existing Chinese contacts, to build closer ties with provincial police forces while investigating the local conditions that permit China's crime syndicates to operate in Japan.[28]

Like the Chinese triads and organized crime in other Asia-Pacific states Japan's crime syndicates are deeply involved in the international drug trade (Shinn 1998a). Japanese crime groups have strong transnational links and cooperate with organized crime in Thailand, Hong Kong, Taiwan, and China (Friman 1991, 1993, 1994, 1996). In the 1990s all of the methamphetamine, Japan's drug of choice, comes from abroad, much of it from Fujian province, compared to Taiwan in the 1980s and South Korea in the 1970s. International syndicates handle transshipment, illegal immigrants, often of Iranian origin, street-level distribution. Japan's *yakuza* acts as an intermediary and derives about one-third of its total revenues from drugs.[29] Since the NPA lacks the power and resources of an organization such as the U.S. Drug Enforcement Agency (DEA), it also lacks precise estimates of the flow of drugs into Japan. But it is clear that Japan's high living standards make it an attractive market for international drug dealers (Kristof 1999b).[30]

Most of the practical police work is facilitated by personal relationships with law enforcement officials from other countries, especially China, Thailand, Taiwan, Burma, Vietnam, Laos, and Cambodia.[31] In the view of the NPA, bilateral police relations are good or excellent with the members of ASEAN, South Korea, and the United States. High-level contacts with Taiwan work well but the problems of Taiwan's ambiguous diplomatic status severely constrain practical police cooperation at lower levels. And relations with China are difficult since the vast bureaucracy of China's Public Security Department exercises strong central control over localities such as Fujian where drugs are produced and shipped to Japan. The ministry's insistence on strict observance of all formalities seriously undermines practical police cooperation.[32] In sum, international drug trafficking by crime syndicates is spreading in the Asia-Pacific. In response, Japan's NPA seeks to build informal cooperative relations with foreign law enforcement officials rather than ceding national sovereignty to formal multilateral institutions.

Since 1996 the smuggling of illegal immigrants has become a problem that Japan's police officials are forced to pay growing attention to (Friman 1998, 2000a, 2000b).[33] Even though the sharpest increases in the arrests of Chinese occurred in the early 1990s, the NPA has only since 1998 intensified its contacts with Chinese police officials. One reason was the extreme caution with which the NPA's Security Bureau had traditionally viewed the building of cooperative ties with police officials from China. But, with the problem of illegal immigration perceived as becoming very serious by 1996, the Security Bureau's opposition has weakened. Since May 1997 the NPA has sought semi-annually to develop cooperative ties at the deputy-chief level.[34]

Even more significant is the beginning of joint operation of the Japanese and Chinese police. The NPA has acted as an intermediary for the cooperation between prefectural police departments and the Hong Kong police since 1997 and Canton and Shanghai police forces since 1998, leading to several arrests (Hirano 1998: 45–6).[35] NPA officials met their Shanghai and Cantonese counterparts after having built up their ties with the Hong Kong police prior to 1997. They are now very interested in creating closer personal relations with police forces in Fujian so as to facilitate future joint operations.[36]

The dramatic decline by the Japan Red Army (JRA), marked by the arrest of nine JRA members since 1995, has not ended the perceived threat that terrorism poses to Japan. In the 1990s Japan has had to cope with some spectacular acts of terrorism both at home (Aum Shinrikyo's sarin gas attack in Tokyo's subway in 1995) and abroad (the attack on the Japanese embassy in Lima in 1996). The target of the NPA's concern is shifting from the JRA to North Korea and to fundamentalist Islamic groups.[37] In line with its policy on other security issues the NPA has sought vigorously to increase trust through the strengthening of bilateral contacts with foreign police professionals and the systematic exchange of information.[38]

Japanese police officers also seek to gather systematic intelligence abroad. More than 100 police officers stationed at Japanese embassies practice cooperative security with local police forces in the host countries. In response to the takeover of the Japanese embassy in Lima, Peru, a terror response team (TRT) was set up in the spring of 1998. It will be dispatched in future crises when Japanese nationals are threatened by international terrorism. The unit trains abroad, and it exchanges information with corresponding units in other countries.[39]

Japan's antiterrorism policy displays clearly the characteristic features of its preferred approach to issues of internal security (Leheny 2000). Multilateral international or regional institutions are relatively unimportant in Japan's approach. Interpol, for example, is of secondary importance in the eyes of NPA officials, even though the director-general of the NPA's International Affairs Department, Toshinori Kanemoto, became the head of Interpol in 1996. On questions of organized crime Interpol does not provide the police with sensitive information. On questions of drug trafficking its information, at best, duplicates what police officers learn through other channels. On questions of illegal immigration Interpol is largely useless. And in Japan's antiterrorism policy its main function is restricted to the posting of international arrest warrants.[40]

In sum, informal bilateralism has been the most important response to the regional spread of transnational crime. The increasing importance of

Asia-Pacific regionalism is noticeable in the intensified efforts of the NPA to create more trust through the improvement of its bilateral ties with national police forces throughout the Asia-Pacific.

Incipient multilateralism in Japan's external and internal security policies

Formal and informal bilateral arrangements in Japan's external and internal security policies shape an incipient form of multilateralism that covers a broad spectrum of different admixtures of bilateral and multilateral elements in the Asia-Pacific's security affairs. Multilateral security arrangements cross the gamut of Track One (government-to-government), Track Two (semi-governmental think-tanks), and Track Three (private institutions) (Stone 1997; Wada 1998).[41] The institutional affiliation of national research organizations participating in Track Two activities confounds the attempt of drawing a sharp line between governmental Track One and nongovernmental Track Two activities. Affiliation varies from being integral to the ministries of foreign affairs (the two Koreas, China, and Laos), to being totally (Vietnam) or partly (Japan) funded and largely (Vietnam) or moderately (Japan) staffed by the Ministry of Foreign Affairs, to very close proximity to the prime minister (Malaysia), to high degrees of independence (Thailand and Indonesia).[42] Whatever their precise character, for most Japanese officials, dialogues that involve semi-official or private contacts are useful to the extent that they help facilitate government-to-government talks; they are not of value in and of themselves.[43]

Japan's interest in and support of stronger multilateral arrangements dates back to the 1960s when its neighbors in Southeast Asia rejected several Japanese proposals to create multilateral economic arrangements (Katzenstein 1997: 12–20). The Japanese government supported the creation of ASEAN and saw it as a useful arrangement to help stabilize Southeast Asia after the end of the Vietnam War. Prime Minister Tanaka's 1974 visit to the region was the first occasion on which the Japanese government referred to ASEAN as a collective political institution rather than to Southeast Asia as a geographic area.[44] Before 1989, like the U.S., but sometimes for different reasons, Japan had no interest in regional security institutions. Looking for a new diplomatic initiative in the wake of the Gulf War and convinced that the cause of Asia-Pacific regionalism was ready to be advanced further diplomatically, in July 1991 the Japanese government proposed a new multilateral security dialogue as part of ASEAN's Post-Ministerial Conference (PMC) (Fukushima 1999a: 143).[45] The proposal by Foreign Minister Taro Nakayama, writes Paul Midford (1998: 2), "represented a dramatic departure from Japan's reactive policy toward regional security, and marked the first time since the end of World War II that Japan made a regional security initiative on its own, and without American support."

Although the Nakayama initiative proved unacceptable to ASEAN members, it did have a threefold effect. It prompted ASEAN to push ahead with its own plans for setting up a multilateral security institution as part of the ASEAN PMC; it contributed to a rapid shift in the hostile stance of the U.S. government toward multilateral security arrangements in the Asia-Pacific; and it prepared the ground for further diplomatic moves by Prime Minister Miyazawa on multilateral regional security initiatives and the growth of multilateralism in the Asia-Pacific in the 1990s. By the end of the decade, Japan's Ministry of Foreign Affairs (MOFA) and JDA had become interested in pushing from "confidence and security-building measures" based on a sharing of information by various participating states about each other's defense posture to "preventive diplomacy" as one way of solving some of the harder security problems in the Asia-Pacific.[46] With varying degrees of enthusiasm the Japanese government has supported all of the new multi-lateral initiatives and has thus followed the recommendations of the Advisory Group on Defense Issues (Advisory Group on Defense Issues 1994; Cronin and Green 1994).

This is not to argue that there were no domestic divisions in Japan. Security multilateralism in the Asia-Pacific meant different things to different groups (Kawasaki 1997). "Realists" viewed all the talk about cooperative security and the ASEAN Regional Forum (ARF) as one additional tool for practicing balance-of-power politics with China.[47] "Idealists" welcomed the ARF as a promising way of moving the Asia-Pacific away from traditional power poli-tics toward the growth of one or several overlapping security communities that might eventually transcend the system of competing alliances. Finally, "realistic liberals" in the MOFA who were crafting the new policy hoped to increase Asia-Pacific stability through institutionalized ways of enhancing transparency and trust.[48] "Their conception of the ARF was an amalgamation of Idealism and Realism: a sort of international community in the narrow realm of information sharing, beneath which the cold reality of power politics and alliance systems persist" (Kawasaki 1997: 495). On balance, Japan's approach to multilateralism has been cautious.

The incipient security multilateralism of the Asia-Pacific takes somewhat different forms. It is, for example, evident in the recent history of several Track Two dialogues. They provide a convenient venue for senior government officials to meet in relatively informal settings. Since 1993, for example, Japan has cooperated with China, Russia, South Korea, and the U.S. in the North East Asia Cooperation Dialogue (NEACD).[49] In addition, since 1994 a Japanese research organization has co-sponsored, with its American and Russian counterparts, the Trilateral Forum on North Pacific Security also attended by senior government officials.[50] Furthermore, since 1998 Japan has conducted semi-official trilateral security talks with China and the U.S. (*Asahi Shimbun*, July 16, 1998, 14th edn; *Japan Times*, September 28, 1999; Fukushima 1999b: 36; Sasaki 1997).

On questions of Asian-Pacific security, however, the most important Track Two dialogues occur in the Council for Security Cooperation in the Asia Pacific (CSCAP) (Simon 1998; Stone 1997: 21–5; Wada 1998: 162–5; Job

2000).[51] Its predecessors were the ASEAN-associated Institutes for Strategic and International Studies. In the early 1990s these institutes played a crucial role in pushing ASEAN to commence systematic security dialogues. And, with the establishment of the Track One ARF, the Track Two activities of these institutes have grown in importance. They prepare studies that may be too sensitive for governments to conduct. And they organize meetings on topics that for political reasons governments may be unwilling or unable to host. CSCAP was created in 1993, and held its first meeting in 1994. It incorporated these institutes into a larger nongovernmental body with a membership that was nearly coterminous with that of the ARF. It is "the most comprehensive, regular, non-governmental forum on Pacific security" (Simon 1998). With its five working groups CSCAP-sponsored dialogues were modeled after those in the Pacific Economic Cooperation Council (PECC) that have brought together, since 1980, business people, government officials in their private capacity, and academic economists (Fukushima 1999a: 131, 154–5; 1999b: 33).[52]

Track Two activities thus can offer governments a variety of informal venues to exchange information and to take stock of the evolving assessments of a variety of governmental and nongovernmental actors. Track Two activities also help shape the climate of opinion in national settings in which security affairs are conducted. They can help in articulating new ideas for national decision-makers. Over time they may socialize elites either directly or indirectly to different norms and identities. And they may also build transnational coalitions of elites that retain considerable influence in their respective national arenas. In brief, they have become an important aspect of Asian-Pacific security affairs.[53]

Multilateral Track Two activities advance also a variety of specific political objectives. All ARF members, for example, are interested in modifying China's political aims through a strategy of engagement (Johnston and Ross 1999; Johnston 1999: 304–15).[54] The Chinese government puts a high premium on its international standing, which is influenced in part by its conduct in regional organizations such as the ARF.[55] Both factors, Alastair Johnston (1999) argues, have helped advance the evolution of the ARF's institutionalization since 1994. China's decision to become a member was a boost for the ARF. After initial opposition China also responded to Japan's suggestion, as part of an ARF initiative, of publishing at least a skeletal National Defense White Paper. This is an indication of a slight shift in China's security policy that reflects its sensitivity to at least some international suggestions; it may augur well for China's willingness to consider giving further support to ARF or other multilateral arrangements some time in the future. Even without a major crisis, such as over Taiwan, China's approach to multilateral security arrangements retains a strong unilateral bent.[56]

Like China, the U.S. also has come to support multilateral security institutions in the Asia-Pacific (Acharya 2000a: 12). This change dates back to the late 1980s and the end of the Cold War. For a variety of reasons the United

States embraced a regional strategy in North America, the Western hemisphere and the Asia-Pacific. The shift was gradual. U.S. grand strategy accepted at the global level regionalism as complementary to its traditional emphasis on universalism. And in the Asia-Pacific it supported multilateral arrangements as complementary but subordinate to established bilateral security treaties. The growing U.S. toleration of and interest in the ARF reflects this change in policy.

Since the mid-1980s a multilateralism centering on the U.S. military has also become important for the armed forces throughout the Asia-Pacific including Japan's.[57] Since 1986, the Commander-in-Chief, Pacific Command (CINCPAC), for example, has brought together military and civilian officials from about fifteen Asia-Pacific countries in a "Seminar for East Asian Security" that was designed primarily to socialize the different militaries.[58] The intent of the U.S. was to increase the level of reassurance and knowledge in the area. In 1994 the U.S. set up an Asia-Pacific Center for Security Studies (APCSS) in Honolulu which is offering a variety of short-term mid-career courses largely for professional military personnel. The U.S.-sponsored Pacific Air Force Chief of Staff Conference (PACC) is held every other year.[59] In the fall of 2000, Japan co-hosted in Tokyo with the U.S. the U.S.-sponsored Pacific Army Management Seminar (PAMS), which brought together officers from thirty to forty states.[60]

Multilateral meetings among officers that are orchestrated by the U.S. military are complemented by the initiatives of some governments in the Asia-Pacific. Through the renegotiation of military-base arrangements, Singapore, for example, has sought to ensure that the U.S. navy remained engaged in maritime Asia-Pacific—since the late 1980s a double hedge against both China's rising political aspirations and Japan's growing economic weight.

Japan's SDF plays a very circumscribed role in such multilateral meetings. At ARF sessions the SDF is represented by JDA officials. Members of the SDF participate in intersessional working groups when technical issues are being discussed.[61] But at the civilian level the sheer scarcity of resources and manpower constrains the degree of involvement of JDA in multilateral meetings. Even within these constraints, the scales are tilted heavily in favor of the political side. MOFA sends very senior officials to the annual ARF meetings while JDA is represented by less senior personnel.[62]

East Timor illustrates the circumscribed role of the JDA in UN-sponsored multilateral peacekeeping operations. Japanese security policy is based on the premise that East Timor and Kosovo, though regionally specific, raise more general issues of international security that require action by the international community rather than regional segmentation.[63] Yet it was only in mid-November 1999, two and a half months after the East Timorese referendum on August 30, that the Cabinet decided on the sending of Japanese personnel to assist this international effort. In the absence of a declared ceasefire between the opposing sides, under the restrictions of Japan's 1992 International Peace Cooperation Law the government was prohibited from sending peacekeeping or humanitarian aid missions to East Timor.[64] According to a top unnamed JDA official, East Timor had requested that aid be delivered by "an Asian nation that is racially similar . . . instead of Australian troops" (Maeda 1999). Compared to the opposition aroused in many quarters in the Asia-Pacific that Australia's active and high-profile role engendered, despite its direct participation in the UN peacekeeping operation, Japan's $100 million support of an intervention force staffed by ASEAN member states, and its pursuit of quiet diplomacy, shielded it from international criticism. It probably consolidated further Japan's political position in Southeast Asia, despite its inability to contribute directly to the UN peacekeeping operation.[65]

Questions of internal security also show incipient forms of multilateralism that reflect a mixture of bilateral and multilateral elements. International meetings are of increasing importance at the professional police level. The annual number of international meetings attended by senior NPA officials has increased from about two or three in the 1970s to about ten in the 1990s.[66] Since 1989, for example, the NPA has hosted annually a three-day meeting on organized crime. Funded by Japan's foreign aid program, this meeting is designed to strengthen cooperative police relationships that facilitate the exchange of information.[67] Although more formal multilateral institutional activities matter much less on questions of internal security, they do occasionally occur.[68] Confronting its third wave of stimulant abuse since 1945, Japan convened an Asian Drug Law Enforcement Conference in Tokyo in the winter of 1999.[69] At that meeting, the director of the UN Office of Drug Control and Crime Prevention (UNDCP) chastized the Japanese government for its limited commitment to curtailing multilaterally the regional trafficking in methamphetamines (Friman 1999). The NPA attended as an observer a May 1999 meeting in which the five Southeast Asian countries and China formally approved an international police strategy (Haraguchi 1999: 36–7). And it organized in January 2000 a conference, attended by officials from thirty-seven countries, on how police cooperation could stem the spread of narcotics (*Asahi Evening News*, January 28, 2000).

Because terrorism is a direct threat to the state, it has been a subject of high-level political meetings of heads of state. In this area, as in the area of multilateral security, Japan has actively sought to create regional institutions.[70] But this is a recent and tentative move. On questions of internal security the absence of multilateral regional institutions in the Asia-Pacific remains striking, especially in comparison to Europe. A recent inventory of a number of transnational crime problems lists several global institutional fora in which these issues are addressed but apart from CSCAP's working group on transnational crime for the Asia-Pacific there is only one regional one, the ASEAN Ministry on Drugs (ASOD) (Shinn 1998b: 170–1).

On questions of both internal and external security the Asia-Pacific's incipient multilateralism and entrenched bilateralism do not contradict one another (Capie *et al.* 1998: 7–8, 16–17, 60–2, IV/3–4, 7). Amitav Acharya (1990: 1–12; 2000b: 18) speaks of an interlocking "spider-web" form of bilateralism that compensates in part for the absence of multilateral security cooperation in the Asia-Pacific. In the 1960s and 1970s, anticommunism provided the political base that allowed joint police operations and cross-border "hot pursuits" of communist guerillas, for example, between Malaysia and Indonesia as well as Malaysia and Thailand. What was true of internal security in the 1960s and 1970s is to some extent true of external security in the 1990s. The North Korean crisis illustrates, as Michael Stankiewicz (1998: 2) observes, "the increasing complementarity between bilateral and multilateral diplomatic efforts in Northeast Asia." Improvement in various bilateral relations in the Asia-Pacific, occasioned by the conflict on the Korean peninsula, is fostering a gradual strengthening of multilateral security arrangements such as the NEACD and Korean Peninsula Energy Development Organization (KEDO). The potential for a flashpoint crisis between North Korea and its neighbors thus is a source for strengthening nascent multilateral security arrangements in Northeast Asia. In April 1999, for example, Japan, South Korea and the U.S. created the Trilateral Coordination and Oversight Group to orchestrate policy toward North Korea.[71] Japanese diplomacy thus is beginning to make new connections between bilateral and multilateral security dialogues.[72]

Japan's external and internal security policies bring together politicians and professionals in regionwide Track One, Track Two and ad hoc meetings. A growth of Asian regionalization in the 1990s is unmistakable in this incipient multilateralism. It reflects a complex mixture of unilateral, bilateral and multilateral aspects. More often than not Japanese policy and Asian-Pacific multilateralism aim at enhancing trust through transparency rather than at transforming state identities.

Conclusion

Multilateralism is often understood to refer to the coordination of national policies in groups of three or more states (Keohane 1990). Some scholars such as David Twining (1998: 3) argue that we need to look beyond formal structures to the content and nature of state interactions in a "qualitative" multilateralism. This comes quite close to John Ruggie's (1992; Sewell 2000) insistence on the existence of collective norms and social purposes as a defining criterion of multilateralism. Proponents of critical security studies go further. Brought together for a large research project under the leadership of Robert Cox, they insist instead that a "new multilateralism" links structural change in world order to the emergence of new multilateral practices shaped in particular by a growing number of nongovernmental organizations (Cox 1997: xvii, xix, xxiv; Schechter 1999: 3–5). Concurrent developments in global and local politics encourage a move "beyond multilateralism [which] must embrace new forms and the widest possible participation, particularly by nongovernmental organizations" (Twining 1998: 143).

The data in this chapter suggest that such movement is not discernible in the security affairs of Japan and the Asia-Pacific. The virtual absence of Track

Three activities on security issues is an indication that no qualitatively new multilateralism has yet taken hold in the Asia-Pacific. Instead, full-blown regionwide intergovernmental dialogues, Track Two processes, and bi- or tri-lateral coordination mechanisms all constitute Asian-Pacific multilateralism in its incipient form. For Track One and Track Two are impossible to distinguish empirically.

Multilateralism often cannot do without bilateralism for reasons of interpersonal relations and mass psychology (Bredow 1996: 109–10). In the case of Japan and the Asia-Pacific, an even more important reason is that multilateralism is not yet a strong and unquestioned collectively held norm either in Tokyo or in any of the other capitals in the Asia-Pacific, not to speak of the fact that non-state actors have acquired no institutionalized standing on security issues. What matters instead is a layering of bilateral and multilateral state policies as the foundation for an incipient security multilateralism.

The distinctiveness of that multilateralism is readily apparent in comparative perspective. Intrusive or transformative multilateralism European-style is not in evidence on questions of Asian-Pacific security. Instead what matters are political practices shaped by a strong tradition of bilateralism and only very recently by an incipient multilateralism. Japanese security policies thus reflect and shape the Asia-Pacific's emerging security order.

Notes

1   Without blaming them for any of the remaining errors of commission and omission we would like to thank for their criticisms, comments, and suggestions on earlier drafts of this paper: Amitav Acharya, Thomas Berger, Robert Bullock, Tom Christensen, Susanne Feske, Michael Green, Walter Hatch, Brian Job, Chalmers Johnson, Alastair I. Johnston, Robert Keohane, Kozo Kato, Stephen Krasner, Ellis Krauss, David Leheny, T. J. Pempel, Richard Samuels, Keiichi Tsunekawa, Robert Uriu, and an anonymous reviewer as well as members of seminars at UC San Diego, Cornell University, and Aoyama Gakuin University. We are also very much indebted to a large number of Japanese and Chinese government officials and policy advisors who gave generously of their time to talk with us.
2   Interview 10-00, Tokyo, January 14, 2000.
3   The report suggested four components which were designed to support U.S. interests in a stable and peaceful Asia-Pacific: maintenance of the forward deployment of U.S. forces in the Asia-Pacific; strengthening of multilateral arrangements in the Asia-Pacific; an adaptation of U.S. alliances, especially with Japan, to the new conditions after the Cold War; and, finally, encouragement of China to define its interests in ways that would be compatible with U.S. interests (Nye 1997; U.S. Department of Defense 1995, 1998).
4   The previous agreement signed in 1996 had stipulated that the SDF and the U.S. military could provide each other with supplies and services in joint exercises, UN peacekeeping operations, and international humanitarian relief operations. Supplies and services covered by the agreement included, among others, fuel, food, medical support, and transportation, but not ammunition (*Gaiko Forum* 1997: 77).
5   The SDF's provision of weapons and ammunition to the U.S. military, and the U.S. military's provision of weapon systems and ammunition to the SDF, are beyond the scope of the agreement (*Gaiko Forum* 1999: 139).

6 Interview 02-99, Tokyo, January 11, 1999. SDF responsibilities in the new guidelines came to include, among others, intelligence-gathering and sharing, rear area support, and manning search-and-rescue operations. The review also committed the Japanese government politically to permit U.S. forces to utilize civilian airports, harbors and private-sector assets (Okimoto 1998: 27).

7 Another change in the revised legislation required prior approval by the Diet of the SDF's rear area support and search-and-rescue operations. In crisis situations, the government has the right to initiate such operations without Diet approval; but the Diet can subsequently refuse its approval and terminate an ongoing operation (*Asahi Shimbun*, April 26, 1999, 16th edn).

8 Interview 10-00, Tokyo, January 14, 2000.

9 Interviews 12-99 and 13-99, Tokyo, January 14, 1999.

10 Interview 03-99, Tokyo, January 12, 1999.

11 These parties had considerable support among the voters on this issue. In a public opinion poll taken in March 1999, 37 percent of the respondents supported and 43 percent opposed the bill. Even among the supporters of the LDP, only 50 percent were for and 34 percent against it (*Asahi Shimbun*, March 19, 1999, 14th edn).

12 Interviews 01-99 and 03-99, Tokyo, January 11–12, 1999.

13 Interview 13-99, Tokyo, January 14, 1999.

14 Military-to-military contacts have expanded greatly since 1999. The two navies have initiated joint military exercises. And the two governments have opened three hotlines between Japan and South Korea to facilitate rapid communications in the case of an incursion of their airspace or territorial waters (Interview 12-99, Tokyo, January 14, 1999). These lines have become operational since May 1999 (Boeicho 1999: 177).

15 Interviews 01-98, 04-98 and 03-00, 04-00, Beijing, June 15 and 16, 1998, and June 13, 2000.

16 In the view of the U.S. media, Japan overreacted to the North Korean missile test of 1998; but in the view of Japanese observers it is the United States that is overexploiting that test politically in using it as the occasion for embarking on a National Missile Defense (NMD) program (Interview 04-00, Tokyo, January 12, 2000). It should be noted that the term TMD is itself contentious. The Japanese government prefers the term "Ballistic Missile Defense" as the focus of "TMD" is on the defense of U.S. military forces stationed abroad (Boeicho 1999: 133).

17 Interviews 03-99 and 04-99, Tokyo, January 12, 1999; Interview 03-00, Tokyo, January 11, 2000.

18 Interviews 01-99 and 02-99, Tokyo, January 11, 1999; Interview 05-00, Tokyo, January 12, 2000.

19 However, that opposition appears not to have been voiced frequently in bilateral contacts at either bureaucratic or political levels in 1999 (Interview 03-00, Tokyo, January 11, 1999).

20 Interview 12-00, Tokyo, January 14, 2000.

21 Interview 13-00, Tokyo, January 14, 2000.

22 These meetings bring together from each country 5–6 persons in "political–military talks" (involving both defense and foreign affairs officials), and 3–4 professional military personnel in "military-to-military talks" (involving only defense officials) (Boeicho 1999: 185; Defense Agency 1998: 171; Interview 02-99, Tokyo, January 11, 1999; *Daily Yomiuri*, February 4, 1997). Military officers of the SDF also have been engaging in "unit-to-unit exchanges" with their counterparts in Russia, South Korea, and Southeast Asian countries (Boeicho 1999: 177–8, 180, 184; Defense Agency 1998: 167–9).

23 Interviews 10-00 and 13-00, Tokyo, January 14, 2000. It is worth noting that, as Japanese public opinion became less critical, military officers have been more free to travel abroad, not only to far-away places in Europe as in the 1970s and

1980s but to neighboring countries in the Asia-Pacific. With the tightening of U.S.–Japan security relations after 1994, Japan has become more self-conscious in developing a broad set of bilateral defense talks and exchanges that complement its persistent dependence on the U.S. and also serve the purpose of cementing the presence of the U.S. in the region. By 1999, Japan was committed to about ten regular bilateral talks, too many for the two officials that the JDA had assigned to this role. India, for example, was interested in commencing bilateral defense consultation, but Japan stalled, not for reasons of policy but simply because of resource constraints (Interview 13-00, Tokyo, January 14, 2000).

24 This intensification of bilateral contacts builds on a small foundation of transnational police links that Japan's National Police Agency (NPA) had developed before the 1990s. For example, the NPA has organized short-term training courses for small numbers of police officials from other Asian-Pacific states, dealing with drug offenses (since 1962), criminal investigations (since 1975), organized crime (since 1988), police administration (since 1989), and community policing (since 1989) (National Police Agency 1998: 62). Furthermore, Japan also runs regular seminars dealing with criminal justice issues which are attended by officials from other countries. Finally, Japanese experts travel to various countries in the Asia-Pacific to train local law enforcement personnel. These seminars and visits serve the purpose of enhancing the capacity of Asia-Pacific police forces, spreading information and establishing contacts that might be useful in subsequent, ad hoc coordinations of police work across national borders (National Police Agency 1997a: 95–9; Donnelly 1986: 628; Katzenstein 1996: 68–71).

25 The NPA's offensive against the *yakuza* and affiliated groups has not altered the fact that, as long as it respects some rules of the game, organized crime in Japan is a tolerated part of society. Even high officials of the NPA do not expect that their efforts will reduce the important role Japan's organized crime syndicates had come to play by the mid-1990s (Interview 09-99, Tokyo, January 13, 1999).

26 Since the beginning of the 1980s, three to four bilateral meetings a year, most importantly with police officials from Hong Kong, the United States and China, have offered a useful informal venue for focusing on concrete cases, such as the smuggling of illegal immigrants.

27 Interviews 09-99 and 10-99, Tokyo, January 13, 1999.

28 Interview 04-00, Tokyo, January 12, 2000.

29 Interview 06-99, Tokyo, January 13, 1999.

30 Interview 06-99, Tokyo, January 13, 1999.

31 In 1998, the NPA organized its 36th seminar for middle-level officials, with the two-week time divided equally between formal meetings and informal socializing and sightseeing. U.S. law enforcement officials attend these meetings as observers, paying their own expenses, making presentations and occasionally joining the informal parts of the program (Interview 06-99, Tokyo, January 13, 1999).

32 Interview 06-99, Tokyo, January 13, 1999.

33 From a figure close to zero in 1990, by 1997 the number of arrests of illegal entrants had increased to 1,360, most of them Chinese. According to police estimates, this is less than a quarter of the total number of illegal entrants (Ishii 1998). Chinese crime syndicates charge about $35,000 for a successful transfer, with payment to be made in China. Furthermore, by overstaying in Japan about 271,000 foreigners are in violation of visa laws (Interview 10-99, Tokyo, January 13, 1999; Keisatsucho 1999: 17).

34 These meetings were followed by ministerial-level exchanges between the Chair of the National Public Safety Commission of Japan, Home Affairs Minister Mitsuhiro Uesugi, and the Chief of the Public Security Department of China, Jia Chuwang, in May 1998, and exchanges between Keizo Obuchi and Jiang Zemin who discussed transnational crime during their November 1998 summit

meeting (Interviews 09-99 and 10-99, Tokyo, January 13, 1999; National Police Agency n.d.). In August 1999, Jia visited Japan and discussed transnational crime with Obuchi. This was the first time a chief of the Public Security Department visited Japan (*Asahi Shimbun*, August 27, 1999, 12th edn). The following month Uesugi's successor, Takeshi Noda, met Jia in Beijing, and discussed, among other things, drug crimes and people smuggling (*Asahi Evening News*, September 15, 1999).

35 Interviews 08-99 and 10-99, Tokyo, January 13, 1999.

36 Interview 10-99, Tokyo, January 13, 1999.

37 Interview 07-99, Tokyo, January 13, 1999. Because terrorism is a direct threat to the state, it has been an important item of the G7/G8 since the mid-1990s, as the agendas of recent summit meetings in Ottawa (December 1995), Sharm-el-Sheik (March 1996), Paris (July 1996), Denver (June 1997), and Cologne (1999) indicate.

38 It runs two types of annual meetings in Tokyo. Funded by the Japan International Cooperation Agency (JICA), since 1995 the NPA has hosted an annual two-week seminar on antiterrorism attended by one or two high- and middle-level police officials from ten to fifteen states of the Asia-Pacific and other regions. And since 1993 the NPA has also organized more intensive, smaller seminars attended by two or three officials from three to five countries. In these seminars the Japanese government provides technical assistance on counterterrorism to developing countries (Interview 07-99, Tokyo, January 13, 1999; Keisatsucho 1999: 231).

39 Interview 07-99, Tokyo, January 13, 1999. It complements the activities of seven metropolitan and prefectural assault teams, with about 200 members, set up in 1996. Since 1997 their activity has been centrally coordinated by the NPA. These teams are being sent abroad for training (*Daily Yomiuri*, August 13, 1997; *Japan Times*, August 30, 1997).

40 Interviews 06-99 and 10-99, Tokyo, January 13, 1999.

41 Since 1994, Track One and Track Two multilateral meetings have been listed regularly (*Dialogue Monitor* 1995–8; *Dialogue and Research Monitor* 1999). The annual number of Track One meetings has varied between a high of 19 in 1999 and a low of 11 in 1998. Corresponding figures for Track Two meetings have fallen between a high of 93 in 1994 and a low of 47 in 1997. In addition there have been additional meetings (varying between a high of 31 in 1996 and a low of 12 in 1998) that do not fit the normal requirements of Track One or Two meetings. These data were kindly provided to us by Professor Brian Job (July 13, 2000). How to count the number of different tracks is a matter of some disagreement among participants and observers. The line separating different tracks is blurred by the fact that government officials often attend Track Two meetings in their private capacity, thus modifying the "private" character of these meetings. This does not necessarily mean that officials are totally free to talk. Discussions are constrained by prior policies and by the information that is prepared prior to the meetings themselves. But, since no verbatim minutes are kept, none of the individuals who participate in the discussion can be assigned any direct responsibility. While there is no formal debriefing by the JDA, the knowledge that individual officials gain is added informally to the information base that the JDA has at its disposal and that can be analyzed for almost any purpose (Interview 13-00, Tokyo, January 14, 2000).

42 Interview 04-00, Tokyo, January 12, 2000.

43 Interview 01-00, Tokyo, January 11, 2000. Track Two institutions thus tend to support rather than undermine the state. There are instances where we should think of them not as nongovernmental organizations (NGOs) but as governmentally organized NGOs (GONGOs). In many states in the Asia-Pacific, the divide between public and private is easily bridged. Prominent businessmen and

scholars, nominally in the private sector, are often linked informally to politicians and bureaucrats whose attendance at Track Two meetings in their "private" capacity is polite fiction. Hence the choice between the multilateralism of different tracks can be a matter of political convenience for states (Stone 1997: 9–19). But both the nature of private-sector participants and the pattern of influence between such participants and their governments vary widely.

44 Interview 02-00, Tokyo, January 11, 2000.

45 Interview 02-00, Tokyo, January 11, 2000.

46 In the absence of the spread of a shared sense of community in all parts of the Asia-Pacific, some officials (at least in the Japanese government) remain skeptical of moving beyond Confidence and Security Building Measures (CSBMs) as do a number of other Asia-Pacific countries, including China (Interviews 11-00 and 13-00, Tokyo, January 14, 2000; Interviews 01-98, 02-98 and 03-98, Beijing, June 15, 1998).

47 Interviews 04-99 and 12-99, Tokyo, January 12 and 14, 1999.

48 Interview 11-99, Tokyo, January 14, 1999.

49 It brings together senior government officials every eight months. The second meeting in May 1994 and the seventh meeting in December 1997 were both held in Tokyo (Boeicho 1999: 193; Fukushima 1999b: 34–5, 43; *Gaiko Forum* 1999: 155). Japan co-chairs NEACD's Study Project on Defense Information Sharing (Fukushima 1999b: 35).

50 The first meeting in February 1994 and the sixth meeting in December 1998 were both held in Tokyo. The forum was originally proposed by Japan. From MOFA the director of the Security Policy Division in the Comprehensive Foreign Policy Bureau is the senior official attending meetings of both the NEACD and the forum (Boeicho 1999: 192–3; Jo 1998b: 4; *Gaiko Forum* 1999: 155; Interview 7-00, Tokyo, January 13, 2000).

51 Interview 04-00, Tokyo, January 12, 2000.

52 National committees and international working groups are common to both. Besides ASEAN members, Australia, Canada, Japan, South Korea, United States, China and others have also joined CSCAP. Rather than as members of a national delegation, Taiwanese participants attend in their personal capacity the sessions of the five working groups on maritime cooperation, security issues in the North Pacific, confidence- and security-building measures, comprehensive security and transnational crime. With Japan co-chairing together with Canada this particular committee, in 1995 and 1997, the North Pacific Working Group held two of its initial three meetings in Tokyo (Cossa 1999: 16; Fukushima 1999a: 131, 154–7; 1999b: 33). The eighth meeting of CSCAP's steering committee was also held in Tokyo in December 1997 (*Gaiko Forum* 1999: 155).

53 The prospect of an increasing number of Track Three meetings would change the picture further.

54 Interviews 03-00, Tokyo, January 11, 1999; 03-98, Beijing, June 15, 1998; and 06-00, Beijing, June 14, 2000. Although reluctant to let China be tied down in any regional arrangement, some parts of the research and advisory community surrounding China's foreign policy bureaucracy have become increasingly convinced of the advantages that multilateral arrangements hold forth for the pursuit of Chinese interests (Johnston and Evans 1999; Interviews 01-98, 02-98, 03-98, 04-98, 07-98, 08-98, 09-98, Beijing, June 15–16, 20–2, 1998). China, however, remains strongly opposed to having multilateral institutions such as the ARF or The Asia–Europe Meeting (ASEM) discuss any controversial territorial or political issues such as the Spratly Islands or Taiwan (Interviews 03-98, Beijing, June 15, 1998; 02-00, Tokyo, January 11, 2000; and 01-00, Beijing, June 13, 2000).

55 Interviews 03-98, 05-98, 06-98, 08-98 and 03-00, Beijing, June 15, 19 and 21, 1998, and June 13, 2000.
56 Interviews 02-00, 03-00, 08-00 and 11-00, Tokyo, January 11 and 13, 2000.
57 Interview 10-00, Tokyo, January 14, 2000.
58 The first uniformed Japanese official attended the seminar in 1993.
59 Japan's Air Self-Defense Forces have participated in the conference since its first meeting in 1989 (Defense Agency 1998: 177).
60 The Ground Self-Defense Forces have been participating in the seminar since its 17th meeting in 1993 (Defense Agency 1998: 176).
61 Interview 10-00, Tokyo, January 14, 2000. The intersessional working group in which the JDA has been most involved, however, was dealing with disaster relief and thus was staffed by several Asia-Pacific states by officials from, among others, their construction ministries. This was such a profound source of irritation for the JDA that it set up the Forum for Defense Authorities in the Asia-Pacific Region. Although not formally affiliated with the ARF, the membership of this Track One meeting is nearly identical with that of the ARF. Since 1996 it has met annually with member states typically sending representatives at the director-general and deputy director-general level (Boeicho 1999: 422; Defense Agency 1998: 372; *Gaiko Forum* 1999: 156; Interview 11-00, Tokyo, January 14, 2000).
62 In the ministerial and senior officials meetings the foreign affairs officials do all the talking. The same applies to ASEAN countries, whose defense officials never talk at meetings at various levels while, as a matter of principle, the JDA representative will talk at least once during the one-and-a-half-day meeting of intersessional working groups. In the last set of talks, which Japan hosted in Tokyo in October 1999, an unofficial lunch only for defense officials was scheduled, to compensate for the silence defense officials endured. In the future, the JDA hopes this will become a permanent innovation at the intersessional working-group-level talks (Interview 13-00, Tokyo, January 14, 2000).
63 Interview 08-00, Tokyo, January 13, 2000.
64 On a humanitarian aid mission covered by the 1992 law, and under the auspices of the United Nations High Commissioner for Refugees, Sadako Ogata, the main contingent of a 150-member Air Self-Defense Force (ASDF) team left Japan in late November 1999 with relief for East Timorese refugees settled in West Timor camps.
65 In fact Japan funded 95 percent of the cost of the operation, with Portugal contributing an additional $5 million and Switzerland $0.5 million; this display of European tightfistedness contrasts sharply with Japan's substantial ($240 million) support for the peacekeeping operation in Kosovo (Interview 03-99, Tokyo, January 11, 1999).
66 Interview 07-99, Tokyo, January 13, 1999.
67 Attempting to build more cooperative international police relations to suppress the smuggling of narcotics, after consultations with the DEA, the NPA has begun since 1996 to host annually two meetings in Tokyo. Each meeting involves about 40–50 high-level police officials, one with China in attendance, the other with Taiwan. Each of the meetings lasts four days but the official part of the program consists of only a one-day plenary. The rest of the time is spent on group tours of Japanese police facilities, sightseeing and socializing (Interview 06-99, Tokyo, January 13, 1999).
68 For developments in ASEAN and the Asia-Pacific more generally, see Calagan (2000). Some of Japan's overseas development assistance, for example, is channeled to foreign law enforcement agencies dealing with international drug trafficking. And in March 1998 the NPA hosted the fourth meeting of an international conference on combating drugs attended by officials from the ICPO and twenty-six countries (Haraguchi 1999: 36).

69 The meeting was attended by five Southeast Asian-Pacific countries (Laos, Vietnam, Thailand, Burma, and Cambodia), China, officials from the UN and observers from eight countries and the EU (Haraguchi 1999: 30, 36–7; Jo 1999; Masaki 1998).
70 In June 1997, for example, the NPA was instrumental in helping create the "Japan and ASEAN Anti-Terrorism Network." It strengthens cooperative ties among national police agencies, streamlines information-gathering, and coordinates investigation when acts of terrorism occur. Following up on an initiative taken by Prime Minister Hashimoto while traveling through Southeast Asia in January 1997, the NPA and MOFA jointly hosted in October 1997 a Japan–ASEAN Conference on Counterterrorism for senior police and foreign affairs officials from nine ASEAN countries (National Police Agency 1998: 53; Interview 07-99, Tokyo, January 13, 1999). And in October 1998 the NPA and MOFA co-hosted a joint Asian Pacific–Latin American conference on counterterrorism. Based on the findings of the Peruvian hostage crisis, it sought to strengthen international cooperation on antiterrorist measures (Gaimusho 1999: 103–4; Hishinuma 1997; Keisatsucho 1999: 231).
71 The group decided to meet at least once every three months (*Asahi Shimbun*, April 26, 1999, evening 4th edn; Tainaka 2000).
72 Interviews 02-99 and 05-99, Tokyo, January 11–12, 1999.

References

Acharya, Amitav (1990) "A Survey of Military Cooperation Among the ASEAN States: Bilateralism or Alliance?," Occasional Paper No. 14, Toronto: Centre for International and Strategic Studies.

Acharya, Amitav (2000a) "Institutionalism and Balancing in the Asia Pacific Region: ASEAN, U.S. Strategic Frameworks, and the ASEAN Regional Forum."

Acharya, Amitav (2000b) "Regional Institutions and Security Order in Asia," paper prepared for the second workshop, Security Order in the Asia-Pacific, Bali, Indonesia, May 29 to June 2.

Advisory Group on Defense Issues (1994) *The Modality of the Security and Defense Capability of Japan: The Outlook for the 21st Century*, Tokyo (August 12).

Alagappa, Muthiah (ed.) (1998) *Asian Security Practice: Material and Ideational Influences*, Stanford, Calif.: Stanford University Press.

Boeicho (1999) *Boei Hakusho* [Defense White Paper], Tokyo: Okurasho Insatsukyoku.

Boeicho (n.d.) *Shin Boei Taiko* ("*Heisei 8 Nendo iko ni kakaru Boei Keikaku no Taiko*"): *21 Seiki ni mukatte no Waga Kuni no Boeiryoku no Arikata* [*The Current Defense Outline* ("National Defense Program Outline in and after FY1996"): Japan's Defense Capability toward the 21st Century].

Bredow, Wilfried von (1996) "Bilaterale Beziehungen im Netzwerk Regionaler und Globaler Interdependenz," in Karl Kaiser and Joachim Krause (eds) *Deutschlands neue Aussenpolitik*, Vol. 3, *Interessen und Strategien*, pp. 119–125, Munich: R. Oldenbourg.

Calagan, Porfirio A. (2000) "Combating Transnational Crime: The Way Forward," paper prepared for the 14th Asia-Pacific Roundtable, Kuala Lumpur, June 3–7.

Cambone, Stephen A. (1997) "The United States and Theatre Missile Defence in North-East Asia," *Survival*, 39, 3 (Autumn): 66–84.

Cantori, Louis J. and Spiegel, Steven L. (1970) *The International Politics of Regions: A Comparative Approach*, Englewood Cliffs, NJ: Prentice-Hall.

Capie, David H., Evans, Paul M., and Fukushima, Akiko (1998) "Speaking Asian Pacific Security: A Lexicon of English Terms with Chinese and Japanese Translations and a Note on the Japanese Translation," working paper, University of Toronto–York University, Joint Centre for Asia Pacific Studies, Toronto, Canada.

Christensen, Thomas J. (1999) "China, the U.S.–Japan Alliance, and the Security Dilemma in East Asia," *International Security*, 23, 4 (Spring): 49–80.

Cossa, Ralph A. (1997) "U.S.–Japan Security Relations: Separating Fact from Fiction," pp. 31–49 in Ralph A. Cossa (ed.) *Restructuring the U.S.–Japan Alliance: Towards a More Equal Partnership*, Washington, DC: Center for Strategic and International Studies Press.

Cossa, Ralph A. (1999) "U.S. Views Toward Northeast Asia Multilateral Security Cooperation," University of California Institute on Global Conflict and Cooperation, Policy Paper No. 51 (June).

Cox, Robert W. (1997) "Introduction," pp. xv–xxx in Robert W. Cox (ed.) *The New Realism: Perspectives on Multilateralism and World Order*, Tokyo: United Nations University Press.

Cronin, Patrick M. and Green, Michael J. (1994) *Redefining the U.S.–Japan Alliance: Tokyo's National Defense Program*. McNair Paper No. 31, Institute for National Strategic Studies, National Defense University, Washington, DC (November).

Crowell, Todd and Usui, Naoaki (1997) "Japan's Missile Vulnerability," *Japan Quarterly* (April–June): 25–31.

Daase, Christopher (1993) "Regionalisierung der Sicherheitspolitik—Eine Einführung," pp. 67–88 in Christopher Daase, Susanne Feske, Bernhard Moltmann, and Claudia Schmid (eds) *Regionalisierung der Sicherheitspolitik: Tendenzen in den internationalen Beziehungen nach dem Ost-West Konflikt*, Baden-Baden: Nomos.

Daily Yomiuri (1997) "Three ASEAN Countries Agree to Hold Regular Security Talks with Japan," February 4.

Defense Agency (1998) *Defense of Japan 1998*, Tokyo: Japan Times.

Defense Agency (2000) *Defense of Japan 1999*, Tokyo: Japan Times.

Dialogue and Research Monitor, No. 1 (February 1999).

Dialogue Monitor, No. 1 (July 1995).

Dialogue Monitor, No. 2 (January 1996).

Dialogue Monitor, No. 3.

Dialogue Monitor, No. 4.

Dialogue Monitor, No. 5 (March 1998).

Dickie, Mure and Fidler, Stephen (1999) "Taiwan Voices Fears over China's Arms Build-up," *Financial Times*, February 11, p. 1.

Donnelly, Jack (1986) "International Human Rights: A Regime Analysis," *International Organization*, 40, 3 (Summer): 599–642.

Fawcett, Louise (1995) "Regionalism in Historical Perspective," pp. 9–36 in Louise Fawcett and Andrew Hurrell (eds) *Regionalism in World Politics: Regional Organization and International Order*, Oxford: Oxford University Press.

Fawcett, Louise and Hurrell, Andrew (eds) (1995) *Regionalism in World Politics: Regional Organization and International Order*, Oxford: Oxford University Press.

Fishlow, Albert and Haggard, Stephan (1992) *The United States and the Regionalisation of the World Economy*, Paris: Organization for Economic Cooperation and Development.

Flynn, Stephen E. (1998) "Asian Drugs, Crime and Control: Rethinking the War," pp. 18–44 in James Shinn (ed.) *Fires across the Water: Transnational Problems in Asia*, New York: Council on Foreign Relations.

Frankel, Jeffrey A. (1997) *Regional Trading Blocs in the World Economic System*, Washington, DC: Institute for International Economics.

French, Howard W. (2000) "U.S. copters? No, No, No. Not in their Backyard," *New York Times*, January 20, p. A4.

Friman, H. Richard (1991) "The United States, Japan, and the International Drug Trade: Troubled Partnership," *Asian Survey*, 31 (September): 875–90.

Friman, H. Richard (1993) "Awaiting the Tsunami? Japan and the International Drug Trade," *Pacific Review*, 6, 1: 41–50.

Friman, H. Richard (1994) "International Pressures and Domestic Bargains: Regulating Money Laundering in Japan," *Crime, Law and Social Change*, 21 (December): 253–66.

Friman, H. Richard (1996) "*Gaijinhanzai*: Immigrants and Drugs in Contemporary Japan?," *Asian Survey*, 36, 10 (October): 964–77.

Friman, H. Richard (1998) "Snakeheads in the Garden of Eden: Immigrants, Smuggling, and Threats to Social Order in Japan," paper prepared for the University of California Comparative Immigration and Integration Project: Managing Migration in the 21st Century, Fall Workshop, University of California, Davis (October 9–10).

Friman, H. Richard (1999) "International Drug Control Policies: Variations and Effectiveness," unpublished paper, Department of Political Science, Marquette University.

Friman, H. Richard (2000a) "Drugs, Migrants and the Politics of Social Order: The Case of Japan," paper prepared for presentation at the International Studies Association 2000 Convention, Los Angeles, Calif., March 14–18.

Friman, H. Richard (2000b) "Evading the Divine Wind through the Side Door: The Transformation of Chinese Migration to Japan," paper prepared for the Last Decade of Migration from the People's Republic of China to Europe and Asia, Institute for Sociology, Budapest, Hungary (May 26–27).

Fukushima, Akiko (1999a) *Japanese Foreign Policy: The Emerging Logic of Multilateralism*, Basingstoke: Macmillan.

Fukushima, Akiko (1999b) "Japan's Emerging View of Security Multilateralism in Asia," University of California Institute on Global Conflict and Cooperation, Policy Paper No. 51 (June).

Fulford, Benjamin (1995) "Gangsters Linked to Bad-loan Morass," *Nikkei Weekly*, November 27.

Gaiko Forum [Foreign Affairs Forum] (1997) No. 113 (December).

Gaiko Forum (1999) Special Issue (November).

Gaimusho (1999) *Gaiko Seisho* [Foreign Affairs Blue Book 1999], Vol. 1, Tokyo: Okurasho Insatsu-kyoku.

Garrett, Banning and Glaser, Bonnie (1997) "Chinese Apprehensions about Revitalization of the U.S.–Japan Alliance," *Asian Survey*, 37, 4 (April): 383–402.

Green, Michael J. (1997) "Theater Missile Defense and Strategic Relations with the People's Republic of China," pp. 111–18 in Ralph A. Cossa (ed.) *Restructuring the U.S.–Japan Alliance: Towards a More Equal Partnership*, Washington, DC: Center for Strategic and International Studies Press.

Green, Michael J. (1999) "Managing Chinese Power: The View from Japan," pp. 152–75 in Alastair Iain Johnston and Robert S. Ross (eds) *Engaging China: The Management of an Emerging Power*, London: Routledge.

Green, Michael J. and Self, Benjamin L. (1996) "Japan's Changing China Policy:

From Commercial Liberalism to Reluctant Realism," *Survival*, 38, 2 (Summer): 35–58.

Grugel, Jean and Hout, Wil (1999) "Regions, Regionalism, and the South," pp. 3–13 in Jean Grugel and Wil Hout (eds) *Regionalism across the North–South Divide: State Strategies and Globalization*, London/New York: Routledge.

Haraguchi, Jiro (1999) "Yakubutsu taisaku no genjo to kadai" [Current state of and problems concerning drug control], *Keisatsu-gaku Ronshu* [Journal of Police Science], 52, 7 (July): 20–37.

Hildreth, Steven A. and Pagliano, Gary J. (1995) "Theater Missile Defense and Technology Cooperation: Implications for the U.S.–Japan Relationship," *Congressional Research Service*, Library of Congress (August 21).

Hirano, Kazuharu (1998) "Hito no mitsuyu? Kokusai soshiki hanzai no genjo to gaiji keisatsu no taio" [Alien Smuggling? Current State of Transnational Organized Crime and Police Countermeasures], *Keisatsu-gaku Ronshu* [Journal of Police Science], 51, 9 (September): 33–51.

Hishinuma, Takao (1997) "Japan to Propose Antiterrorism Meeting at G-7 Summit," *Daily Yomiuri* (May 9).

Hughes, Christopher W. (1996) "The North Korean Nuclear Crisis and Japanese Security," *Survival*, 38, 2 (Summer): 79–103.

Igarashi, Takeshi and Watanabe, Akio (1997) "Beyond the Defense Guidelines," *Japan Echo*, December, pp. 34–7.

Ina, Hisayoshi (1997) "An Inside Look at the Defense Guidelines Review: Tanaka Hitoshi Interviewed," *Japan Echo*, December, pp. 30–3.

Inoguchi, Takashi (ed.) (2002) *Japan's Asian Policy: Revival and Response*, New York: Palgrave Macmillan.

Institute of Social Science, University of Tokyo (1998) "Okinawa," *Social Science Japan*, 14 (November).

Ishii, Toshinao (1998) "China to Crack Down on Arms, Drugs Smuggling," *Daily Yomiuri* (May 7).

Jo, Toshio (1998a) "Cabinet Approves Bill on Defense?," *Asahi Evening News* (April 28).

Jo, Toshio (1998b) "Call for Japan, U.S., Russia to Conduct Rescue Drills," *Asahi Evening News* (December 10).

Jo, Toshio (1999) "Tokyo Pledges to Finance UN Anti-drug Plan," *Asahi Evening News* (February 3).

Job, Brian L. (2000) "Non-governmental Regional Institutions in the Evolving Asia Pacific Security Order," paper prepared for the Second Workshop on Security Order in the Asia Pacific, Bali, May 30 to June 2.

Johnson, Chalmers (1997) *The Failure of Japanese and American Leadership after the Cold War: The Case of Okinawa*, Woodrow Wilson Center for Scholars, Asia Program, Occasional Paper No. 74 (February 6).

Johnston, Alastair Iain (1999) "The Myth of the ASEAN Way? Explaining the Evolution of the ASEAN Regional Forum," pp. 287–324 in Helga Haftendorn, Robert O. Keohane and Celeste Wallander (eds) *Imperfect Unions: Security Institutions over Time and Space*, Oxford: Oxford University Press.

Johnston, Alastair Iain and Evans, Paul (1999) "China's Engagement with Multilateral Security Institutions," pp. 235–72 in Alastair Iain Johnston and Robert S. Ross (eds) *Engaging China: The Management of an Emerging Power*, London: Routledge.

Johnston, Alastair Iain and Ross, Robert S. (eds) (1999) *Engaging China: The Management of an Emerging Power*, London: Routledge.

Kaplan, David (1996) "Japanese Organized Crime and the Bubble Economy," *Woodrow Wilson Center Asia Program Occasional Paper*, No. 70 (December 13).

Katzenstein, Peter J. (1996) *Cultural Norms and National Security: Police and Military in Postwar Japan*, Ithaca, NY: Cornell University Press.

Katzenstein, Peter J. (1997) "Introduction: Asian Regionalism in Comparative Perspective," pp. 1–44 in Peter J. Katzenstein and Takashi Shiraishi (eds) *Network Power: Japan and Asia*, Ithaca, NY: Cornell University Press.

Kawasaki, Tsuyoshi (1997) "Between Realism and Idealism in Japanese Security Policy: The Case of the ASEAN Regional Forum," *Pacific Review*, 10, 4: 480–503.

Keisatsucho (1999) *Keisatsu Hakusho* [Police White Paper], Tokyo: Okurasho Insatsukyoku.

Keohane, Robert O. (1990) "Multilateralism: An Agenda for Research," *International Journal*, 45, 4 (Autumn): 731–64.

Kristof, Nicholas D. (1999a) "Intruders Turn Tail, and Japan Thrills to Echoes of Its Own Roar?," *New York Times*, March 25, p. A9.

Kristof, Nicholas D. (1999b) "Oh, Those Poor *Yakuza*: Japanese Gangs on Defensive as Chinese Arrive," *International Herald Tribune*, June 18, p. 1.

Kynge, James (1999a) "Beijing Condemns U.S.–Japan Pact," *Financial Times*, June 7, p. 1.

Kynge, James (1999b) "U.S. and China Clash over Missile Shield for Asia," *Financial Times*, March 2, p. 1.

Lake, David A. and Morgan, Patrick M. (1997) "The New Regionalism in Security Affairs," pp. 3–19 in David A. Lake and Patrick Morgan (eds) *Regional Orders: Building Security in a New World*, University Park, Pa.: Pennsylvania State University Press.

Leheny, David (2000) "Watch or Die: Two Rocks and a Hard Place in Japan's Counterterrorism Policies," paper prepared for the 96th Annual Meeting of the American Political Science Association, Washington, DC (August 31 to September 3).

Maeda, Toshi (1999) "SDF Ai Flights Fly Legalistic Tightrope," *Japan Times* (November 24).

Mansfield, Edward D. and Milner, Helen V. (1997) "The Political Economy of Regionalism: An Overview," pp. 1–19 in Edward D. Mansfield and Helen V. Milner (eds) *The Political Economy of Regionalism*, New York: Columbia University Press.

Masaki, Hisane (1998) "Seven Nations to Gang Up against Illegal Stimulant Use," *Japan Times* (December 6).

Midford, Paul (1998) "From Reactive State to Cautious Leader: The Nakayama Proposal, the Miyazawa Doctrine, and Japan's Role in Promoting the Creation of the ASEAN Regional Forum," paper prepared for the Annual Conference of the International Studies Association, Minneapolis, Minn. (March 17–21).

Mochizuki, Mike M. (1997) "A New Bargain for a Stronger Alliance," pp. 5–40 in Mike M. Mochizuki (ed.) *Toward a True Alliance: Restructuring U.S.–Japan Security Relations*, Washington, DC: Brookings Institution Press.

Morgan, Patrick M. (1997) "Regional Security Complexes and Regional Orders," pp. 20–42 in David A. Lake and Patrick Morgan (eds) *Regional Orders: Building Security in a New World*, University Park, Pa.: Pennsylvania State University Press.

National Police Agency (1997a) *White Paper on Police 1997 (Excerpt)*, Tokyo: National Police Agency.

National Police Agency (1997b) "Problem with Foreign Visitors and Counter-measures (January–June 1997)" (August).

National Police Agency, International Cooperation Division, International Affairs Department (1998) *Police of Japan '98*, Tokyo: National Police Agency.

National Police Agency (n.d.) *Identification, Localization and Dissolution of Transnationally Active, Organized Groups of Smugglers*, Tokyo: National Police Agency.

Nye, Joseph S. (1997) "An Engaging China Policy," *Asian Wall Street Journal* (May 14).

Okimoto, Daniel (1998) "The Japan–America Security Alliance: Prospects for the Twenty-first Century," Stanford University, Institute for International Studies, Asia/Pacific Research Center.

Ross, Robert S. (1999) "The Geography of the Peace: East Asia in the Twenty-first Century," *International Security*, 23, 4 (Spring): 81–118.

Ruggie, John (1992) "Multilateralism: The Anatomy of an Institution," *International Organization*, 46, 3 (Summer): 561–98.

Russett, Bruce M. (1967) *International Regions and the International System: A Study in Political Ecology*, Chicago, Ill.: Rand McNally.

Sasaki, Yoshitaka (1997) "Asian Trilateral Security Talks Debut," *Asahi Evening News* (November 7).

Schechter, Michael G. (1999) "International Institutions: Obstacles, Agents or Conduits of Global Structural Change?," pp. 1–28 in Michael G. Schechter (ed.) *Innovation in Multilateralism*, Tokyo: United Nations University Press.

Sewell, James P. (2000) "Congenital Unilateralism in a Multilateralizing World: American Scholarship on International Organization," pp. 1–42 in James P. Sewell (ed.) *Multilateralism in Multinational Perspective: Viewpoints from Different Languages and Literatures*, Tokyo: United Nations University Press.

Shimada, Haruo (1997) "The Significance of the Okinawa Issue: The Experience of the Okinawa Problem Committee," pp. 83–97 in Ralph A. Cossa (ed.) *Restructuring the U.S.–Japan Alliance: Towards a More Equal Partnership*, Washington, DC: Center for Strategic and International Studies Press.

Shinn, James (1998a) "Introduction," pp. 1–17 in James Shinn (ed.) *Fires across the Water: Transnational Problems in Asia*, New York: Council on Foreign Relations.

Shinn, James (1998b) "American Stakes in Asian Problems," pp. 158–74 in James Shinn (ed.) *Fires across the Water: Transnational Problems in Asia*, New York: Council on Foreign Relations.

Simon, Sheldon W. (1998) "Security Prospects in Southeast Asia: Collaborative Efforts and the ASEAN Regional Forum," *Pacific Review*, 11, 2: 195–212.

Sims, Calvin (1999) "U.S. and Japan Agree to Joint Research on Missile Defense," *New York Times*, August 17, p. A4.

Stankiewicz, Michael (1998) "Preface: The Bilateral–Multilateral Context in Northeast Asian Security," *Korean Peninsula Security and the U.S.–Japan Defense Guidelines*, IGCC Policy Paper No. 45, Northeast Asia Cooperation Dialogue VII (October).

Stone, Diane (1997) "Networks, Second Track Diplomacy and Regional Cooperation: The Role of Southeast Asian Think Tanks," paper presented to the 38th Annual International Studies Association Convention, Toronto, Canada (March 22–26).

Tainaka, Masato (2000) "Nations Renew N. Korea Efforts," *Asahi Evening News* (March 31).

Takayama, Hideko (1995) "Tokyo's Dirty Secret: Banks and the Mob," *Newsweek*, December 18, pp. 42–3.

Thompson, William R. (1973) "The Regional Subsystem: A Conceptual Explication and Propositional Inventory," *International Studies Quarterly*, 17, 1: 89–117.

Twining, David T. (1998) *Beyond Multilateralism*, Lanham, Md.: University Press of America.

United States Department of Defense, Office of International Security Affairs (1995) *United States Security Strategy for the East-Asia Pacific Region* (February).

United States Department of Defense, Office of International Security Affairs (1998) *United States Security Strategy for the East Asia-Pacific Region: 1998* (November).

Wada, Jun (1998) "Applying Track Two to China–Japan–U.S. relations," pp. 154–83 in Ryosei Kokubun (ed.) *Challenges for China–Japan–U.S. Cooperation*, Tokyo: Japan Center for International Exchange.

Walker, Tony and Fidler, Stephen (1999) "U.S. Fears on China Missile Build-up," *Financial Times*, February 10, p. 1.

Wang, Jianwei and Wu, Xinbo (1998) *Against Us or with Us? The Chinese Perspective of America's Alliances with Japan and Korea*, Stanford University, Institute for International Studies, Asia/Pacific Research Center (May).

Watanabe, Akio and Ina, Hisayoshi (1998) "Anzen hosho kankyo no henka to nichibei kankei e no inpakuto" [Changes in the security environment and impact on Japan–U.S. relations], pp. 19–38 in Chihiro Hosoya and Tomohito Shinoda (eds) *Shin Jidai no Nichibei Kankei: Partonarshippu o Saiteigi suru* [Japan–U.S. Relations in a New Age: Redefining Partnership], Tokyo: Yuhikaku.

Wiltse, Jeffrey S. (1997) "The 'China Factor' in Japanese Military Modernization for the 21st Century," PhD dissertation, Naval Postgraduate School, Monterey, Calif.

Yamaguchi, Noboru (1997) "Why the U.S. Marines Should Remain in Okinawa: A Military Perspective," pp. 98–110 in Ralph A. Cossa (ed.) *Restructuring the U.S.–Japan Alliance: Towards a More Equal Partnership*, Washington, DC: Center for Strategic and International Studies Press.

6 Immovable object? Japan's security policy in East Asia

H. Richard Friman, Peter J. Katzenstein,
David Leheny, and Nobuo Okawara (2006)

The external and internal security environments confronting Japan are changing. Japan faces new challenges such as missile defense, the spread of weapons of mass destruction, relations with North Korea, and, significantly, the deployment of the Self Defense Forces (SDF) in Iraq, and the broader war on terrorism. Internally, Japan faces an array of challenges to stability and order including illegal immigration and illicit drug trafficking, both of which are becoming more diverse and less amenable to control. Despite challenges to both security environments, Japan's policies have not adjusted evenly. In the post-9/11 world, Japan's external security policies—purportedly the sacrosanct hallmark of postwar Japanese pacifism—appear to have changed more than its internal policies.

On questions of external security, tight constitutional constraints on Japanese military operations abroad and Japan–U.S. defense coordination continue to frame political debates. In this context, the government's support for U.S. activities in the war on terrorism remains highly qualified and contingent. But international events, combined with political and social change in Japan, have undermined the strength of the pacifist side in the domestic struggle over Japan's security. Conservatives have pushed successfully for a larger military role for Japan, in accordance with American requests. The government also has sought to embed itself in a multilateral security framework while remaining fully attuned to domestic political constraints over the terms on which Japan is prepared to engage the world.

Japan's internal security policies remain deeply rooted in notions of a Japanese homogeneity and uniqueness that should be defended in distinctive ways. As noted by William Kelly and Merry White (2006), Japan's social dynamism has been an uneasy fit with prevailing notions of the country's timeless homogeneity and enduring national character, ideological motifs that also mark the political immobilism described by T. J. Pempel (2006). Asia's dramatic social changes have not left Japan unaffected. With the rise in immigration to Japan, the police have been exceptionally keen to clamp down on drug trafficking and the growth of foreign crime syndicates. Officials continue to cling to the image of Japan as a society that, by virtue of its homogeneity, guarantees an exceptional level of safety to its citizens. The image persists even as important domestic institutions, such as the traditional, order-enhancing role of organized crime (*boryokudan*, or, more commonly, the *yakuza*), have sharply diminished in the 1990s, and police links to immigrant communities remain tenuous. Internal security policy thus seems more like a faithful mirror of the public ideology of Japan than of changing social practices that are altering Japanese society.

Operating within the political constraints of Article 9 of its Peace Constitution and shielded for decades from possible external attacks by a security treaty with the United States, the Japanese government is continuing to put close relations with the United States at the center of its broadly conceived security policy. The disintegration of the Japan Socialist Party in the 1990s has given Japan's government political space to adjust to changing external demands that the country play a larger international and regional role, within the constitutional restraints that are always open to continuous reinterpretation. And, since it shies away from any unilateral initiatives on military matters, Japan's government is in general fully supportive of newly emerging multilateral security institutions in Asia.

Counterterrorist policies, especially after the September 11 attacks, illustrate how external and internal security are linked inextricably. Until recently, anticommunism at home and constrained case-by-case efforts marked Japan's counterterrorism policies, and even the 1995 Aum Shinrikyo attack provoked only limited policy and administrative changes, due to resistance by domestic religious organizations and parties. Police and diplomatic efforts that focused primarily on the safety of Japanese from depoliticized overseas threats also reinforced the idea of Japan as a family polity, with a benevolent and protective government willing to step in to protect citizens from a world they did not make and cannot understand. Since 9/11, however, Japanese conservatives have successfully mobilized domestic fears, especially of North Korea, to justify an expanded antiterrorism role alongside the United States. Legitimized by U.S. efforts to remake security as a comprehensive phenomenon, the government has successfully pushed for a more muscular presence overseas while maintaining institutionalized motifs of homogeneity and state responsibility at home to keep at bay fears of a changing region and a changing nation.

In an Asian security environment increasingly marked by porous boundaries between internal and external security, limited change in Japan's external security policy has outpaced changes in Japan's internal security policy. Japanese officials have adopted a comprehensive approach to the country's national and societal security that extends well beyond marshaling the military force necessary to defend against external military threats. The effects of the 9/11 attacks thus have not forced any fundamental rethinking in Japan's security policies. Continuity in policy rather than dramatic policy change marks Japanese security policies both abroad and at home. For most Japanese security policymakers, an ideal Asian security environment would feature atomized nation-states, open to legal trade but with tight controls on migration and trafficking and tied in loose multilateral networks under American security guarantees. While promoting multilateral cooperation in the Asia-Pacific region, however, Japan has taken incremental steps toward expanding the military's international role. Furthermore, Japan's internal security initiatives betray durable though outdated notions of Japanese homogeneity. The government's policy thus is caught between building an Asia that requires a further opening of Japan and maintaining the illusion of a Japan that never really was and never will be.

Japan's societal security policy

Japan's societal security policy has long sought to ensure domestic order by embedding the police in society and relying on the police and, to a lesser extent, other agencies in the enforcement bureaucracy to prevent inroads by foreign threats (Katzenstein 1996). The policy draws heavily on an institutionalized norm of collective identity that links Japan's successes in domestic social order to the country's ethnic homogeneity. The homogeneity myth shapes expectations of how policing can link the state and society in a shared enterprise as well as how Japanese society is able to resist threats to social order that have plagued other advanced industrial countries (Hoshino 1994; Friman 2001). Social and economic changes increasingly pose challenges to the homogeneity myth; but, rather than exploring new paths to social order, the enforcement bureaucracy has redoubled efforts to preserve homogeneity and embed the police in society.

The police have long maintained the image of Japan's social order by isolating minority populations such as the *burakumin* (a lower caste facing continuing discrimination) and permanent foreign residents from Korea and China (Weiner 1997). They have relied on Japanese organized crime groups (the *yakuza*) to facilitate this image by acting as paths for socioeconomic opportunity for marginalized Japanese youth and some minority groups, such as permanent foreign resident Koreans, while curtailing the activities of others (De Vos 1992; Kaplan and Dubro 2003). During the 1990s, revenue shortfalls in the post-bubble economy weakened accommodations between and within the major crime syndicates. The result was a wave of gang violence that spilled over into the broader public sphere and eroded an unspoken public and police tolerance of organized crime. Antigang legislation introduced during the 1990s, the Botaiho (Boryokudan Taisaku Ho, Organized Crime Countermeasures Law), increased state scrutiny of criminal groups, criminalized a range of gang activities, and led to increasingly intrusive law enforcement techniques. Though the impact of the measures should not be overstated, they had the intended effect of decreasing the public profile of organized crime (Friman 1999; Herbert 2000; Kaplan and Dubro 2003; Hill 2003). Combined with the economic downturn, however, the legislation also had unintended effects on illegal immigration and the transnational drug trade into Japan.

During the 1980s, immigration policies and a booming economy had encouraged new waves of legal and illegal migration. Initially Japanese law enforcement officials expressed only limited concern over the potential threats to social order from the new migrants. National Police Agency reports in the early 1980s noted an increase in violations of immigration regulations, work permits, and laws prohibiting prostitution. The reports did not conceptualize this increase as a major threat. In the context of increasingly visible foreign populations and a broader national debate over immigration policy reform during the late 1980s, however, the police position became more strident. The 1987 White Paper on Police (*Keisatsu Hakusho*) prioritized threats posed by Japan's internationalization and explicitly focused on the problems posed by the new foreign workers (Keisatsucho 1987; see also Herbert 1996: 196). This pattern continued during the 1990s, with law enforcement officials often making little distinction in the legality of the migrant status of foreign workers and alleging linkages between the new wave of visiting foreigners (*rainichi gaikokujin*) and organized foreign crime groups. By 2003, the linkage between foreigners and crime had reemerged as part of a broader national politicization of crime as challenge to social order.

The interrelated threats of the transnational drug trade and illegal immigration have received special attention in Japan. Japan has long been a transshipment point for the Southeast Asian drug trade into Europe and the United States. And it is one of several money-laundering centers for transnational crime in Asia (Friman 1996; U.S. Department of State, Bureau For International Narcotics 2003, 2004). Although Japan's domestic drug market is relatively small by international standards, drug trafficking remains an issue of domestic concern. Stimulants, especially methamphetamine, are the primary drugs of choice, while marijuana and hashish, cocaine, heroin, and various psychotropic drugs attract more limited interest. The police, and to a lesser extent narcotics officers of the Ministry of Health, Welfare, and Labor, are responsible for drug enforcement. Due in part to the legacy of extensive police penetration of Japanese society during the 1930s, Japanese enforcement methods have been less intrusive than those found in other advanced industrial countries. Authorities have moved only slowly to introduce undercover operations, paid informants, controlled delivery, money-laundering investigations, and wiretapping (Friman 1996; Katzenstein 1996; *Japan Times*, May 24, 2002; *Japan Today*, November 26, 2002).

The *yakuza* play a dominant role in the transnational drug trade, integrating methamphetamines from Asian suppliers, most recently China, North Korea, the Philippines, and Taiwan, into extensive domestic distribution networks (Friman 1999; U.S. Department of State, Bureau For International Narcotics 2004). Drug distribution networks in stimulants that exclude the *yakuza* are relatively rare. Due in large part to the limited interest of the *yakuza* in extending their networks to dealing in other drugs, external suppliers of narcotics, marijuana and hashish, and psychotropic drugs have made only limited inroads into the Japanese market. This pattern began to shift during the 1990s. Apprehensions of foreigners for drug offenses increased dramatically, especially those involving narcotics and marijuana. However, these patterns partially reflected Japanese law enforcement's refocusing of resources and manpower on foreigners. And they revealed a deep reluctance to use controlled delivery practices to trace drug shipments from point of entry to upper- and middle-level Japanese wholesalers. Still, large-scale, foreign-controlled distribution networks remain relatively rare (Friman 1999, 2004).

Emigration to Japan has been influenced negatively by immigration regulations that restrict access by unskilled workers, especially those of non-Japanese descent, and positively by the pull effects of the economy's growing structural dependence on such labor (Mori 1997; Sellek 2001). Island geography and the relative ease of exploiting inconsistencies in the country's enforcement of visa practices have made overstaying more common than illegal entry with false documents or by clandestine means (Herbert 1996: 43–5; Friman 2003). During the 1980s, migrants exploited tourist visa exemption accords and precollege student visa programs to gain access to the country. Tighter monitoring of these programs by the early 1990s shifted migration to other paths. Chinese snakehead (*jato*) smuggling networks emerged as sources of altered Japanese passports, Taiwanese identity cards, and assistance in identity theft and deception. This last included arranging fake marriages and applications for entry as "war-orphan" spouses or relatives of Japanese stranded in China after 1945 (e.g., *Mainichi Daily News*, December 17, 1997; *Daily Yomiuri*, July 17, 2001; *Japan Today*, August 27, 2002). Through the 1990s, these networks also turned to large-scale migrant smuggling into Japan using fishing boats and cargo ships (Mo 1994; Friman 2001; *Daily Yomiuri*, April 30, 2001).

The police responded to these challenges by adding to, and shifting existing, resources into task forces prioritizing international crime, emphasizing foreign crime in annual and biannual reports, and stressing the foreign crime threat in media and public relations campaigns (Herbert 1996; Friman 2001). The police academy introduced foreign-language training and study tours. Metropolitan police departments turned to a combination of a limited pool of civilian interpreters and digital translators to facilitate basic investigations. The National Police Agency also turned to the selective deployment of police officers abroad for experiential training (Keisatsucho 1999; Friman 2001). These programs were geared primarily toward aiding the police in dealing with foreigners who, disturbingly from the police standpoint, did not follow the idealized Japanese pattern of interaction with authority. The results through the 1990s were uneven at best. Especially missing from these efforts was a systematic exploration of how to build better police ties with new immigrant communities.

The combination of Botaiho and economic pressures also facilitated the fragmentation of illicit drug and migrant trafficking networks. In the case of methamphetamine, the *yakuza* began to move upstream into smuggling while reducing their public profile at home by clandestinely subcontracting retail distribution operations to networks of non-Japanese. Those *yakuza* less well placed in dominant drug distribution networks also began to expand into the smuggling and distribution of marijuana and synthetic drugs (Friman 1999; Kaplan and Dubro 2003; Friman 2004). Long active in the smuggling and trafficking of women for the Japanese sex industry, the *yakuza* also began to diversify into the issuing of illegal work permits and the smuggling of male migrant labor. Drawing on new ties with *yakuza* organizations, Chinese smuggling networks began to offer package deals for transportation, employment, and accommodation in Japan (Friman 2001, 2003).

Although not so well acknowledged by the police, the intersection of diversification, syndicate infighting, and *yakuza* efforts to avoid greater public scrutiny also began to erode the ability of Japanese organized crime to help regulate public order. Operating on a smaller scale and better able to prey on new migrant communities, groups of mainland Chinese and other foreigners soon began to displace the *yakuza* from protection, gambling, and prostitution rackets in major entertainment districts. Faced with what appeared to be reckless threats and acts of violence from Chinese gangs, and already under public scrutiny, the *yakuza* began to retreat from these traditional strongholds. Highly publicized police crackdowns in areas such as Tokyo's Kabukicho district led some Chinese to leave Japan, others to move out of Tokyo into other Japanese cities, and still others to temporarily lie low as the *yakuza* sought to reinsert themselves into the vacuum. This pattern was repeated several times into the new millennium (Mo 1998; Friman 1999; *Mainichi Daily News*, August 21, 2001; *Japan Times*, February 3, 2002, October 27, 2002; Kaplan and Dubro 2003).

By 2003, a combination of crime rates rising to postwar highs and arrest rates falling to postwar lows focused public and political attention on the erosion of social order. Facing public scrutiny, police officials sought to explain crime and arrest patterns as stemming from increasing juvenile, organized, and foreign crime, and a police force lacking the necessary resources to facilitate order. Organized foreign crime, however, soon emerged as the primary threat in official discourse, and the need for the protection of homogeneity and the increased embedding of the police in Japanese society as the primary solutions (Keisatsucho 2003; Reynolds 2003). In August 2003, the National Police Agency (NPA) announced that it would be adding 10,000 new police officers by 2006 to restore public safety, on top of an additional 10,000 officers already scheduled for 2002–4 (*Asahi Shimbun*, August 27, 2003). The same month Tokyo Governor Ishihara Shintaro announced the formation of a new security task force headed by Tokyo's vice-governor for security, the former NPA and noted Hiroshima Police official Takehana Yutaka. By September, Ishihara was pledging to deploy Tokyo police and immigration authorities to seven area prefectures to help decrease crime by foreigners (Utsunomiya 2003a, 2003b).

Foreign crime emerged as a central theme in the September 2003 the Liberal Democratic Party (LDP) presidential elections and the national parliamentary elections the following month. Leading candidates in both emphasized the need for a stronger stand on crime, especially foreign crime (Reynolds 2003; *Japan Today*, September 20, 2003). In the Japanese National Diet campaign, top LDP officials blanketed the media with the party's pledge to address the threat of foreign crime. Justice Minister Nozawa Daizo pledged to make Japan safe again so that "women and children can walk alone on the streets at night," through the introduction of new law enforcement measures, additional prisons, and biometric identifiers in foreign passports to curtail illegal immigration (Matsubara 2003; *Japan Times*, September 20, 2003). By December 2003, the Tokyo Metropolitan Government had begun to act on a provision in the LDP party platform, announcing new joint task forces with the Ministry of Justice's Immigration Bureau intended to "halve the number of illegal residents in Tokyo in five years" (*Japan Today*, December 30, 2003). The Ministry of Justice also announced tighter regulations on residency permits for Chinese students seeking to study in Japan and the introduction of profiling measures aimed at identifying likely illegal foreigners (*Mainichi Daily News*, December 4, 2003; *Asahi Shimbun*, March 8, 2004). The NPA announced a major institutional reorganization through amendment of the Police Law in 2004 that would "integrate divisions that focus exclusively on crime syndicates, foreigners, drugs and guns" (*Daily Yomiuri*, December 23, 2003). Amid the politicized uproar and anecdotal evidence of rising foreign criminal activity, little attention was focused on the relatively small amount of crime committed by foreigners as a percentage of overall crime, potential flaws in statistics on crimes by foreigners, and the rather limited and declining numbers of illegal immigrants.

It is unsurprising in this domestic context that the international response of Japanese law enforcement to societal security challenges also has reflected an emphasis on preserving homogeneity as the path to societal security. In general, the Japanese government has sought international assistance to impede the entry of persons posing potential threats while deflecting foreign pressure for more extensive cooperation that could lead to potential interference in the Japanese approach. On drug control issues, Japanese compliance with U.S. requests for greater formal cooperation, especially at the enforcement level, traditionally has been slow (Friman 1996). Japanese authorities have sought to extend bilateral ties with drug source countries, especially those in Northeast and Southeast Asia. These ties have consisted of occasional government missions, temporary deployment of Japanese enforcement personnel abroad, and limited steps toward cooperative law enforcement. More commonly they have entailed training programs for foreign law enforcement personnel in Japanese policing methods. Japan's multilateral drug control efforts include participation in major United Nations drug control treaties as well as task forces and conferences, including those organized under the auspices of the UN, G8, OECD, Interpol, and the ASEAN Regional Forum. The gap between such Japanese participation and implementation of treaty and task force provisions in practice remains, however, in bilateral as well as multilateral relations (Friman 1996; U.S. Department of State, Bureau for International Narcotics 2004).

On illegal immigration issues, Japan has turned to bilateral efforts primarily with migration source countries in Asia. Deliberations over visa exemption accords and student visa programs, and to a lesser extent lax entertainment visa programs, initially distinguished these negotiations. By the mid-1990s, bilateral negotiations were focused on China. In an attempt to curtail incidence of large-scale migrant smuggling, in March 1997 a Japanese delegation of enforcement and Foreign Ministry officials met with Chinese counterparts in Beijing and Shanghai. In 1998, Japanese and Chinese officials completed negotiations on a framework agreement of cooperation that included provisions for the deployment of Japanese police officials to Beijing, Fuzhou, Guangzhou, and Shanghai (*Japan Times*, March 2, 1997, March 20, 1997; *Daily Yomiuri*, May 7, 1998). More recent cooperation has focused on efforts to track down Chinese perpetrators of violence in Japan (*Japan Times*, September 21, 2003; *Japan Today*, October 2, 2003). Though solutions do lie in coordinated efforts of source and host countries, the bilateral efforts with China illustrate a broader pattern of Japanese authorities failing to adequately address the domestic dynamics that influence illegal immigration (*Japan Today*, June 6, 2002). In brief, Japan's policy has been aimed at enhancing its societal security, bilaterally where it can and multilaterally where it must.

Japan's counterterrorism policies before September 11, 2001

Because Japan, like many other advanced industrial nations, has largely treated terrorism as a law enforcement rather than military or political issue, it is unsurprising that the country's pre-2001 counterterrorism programs would resemble its approach to crime. By working within unyielding political constraints and a conceptual frame emphasizing a safe, conservative core for Japanese society, the police have shifted from isolating and expelling citizens with radical leftist leaning toward the careful management of such domestic threats as new religious movements. Without a clear sense of how best to deal with the threat of international terrorism, police and diplomats have traditionally operated on a case-by-case basis. Although they have tried to adhere to international conventions on terrorism, they have been more concerned with maintaining some flexibility so as to save Japanese lives in specific terrorist incidents. The consistent notion here has been that Japan's unruly elements could be expelled or controlled, thereby creating a safe and untroubled social core for Japanese security; foreign terrorist threats were, as much as possible, seen as uncoordinated, nearly random examples of a dangerous and chaotic world from which Japan required protection.

Throughout the 1970s, the Japanese government found itself plagued by uncoordinated but coinciding threats that left the impression of a nation under siege. Organized in the late 1960s and early 1970s, the Japanese Red Army (JRA) became one of the world's more fearsome terrorist organizations, its small size notwithstanding. In the 1970s, JRA operatives massacred twenty-four people at Lod Airport in Tel Aviv, following it with airplane hijackings that netted the group large ransoms from the Japanese government; it even tried to take over the U.S. embassy in Kuala Lumpur. In the face of heavy pressure from international police organizations, JRA members were largely forced to stay in a small number of countries (North Korea, Syria-controlled Lebanon, Libya) willing to give them cover, but during the 1980s the bulk of Japanese counterterrorism policy focused on the group.

During the JRA's exile, a homegrown crisis developed, as the Japanese government sought to use farmland in Chiba Prefecture to build a new airport. It inspired an odd but surprisingly durable alliance between conservative farmers and radical students convinced that the government's efforts were directed at helping the U.S. prosecute the war in Vietnam. The government tried for years to remove the farmers from their land, by force if necessary. The standoff has ultimately ended only because of the old age of the remaining farmers and because of intensely unfavorable press associated with some of the government's early strong-arm tactics. The situation endured as a tense fact of life in Narita rather than as a full-fledged insurgency or crackdown. Even occasional bombings of the homes of government bureaucrats associated with the plan did not lead the police to react with overwhelming force against the farmers (Keisatsucho 1988: 7–85; see also Apter and Sawa 1986).

Japan's police have been able to take advantage of their community relations —perhaps best symbolized by the *koban* (police box) system—to monitor the development of antigovernment organizations with violent capabilities in postwar Japan. Of critical importance was the antisystemic bent of the leftist groups, whose motives were seen as more threatening than those of violent right-wing organizations. Though constrained in part by constitutional protections of civil liberties and by restrictions on the use of force, the Japanese government has occasionally been able to pull off extraordinary shows of force, including the massive search of apartments in Tokyo along the parade route for the funeral of the Showa Emperor in 1989 (Katzenstein 1996).

Partly because of its experience during the tumultuous 1960s and 1970s, the NPA focused nearly exclusively on leftist radical movements, a strategy whose limitations became painfully apparent in 1995 when the government suffered a massive intelligence failure culminating in Aum Shinrikyo's sarin gas attack on Tokyo's Kasumigaseki subway station. This millenarian cult had, in the process of building a fanatical base around its leader, Asahara Shoko, apparently been involved in a 1989 murder of a Japanese lawyer and a "test case" sarin gas attack in Matsumoto in 1994. They are also suspected of attempted attacks with botulinum toxin, anthrax, and VX gas, in addition to various and sundry cases of extortion, murder, and possibly even the 1995 shooting of NPA chief Kunimatsu Takaji. Moreover, by 1995 the cult had global assets in excess of $1 billion, operated more than thirty branches in six countries, and claimed 50,000 members worldwide. The resourceful cult used its connections, especially those in Russia, to build significant chemical and biological weapons capabilities, acquire an attack helicopter, and even get a model for an AK-74 assault weapon, which it may have been readying for mass production (Sansoucy 1998: 3–4, 11–16, 19, 27; Miyasaka 2001: 1, 78). Even without direct evidence of its various crimes, the police might have been expected to find it worrisome that a large, rich religious cult with millenarian overtones and end-of-the-world fantasies might have counted among its members so many science graduates of Japan's top universities.

Since 1945 the taboo against police interference in the affairs of religious sects has run very deep in Japan. While the police were well attuned to the activities of left-wing radicals in the 1970s and 1980s, they were less concerned with the potential criminal activities of religious organizations. Aum Shinrikyo is one of 1,500 religious organizations officially recognized by the government between 1984 and 1993. These sects fill the political space left vacant when Shintoism disappeared as the conservative state religion after 1945. Once granted recognition, these groups have generally enjoyed numerous privileges, tax exemptions, and de facto immunity from any form of political oversight (Sansoucy 1998: 17–23). Resistance to government interference in religion has been institutionalized largely through the emergence of the political party Komeito (from 1998 New Komeito, Clean Government Party), tightly linked to the Soka Gakkai, a "new religious movement" that claims 12 million members. Although the Soka Gakkai and other optimistic, life-affirming offshoots of Buddhism and Shintoism shared little ideologically with the "new-new religions"—usually called *karuto* (cults) in Japanese— Komeito's determined efforts to protect the financial and political privileges of its parent religion have likewise made it easier for groups such as Aum to escape scrutiny (Hardacre 2003).

The Aum attack was therefore a massive intelligence failure steeped deeply in politics. Although there was ample evidence, and despite numerous complaints about the cult, the Japanese police "studiously avoided investigating Aum" (Steinhoff 1996: 17). The Public Security Intelligence Agency, responsible for investigations connected with the Anti-Subversive Activities Law, had almost invariably focused on left-wing movements, and had virtually no experience with surveillance of religious groups; before the 1995 attack, it had virtually no information on Aum (Hardacre 2003: 148–9). Although the group's attacks revealed it to be heavily antistate in its goals, its status as a religious movement and its distance from traditional left-wing groups had shielded it from the government scrutiny that almost certainly would have shut down a similarly destructive communist organization.

When prosecutors drew up charges against the offenders, they chose to treat the attacks as individual murders and assaults rather than invoking Articles 77 (carrying out civil war) and 78 (preparing for civil war) of the Japanese Criminal Code. The prosecution thus sidestepped investigating the group's extensive transnational links, especially with Russia (Miyawaki 2001: 2–3). While in the opposition, Komeito had been unable to prevent revision of the Religious Corporations Law, which required religious groups to provide the government with more information about group activities and finances; in theory, this afforded the government the means to pursue organizations suspected of criminal activity. Indeed, the LDP had forced through the revisions in part to link Komeito with Aum and thereby discredit the opposition (Hardacre 2003: 146–8). But, if politics makes for strange bedfellows, Japan's political promiscuity in the past decade has been truly remarkable. Komeito has been a member of the LDP-led ruling coalition since 1999, and it has apparently enforced some restraint on the creation of new post-Aum laws. The most important piece of legislation, passed in late 1999, has been the Law to Control Organizations That Have Committed Acts of Indiscriminate Mass Murder. Though written as a law ostensibly providing the authority to investigate "all" such organizations, the law's convoluted title and the surrounding politics make it clear that this was a law designed specifically to permit government scrutiny of Aum (now renamed Aleph)— and of virtually no other Japanese organizations.

After the Aum attack, what has struck many observers is the tepidness and the slow pace of the government's response. This was in agreement with the Japanese public's view of Aum as a bizarre religious cult with no clear political objectives and little likelihood of a repetition of its terrorist attacks with weapons of mass destruction (Japan Society 2001: 21; Miyasaka 2001: 76). The LDP government tried to strengthen the counterterrorist capabilities of the police by revising the basic legislation governing the National Police Agency and by adding new laws facilitating the detection of future terrorist attacks. Yet the opposition, which was rooted in a deep mistrust of the potential abuse of executive authority, prevented any comprehensive measures against suspicious organizations. With the support of the Japan Federation of Bar Associations, human rights activists and the mass media argued against the invocation of the Anti-Subversive Activities Law, and Aum was permitted to survive as a religious organization (Mullins 1997; Miyasaka 2001: 69, 77; Pangi 2003: 40).

In fact, most of the government's responses should be categorized not as "counterterrorism" but rather as the more politically neutral "crisis management." Coming shortly after the Kobe earthquake, in which the Japanese government manifestly failed to act quickly enough to save at least some of the more than 6,000 people who perished in the quake (Pekkanen 2000), and in the midst of embarrassing financial débâcles that it seemed powerless to prevent, Aum Shinrikyo's attack seemed to be more evidence that the Japanese government was incapable of dealing with crises. Critics seemed preoccupied with the roots of Japan's crisis management problems, whether in the murky soil of the Japanese national character or the banal haze of organizational culture (Sassa 1997: 183–5).

Responsibility for crisis management was lodged in the Cabinet Office for National Security Affairs. A subsequently enacted radical administrative reform program makes it virtually impossible to gauge how and in what agency Japan's crisis management policy might be conducted in the future (Itabashi, Ogawara, and Leheny 2002). Even where the NPA, for example, succeeded in developing new capabilities, it has found itself unable to make much use of them. After the Aum attack, the NPA cooperated with prefectural police to create *tokushu butai* ("special units," but generally known by the acronym SATs, for Special Assault Teams) designed to handle terrorist crises such as hijackings. Although the NPA took the opportunity to announce the creation of the SATs in a white paper written in the midst of the Peru crisis, when the Japanese ambassador's house was occupied for four months by Tupac Amaru members, the connection was tenuous; no one suggested that the SATs should have taken part in a rescue effort (Keisatsucho 1997). Not even Japan's hawks have seriously proposed that SATs should be allowed to operate in overseas crises. Instead, they tend to save their political capital for the promotion of larger-ticket military items for Japan's national defense.

If the Japanese government's counterterrorism efforts at home have been marked by tightly focused investigations on specific and publicly acknowledged threats, overseas they reflect a case-by-case approach that does not focus on specific movements but on protecting the lives of Japanese citizens in specific incidents. Keenly aware of the difficulty of preventing attacks before they occur or of handling crises with the use of force, Japanese policymakers have become extraordinarily sensitive about their inability to protect Japanese citizens. Japan publicly maintains a "no concessions to terrorists" policy in accordance with international conventions, but the Japanese government has found itself with the reputation as a bargainer. To be fair, the most visible instance of Japan's willingness to negotiate with terrorist groups—its payment of $6 million to the JRA to end a 1977 hijacking in Bangladesh—took place before international conventions proscribed deals. But Japanese newspapers reported in 1997 that the Japanese government paid a ransom of between $2 million and $5 million to the Islamic Movement of Uzbekistan to release several Japanese aid workers taken hostage in Kyrgyzstan (Leheny 2001–2). The government's decision to work nonstop for the release of the hostages reveals a little-discussed component of Japan's counterterrorism policy: whether correctly or incorrectly, Japanese policymakers believe that the political costs of allowing hostages to die would be unacceptably high.

This approach was, until recently, further reinforced by the structure of Japanese counterterrorism policymaking in the Ministry of Foreign Affairs (MOFA). Unlike the United States, where the Office of the Coordinator for Counterterrorism operates as an independent section within the State Department, the Japanese counterpart organization was nested in the Consular and Migration Affairs Department—the division chiefly responsible for the protection of Japanese citizens overseas. Although known in English as the Anti-Terrorism Office, the Japanese title—Hojin Tokubetsu Taisakushitsu—is better translated as "The Office for Special Measures for Our Citizens Overseas." With the NPA able to play only a limited role in counterterrorism overseas due to stringent restrictions on the exercise of police or military force outside of Japan's borders, the Consular and Migration Affairs Department was the primary actor in Japan's overseas counterterrorism efforts.

Hamstrung by constitutional and normative constraints, however, MOFA's office pushed as much as possible the idea that Japanese had to take better care of themselves overseas because the Japanese government might be unable to do so. MOFA's offices helped to publicize several *kaigai anzen animeshon bideo* (overseas safety animation videos) that depict the world as a menacing place, especially to the trusting and therefore vulnerable Japanese. These videos, made by the Council for Public Policy—an NPA-affiliated think-tank—feature a rich variety of themes. The humorous *Sakusen Kodo Tokyo* (Battle Code Tokyo) follows a Japanese man who has been kidnapped and tricked into believing that he is in Tokyo, when he is in fact in a cheap facsimile made by foreign spies. The facsimile fails because the foreigners are simply unable to make it safe enough to keep the man (and, apparently, his kidnapped predecessors) from being killed on roads and beaches that, unlike the real Tokyo, are actually unsafe. A more dramatic video, *Kidnap*, follows the efforts of a Japanese salaryman overseas to rescue his boss, who has been taken captive by terrorists. The message is clear: the Japanese state makes the Japanese secure at home, but the world is not Japan. Paradoxically, of course, it is the state's responsibility to make Japanese aware of its inability to protect them overseas.

The impact of 9/11

Judging by the Japanese government's rhetoric, al Qaeda's September 11 strikes on New York and Washington changed everything. Japan was firmly on the side of the United States in the war on terror, and Foreign Minister Kawaguchi Yoriko argued that Japan would need to make changes in its laws to align its policies with those of the United States and Great Britain. In December 2001, MOFA added a new counterterrorism organization, the International Counterterrorism Cooperation Office, within the Foreign Policy Bureau. Its members complement the staff still in the Hojin Tokubetsu Taisakushitsu, but they now have responsibility for promoting Japan's counterterrorism work with the United States, the G8, the United Nations, and other states.[1] Although the Diet was slower than Prime Minister Koizumi in promising Japanese support for the U.S. campaign against the Taliban and al Qaeda in Afghanistan, it ultimately responded with the Anti-terrorism Special Measures Law. This law was not an effort to engage in counterterrorism *per se*, but rather to support American activities in this specific instance. The law does little, if anything, however, to prepare either the government or the public for the possibility that the war on terror may have implications for Japanese interests, especially in Southeast Asia (Leheny 2001–2).

Some of the government's other "counterterrorism" initiatives may have longer-term security implications, and they have been built on Japanese concerns over more proximate threats, such as Chinese criminals and North Korean spies, rather than a barely understood specter called al Qaeda. Long haunted by the concerns over clear North Korean violation of Japanese waters for drug smuggling, espionage, and, most disturbingly, kidnapping Japanese citizens, the LDP used the opportunity posed by 9/11 to link a revision of the Japan Coast Guard's governing law to the overall threat of terrorism (Maeda 2002: 187–8; Shinoda 2002). In so doing, it essentially loosened restrictions on the Coast Guard's use of force against the euphemistically named "unknown vessels" (*fushinsen*) constantly violating Japanese territorial waters. Not two months later, in December 2001, Japanese Coast Guard vessels surrounded and fired on a presumed North Korean spy boat, which then exploded and sank, presumably because of a self-destruction mechanism. Although the incident actually ended in China's economic zone (Valencia and Ji 2002: 724), rather than Japan's, criticism at home was muted largely because of the increasing visibility of numerous North Korean menaces.

Japanese security specialists argued that Japan's support of U.S. counterterrorism permitted Japanese actions overseas, a bizarre mismatch with the government's inability to use the SDF effectively at home in the event of an invasion or similar incursion. In the words of one of Japan's leading specialists on international relations, Akihiko Tanaka, "We have laws for when there is a crisis in the region, and now we will probably have a law when there is a crisis far overseas. But the laws for when Japan is attacked are inadequate" (Harney 2001: 2). In the spring of 2002 the Cabinet also approved a package of three bills addressing the eventuality of an armed attack on the home islands of Japan (Nabeshima 2002). The unexpected admission by Kim Jong-Il, during a state visit by Koizumi to Pyongyang, that agents of his government had kidnapped fifteen Japanese, and that a majority of them had died while working as language teachers to North Korean spies, had by this time left little doubt in the minds of many Japanese about where the threat lay. When a March 2002 poll by Central Research Services (Chuo Chosasha) inquired about threats to Japan, the four most popular answers—"terrorism," weapons of mass destruction attacks, overseas guerillas (specifically including those onboard "suspicious boats"), and missile attacks—were all clearly or arguably tied to North Korea (MOFA 2002b).

The most important of the three bills defined more precisely the responses that would be permitted in the eventuality of a direct attack. The other two bills amended the Self-Defense Forces Law and the law governing the Security Council of Japan. At issue, politically, was not preparation for the most acute of Japan's security threats, North Korean spy ships (already covered by the Coast Guard law revision) and missile or terror attacks. Although the government's interpretation of Article 9 clearly recognizes Japan's right to use military force in the face of an external attack, thereby allowing the emergency legislation, critics saw the legislative package as a Trojan horse designed to chip away even further at constitutional restrictions. With many legislators quietly uneasy in the governing coalition and vociferously critical in the opposition, the government made no attempt to push the bills through the Diet in 2002. In May 2003 the governing coalition accepted some of the amendments to the main bill proposed by the Democratic Party of Japan (DJP), the largest opposition party in the Diet. They included a government commitment to maximum respect for the constitutional rights of citizens in countering any armed attack and giving the Diet the power to terminate the military operations covered by the bill. Compromise effected, all three bills passed the lower house in May and the upper house in June 2003, with the support in each house coming from over 80 percent of the members. Prime Minister Koizumi thus successfully instituted an emergency security law, something that was not feasible when his father, Junichiro Koizumi, headed the Defense Agency in the 1960s (Samuels 2003).

For military matters, the post-September 11 security environment became an opportunity for the LDP to achieve policies it had long wanted to pursue but believed to be impossible. Using the demands of an attacked and enraged ally as a foot in the door, and then relying on widespread public fears of a dangerously unbalanced neighbor, the government took steps that had long been planned. Rather than using the issue of terrorism to reassess societal security, however, Japanese authorities remained focused on foreigners and eroding homogeneity and the challenges posed by organized crime. By late 2002, the authorities had made explicit their view that terrorism was inextricably linked to transnational drug trafficking, illegal migration, and North Korea (*Asahi Shimbun*, December 7, 2002; *Japan Today*, September 27, 2002, November 18, 2002, December 6, 2002). Police expansion and NPA reorganization, as well as NPA and Ministry of Justice calls for prison and detention-house expansion, were the solutions enacted to the challenges to homogeneity (*Daily Yomiuri*, August 27, 2001; *Japan Times*, July 24, 2002). Former NPA official Sassa Atsuyuki neatly captures the prevailing police mood in a 2004 article in the influential opinion monthly *Chuo Koron*. Japan is unprepared for international terrorism, he argues, because there were too many restrictions placed on the government by liberals who have ignored the need for public safety. What Japan needs, therefore, is a much larger police force that can ensure that police boxes are always staffed, that people can be appropriately searched at public locations, and that special attention be paid to Arabs and Muslims. He admits that this requires racial discrimination but calls it *sezaru o enai* (unavoidable) (Sassa 2004: 89). In effect, terrorism becomes one more in a larger constellation of threats for which the prescription is always the same: more police, larger budgets, and, where possible, fewer restrictions on investigations.

Some of the NPA's activities reflect direct pressure from the United States as well as the provisions of UN conventions on terrorism. Japan has signed on to, and begun to implement, new international conventions on suppressing terrorism and curtailing the financing of terrorist organizations. Following Prime Minister Koizumi's announcement of a seven-point antiterrorism plan in September 2001, President George Bush noted with appreciation Japanese measures to "strengthen international cooperation in sharing information and immigration control" (U.S. Department of State 2001; MOFA 2002a). To date, Japan has frozen the assets of terrorist organizations and has tried to align its money-laundering laws with the international convention on the financing of terrorism. The government also ordered its embassies and consulates to be more assiduous in screening visa applicants, doubled the number of visa and immigration trainees (MOFA 2002a), and even exchanged customs officials as part of a Container Security Initiative designed to protect the United States from the smuggling of terrorist weapons via container vessels (*Japan Today*, September 26, 2002). Japan also has joined the United States in six-party talks with North Korea on nuclear threats and in broader multilateral cooperation as part of the 2003 Madrid Initiative aimed at curtailing North Korean weapons of mass destruction as well as drug and currency smuggling (Kim 2003; Kralev 2003; Nabeshima 2004). The most visible evidence of this cooperation has been Japan's large-scale monitoring and inspection of North Korean ships entering Japanese ports (*Asahi Shimbun*, June 2, 2003; *Japan Times*, August 26, 2003).

On occasion, however, Japanese policy had resisted as much as accommodated the demands of the United States, illustrated here by the longstanding negotiations over concluding the Mutual Legal Assistance Treaty (MLAT). Such treaties allow for direct communication and cooperation between law enforcement authorities rather than requiring them to work through diplomatic channels. Initial negotiations had proved time consuming, with some observers speculating that the Japanese government was loath to allow direct U.S. intervention in Japanese investigations (*Japan Times*, August 24, 2002, October 22, 2002; U.S. Department of State 2002). While delaying on the MLAT, the Japanese government took incremental steps to protect the Japanese from foreign criminals and drugs. Finally, facing heavy and consistent pressure from the United States, the Japanese government concluded the MLAT negotiations and signed the treaty in August 2003, stipulating that it was aimed primarily at terrorism and crimes involving the Internet (*Yomiuri Shimbun*, June 20, 2003). U.S. government interpretations of the MLAT, however, appear to be much broader than those held by Japan, suggesting that the pattern of Japanese resistance and accommodation will continue (U.S. Department of Justice 2003).

Observers have frequently commented on the constitutional and political constraints on Japan's security stance, but have been far slower to notice the comprehensiveness of Japanese policies. In the aftermath of September 11, Japan now faces a world more attuned to the interrelationship between internal and external security, as well as a changing region replete with myriad dangers for citizens and policymakers alike to ponder. Changes in the international environment have complemented political and social transformations in Japan. Yet, in the post-9/11 world, Japan's external and internal security policies appear to be shifting unevenly.

The blueprint for a more assertive Japan has existed for decades, especially since the Nakasone years in the 1980s. Though deeply controversial, hopes that the Self-Defense Forces would be given an expanded international role have animated political debate, especially since the end of the Cold War, and with the atrophy of the traditional Japanese left, there are fewer brakes than ever before on government action. In contrast, the constraints on internal security policy change are as much intellectual as they are political. The only way to deal fully with the challenges of the transnational drug trade, illegal immigration, and terrorism is to acknowledge that security is not served by seeking to re-create Japan as a hermetically sealed, homogenous nation. Put simply, there is no blueprint in Japan for looking beyond the defense of homogeneity as the path to internal security.

Ideally, a Japanized security environment in Asia would consist of atomized, independent nation-states, all cooperative, economically open but physically distinct, and able to trust in one another's good intentions. By promoting multilateral cooperation, the Japanese government has sought to mitigate domestic and Asian concerns over the iron-clad U.S.–Japan alliance, which it sees as the ultimate guarantor of Japanese security. In the post-9/11 world, security specialists around the globe are grappling with what a U.S.-led war on terror means for different regions and for the world in general. For the Japanese government, it provides an opportunity to harness wider and more comprehensive national fears over security, using them to justify a more assertive international stance. But the government shows few signs of peering too closely at what rapid social and regional transformation will likely mean over the long term. Staring into the abyss of the changes might reveal something about Japan's future that the government would rather not see.

Note

1   Interview, March 2004.

References

Apter, David and Sawa, Nagayo Sawa (1986) *Against the State: Politics and Social Protest in Japan*, Cambridge, Mass.: Harvard University Press.

Asahi Shimbun (2002) "Spy Ship, Drug Smuggling Boat 'One and the Same' ," December 7.

Asahi Shimbun (2003) "Tight Inspections for N. Korean Ship," June 2.

Asahi Shimbun (2003) "NPA to Bulk Up, Target Gangs," August 27.

Asahi Shimbun (2004) "Screening Cuts Chinese Student Numbers," March 8.

Daily Yomiuri (1998) "China to Crack Down on Arms, Drug Smuggling," May 7.

Daily Yomiuri (2001) "Smuggling of People Doubles since January," April 30.

Daily Yomiuri (2001) "Arrests Made over Marriage Scam," July 17.

Daily Yomiuri (2001) "NPA Unveils Plan to Increase Officers by 10,000 in 3 Years," August 27.

Daily Yomiuri (2003) "NPA Plans Steps against Terrorists Gangs," December 23.

De Vos, George A. (1992) *Social Cohesion and Alienation: Minorities in the United States and Japan*, Boulder, Colo.: Westview.

Friman, H. Richard (1996) *NarcoDiplomacy: Exporting the U.S. War on Drugs*, Ithaca, NY: Cornell University Press.

Friman, H. Richard (1999) "Obstructing Markets: Organized Crime Networks and Drug Control in Japan," pp. 173–97 in H. R. Friman and P. Andreas (eds), *The Illicit Global Economy and State Power*, Boulder, Colo.: Rowman & Littlefield.

Friman, H. Richard (2001) "Immigrant Smuggling and Threats to Social Order in Japan," pp. 294–317 in D. Kyle and R. Koslowsky (eds) *Global Human Smuggling: Comparative Perspectives*, Baltimore, Md.: Johns Hopkins University Press.

Friman, H. Richard (2003) "Evading the Divine Wind through the Side Door: The Transformation of Chinese Migration to Japan," pp. 9–33 in P. Nyri and I. R. Saveliev (eds) *Globalizing Chinese Migration: Trends in Europe and Asia*, Aldershot/Burlington, Vt.: Ashgate Press.

Friman, H. Richard (2004) "The Great Escape? Globalization and Immigrant Entrepreneurship in the Criminal Economy," *Review of International Political Economy*, 11, 1: 98–131.

Hardacre, Helen (2003) "After Aum: Religion and Civil Society in Japan," pp. 135–53 in F. J. Schwartz and S. Pharr (eds) *The State of Civil Society in Japan*, Cambridge: Cambridge University Press.

Harney, Alexandra (2001) "Japan Drafts Law to Allow Its Military to Operate Overseas," *Financial Times*, October 17: 2.

Herbert, Wolfgang (1996) *Foreign Workers and Law Enforcement in Japan*, London/New York: Kegan Paul.

Herbert, Wolfgang (2000) "The Yakuza and the Law," pp. 143–58 in J. S. Eades, T. Gill and H. Befu (eds) *Globalization and Social Change in Contemporary Japan*, Melbourne: Trans Pacific Press.

Hill, Peter (2003) *The Japanese Mafia: Yakuza, Law and the State*, Oxford: Oxford University Press.

Hoshino, Kanehiro (1994) *Organized Crime and Its Origins in Japan*, National Research Institute of Police Science.

Itabashi, Isao, Ogawara, Masamichi with Leheny, David (2002) "Japan," pp. 337–73 in Y. Alexander (ed.) *Countering Terrorism: Strategies of Ten Nations*, Ann Arbor, Mich.: University of Michigan Press.

Japan Society, the National Institute for Research Advancement (Tokyo), and the Research Institute for Peace and Security (Tokyo) (2001) "New Approaches to U.S.– Japan Security Cooperation: Conference Report," pp. 11–37 in M. Green (ed.) *New Approaches to U.S.–Japan Security Cooperation: Terrorism Prevention and Preparedness*, New York: Japan Society.

Japan Times (1997) "China Pushed on Illegal Entry," March 2.

Japan Times (1997) "China to Curb Illegal Immigrants," March 20.

Japan Times (2002) "Shinjuku's Boom–Bust Underground Economy," February 3.

Japan Times (2002) "Drug Ring Bugged," May 24.

Japan Times (2002) "Nation at Crime and Punishment Crossroad," July 24.

Japan Times (2002) "Osaka Seminar Clarifies Provision of UN Crime Convention," August 24.

Japan Times (2002) "U.S. Urges Signing of Bilateral Treaty for Exchanging Crime Information," October 22.

Japan Times (2002) "Chinese, Japanese Clash in 'Mafia Town' ," October 27.

Japan Times (2003) "Show of Force Greets North Korean Ferry," August 26.

Japan Times (2003) "Two Held in China over Fukuoka Killings," September 21.

Japan Times (2003) "The Zeit Geist: Time to Come Clean on Foreign Crime Wave," October 7.

Japan Today (2002) "U.S. Presses Japan to Crack Down on Human Trafficking," June 6.

Japan Today (2002) "Police Bust Counterfeit Passport Ring," August 27.

Japan Today (2002) "Japan, U.S. to Block Weapons Smuggling," September 26.

Japan Today (2002) "Drug Smuggling to Be on Japan–N. Korea Agenda," September 27.

Japan Today (2002) "Japan Suspects N. Korea Abducted 70–80 More Japanese," November 18.

Japan Today (2002) "Police Arrest Iranians in Undercover Drug Sting," November 26.

Japan Today (2002) "Ship Smuggled $2.5 Bil from Japan to North Korea," December 6.

Japan Today (2003) "PM: Influx of Foreign Workers Will Cause Security Problems," September 20.

Japan Today (2003) "Police Start Probe in China on Fukuoka Family Murder," October 2.

Japan Today (2003) "Two Hundred Officers to Crack Down on Illegal Residents," December 30.

Kaplan, David E. and Dubro, Alec (2003) *Yakuza: Japan's Criminal Underworld*, Berkeley, Calif.: University of California Press.

Katzenstein, Peter J. (1996) *Cultural Norms and National Security: Police and Military in Postwar Japan*, Ithaca, NY: Cornell University Press.

Keisatsucho (1987) *Keisatsu Hakusho* [White Paper on Police], Tokyo: Zaimusho Insatsu-kyoku.

Keisatsucho (1988) *Keisatsu Hakusho* [White Paper on Police], Tokyo: Zaimusho Insatsu-kyoku.

Keisatsucho (1997) *Keisatsu Hakusho* [White Paper on Police], Tokyo: Zaimusho Insatsu-kyoku.

Keisatsucho (1999) *Keisatsu Hakusho* [White Paper on Police], Tokyo: Zaimusho Insatsu-kyoku.

Keisatsucho (2003) *Keisatsu Hakusho* [White Paper on Police], Tokyo: Zaimusho Insatsu-kyoku.

Kelly, William W. and White, Merry I. (2006) "Students, Slackers, Singles, Seniors, and Strangers: Transforming a Family-Nation," pp. 63–82 in P. J. Katzenstein and T. Shiraishi (eds) *The Dynamics of East Asian Regionalism*, Ithaca, NY: Cornell University Press.

Kim, Ah Young (2003) "End North Korea's Drug Trade Addiction," *Japan Times Online*, June 26, <http://www.japantimes.co.jp>.

Kralev, Nicholas (2003) "U.S. Seeks Asian Aid for Ship Searches," *The Washington Times*, June 18, A1.

Leheny, David (2001–2) "Tokyo Confronts Terror," *Policy Review*, 110 (December/ January): 37–47.

Maeda, Tetsuo (2002) "Kaijo Hoancho Ho no kaitei to ryoiki keibi" [Territorial Security and the Revision of the Japanese Coast Guard Law], pp. 184–200 in Y. Toshihiro (ed.) *Yuji hosei wo kento suru* [Investigating the Emergency Laws], Tokyo: Horitsubunkasha.

Mahathir, Mohamad and Ishihara, Shintaro (1995) *The Voice of Asia: Two Leaders Discuss the Coming Century*, Tokyo: Kodansha International.

Mainichi Daily News (1997) "Osaka Authorities to Crack Down on Fake Chinese 'War Orphans' ," December 17.

Mainichi Daily News (2001) "Gang Boss Gunned Down as Yakuza War Escalates," August 21.

Mainichi Daily News (2003) "Japan Denies 90% of Chinese Students Resident Permits," December 4.

Matsubara, Hiroshi (2003) "Justice Minister Pledges to Make Japan 'Safe Again,' Tighten Border Controls," *Japan Times Online*, September 28, <http://www.japantimes.co.jp>.

Miyasaka, Naofumi (2001) "Terrorism and Antiterrorism in Japan: Aum Shinrikyo and After," pp. 67–81 in M. Green (ed.) *Terrorism Prevention and Preparedness: New Approaches to U.S.–Japan Security Cooperation*, New York: Japan Society.

Miyawaki, Raisuke (2001) "Lessons in Fighting Terrorism: American and Japanese Perspective [sic]," remarks prepared for the Global Security Roundtable, Japan Society, New York, November 7.

Mo, Bangfu (1994) *Jato: Suneku Heddo* [Snakehead], Tokyo: Shinsho Bunko.

Mo, Bangfu (1998) "The Rise of the Chinese Mafia in Japan," *Japan Echo* 25, 1 (February): 44–7; translation of "Kyuzosuru Zainichi Chugokukjin Mafia no Hanzai," *Sekai* (November 1997): 240–7.

MOFA (2002a) *Japanese Report on Implementation of the APEC Leaders' Statement on Counter-Terrorism*, <http://www.mofa.go.jp>.

MOFA (2002b) *Anzen hosho ni kan suru yoron chosa* [Opinion Poll on National Security], reported on MOFA website, <http://www.mofa.go.jp/mofaj/gaiko/ah_chosa/index.html>.

Mollman, Steve (2001) "No Fly Zones," *Asiaweek*, November 30.

Mori, Hiromi (1997) *Immigration Policy and Foreign Workers in Japan*, New York: St Martin's Press.

Mullins, Mark R. (1997) "The Political and Legal Response to Aum-Related Violence in Japan: A Review Article," *The Japan Christian Review* (Tokyo), 63: 37–46.

Nabeshima, Keizo (2002) "Defense Bill Only a First Step," *Japan Times Online*, April 22, <http://www.japantimes.co.jp>.

Nabeshima, Keizo (2004) "Northeast Asian Safety Valve," *Japan Times Online*, March 8, <http://www.japantimes.co.jp>.

Pangi, Robyn (2003) "Consequence Management in the 1995 Sarin Attacks on the Japanese Subway System," *BCSIA Discussion Papers 2002–4*, EDSP Discussion Paper ESDP-2002–01, John F. Kennedy School of Government, Harvard University, February.

Pekkanen, Robert (2000) "Japan's New Politics? The Case of the NPO Law," *Journal of Japanese Studies*, 26, 1: 111–43.

Pempel, T. J. (2006) "A Decade of Political Torpor: When Political Logic Trumps Economic Rationality," pp. 37–62 in P. J. Katzenstein and T. Shiraishi (eds) *The Dynamics of East Asian Regionalism*, Ithaca, NY: Cornell University Press.

Reynolds, Isabel (2003) "Japan's Politicians Turn to Crime—to Win Votes," Reuters, October 27.

Samuels, Richard J. (2003) "Gunning for Reform," *Time* (Asia), September 22.

Sansoucy, Lisa (1998) "Aum Shinrikyo and the Japanese State," unpublished paper, Government Department, Cornell University (March 13).

Sassa, Atsuyuki (1997) *Kiki kanri* [Crisis Management], Tokyo: Gyosei.

Sassa, Atsuyuki (2004) "Chian wo keishi shitekita tsuke wo ima harawasareteiru" [We Are Now Paying the Price for Having Neglected Public Order], *Chuo Koron* 119, 2 (February): 86–91.

Sellek, Yoko (2001) *Migrant Labor in Japan*, Basingstoke/New York: Palgrave Macmillan.

Shinoda, Tomihito (2002) "Japan's Response to Terrorism and Implications for the Taiwan Straits Issue," *Japan–Taiwan Security Forum*, January 22, <http://taiwansecurity.org/TS/2002/JTRF-Shinoda-0102.htm>.

Steinhoff, Patricia G. (1996) "From Dangerous Thoughts to Dangerous Gas: A Frame Analysis of the Control of Social Movements in Japan," paper presented at the American Sociological Association Meetings, New York, August 16–20.

United States Department of Justice (2003) "United States–Japan Mutual Legal Assistance Treaty Signed to Enhance Law Enforcement Cooperation," *Department of Justice Press Release #443* (August 5), <http://www.usdoj.gov>.

United States Department of State, Bureau for International Narcotics and Law Enforcement Affairs (Annual) *International Narcotics Control Strategy Report*, Washington, DC, <http://www.state.gov/g/inl/rls/nrcrpt/>.

United States Department of State (1991) "Text of Joint Ministerial Press Conference, Third APEC Ministerial Meeting as released by the U.S. Department of State, Office of the Assistant Secretary/Spokesman, Shilla Hotel, Seoul, Korea," *Federal News Service*, November 14.

United States Department of State (2001) "U.S. Welcomes Japan's Anti-Terrorism Assistance Package," <http://usinfo.state.gov>.

United States Department of State (2002) "Japan Seeks Greater Law Enforcement Cooperation," U.S. Embassy Transcript, October 22, <http://usembassy.state.gov/tokyo/>.

Utsunomiya, Yuji (2003a) "Tokyo Sets Up Security Force," *Japan Times Online*, August 2, <http://www.japantimes.co.jp>.

Utsunomiya, Yuji (2003b) "More Police, Immigration Officers Sought," *Japan Times Online*, September 23, <http://www.japantimes.co.jp>.

Valencia, Mark J. and Ji, Guoxing (2002) "The 'North Korean Ship' and U.S. Spy Plane Incidents: Similarities, Differences, and Lessons Learned," *Asian Survey*, 42, 5 (September/October): 723–32.

Weiner, Michael (ed.) (1997) *Japan's Minorities: The Illusion of Homogeneity*, London/New York: Routledge.

Yomiuri Shimbun (2003) "Nichibei de sosa kyojo joyaku, natsu ni mo teiketsu" [U.S.–Japan MLAT Expected to Be Completed This Summer], June 20.

Part II

Japanese and Asian security in comparative perspective

7 Coping with terrorism: norms and internal security in Germany and Japan

Peter J. Katzenstein (1993)[1]

Germany and Japan have been deeply affected by the traumatic defeat they suffered in World War II. Their "Hollandization" (Mueller 1989: 95–6) as a consequence of that war is reflected in the transformation of both countries from the leading challengers in the international state system in the first half of the twentieth century to the leading trading states in the international economy at the onset of the twenty-first century (Rosecrance 1986). Profoundly suspicious of military issues and deeply afraid of being drawn into military engagements, both states have been unable to sidestep security policy altogether. For they have been compelled to defend the state's security inside their borders. In comparison with their practices in the recent past, the physical coercion that these two trading states apply in securing their internal security is very small. Nonetheless, the power of the police in both states has measurably increased during the past two decades. And in both cases that growing police power has moved away from a preoccupation with reacting to the threat of civil war or massive social unrest to focus on generating the social intelligence necessary to prevent the threats that terrorism and violent social protest pose for the state.

Informed by different norms, Germany and Japan have accomplished this task in different ways. The strengthening of state power through changes in legal norms in Germany betrayed a profound fear that terrorism was challenging the core fiber of the state and thus of the social order. Eradicating terrorism and minimizing the effects of violent social protest were tantamount to overcoming the specter of a Hobbesian state of nature. In Japan, the close interaction of social and legal norms revealed a state living symbiotically within its society and not easily shaken in its very foundation. Eliminating terrorism or containing violent social protest was the task of a Grotian community. Conversely, Germany's active involvement in the evolution of international legal norms conveyed a conception of belonging to and participating in an international Grotian community. Japan's lack of concern for the consequences of pushing Japanese terrorists abroad and its generally passive stance were based on a Hobbesian view of the international system.

Germany and Japan have operated under similar international constraints and opportunities provided by the United States' hegemony and its gradual decline. And both have organized their domestic politics for the pursuit of economic prosperity and competitiveness in international markets rather than national grandeur and power in the international state system. But why do these structural similarities fail to account for the differences in the ways Germany and Japan have accomplished such important tasks as defending state security against internal threats?

The answer to this question lies in the fact that most variants of structural analysis take as a given the normative context in which actors define their interests. But structures often embody different norms and thus give different cues as to what actors should do. And in times of change, when structures crumble, these norms acquire particular importance in informing actors about the interests they hold. Should the German army send East German equipment to the Middle East while permitting its air force to fly missions from Turkish airfields, or should Germany be adamant about not participating in the out-of-area engagement of NATO troops? Should Japan send unarmed soldiers to the Mideast, pay a lot of money, or do nothing? The situation was analogous when the social environment of the German and Japanese states changed in the late 1960s in reaction to the Vietnam War, among other things. German and Japanese officials confronted difficult choices. Should large-scale social protest be tolerated? Should it be crushed with a massive display of police or paramilitary force? Or should it be contained through a reorganization and reequipment of national police forces? And was the upsurge of terrorism in Germany and Japan best combated with new or traditional security policies? The answers to these questions were not obvious to either the Germans or the Japanese.

In such situations of uncertainty actors fall back on the worldview they have acquired over time—that is, a mixture of causal and principled beliefs about how the world works, and how one should behave in it. On questions of security policy German and Japanese views have been molded decisively by the memories of the enormous costs of the Nazi regime and Japan's military dictatorship as well as the disastrous loss of World War II. Thus, normative context that informs the interests of actors matters a great deal.

Norms that are institutionalized matter in particular because they more easily find expression in law and culture. Institutionalized norms express a worldview that influences behavior not only directly, by setting standards of appropriateness for behavior, but also indirectly, through selective prefabri-cated links between values that individuals or collectivities habitually rely upon to address specific problems. Institutionalized norms thus are not only a set of preferences or values motivating behavior. And they do not influence behavior merely by prescribing the ends of action. Institutionalized norms affect behavior also indirectly by offering a way of organizing action rather than specifying only the ends of action (Swidler 1986).

Some may call this style of analysis "loosely rationalistic"; others may prefer to call it "loosely culturalist." But this perspective permits us to side-step the weakness that impairs much of the analysis that focuses only on interests. Both interest-driven and norm-driven styles of analysis often assume the ends of action: "rational," individualistic, arbitrary preferences or "irrational," consensual, cultural values. These two perspectives fail to appreciate the normative context of the process by which interests are defined. And they frequently overlook the fact that social or individual action is typically part of an institutionalized repertoire of action. Indeed, the styles or strategies of action are more persistent than the ends that individuals or societies seek to attain. The prefabricated links that institutionalized norms establish are part of a collective consciousness that creates habits of interpretation and repertoires of action (Adler 1987: 11, 15; Rosenau 1986).

Norms do not float freely in social and political space. They are shaped by history and institutions. To most observers the dramatic decline in Germany's and Japan's militarist norms since 1945 is self-evident. The epochal events of the 1930s and 1940s, embodied in institutional structures such as the demilitarization of the police, had significant effects on subsequent policies of internal security. The analysis falls squarely into the historical rather than anthropological mode of political culture studies (Berger 1991: 13–14). Norms work their effects through historically created institutions and experiences; they are not determined solely by such deep social structures as religion and language. And while the norms that help historically evolving national cultures can be studied among larger collectivities rather than small groups, they are not all made out of one piece of cloth. The degree of divergence between legal and social norms, for example, is a matter of some importance.

Domestic and international norms cannot be analyzed only through the study of behavior (Kratochwil and Ruggie 1986; Adler 1988; Ruggie 1988; Tannenwald 1988). Norms reflect unspoken premises. Their importance lies not in being true or false but in being shared. For these premises themselves often create the evidence that confirms their validity. Norms can be violated by behavior; but they cannot be invalidated. They specify rules rather than regularities. Friedrich Kratochwil and John Ruggie insist that shared meanings are the center of any study of norms. We must grasp, by whatever method appears appropriate, how actors interpret themselves and the world. For the norms that inform action emerge in and through the shared interpretations and shared expectations that constitute standards for judging action. Norms offer a context that affects the interest and behavior of actors in complex ways. They cause, guide, and inspire action. What matters is not only the compliance of actors with forces that determine their behavior and thus make it amenable to explanation and prediction. What matters also is the competence of actors to interpret themselves and the world and to share these interpretations with others.

What is true of domestic norms holds also for international norms. Agreement on norms in the international community is achieved either through parallel or converging national legislation or through international treaties. Treaties may directly specify norms that become binding after they have been translated into national legislation. Or, alternatively, they may articulate general principles that inform the process of norm-setting through national legislation without specifying the norm itself. The difference between international and domestic societies lies in the number of people and the density of institutions involved in defining and interpreting norms. In international society that task is reserved to a few scores of scholars of international law whose writings constitute many of the data that provide the basis for the advice they give to their national governments about the evolution of international norms.

We can fruitfully explore the role of norms by looking at the domestic and international politics of Germany's and Japan's policies of internal security. The definition of terrorism is strongly contested politically. There are two basic types of terrorism: individual terrorism and state terrorism. Furthermore, terrorism can be waged by right-wing or left-wing political radicals. Because groups on the radical left were at the center of the concern of the German and Japanese governments on questions of internal security during the last two decades, I shall deal only with acts of terrorism perpetrated by those groups. Among the political elites of Western democracies a shared if imprecise definition of terrorism has emerged during the last two decades. Terrorist acts are crimes designed to affect at least one putative social norm, to attract maximum publicity, and to instill fear. Many terrorist acts violate the rules of war. All of them depend on violence or the threat of violence directed against private or public targets. Terrorists are politically motivated and often work in small groups. Unlike other criminals, they often take credit for their actions while also seeking to conceal their individual identities (Jenkins 1980: 2–3; Gal-Or 1985; Hailbronner 1982; Kittrie 1978; Gibbs 1989).

Terrorism and government response

Terrorism and violent social protest

Although Germany has not been immune to international terrorism, most incidents of terrorist activity have been committed by domestic groups. The Red Army Faction and the Revolutionary Cells on the left and some neo-Nazi groups on the right have targeted prominent politicians and businessmen as well as United States military installations and personnel. Between 1970 and 1979, 649 attacks by left-wing groups killed 31 people and injured 97; 163 other people were seized as hostages. Terrorist groups committed at least thirty bank robberies, which netted millions of Deutschmarks. Between 1980 and 1985 the total number of terrorist acts rose to 1,601 (Horchem 1980: 51; Kolinsky 1988: 61, 73).

Since there are no reliable data on the number of German terrorists, the media always repeat government estimates of about 20 activists, 200 sympathizers who may help with money, cars, or apartments, and a supportive social milieu of about 2,000 to 20,000 people among whom sympathizers and activists are recruited. Compared to the official data on the membership of radical organizations of the left (63,000), of the right (22,000), and among foreigners (117,000), these are small figures (Borgs-Maciejewski 1988: 44–5). Furthermore, terrorist acts pale numerically in comparison with the total annual numbers of estimated criminal acts (10 million), recorded criminal acts (4 million), and suspects investigated by the police (1.5 million). Less than half of the suspects are prosecuted and less than a third of those prosecuted are convicted; only a tiny portion of those convicted are sent to jail (Wehner 1980: 538; Busch *et al.* 1985: 260–9). These aggregate figures reveal how seriously the police and the government take terrorism in Germany. Terrorist acts and violent demonstrations account for about 15,000 crimes against state security, that is, about one-third of 1 percent of all recorded criminal acts. Yet between 5 and 10 percent of all police personnel in Germany are assigned to the state security divisions of the various police forces, excluding a force of about 25,000 that protects Germany's border and acts as a reserve in the case of large-scale public demonstrations (Brand 1989: 142; Gössner 1987).

Like Germany, Japan has experienced a spate of terrorism and violent social protest during the last three decades that has originated from within its own society. But, in contrast to the German Red Army Faction, Japan's Red Army, after a brief period of operation at home in the late 1960s and early 1970s, moved abroad. North Korea and the Mideast became staging areas for a series of spectacular and brutal international operations during the next two decades (Steinhoff 1989). At home massive demonstrations against the U.S.–Japan Security Treaty in 1960 and the antiwar movement in the late 1960s as well as the renewal of the treaty in 1970 spawned a number of social movements. Some of them, such as the movement opposing the construction of an airport at Narita, on the outskirts of Tokyo, relied on violence as a symbolic tool as much as a method of self-defense (Apter and Sawa 1984). But other groups, such as Chukaku, mobilized a small cadre of professional militants involved in bombing attacks or the launching of homemade, primitive missiles from apartment houses or cars. The targets of these attacks typically were members of Japan's political and economic establishment, including in recent years the Emperor system. These attacks have occurred in waves over the last two decades. Between 1969 and 1988 the Japanese police reported 236 bombing attacks and 531 guerilla actions (Katzenstein and Tsujinaka 1991: appendix). The international scope of its actions may have earned the Japanese Red Army greater international notoriety than its German namesake. But Japan, with twice the population of Germany, has probably had only half as many incidents of terrorism.

This is not to argue that terrorism and social violence are less important politically in Japan than in Germany. Japan's low overall crime rate, after all, is unique among the advanced industrial countries. Though Germany is a relatively orderly and crime-free society by American standards, Japan's crime rates are lower by a factor of three for murder, four for burglary, six for rape, and thirty-one for robbery. Estimates of the number of militant cadres

operating inside such organizations as Chukaku vary greatly. Four of Japan's
five radical groups and ten of about thirty affiliated sects are prone to violent
or terrorist actions. Estimates provided by various branches of the Japanese
police indicate that the radical left, which in Japan, too, accounts for the bulk
of violence and terrorism, appears to have about 14,000 activists and another
20,000 sympathizers. The number of professional militant cadres in large
organizations such as Chukaku lies in the hundreds. Other militant organizations have many fewer. The Red Army, for example, has about two dozen
cadres abroad and a few hundred sympathizers inside Japan. As in Germany,
the police mobilize a disproportionate number of their forces to deal with
these few radicals. The police's penchant for secrecy is so great that only
rough estimates are possible. While the official number of security police is
probably only about 5,000—that is, about 50 percent fewer than the analogous forces in Germany—the flexible deployment of personnel in Japanese
bureaucracies makes it possible to allocate, on a temporary basis, perhaps up
to one-quarter of Japan's total police force of 240,000 to the issue of internal
security (Katzenstein and Tsujinaka 1991: 8, 25–9, 47–84; Katzenstein
1990: 12–13).

Government policy

In Germany the incidence of terrorism and large-scale social protest reinforced
a modernization and quantitative expansion of the police that was a key part
of the Social Democratic reform program of the 1970s. More important than
the considerable quantitative expansion in personnel and financial resources
were the qualitative improvements and the change in the basic mission of the
police. The guiding image was no longer a state of emergency caused by civil
war and insurrection incited by East German infiltrators. Instead the line
separating normality and emergency became blurred. In trying to anticipate
possible threats to state security, the police changed from reacting to social
developments to trying to prevent them from arising in the first place.
Improved methods of collecting, storing, and using information were seen as
the most promising approach to dealing with the terrorist threat even at the
cost of what liberal democrats charged was a serious loss of civil liberties.

New forms of police investigation have come to supplement traditional
police work. "Computer matching" (*Rasterfahndung*) was developed in the
1970s to combat terrorism. In the hope of making police work more efficient
and effective, large numbers of data were scanned to identify overlapping
clusters of what were considered to be suspicious traits of target populations.
In the 1970s the police got access to the files of utility companies, for example,
and thus could identify those customers who paid their bills in cash or
through third parties. This group of potential suspects was narrowed further
through checks with data on residence registration (which is compulsory in
Germany), automobile registration, receipt of social security or child-care
payments, and the like. The names that remained on the list were potential

terrorist suspects: they were young and single, were not registered, had no automobiles, and paid their bills in cash. Traditional police searches then focused on this target group. If, in addition, these suspects lived in large apartment buildings with underground garages and exits that were unrestricted even during rush hour, they were put under police surveillance, especially if they had changed their locks as soon as they moved in, received little or no mail, insisted on having a telephone installed right away, paid their rent in cash in advance, and kept their curtains closed even during the day (Brand 1989: 69; *Bürgerrechtt und Polizei* 1980: 16–21; Flaherty 1989: 73). "Preventive" and "intelligent" police work in the name of internal security was thus informed by abstract social categories that the police had defined, rather than concrete evidence that a suspect had been involved in specific terrorist acts.

The home-grown high-tech approach to problems of internal security was complemented by an activist stance that favored international policy coordination to contain the threat of terrorism in Germany. A policy statement from the mid-1980s articulates the position of the German government very clearly: a liberal sharing of information to facilitate a preventive search of international terrorists by national police forces; far-reaching agreements on police cooperation across national borders; simplification of intergovernmental judicial assistance in general and of extradition in particular; and harmonization of national legislation in areas pertaining to antiterrorist policy. The German government has displayed its activist stance wherever it could in multilateral arenas, among others in the United Nations; at the economic summit meetings; in Interpol; in the Schengen Agreement, recently concluded among some members of the European Community; and in the Working Group for Combating Terrorism, convened within the framework of European political cooperation.

Perhaps most far-reaching during the last fifteen years has been the international coordination of antiterrorist policies under the auspices of the key intergovernmental system of cooperation, TREVI (Terrorism, Radicalism, Extremism, Violence, International). A standing conference of the ministers of interior and justice of the member states of the European Community (EC), TREVI is not a part of the European Community, probably because it wants to avoid parliamentary oversight. But the ministers meet, often on the same day, both under the auspices of TREVI and in their capacity as members of the Council of Ministers of Interior of the EC. TREVI was the result of what was largely a German initiative in 1975, at the height of one of the terrorist waves in Germany. TREVI and its various working groups provide not only for regular high-level contacts but also for regular, institutionalized cooperation in the area of practical police work affecting antiterrorist policy (Katzenstein 1990: 23–7, 52–3).

TREVI and the other multilateral arrangements provide arenas that facilitate the intense bilateral contacts that tie the German police to their partner organizations in other European states. These contacts often involve the sharing of intelligence information and the furthering of professional contacts with the police forces of other states, including an exchange program of police officers with France. More important, they facilitate cooperation of the police at the local level, in particular in border areas, which has become quite extensive after a 1987 administrative agreement concluded between Germany and France.

In sharp contrast to the high-tech image that Japanese industry has projected during the last two decades, the Japanese police have relied primarily on their traditionally close relations with the public in their efforts to defend Japan's internal security. The access to society that the German police apparently sought in the computer in the 1970s has always been available to the Japanese police through numerous organizations that link them to civil society. The local police station (*koban*) has always served as an instrument of surveillance. Annual house calls by policemen are still standard and are designed to elicit regular and detailed information on individual citizens. Such innovations as massive searches of apartment complexes and the creation or extension of myriads of other police support organizations with a combined total of millions of individual contact points have provided the Japanese police with rich sources of information that the German police, lacking such an osmotic relation with society, have sought to gain through high technology. The Japanese police strategy appears less like the proclaimed German shift from reactive to preventive policing than as an adaptation and extension of a social surveillance system that was already in place.

The Japanese approach was very successful in the early 1970s. Whereas successive generations of the Red Army Faction have operated inside Germany, the Japanese police succeeded in pushing the Japanese Red Army offshore within a couple of years. In the 1970s it was said that Japan was good at exporting TV sets and terrorists. Yet these methods have not had much effect in containing the attacks staged by the militant cadres of such organizations as Chukaku. When radicals hold down steady white-collar jobs, do not participate in any political activities, and lead apparently normal lives, as these militant cadres do, it is almost impossible to track them down.

Japan has taken a much less activist stance than Germany in the international dimensions of its policy of internal security. The apparent shift from an accommodating policy toward terrorist demands in the 1970s to an unyielding one in the 1980s has not yet been tested seriously; to date the Japanese government has been spared the agonizing choices that the Red Army posed in the 1970s. But during the last decade the rhetoric of internationalism has increased on questions of internal security, as on most other important issues the government has faced. But translating this general political commitment to international policy coordination into concrete initiatives has been an excruciatingly difficult process for the Japanese. The convening of the Conference on Security Matters for the Asia-Pacific Region in June 1988, under the auspices of the National Police Agency (NPA), is a case in point. It was the first such high-level meeting that the NPA had convened since 1945 and thus it represented a watershed in the postwar history of Japan's policy of internal security. But at the conclusion of the meeting several governments were simply unwilling to sign the final communiqué.

Furthermore, in contrast to Europe, Asia has no indigenous legal framework that might offer the kind of multilateral forum that Japan is interested in creating. With its residue of Chinese, French, German, and American legal traditions, Japan is living side by side in Asia with India and the Philippines, for example, which are shaped by the legacy of the English and the American judicial and police systems. Weak as it is for reasons of geographic isolation, the operative police cooperation that ties Japan to other countries thus is restricted to bilateral relations in particular crisis situations. Confronted with explicit threats from the Red Army and other extremist groups, Korea and Japan, for example, cooperated, for the first time since 1973–4, in making the security preparations for the Seoul Olympic Games of 1988. And with the exception of its relations with the United States, in contrast to Germany and most other continental European states, Japan deals with the issue of extradition not on the basis of treaties but on the basis of reciprocity.

Domestic norms and internal security policy

Germany

The norms characterizing Germany's domestic policy of internal security are centered on the idea of the lawful state (*Rechtsstaat*). It is the central concept that informs the self-understanding of the police, the elite civil servants, and the politicians as they deal with questions of terrorism. The lawful state is an abstraction that is not based on any substantive rule of law. It is the state, not social norms or moral values, that is the foundation for Germany's legal norms (Cowen 1986: 31–3; Finn 1989: 346). The concept of the state is "imbued with connotations of 'right' and 'law' which logically as well as normatively precede any particular type of regime such as democracy or authoritarianism" (Katzenstein 1987: 383). The police do not simply enforce the law. In the words of the Police Administrative Law of 1931, the police are the business of the state. "In effect, the police emanate from the state, not from the people, in philosophy as well as in practice" (Fairchild 1988: 121). The state thus transcends the role of mere enforcer of a set of rules. The power of the state is legally controlled, but in the interest of defending state security it also can be legally imposed. West Germany's Basic Law balances its commitment to the primacy of individual rights with the provision that they can be limited, by, among other things, the principle of loyalty to the Constitution. Organizations hostile to the constitutional order are explicitly prohibited (art. 9, sec. 2) (Weiss 1976: 63–4; Denninger 1977; Hammans 1987). On questions of state security, and perhaps more broadly, the state legitimates itself.

It is important to note that in Germany changing social norms are typically codified in legal language. Constitutional amendments in this legalistic culture are thus passed with great regularity. Between 1949 and 1983 forty-nine articles of the Basic Law were altered, thirty-three were added, and seven were deleted. By contrast, Japan's Constitution has not been altered since the end of World War II, and the Constitution of the United States has been changed only about two dozen times during the last two hundred years (Seifert 1977, 1983). In Germany the lawful state plays a central role in guaranteeing that government activity rests on a solid foundation of constitutional legality.

This normative context explains why the German political elite responded to the rash of terrorist attacks in the 1970s and 1980s with twenty amendments of the penal code passed between 1970 and 1989 (Katzenstein 1990: 32–3). Before the 1970s the provisions of the penal code tended to make it difficult to open criminal proceedings against suspects without specific evidence. The definition of an offense against the state was narrowly drawn. Public prosecutors had to identify and charge principal suspects. Citizens were under no general obligation to report terrorist activities to the police. But the changes in the law that have been made during the last two decades amounted to ensuring the state's right to security against attacks from radicals, even at the cost of infringing on traditional civil liberties.

Article 129a illustrates with particular clarity this shift in legal norms to facilitate the protection of state security. Revised in 1976 and again in 1986, it has granted state officials broad discretionary powers. It forbids the "support" or "advertisement" of terrorist organizations and, under certain conditions, permits the police to arrest individuals even in the absence of any suspicion of criminal activity. In fact, it subjects to criminal proceedings issues concerning criminal intent rather than criminal behavior. The extension of the government's coercive power beyond criminal behavior is virtually unknown in other European countries, as well as Japan. But it has been an essential element of German political practice. Furthermore, Article 129a centralized the power to prosecute all cases involving terrorist activities in the hands of the Office of the Federal Prosecutor, sidestepping the possibility of a long appeals process. And it linked the judicial treatment of terrorist suspects to some of the most controversial procedural reforms of the penal code in the 1970s. According to Article 129a, merely being suspected of supporting a criminal organization constitutes a criminal act and thus provides legal justification for the issuance of a search or arrest warrant. The conviction rate of suspects charged under Article 129a has been extremely low. Between 1980 and 1987 only thirty of the 2,700 preliminary investigations initiated by the federal prosecutor under the provisions of Article 129a, or a little more than 1 percent, have led to convictions (*Der Spiegel*, November 14, 1988: 66; Werkentin 1989: 6). Another study cites a figure of 6 percent for all court cases brought under the authority of Article 129a (Brand 1989: 174; Gössner 1987: 156). The legal restrictions under which the police and prosecutor operate thus have been weakened, and so have individual rights; the power of the police and the protection of state rights have been strengthened (Krauss

1979: 209–10; Cobler 1984: 407). In sum, the legal norms that are invoked against terrorist activity and suspects reveal a state intent on strengthening its own security as the sole source of law. A working group of NATO concurred with this conclusion in the late 1980s when it noted that "antiterrorist legislation in West Germany is extremely severe" (North Atlantic Assembly 1987: 37).

Japan

Japanese legal norms, unlike those of Germany, are deeply embedded in social norms rather than constitutive of them. This difference is reflected in the sizes of the legal professions of the two countries. With only half the population of Japan, Germany in the 1980s had, in proportional terms, six times as many judges, five times as many lawyers, three times as many private attorneys, and a third more procurators (Haley 1982: 274; Henderson 1965: 195–6; Smith 1985: 43; Citizens Crime Commission of Philadelphia 1975: 33; Oki 1984: 5). But the difference is also a matter of quality. In contrast to Germany, Japan has declared none of its radical organizations illegal since 1945. The normative context in which Japan's internal security policy is conducted is distinguished by a porous border between formal and informal authority. In Japan, argues David Bayley, government "is not the result of an explicit act of fabrication by an existing community, the product of making a constitution. Government is not added on to community; it is intrinsic to community, as parentage is to family" (Bayley 1976: 65–6). In contrast to Germany, Japan has avoided passing a spate of legislation on questions of internal security. In the 1970s and 1980s the Diet passed only a handful of laws or amendments dealing with internal security (Katzenstein and Tsujinaka 1991: table 5). The reason for this legal passivity lies in a political stalemate over an attempt to strengthen the legal and political position of the police that has continued since the late 1950s, despite recurrent efforts by conservatives in the Liberal Democratic Party (LDP) to review this issue. Confronted with this political reality, the police have adapted Japan's tradition of bureaucratic informalism to deal with problems of internal security.

The police practice of informalism (*unyo*) does not amount simply to arbitrary police discretion. But in permitting a very flexible application of police powers it gives a very broad definition to the legal restraints under which the police operate. The practice of informalism is, generally speaking, the most important norm guiding police action on questions of internal security. It describes the basic intentions of police officials rather than the surface appearance of their public statements. It does so in two distinct ways. It systematically applies a variety of minor laws and ordinances to cover the legal void left by political stalemate in the Diet. And it systematically, and on the whole successfully, has broadened the interpretation of the small number of security and police laws that do exist, in particular Article 2 of the Police Law as well as the Police Duties Execution Law. Leading police officials in the 1980s were very explicit about the fact that in providing "comprehensive security" the police self-consciously made intelligent use of their powers to conduct investigations under all existing laws and ordinances.

Many police practices that appear highly questionable in light of minimal existing legislation thus are not deemed illegal by the courts, which have normally taken a conservative and passive attitude toward the practice of bureaucratic informalism. The police have remained untouched by the provision for the compulsory prosecution of the abuse of authority. Of the 1,785 charges brought against the police between 1948 and 1977, only seven cases were prosecuted; and of these only four ended in convictions. "Not only is the small number of cases being prosecuted conspicuous, but so is the low conviction rate, especially in view of the fact that the average conviction rate of all Penal Code violations has been more than 95 percent in Japan" (Murayama 1980: 69).

But legal norms are by no means the only normative context for Japan's policy of internal security. Public opinion, as revealed by surveys and by published commentary, weighs heavily on the behavior of the police and the decisions of the public prosecutors and judges. Karel Van Wolferen, for one, concludes that "the social sanctioning role played by the Japanese press must be seen in the perspective of the practical shortcomings of the Japanese legal system" (Van Wolferen 1989: 225; Beer 1984; Whittemore 1961). Informal processes of social control have been very important in conditioning police policy since 1945, and the police have made self-conscious efforts to cultivate public opinion and not to act against public sentiment. In the face of widespread student unrest in the late 1960s, the security and riot police delayed a crackdown on student radicals for almost two years, until 1969, when public sentiment had swung away from the students and behind the government and the police.

This attention to public opinion has had stunning results. An institution that was totally delegitimized between 1945 and 1960 has now become fully accepted by the public. "Even people who tend to have a skeptical attitude toward the police . . . admit that abuses of power by the police are minimal" (Bayley 1984: 192). Complaints lodged against the police with the civilian review boards of the Ministry of Justice have declined steadily since 1948 and numbered about 100 a year in the 1980s, in a population of more than 100 million (Smith 1985: 125). We do not know whether the number is so low because the public has a favorable perception of the police or because the public is aware that complaints against the abuse of police authority are very rarely prosecuted. But three national surveys conducted in 1983 revealed that, among eight major public institutions, the police were rated most favorably, ahead of the press, business, and government. It is thus no accident that the public views the police as the main defenders of human rights in Japan (Katzenstein and Tsujinaka 1991: 133–5). Much of that goodwill derives from the daily activity of the police in community life and their deliberate efforts to convince the public that public and police are on the same side in the effort to maintain a civil society. But, whatever its source, the public's support allows security and riot police great flexibility in their daily concern with internal security.

International norms and internal security

Germany

The abstract universalism that typifies Germany's domestic norms has made it easy for German officials to view the German state as part of an international community of states seeking to protect itself against subversive attacks. Embodied in the Holy Roman Empire of the German people, the ancient concept of universal sovereignty stood for an international community that encompassed various parts of Germany (Dumont 1986: 591). Germany's interest in the strengthening of international community since 1945 thus has an important historical precedent. Specifically, Germany has participated with great energy in the process of furthering the evolution of international norms prohibiting terrorist activities, and in several key episodes has in fact played a leading international role. Its active role in furthering the evolution of international legal norms since 1949 was partly a concerted attempt to regain a measure of the legitimacy that the Nazis and their international legal specialists of the New Order had squandered (Vagts 1989). More important, in the last two decades this active role has been shaped by the characteristic weight that German political leaders have accorded legal norms in domestic politics.

Although, in part for reasons of bureaucratic politics, Germany's involvement in the process of norm definition has been more circumscribed in the UN than in various European fora, Germany did take the leading part in the formulation of the 1977 UN Convention on Terrorism. The subject of terrorism was included on the agenda of the General Assembly at the request of the Federal Republic, and a German chaired the group that drafted the convention (Lagoni 1977; Rosenstock 1977). The German government did not press ahead with this initiative in the hope of overcoming the political disagreements over the definition of terrorism that had divided the General Assembly during the preceding decade. Rather it evidently wanted to put its domestic antiterrorist policy on the broadest conceivable footing. Clarifying and universalizing the principles that informed that policy were integral parts of this political effort.

The same impulse is noticeable in other international arenas, such as the economic summits convened by the advanced industrial states since 1977. The subject of terrorism was raised for the first time at the Bonn summit in 1978, apparently without prior staff work, at a time when Chancellor Helmut Schmidt was very much preoccupied by the issue. In their final communiqué the seven heads of state condemned terrorism and threatened to discontinue air service to any country that offered sanctuary to terrorists or hijackers

(Putnam and Bayne 1987: 86–7). Since the Group of Seven is politically more homogeneous than the United Nations and accounts for 70 percent of the total air traffic in the Western world, the summit was a promising international arena for the German government. But it was also clear that the political consensus that emerged at the Bonn summit did not really set any norm and had no legally binding force according to customary international law.

From the perspective of the German government, Europe offered the advantage of furthering the evolution of international norms in a setting of relative political homogeneity. In the hope of informing or guiding national legislation, for example, the Council of Ministers of the Council of Europe summarizes existing international practices and interpretations in regard to various issues, including those that involve international criminal activity. Working under the auspices of the Council, the European Committee on Crime Problems has facilitated the signing of a number of international conventions (Harremoes 1981). And the decisions of the European Court of Human Rights in Strasbourg are binding on national courts and governments. In the area of human rights, which includes the norms affecting state reaction to terrorism, Western Europe has developed a regime as strong as any to be found in other regions of the world (Donnelley 1986: 620–4). Because they touch on key aspects of state sovereignty, norms concerning the evolution of the practices of state coercion, embodied in international penal law, are hampered by obstacles that are greater than any in the areas of international civil or commercial law. But, despite these impediments, international norms have in fact spread also in the area of public law and have partially converged in national legal practice.

Germany's confident participation in the process of furthering the evolution of international law was very apparent in the central role it played in developing the European Convention on the Suppression of Terrorism, passed in 1977—arguably the most important international convention to establish international norms and procedures for combating terrorism. The convention derives from the 1957 European Convention on Extradition, amended in 1975 and 1978, and the 1959 European Convention on Mutual Assistance in Criminal Matters, which was amended in 1978. Based on a political initiative by the German minister of justice, the convention was drafted by the Council of Europe (Friedlander 1982; Freestone 1981; Gal-Or 1985). The Federal Republic was strongly committed to the passage of the convention and ratified it without reservation as early as 1978, in the hope of setting an example for the other members of the Council of Europe (Gal-Or 1985: 256). Eventually all members except Malta and Ireland followed suit. With some justification one critic of the convention has argued that it is an "international manifestation of the theory of the 'strong state'—that states hold in reserve strong and wide-ranging powers with which to suppress possible dissent. Germany particularly . . . is generally associated with this view" (Freestone 1981: 215).

Broadly speaking, the convention shifts attention away from the individual right to political asylum, a concern characteristic of the 1930s, 1940s, and 1950s, toward the threat of terrorism, a preoccupation of the 1960s and 1970s. In a sharp break with earlier agreements articulating international norms of conduct, Articles 1 and 2 of the convention stipulate that certain kinds of crime shall never be considered political, notwithstanding their political motivation or content (Schubert 1986). The convention lists the offenses covered by the term "terrorist crime" and requires signatories to cooperate as widely as possible on all criminal activities covered by its text and, when necessary, to rely on binding arbitration.

Germany's active involvement in the spread of international norms of antiterrorism, especially in Europe, has also found a receptive forum in the Conference on Security and Cooperation in Europe (CSCE). This is arguably the most important institution for moving Western and Eastern Europe in the direction of a pan-European peace order, an idea that has inspired Germany's Eastern policy during the last two decades. The final document of the CSCE, signed in Vienna in January 1989 by all European states except Albania, as well as by the Soviet Union, the United States, and Canada, echoes the European Convention of 1977. "The participating states unreservedly condemn as criminal all acts, methods and practices of terrorism, wherever and by whomever committed . . . and agree that terrorism cannot be justified under any circumstances" (*New York Times* 1989: A12). The signatories of the final document agreed also to stand firm in the face of terrorism, to strengthen bilateral and multilateral cooperation to combat and prevent terrorism, and to ensure the extradition or prosecution of all persons implicated in acts of terrorism. In short, the international norm against terrorism has evidently spread during the last two decades and Germany has been very much in the forefront of attempts to strengthen that development.

Japan

With only a few exceptions, Japan is in full agreement with the evolving international human rights foundation that informs the antiterrorist policy of the major Western democracies. But the social embeddedness of Japanese law and its situational logic have made it more difficult for Japan than for Germany to involve itself actively in furthering the evolution of international legal norms prohibiting terrorism. Furthermore, Japan's social consensus has favored the notion of Japan's uniqueness in the contemporary international system. The extension of the abstract universalism of German law into a larger European space has no Japanese analogue. The process appears to have worked rather in reverse. When the Japanese government confronted a dangerous threat from the Red Army, operating abroad in the 1970s, it enacted six domestic laws so that it could ratify five international treaties that it had signed previously. In other words, the existence of international norms shaped the evolution of Japan's domestic legal norms on questions of internal security. But the effect of these security laws remained largely symbolic and had little bearing on the practical work of the police and the legal profession dealing with questions of internal security.

Furthermore, Japan has not yet been forced to act on the strength of the international antiterrorist conventions it has signed and ratified and thus to demonstrate that in fact it regards them as binding. And in none of the international organizations has Japan taken a leading role in seeking to further international norms of antiterrorist policy. In 1973, for example, it voted together with France in the legal committee of the International Civil Aviation Organization against a proposal, supported by the United States, Britain, and Canada, among others, backing collective action against states that refused to interrupt air service with states that were granting safe haven to terrorists (Fingerman 1980: 141). And in the 1980s Japan failed to ratify two international conventions dealing with the security of airports and of oil-drilling platforms, even though it had sponsored one of them. Finally, Asia simply has not evolved any kind of regional framework of organizations that would give Japan an opportunity to play a more active role. On the question of human rights, as on many other issues of international law, "in Asia there are neither regional norms nor decision-making procedures" (Donnelley 1986: 628).

In contrast to Germany and other European states, Japan views international legal norms not as a process but as a product, not as part of the evolution of its domestic law but as a given attribute of international society to which it must adjust. International law is a tool of diplomacy to further the interests of states. It is not a process by which the creator of norms is in turn bound. The Japanese approach to international legal norms is more narrow and tactical than the German. It lacks an "internationalism in the sense of identification with the international community, with human kind as a whole, that is, rather than in the sense of 'good neighbour' punctiliousness about international obligations—which the Japanese have in good measure" (Dore 1986: 245).

This is not to argue that the Japanese lack any conception of international norms. Like the people of other states, they seek to generalize to the international realm the institutions and practices that shape domestic norms. But their avenue for doing so is through the process of international technology, as any student of the American or European automobile industry will readily testify, rather than through international law. In contrast to Germany, Japan lacks in international society what it has in domestic society, an ideology of law and a moral vision of the good society. Without the dense set of social relations that characterize domestic society, what remains in international society is a world of "connections," of interests and reciprocity that look merely opportunistic when stripped of their thick domestic social context. For the Japanese, to act in accordance with one's international responsibility means to do what is expected of a country whose influence in the world is rapidly rising. It means conceiving of Japanese interests in the longer term. It does not mean conceiving of the "self" in broader terms, on the basis of a vision that might resemble the abstract universalism of German legalism or the self-confident assertiveness of Anglo-Saxon liberalism. For Japan to transcend its interest-driven approach to questions of international norms would require nothing less than a fundamental domestication of international society by Japan—the extension, that is, of its deep social fabric abroad. While this process is certainly under way in several economic and social policy domains, any substantial and sustained change along these lines would constitute a very important break in the domination of the international system by the West.

Norms as analytical constructs for empirical analysis

The normative context of policy is important if we wish to understand better the constitution of policy interests. Since norms and interests are normally converging, it is very difficult to establish empirically the primacy of one over the other. We should therefore make problematic what is often taken to be axiomatic: the interests of actors. To stipulate actors' interests on the basis of abstract notions of structure is often to bypass a significant question we must grapple with if we wish to understand why political actors behave the way they do. To focus on the norms that inform the interests that drive policy, however, is not to assume that norms provide the only plausible explanations, to the exclusion of all other factors. Norms do not determine outcomes for two simple reasons. They are contested, and they are contingent.

Norms are contested

Terrorism is a violent contestation of prevailing norms. A focus on the normative context in which Germany and Japan debated and implemented their antiterrorist policies thus must consider the elementary fact that norms are normally contested. These focal "points of concern" (Laitin 1988: 590) reveal an agreement within society or between societies about what it is that is worth arguing about, a source of significant data for an understanding of the normative context of policy. In both Germany and Japan that point of concern in the domestic debate involved the dominant legal and political establishment on the one hand and a civil libertarian countergroup and occasional court judgments on the other. In the evolution of international norms there was some opposition among German and European specialists in international law (a small elite group that at the same time both constitutes and interprets to their respective governments the evolution of international norms) as well as among politicians to the spread of Germany's strong state norm. Japan's apparent passivity on questions involving the evolution of international norms, on the other hand, voided any substantive public debate because of a broad social consensus on the uniqueness of Japanese culture in the modern world.

In Germany the Basic Law itself reveals a tension between the rule of law that constitutes the state as the sum of laws duly passed by Parliament and individual rights securely anchored in a natural rights tradition, on the one hand, and legal strictures imposed on state—that is, executive—power without constituting the state in a truly liberal, parliamentary fashion, on the other (Busch *et al.* 1985: 53–8; Funk, Kauß, and Zabern 1980: 71–6). This ambiguity has been at the center of debate between the German mainstream and its more radical democratic critics who champion a more vigorous defense of civil liberties. Occasional partisan disagreements in Germany, as elsewhere in Europe, have centered on the trade-off between the need for effective protection against terrorism and executive discretion on the one hand and a concern for freedom of expression, the protection of individual rights, and parliamentary supervision on the other. Finally, some of the German responses, such as the redrafting of Article 129a of the Penal Code, which now includes issues of motivation and intent as well as overtly criminal behavior, are in such substantial disagreement with the legal doctrine and practice of other European states that they are typically not covered in any of the bilateral and multilateral treaties that Germany has signed. In a couple of cases this has been the cause of considerable friction between Germany and some of its neighbors.

Conflicts over the evolution of domestic norms that affect international security policy have been rare and more muted in Japan than in Germany. Occasionally, as in the late 1960s and early 1970s, a conservative legal establishment that has favored a passive stance in the face of the informal practices of the police has been confronted by a small group of reform-minded lawyers and judges intent on protecting the civil rights of political demonstrators. But, generally speaking, the Supreme Court in particular has gone out of its way to avoid ruling on politically sensitive cases, has tried to muffle reformist lawyers, and thus has had a substantial effect on lower-court rulings. Japan's relative lack of political conflict over and passive attitude toward the evolution of international norms demonstrate that this issue has simply not been a focal point of concern (Laitin 1988). A widely shared assumption holds that Japan is unique in the international system and that the specific requirements of Japanese society as well as the situational logic of Japan's legal norms do not connect easily with the evolution of more abstract Western norms as codified in international public law. The comparison between Japan and Germany demonstrates that different focal points for political conflict will yield different equilibria. Different political systems exhibit different forms of rationality.

Norms are contingent

Norms themselves are not the sole determinants of the interests that shape actors' political choices and political outcomes. At a minimum, any comprehensive analysis must also include the structural conditions that shape interests, choices, and outcomes. These structures differ in Germany and Japan along three dimensions: the organizational structure of the state, the relations between state and society, and the links between the state and transnational structures.

On questions of internal security, Germany's federal system and the system of alternating coalition governments has been modified by procedural and institutional responses that have sought to integrate the police and intelligence services into one centralized structure. In comparison with other policy domains in Germany, the issue of internal security is characterized by a remarkably centralized state structure. But the proliferation of coordinating interagency bodies, standing committees of the various state governments, and the political and bureaucratic conflicts between ministries headed by politicians belonging to different parties leave the image of a decentralized structure in comparison with the flexible centralized organization of the Japanese security policy in the National Police Agency and the Metropolitan Police Department. The difference in structure is equally clear in the relations between state and society on questions involving internal security. The distance that the stark German differentiation between state and society (*Obrigkeitsstaat*) imposes is incomparably greater than one finds in the osmotic relation between formal and informal centers of authority in Japan's familial state. Finally, for reasons of geography and history alone, the German state is much more closely linked to other state structures, especially in Europe, than is Japan, which still suffers from a deep sense of isolation from the world community. While the organization of the state is not unconnected to the role of norms that help shape policy formulation, its primary effect is on the implementation of policy. The structure of state–society relations in these two cases corresponds clearly to the directive role of legal norms in Germany as contrasted with the social embeddedness of Japan's legal norms. And the links between the state and transnational structures which are so much stronger in Germany than in Japan correlate with the activist stance Germany has chosen in furthering the evolution of international norms in contrast to Japan's passivity. In short, the effects of at least two of the three dimensions of structure parallel the domestic and international norms of the two countries.

Both norms and structures predispose Germany to abstract universal norms that facilitate the government's choice of a high-tech approach to the gathering of social "intelligence" and of active involvement in the international process of strengthening universal norms of antiterrorism. Conversely, Japan's norms and structures favor socially embedded and thus nationally specific norms that make plausible the government's effort to elicit social "intelligence" through the adaptation of existing institutions and practices and to remain passive in the furthering of international norms of antiterrorism.

Conclusion

Important differences in Germany's and Japan's policies of defending state security against threats posed by terrorism and violent social protest cannot be explained solely in terms of their domestic structures or the international structures that condition policy in the international system. An explanation of Germany's and Japan's policies of internal security must also pay attention to the normative context that frames political choices. Does this argument hold for other instances of internal security policy, such as Germany's and Japan's antidrug policies? And could it be extended to the issue of external security?

Antidrug policies are accorded very high priority in Germany's and Japan's internal security policies. In domestic affairs as in antiterrorism policy, a great gulf yawns between a German policy that expresses primarily the legal norms of a relatively autonomous state and a Japanese policy that relies heavily on the social embeddedness of the Japanese state. And in international affairs Germany has chosen a more activist and cooperative approach to the containment of the flow of illegal drugs than Japan has taken.

Modeled on the American approach, Germany's antidrug policy is informed by the concept of "extended defense." The government's 1988 antidrug report defines the concept clearly. "Of decisive importance for inhibiting the import of stimulants is the effort to build a line of defense in producer and transit countries. This requires close international cooperation" (Thamm 1989: 182). In the 1980s Germany stationed thirty-seven police officers in twenty-one countries, primarily in the Third World. "The European government with the greatest number of law enforcement agents stationed abroad is West Germany," writes Ethan Nadelmann. "[Police] agents also demonstrated their willingness to conduct operations on foreign soil, even to the extent of riling foreign governments. In these respects as well as in its adoption of . . . proactive investigative techniques [of the sort employed by the Drug Enforcement Agency (DEA) in the United States], the German federal police agency has consciously emulated the DEA." Furthermore, the networks of European police that operate in the area of antiterrorism policy—such as TREVI and the Schengen Accord—also support Germany's active international stance. In domestic politics Germany's antidrug police units have become "the most innovative and aggressive in Europe. . . . In Germany, more than in any other country, both the Länder [state] and the federal police have adopted the DEA models of investigation with few inhibitions." Backed by legislative changes among all of the European police forces, the German police use undercover operations most extensively (Nadelmann 1987: 86, 295, 269, 285, 288).

Japan's antidrug policy rests on one main strategy, "to isolate not only drug dealers, but also the users from the rest of the population" (National Police Agency 1990: 3). In this as in all other areas of crime, Japan's police have been very effective. Only when Japan's social structure was deeply disrupted, as it was in the first postwar decade, did the drug problem take on epidemic proportions. But the restabilization of Japan and the tough penalties that were imposed quickly ended that epidemic and left Japan, despite some sharp increases in drug-related offenses in the 1970s and 1980s, with a drug problem that by American standards is minuscule (Friman 1991; Yokoyama 1988; Tamura n.d.). The close involvement of the Japanese police with local communities is a key to policy success. Since drugs are widely seen as a risk not only to the individual but to society at large, drug users are regularly reported to the police even by family members. And the police remain confident that the social barriers to drugs will hold up. With arrests for drug-related offenses decreasing sharply in 1989, the Japanese police exuded optimism. "What we are thinking of is how to create an anti-drug society" (National Police Agency 1990: 5).

Japan has frequently professed its readiness to cooperate internationally despite a domestic drug problem that is not of grave concern; but it never ratified the 1971 UN Convention on Narcotics and Psychotropic Substances. Despite the criminalization of drug-related offenses, enforcement measures in Japan have remained relatively lax by American standards. The Ministry of Justice was successful in blocking long-standing demands by the National Police Agency that the police be granted legal powers that are considered quite normal in the United States and to some extent in Germany, including undercover operations, surveillance, wiretaps, and access to bank records. The limitations under which the police are operating in Japan have occasioned constant complaints by DEA representatives stationed in Japan. For lack of national legislation, even the monitoring of money-laundering operations, regarded as essential if the police are to close in on the drug-related activities of organized crime, has been stalled for years despite intense international pressure. Japan's participation in a "global partnership" in the American war against drugs, signed by Prime Minister Kaifu and President Bush in September 1989, thus was not motivated by serious concern about drugs. It was instead seen as a way of cementing relations with Japan's most important trade partner and security guarantor at a time of mounting political friction between the two countries. Because the deployment of military forces abroad is prohibited by its constitution, Japan has refused to participate in the eradication or interdiction of drugs abroad, a major part of America's war on drugs. Instead Prime Minister Kaifu agreed in September 1989 to provide economic and technical assistance and cooperation to encourage drug-exporting countries to diversify their economic bases. It did so apparently with little interest in the substance of policy. A special Japanese assistance program to Colombia which was part of the war on drugs, for example, provided funds for a new sewer system for Bogotá and the purchase of audiovisual equipment for the government's music archive (Friman 1991: 885–6, 888).

Germany's and Japan's external security, like their internal security, cannot be explained fully by structural factors alone. Nearly fifty years after their unconditional surrender to the Allied forces, Germany and Japan appear to have won the cold war that the United States and the Soviet Union waged. Under the protective umbrella of the United States, these two trading states are no longer subject to the temptations of military glory and territorial conquest, which had led to their cataclysmic defeat in World War II. Instead

Germany and Japan have focused their political attention on enhancing their competitiveness in international markets while at the same time maintaining viable political relations with the United States as well as with their European and Asian neighbors. The widespread aversion to the use of military force "has become institutionalized in Japanese and West German societies and has become a central feature of their new political culture" (Berger 1991: 1–3). Their reaction to the Gulf War in 1991 demonstrated that Germany and Japan are facing political possibilities for growing international influence that they are unwilling to exploit. Hundreds of thousands of antiwar demonstrators in the streets of Bonn and unseemly wrangling in the Japanese Diet reinforce the impression that the trauma of the defeat of 1945 continues to have deep effects on Germany's and Japan's national security policies.

These effects can be gauged only through a consideration of the normative contexts in which policies are formulated and implemented. And the normative contexts of Germany and Japan differ. In domestic politics, German policy has been informed by norms expressed in the concepts of "moral leadership" and the "citizen in arms." These concepts were coined deliberately to forestall the reappearance of German militarism. And they were deliberately institutionalized to foster the growth of an army that was actively supportive of democratic values. As the two concepts indicate, the reform effort aimed at the exercise of authority within the armed forces as well as the pattern of relationship between the military and society. Although the issue of Germany's rearmament was hotly contested in the 1950s, there was virtual unanimity in all political quarters that an unconstrained military would be an invitation to total disaster. The concept of moral leadership was designed to instill political consciousness and responsibility in West German soldiers without endangering military preparedness. Some of the ideas that informed the concepts of moral leadership and the citizen in arms were patterned along the lines of the concept of social partnership that has informed labor–management relations in West Germany since 1945. The modern soldier has become a professional with a distinctive competence, including courage, leadership qualities, and commitment, but he no longer has any claim to uniqueness. The principles that were to guarantee the full integration of the military into a civilian society and its subordination to a democratic system of government, though at times sharply contested in politics, were in the end legally codified between 1954 and 1957 and "signified a dramatic break with the Prussian-German military tradition" (Abenheim 1988: 167). These moral norms were also institutionalized in a School of the Armed Forces for Moral Leadership, created in the 1950s, and in two military academies set up in the early 1970s.

In the international realm German policy since 1945 has been informed by the concept of security partnership. Konrad Adenauer's Western policy embraced West Germany's membership in NATO and the European Community because they promised both to help defend the Federal Republic against the threat from the Soviet Union and to regain West German sovereignty. But, with political conditions changing in the 1960s, the Federal

Republic became a leading proponent of NATO's adoption of the Harmel Report in 1967. The report stated that NATO should transcend its trad- itional role as a defense alliance and involve itself actively in furthering the process of détente. The Harmel Report provided the international basis for West Germany's Eastern policy in the 1970s and 1980s, which helped nor- malize relations between West Germany, the Soviet Union, and the Eastern European states, including the German Democratic Republic. The process of normalization with the East, like that of Western integration, was informed by the concept of security partnership in an international community of nations. Before 1945 the concept of community was coupled almost by definition with the adjective "national." After 1945, however, Germans thought and talked about domestic affairs primarily in terms of civil society. Germany did belong, however, to the Atlantic Community, the European Community, and now an emerging pan-European peace order. The idea of the international state system as a security partnership is evidently patterned in part on the West German system of social partnership which has regulated conflict between business, unions, and some of the other major interest groups. Though the precise mean- ing of the concept of security partnership has been politically contested, the wish to see Germany fully integrated in a variety of international partnerships in the broader community of nations is generally shared.

This view of the world is alien to Japan. Economic and social consider- ations have been central to Japan's definition of "comprehensive security." Japan's economic reconstruction created stunning successes in export markets in the United States and throughout the world. The story of economic success marred by protectionist backlash abroad has become repetitive as Japan has conquered world markets first in mature industries and subsequently in mod- ern ones. Japan's response to the political consequences of its economic suc- cess has been very consistent. Until the mid-1980s Japan engaged in tough bargaining and eventual pragmatic compromise on some kind of "voluntary" export restrictions. Only in the last few years has an uncomfortable awareness spread in Tokyo that Japan may be called upon to develop more comprehensive political solutions to the international political disruptions that its economic prowess is creating.

Japan's normative vision centers on the notion of an economic partnership in an international society of states. In this worldview what holds the world together, both at home and abroad, is interests, not common norms that tie actors together in common projects. Cooperation is made possible by flexibility in the redefinition of short-term interests as long-term interests. The extraordinary ability to redefine one's interest is based on the deliberate attempt to foster ongoing interest-based relationships, in domestic politics as well as in international affairs. The Japanese "self" is extended to incorporate at least some relevant portions of the "other" so that the expectation of an ongoing interest-based relationship is met (Hamaguchi 1985). This approach differs greatly from the purely market-based approach of the United States, with its assumption of self-contained and autonomous actors. But it differs also from the German and European experience, which increasingly is putting into question the very notion of a national self. Japan's approach to international life is more accepting than Germany's of vulnerability in economic and security affairs. But Japan lacks the German experience of becoming enmeshed with the political structures of numerous neighbors in international institutions and policy projects.

Our analysis of international and domestic politics will remain incomplete if it neglects the normative context that helps define the interests of actors. Incompleteness is of course essential to the enterprise of developing compelling explanations in the social sciences. But the assumption that actors know their interests, though convenient for analytical purposes, sidesteps some of the most important political and intriguing analytical questions in contemporary politics. With established political structures crumbling in various parts of the world, conventional structural analysis needs to be modified and extended. The idea of letting go of the assumption that interests are fixed will disturb those who look for a definite Archimedean point to plant their feet on and gain the analytical leverage that they assume will help them to explain the world. I hope I have shown that in a fluid world some advantage may derive from being more nimble-footed. It is possible to do theoretically informed and empirically oriented research on the normative context that informs the interests political actors hold.

Note

1   Some of the material in this chapter is drawn from Peter J. Katzenstein, *West Germany's Internal Security Policy: State and Violence in the 1970s and 1980s*, Cornell University, Center for International Studies, Western Societies Program, Occasional Paper no. 28 (1990), and Peter J. Katzenstein and Yutaka Tsujinaka, *Defending the Japanese State: Structures, Norms, and the Political Responses to Terrorism and Violent Social Protest in the 1970s and 1980s*, Cornell University, East Asia Program (1991). I thank Judith Goldstein, Robert Keohane, David Laitin, T. J. Pempel, and Robert Smith for their criticisms and suggestions on a previous version of this chapter.

References

Abenheim, Donald (1988) *Reforging the Iron Cross: The Search for Tradition in the West German Armed Forces*, Princeton, NJ: Princeton University Press.

Adler, Emanuel (1987) *The Power of Ideology: The Quest for Technological Autonomy in Argentina and Brazil*, Berkeley, Calif.: University of California Press.

Adler, Emanuel (1988) "Cognitive Evolution: A Dynamic Approach for the Study of International Relations and Their Progress," unpublished manuscript, Harvard University.

Apter, David E. and Sawa, Nagayo (1984) *Against the State: Politics and Social Protest in Japan*, Cambridge, Mass.: Harvard University Press.

Bayley, David H. (1976) "Learning about Crime—the Japanese Experience," *Public Interest*, 44 (Summer): 55–68.

Bayley, David H. (1984) "Police, Crime, and the Community in Japan," pp. 177–98 in George DeVos (ed.) *Institutions for Change in Japanese Society*, Berkeley, Calif.: Institute of East Asian Studies, University of California.

Beer, Lawrence Ward (1984) *Freedom of Expression in Japan: A Study in Comparative Law, Politics, and Society*, Tokyo: Kodansha.

Berger, Thomas (1991) "The Reluctant Allies: The Genesis of the Political Military Cultures of Japan and West Germany," unpublished manuscript, Massachusetts Institute of Technology, Department of Political Science.

Borgs-Maciejewski, Hermann (1988) *Was jeder vom Verfassungschutz wissen sollte: Aufgaben, Methode, Organisation*, Heidelberg: Decker & Müller.

Brand, Enno (1989) *Staatsgewalt: Politische Unterdrückung und Innere Sicherheit in der Bundesrepublik*, Göttingen: Verlag die Werkstatt.

Bürgerrecht und Polizei (1980) (CILIP 6) "Rasterfahndung," August/September/October, pp. 16–21.

Busch, Heiner, Funk, Albrecht, Kauß, Udo, Narr, Wolf-Dieter, and Werkentin, Falco (1985) *Die Polizei in der Bundesrepublik*, Frankfurt: Campus.

Citizens Crime Commission of Philadelphia (1975) *Tokyo: One City Where Crime Doesn't Pay*, Philadelphia, Pa.: Citizens Crime Commission.

Cobler, Sebastian (1984) "Plädoyer für die Streichung der Artikel 129, 129a StGB," *Kritische Justiz*, 17, 4: 407–17.

Cowen, Regina H. E. (1986) *Defense Procurement in the Federal Republic of Germany: Politics and Organization*, Boulder, Colo.: Westview.

Denninger, Erhard (ed.) (1977) *Freiheitliche demokratische Grundordnung: Materialien zum Staatsverständnis und zur Verfassungswirklichkeit in der Bundesrepublik*, 2 vols, Frankfurt: Suhrkamp.

Donnelley, Jack (1986) "International Human Rights: A Regime Analysis," *International Organization*, 40 (Summer): 599–642.

Dore, Ronald (1986) *Flexible Rigidities: Industrial Policy and Structural Adjustment in the Japanese Economy, 1970–80*, Stanford, Calif.: Stanford University Press.

Dumont, Louis (1986) "Are Cultures Living Beings? German Identity in Interaction," *Man*, (n.s.) 21: 587–604.

Fairchild, Erika S. (1988) *German Police: Ideals and Reality in the Post-War Years*, Springfield, Ill.: Charles C. Thomas.

Fingerman, Mark E. (1980) "Skyjacking and the Bonn Declaration of 1978: Sanctions Applicable to Recalcitrant Nations," *California Western International Law Journal*, 10, 1 (Winter): 123–52.

Finn, John E. (1989) "Constitutional Reconstruction, Militant Democracy, and Antiterrorism Legislation in the Federal Republic of Germany," unpublished manuscript, Wesleyan University.

Flaherty, David H. (1989) *Protecting Privacy in Surveillance Societies: The Federal Republic of Germany, Sweden, France, Canada, and the United States*, Chapel Hill, NC: University of North Carolina Press.

Freestone, David (1981) "Legal Responses to Terrorism: Toward European Cooperation?," pp. 195–226 in Juliet Lodge (ed.) *Terrorism: A Challenge to the State*, New York: St Martin's Press.

Friedlander, Robert A. (1982) "Terrorism and International Law: Recent Developments," *Rutgers Law Journal*, 13, 3 (Spring): 493–511.

Friman, Richard H. (1991) "The United States, Japan, and the International Drug Trade: Troubled Partnership," *Asian Survey*, 31, 9 (September): 875–90.

Funk, Albrecht, Kauß, Udo and Zabern, Thomas von (1980) "Die Ansätze zu einer neuen Polizei: Vergleich der Polizeientwicklung in England/Wales, Frankreich und der Bundesrepublik Deutschland," pp. 71–6 in Erhard Blankenburg (ed.) *Politik der Inneren Sicherheit*, Frankfurt: Suhrkamp.

Gal-Or, Noemi (1985) *International Cooperation to Suppress Terrorism*, New York: St Martin's Press.

Gibbs, Jack P. (1989) "Conceptualization of Terrorism," *American Sociological Review*, 54, 4 (June): 329–40.

Gössner, Rolf (1987) "Auf der Suche nach den verlorenen Maßstäben," *Demokratie und Recht*, 2: 142–66.

Hailbronner, Kay (1982) "International Terrorism and the Laws of War," *German Yearbook of International Law*, 25: 169–98.

Haley, John O. (1982) "Sheathing the Sword of Justice in Japan: An Essay on Law without Sanctions," *Journal of Japanese Studies*, 8 (Summer): 265–81.

Hamaguchi, Esyun (1985) "A Contextual Model of the Japanese: Toward a Methodological Innovation in Japanese Studies," *Journal of Japanese Studies*, 11, 2: 289–321.

Hammans, Peter (1987) *Das politische Denken der neueren Staatslehre in der Bundesrepublik: Eine Studie zum politischen Konservatismus juristischer Gesellschaftstheorie*, Opladen: Westdeutscher Verlag.

Harremoes, Erik (1981) "Activités du Conseil de l'Europe dans le Domaine des Problèmes Criminels (1975–1980)," *Revue de Science Criminelle et de Droit Pénal Comparé*, 1 (January–March): 57–70.

Henderson, Dan Fenno (1965) *Conciliation and Japanese Law: Tokugawa and Modern*, Vol. 2, Seattle, Wash.: University of Washington Press.

Horchem, Hans Josef (1980) "Terrorism and Government Response: The German Experience," *Jerusalem Journal of International Relations*, 4, 3: 43–55.

Jenkins, Brian M. (1980) "The Study of Terrorism: Definitional Problems," unpublished manuscript, Santa Monica, Calif.: Rand Corporation.

Katzenstein, Peter J. (1987) *Policy and Politics in West Germany: The Growth of a Semisovereign State*, Philadelphia, Pa.: Temple University Press.

Katzenstein, Peter J. (1990) *West Germany's Internal Security Policy: State and Violence in the 1970s and 1980s*, Ithaca, NY: Western Societies Program, Center for International Studies, Cornell Studies in International Affairs, Occasional Paper No. 8.

Katzenstein, Peter J. and Tsujinaka, Yutaka (1991) "Defending the Japanese State: Structures, Norms, and Political Responses to Terrorism and Violent Social Protest in the 1970s and 1980s," Ithaca, NY: East Asia Program, Cornell University.

Kittrie, Nicholas G. (1978) "Reconciling the Irreconcilable: The Quest for International Agreement over Political Crime and Terrorism," *Yearbook of World Affairs*, 32: 208–36.

Kolinsky, Eva (1988) "Terrorism in West Germany," pp. 57–88 in Juliet Lodge (ed.) *The Threat of Terrorism*, Brighton: Wheatsheaf.

Kratochwil, Friedrich and Ruggie, John Gerard (1986) "International Organization: A State of the Art on an Art of the State," *International Organization*, 40, 4 (Autumn): 753–75.

Krauss, Detlev (1979) "The Reform of Criminal Procedure Law in the Federal Republic of Germany," *Juridical Review*, (n.s.) 24 (December): 202–23.

Lagoni, Rainer (1977) "Die Vereinten Nationen und der internationale Terrorismus," *Europa-Archiv*, 32, 6: 171–80.

Laitin, David (1988) "Political Culture and Political Preferences," *American Political Science Review*, 82, 2 (June): 589–93.

Mueller, John (1989) *Retreat from Doomsday: The Obsolescence of Major War*, New York: Basic Books.

Murayama, Masayuki (1980) "A Comparative Study of Police Accountability: A Preliminary Work," unpublished manuscript, University of California, Berkeley.

Nadelmann, Ethan Avram (1987) "Cops across Borders: Transnational Crime and International Law Enforcement," PhD dissertation, Harvard University, Department of Government.

National Police Agency (1990) *Anti-Drug Activities*, Tokyo: Japan International Cooperation Agency and National Police Agency of Japan.

New York Times (1989) "Excerpts from East–West Agreement on the Protection of Human Rights," January 17, p. A12.

North Atlantic Assembly, Working Group on Terrorism (1987) *Final Report*, Brussels: North Atlantic Assembly.

Oki, Masao (1984) "Japanese Rights' Consciousness: The Nature of Japan's Judicial System," *Look Japan* (January 10): 4–5.

Putnam, Robert D. and Bayne, Nicholas (1987) *Hanging Together: Cooperation and Conflict in the Seven-Power Summits*, Cambridge, Mass.: Harvard University Press.

Rosecrance, Richard (1986) *The Rise of the Trading State: Commerce and Conquest in the Modern World*, New York: Basic Books.

Rosenau, James N. (1986) "Before Cooperation: Hegemons, Regimes, and Habit-Driven Actors in World Politics," *International Organization*, 40, 4 (Autumn): 849–94.

Rosenstock, Robert (1977) "U.S. Supports Establishment of UN Ad Hoc Committee on Drafting of Convention against Taking of Hostages," *U.S. Department of State Bulletin*, 76 (240177) (January 24): 72–5.

Ruggie, John Gerard (1988) "International Structure and International Transformation: Space, Time, and Method," unpublished manuscript, La Jolla, Calif.

Schubert, Michael (1986) " 'Terrorismusbekämpfung' als Vorwand für die Kriminalisierung politischer Konflikte," *Vorgänge*, 25, 2: 87–114.

Seifert, Jürgen (1977) *Grundgesetz und Restauration*, 3rd edn, Neuwied: Luchterhand.

Seifert, Jürgen (1983) *Das Grundgesetz und seine Veränderung*, 4th edn, Neuwied: Luchterhand.

Smith, Robert J. (1985) *Japanese Society: Tradition, Self, and the Social Order*, Cambridge: Cambridge University Press.

Spiegel, Der (1988) "Gewalt Weihnachten," November 14, p. 66.

Steinhoff, Patricia G. (1989) "Hijackers, Bombers, and Bank Robbers: Japanese Managerial Style in the Radical Left," *Journal of Asian Studies*, 48 (November): 724–40.

Swidler, Ann (1986) "Culture in Action: Symbols and Strategies," *American Sociological Review*, 51, 2 (April): 273–86.

Tamura, Masayuki (n.d.) "Yakuza and Stimulants: Drug Problems in Japan," unpublished manuscript, Tokyo, National Research Institute of Police Science.

Tannenwald, Nina (1988) "How Norms Matter in International Relations: Berlin 1948 and the Cuban Missile Crisis," unpublished manuscript, Cornell University.

Thamm, Berndt Georg (1989) *Drogenfreigabe: Kapitulation oder Ausweg? Pro und contra zur Liberalisierung von Rauschgiften als Maßnahme zur Kriminalitätsprophylaxe*, Hilden: Verlage Deutsche Polizeiliteratur.

Vagts, Detlev F. (1989) "International Law in the Third Reich," *American Journal of International Law*, 84, 3 (July): 661–704.

Van Wolferen, Karel (1989) *The Enigma of Japanese Power: People and Politics in a Stateless Nation*, New York: Knopf.

Wehner, Bernd (1980) "Wir wissen nicht, was wir wissen ... obwohl wir es könnten," *Kriminalistik*, 12 (December): 538.

Weiss, Peter (1976) "Joe McCarthy Is Alive and Well and Living in West Germany: Terror and Counter-Terror in the Federal Republic," *New York University Journal of International Law and Politics*, 9, 1 (Spring): 61–88.

Werkentin, Falco (1989) "Stellungnahme zur Frage der ersatzlosen Auflösung der P-Abteilungen in der Staatsanwaltschaft Berlin," unpublished manuscript, Humanistische Union, Landesverband Berlin.

Whittemore, Edward P. (1961) *The Press in Japan Today . . . A Case Study*, Columbia, SC: University of South Carolina Press.

Yokoyama, Minoru (1988) "Development of Japanese Drug Control Laws toward Criminalization," paper presented at the International Conference on Crime, Drugs, and Social Control, Hong Kong, December 14–16.

8 Why is there no NATO in Asia? Collective identity, regionalism, and the origins of multilateralism

Christopher Hemmer and Peter J. Katzenstein
(2002) [1]

Regional groupings and regional effects are of growing importance in world politics. Although often described in geographical terms, regions are political creations and not fixed by geography. Even regions that seem most natural and unalterable are products of political construction and subject to reconstruction attempts. Looking at specific instances in which such constructions have occurred can tell us a great deal about the shape and the shaping of international politics.

In the aftermath of World War II, the United States attempted to create and organize both a North Atlantic and a Southeast Asian region. The institutional forms of these regional groupings, however, differed dramatically. With its North Atlantic partners, the United States preferred to operate on a multilateral basis. With its Southeast Asian partners, in contrast, the United States preferred to operate bilaterally. Why? Perceptions of collective identity, we argue, played an underappreciated role in this decision. Shaped by racial, historical, political, and cultural factors, U.S. policymakers saw their potential European allies as relatively equal members of a shared community. America's potential Asian allies, in contrast, were seen as part of an alien and, in important ways, inferior community. At the beginning of the Cold War, this difference in mutual identification, in combination with material factors and considerations of efficiency, was of critical importance in defining the interests and shaping the choices of U.S. decisionmakers in Europe and Asia. Different forms of cooperation make greater or lesser demands on shared identities. Multilateralism is a particularly demanding form of international cooperation. It requires a strong sense of collective identity in addition to shared interests.

This case is of more than passing historical interest. In recent years, realist and liberal theorists of international relations have debated, more than once, the relative importance and efficacy of material capabilities versus institutions in world politics. Realists have argued that international anarchy and the security dilemma it creates make international institutions epiphenomenal or, at best, marginal to world politics. Liberals have claimed instead that institutions have noticeable effects that can ameliorate the security dilemma. After the end of the Cold War and the collapse of the Soviet Union, neorealist theory, for example, expected the North Atlantic Treaty Organization (NATO) to disintegrate quickly. Neoliberalism did not. Instead, neoliberals argued that NATO helped create conditions that were conducive to peace in Europe after 1945 and that, therefore, NATO was likely to prosper and endure (Duffield 1998; Haftendorn, Keohane, and Wallander 1999; Wallander 1999, 2000). More than a decade has passed since the end of the Cold War and, far from disappearing, NATO is expanding.

The empirical research program of neoliberal institutionalism remains, however, largely restricted to a small pool of successful Western institutions such as NATO, the General Agreement on Tariffs and Trade/World Trade Organization (GATT/WTO), or the European Union (EU) (Kohno 1996). Even in these cases, neoliberal theory encounters uncomfortable difficulties. Why did the Warsaw Pact not persist as uncertainty increased in Eastern Europe's security environment in 1989–90? And why did NATO rather than the Organization for Security and Cooperation in Europe become Europe's preferred security regime in the 1990s? An exclusive focus on unmeasured institutional efficiencies that are created by a stipulated lowering of transaction costs and a variety of institutional asset specificities risks slighting the causal importance of material capabilities and collective identities. "Institutional assets," writes Celeste A. Wallander, "affect the costs and effectiveness of alternative strategies, but they do not determine purpose" (Wallander 2000: 712).

Neoliberal institutionalism's central claim—that institutions develop when states foresee self-interested benefits from cooperation under conditions that are propitious for overcoming obstacles to cooperation—remains in need of further testing and refinement. "A single, deductive model is a bridge too far," conclude Barbara Koremenos, Charles Lipson, and Duncan Snidal, further stating that "Bedrock preferences are constant—a hallmark assumption and limitation of the rational approach" (Koremenos, Lipson, and Snidal 2001: 1065, 1074). Security arrangements in Asia remain a puzzle. Multilateral institutions failed despite the presence of self-interested benefits from cooperation. Even though, as in Europe, multilateral security arrangements would have provided information, reduced transaction costs, made commitments more credible, and established focal points for coordinating policies, after 1945 the U.S. government opted for a hub-and-spokes system of bilateral alliances in Asia with the United States at the center. "If NATO was so successful in Europe," asks Masaru Kohno (1996: 7), "why was it not copied in East Asia in the aftermath of World War II?" Neoliberal theory, by itself, offers no compelling answer to this question.

Neither does a realist analysis that focuses exclusively on capabilities and interests. Realist scholars are right to insist that the main U.S. interests were served well by forming a set of bilateral alliances in Asia (Kohno 1996: 29–33). But they remain silent on the issue of why those interests favored multilateral arrangements in Europe and bilateral ones in Asia. Material capabilities alone offer little help in answering the question of why there was no NATO in Asia.

Strict formulations of both liberalism and realism are less convincing than eclectic variants that also incorporate important insights from constructivist theory (Wendt 1999; Ruggie 1998; Katzenstein 1996b). Eclectic explanations highlight the causal importance of social facts such as power status and threat perceptions, in addition to the material facts and efficiency considerations stressed by rationalist approaches. Eclectic explanations also undercut reifications such as the distinction between domestic and international levels of analysis. Theoretical eclecticism cuts against the paradigmatic organization of most contemporary scholarship on international relations. Thinking in terms of schools of thought, as James Fearon and Alex Wendt argue, at the very least can "encourage scholars to be method-driven rather than problem-driven in their research, which may result in important questions or answers being ignored if they are not amenable to the preferred paradigmatic fashion" (Fearon and Wendt 2001: 1). To liberalism, constructivism adds consideration of the effects identities have on both formal and informal institutions. To neorealism, it adds consideration of the effects of ideational rather than material structures, specifically the effects of identity on actor interests (Adler and Barnett 1998; Neumann 1999; Acharya 2000, 2001).

In the second section of this chapter, we briefly contrast the policies the United States pursued in Europe and Asia during the early Cold War. Although strikingly little comparative work has been done contrasting U.S. foreign policy in Asia and in Europe, in the following section we briefly explore explanations that can be gleaned from the existing literature on why the United States preferred multilateral organizing principles in Europe and bilateral ones in Asia. Next, we put forward three eclectic explanations that combine the material and efficiency factors stressed in realist and liberal explanations with social factors stemming from the different levels of identification American policymakers felt with regard to their European and Asian allies. Finally, we explore some of the theoretical and empirical implications of this argument.

Constructing regions and regional institutions after 1945

When the U.S. Senate first began to debate the issue of a formal U.S. commitment to Europe following World War II, Senator Henry Cabot Lodge, Jr, was puzzled as his colleagues began to discuss the relationship between the United States and its potential European allies as a regional one. "Certainly," he argued, "the United States and Western Europe" could not be part of the same region. "Certainly" they could, Senator Arthur Vandenberg responded, "because this is a North Atlantic region." This exchange initiated a short debate over how far the concept of a region could be stretched. Could a region be anything a state wanted it to be, or did 3,000 miles of ocean render absurd any talk of a common region (U.S. Senate 1973: 14–19, 315–17)? This brief exchange underscores the fact that regions do not just exist as material objects in the world. Geography is not destiny (Paasi 1986). Instead, regions are social and cognitive constructs that can strike actors as more or less plausible.

The creation of NATO and the Southeast Asian Treaty Organization (SEATO) form a natural parallel that has sparked surprisingly little attention from students of international politics (Duffield 2001: 69–72). Comparing the two offers the historian of international relations something like a natural experiment. In the early Cold War, the United States initiated a number of regional alliances to help organize some recently defined regions. The form of these regional alliances, however, varied significantly. The United States consistently treated the newly minted North Atlantic region differently than the newly minted Southeast Asian region. In Europe, it opted to promote a multilateral framework. The United States preferred to deal bilaterally with its Asian allies. Why? Because most of the secondary literature on the creation of these two alliances predates the current theoretical concern with the question of bilateralism versus multilateralism, it is not very illuminating on this issue.

Noting that more than two states make up the SEATO alliance, much secondary literature treats it as a multilateral alliance. SEATO, however, is not multilateral in the same sense as NATO (Ruggie 1997: 105). First, the language of the treaty commitment is much weaker. Instead of the NATO commitment to collective defense as outlined in article V, which states that an attack on one will be considered an attack on all, article IV of the SEATO treaty merely classifies such an attack as a threat to peace and safety. Furthermore, in SEATO the United States made it clear that it retained its prerogative to act bilaterally or unilaterally. This was formalized in the Rusk–Thanat joint statement of 1962, in which the United States stressed that its commitment to Thailand "does not depend upon prior agreement of all the other parties to the treaty, since the obligation is individual as well as collective" (Rusk and Thanat 1962: 498–9). Organizationally, the differences were just as apparent. In SEATO, there was no unified command and no specifically allocated unified forces; and any actions taken under SEATO auspices were handled individually by the member states and not by the institution as a whole (Modelski 1962: 38–9; Webb 1962: 66).

U.S. policymakers contemplated the possibility of establishing an Asian NATO. Indeed, many of its prospective members favored the creation of a NATO-type institution (Lundestad 1999: 208; Kohno 1996: 29; Kim 1965: 65–6). The United States, however, remained adamantly opposed to using NATO as the model and even discouraged the use of the term SEATO, fearing unwanted comparisons of the acronyms. As one member of the U.S. State Department wrote to John Foster Dulles:

> In accordance with your suggestion . . . we have attempted to get away from the designation "SEATO" so as to avoid fostering the idea than an organization is envisioned for SEA [Southeast Asia] and the Pacific similar to NATO. . . . In spite of our efforts, the designation "SEATO" has

stuck. . . . *I suggest that we accept that "SEATO" is here to stay and that we*
continue to make clear in our substantive discussions that so far as the U.S. is
concerned, the SEA Pact is not conceived as a parallel to NATO.

(U.S. Department of State 1984: 740–1; emphasis in original)

In the following section, we discuss existing arguments regarding the
rise of multilateral or bilateral institutions to see what they can offer in the
way of explanation for why the United States treated NATO and SEATO so
differently.

Universal and indeterminate explanations

Even though most studies of the security arrangements the United States
sought to create after World War II are regionally limited to Europe or Asia,
many seek universal explanations for the rise of multilateral or bilateral
institutions. Once Europe and Asia are placed in a comparative perspective,
however, the problem with these explanations becomes obvious. As universal
explanations, they are unable to account for the regional differences in U.S.
policy. A second set of explanations for America's preference for multilateral
mechanisms in Europe and for bilateral mechanisms in Asia is underdetermined. The opportunities and constraints to which these accounts point as
the driving force behind U.S. choices could have been satisfied by either
bilateral or multilateral security arrangements. Therefore, by themselves,
these explanations are insufficient.

Universal explanations

More than any other scholar, John Ruggie has drawn our attention to the
importance of multilateralism as a novel social institution in twentieth-
century diplomacy. Ruggie focuses mostly on Europe in this context (Ruggie
1993, 1994). He interprets the expansion of multilateral principles after
World War II as the result of the U.S. "vision as to what constitutes a desirable
world order" (Ruggie 1994: 560; Legro 2000). According to this view, the
United States has pushed multilateral principles abroad for a number of
reasons. The principles are a convenient mask for U.S. hegemony. They
duplicate U.S. domestic order. And they are consistent with the U.S. view of
itself (Ruggie 1994: 561–5). While this explains why the United States
may find multilateral principles attractive, it cannot explain why the United
States pushed multilateralism much more in Europe than in Asia. Ruggie
notes this difference, but does not attempt to account for it beyond noting that it "was not possible" to embrace multilateralism in Asia (Ruggie
1993: 4, 29).

Anne-Marie Burley offers a similarly universal explanation (Burley 1993).
Following Charles Maier (1978), Burley argues that U.S. support for multilateralism was an attempt to apply the lessons the United States had learned

from the Great Depression on an international scale. In essence, Burley argues, the United States attempted to implement a global New Deal following the war. However, this account suffers from the same limitations as Ruggie's. It cannot explain why the United States applied these global principles differently in different world regions. As David Lake notes, the United States projects its norms onto the global scene "in a highly selective fashion that itself needs to be explained" (Lake 1999: 218).

Universal explanations derived from studies focusing on U.S. policy toward Asia during the Cold War are equally limited. One such explanation highlights the unwillingness of the United States to delegate authority. If the United States was going to bear the largest share of the burden for the military defense of Asia, why should it cede control or limit its freedom of action in a multilateral institution (Kim 1965: 68; Webb 1962: 66)? In the words of one U.S. Department of Defense official, a "NATO pattern" in Asia would be "inimical to U.S. interests in that it could . . . tend to reduce, without compensating military advantage, United States military freedom of action" (U.S. Department of State 1984: 767–8).

This explanation also fails to account for the different policies the United States pursued in Europe and Asia. Why would the United States accept the loss of control entailed in the creation of multilateral institutions in Europe, but not in Asia? A realist could answer that the United States accepted this loss of control in Europe because the European states offered a "compensating military advantage." Such an explanation is undoubtedly partly correct. In their material power resources, European states offered more advantages to the United States than did Asian states. This, however, can only be part of the story. During the early Cold War, the United States was so far ahead of both the war-destroyed European states and the newly emerging states of Asia that any differences between these two regions was probably marginal compared to the huge gulf separating the United States from both. By itself, therefore, a general unwillingness to cede control to weaker allies in multilateral institutions cannot explain the regional difference in U.S. policy.

Underdetermined explanations

Steven Weber's important work on the evolution of multilateralism in NATO argues that U.S. policymakers believed a multipolar world would be more stable than the bipolar world they saw come into existence following World War II (Weber 1991, 1993). The only way for a multipolar world to come into being, however, would be for centers of power to emerge that were independent of the United States and the Soviet Union. The United States promoted multilateralism in Europe, according to Weber, to encourage the emergence of an independent center of power that could usher in a more peaceful period of multipolarity.

The logic of this argument, as Weber notes, would lead him to expect that the U.S. preference for multipolarity should also have led it to promote the development of independent centers of power in Asia as well as in Europe (Weber 1991: 16). In part, this expectation is confirmed—the United States did try to restore Japan's power. However, in building up an independent center of power in Asia, the United States chose to do so in terms of its bilateral relationship with Japan, rather than in terms of a regional multilateral institution. Thus, by itself, the U.S. desire to see the emergence of independent centers of power has no direct relationship to the choice between bilateral or multilateral security arrangements.

A second underdetermined explanation points to the hostilities that existed between Japan and its neighbors after 1945. Fearful of Japan's reemergence as an imperialist power, many Asian states were hesitant to join any Pacific alliance that had Japan as a member (Duffield 2001: 80–1; Kohno 1996: 31–2). For example, John Foster Dulles discovered that many prospective members of any Asian alliance "have memories of Japanese aggression that are so vivid that they are reluctant to create a Mutual Security Pact with Japan" (Dulles 1952: 182).

Yet fear of Japan does not offer a complete explanation for the U.S. decision to work bilaterally in Asia. Germany's pariah status following World War II was equal to if not greater than Japan's. Yet this pariah status did not prevent the United States from supporting and pursuing multilateral initiatives in Europe that would soon include Germany (Trachtenberg 1999). There were many calls for the United States to rehabilitate Japan in the eyes of its neighbors so that it could become a member of a wider Pacific pact. Such a policy would have required a sharper break with the past than General MacArthur and the U.S. occupation of Japan were prepared to make, particularly with respect to the political status of Emperor Hirohito (Bix 2000: 533–80). In fact, the United States government never made the same efforts to integrate Japan into Asia through multilateral institutions as it did for Germany in Europe (Hampton 1998/9). Had the United States pushed its Asian allies to accept Japan as hard as it pushed its European allies to integrate with Germany, similar institutions might have evolved in the two regions (U.S. Department of State 1984: 425–6).

A third underdetermined argument centers on the Eisenhower administration's New Look policy. Central to this policy was reducing the defense budget by limiting reliance on costly ground troops and focusing on a less expensive nuclear deterrent. Some argue that the limited nature of the U.S. commitment to SEATO flowed from the fiscal conservatism and massive retaliation strategy of the Eisenhower administration, reinforced by the lessons of the Korean War (Marks 1993: 51–2; Hess 1990: 280). As Secretary of State Dulles put it during Senate hearings on the SEATO treaty:

> We do not expect to duplicate in this area the pattern of the NATO [organization] and its significant standing forces. That would require a diversion of and commitment of strength which we do not think is either practical or desirable or necessary.

Instead, Dulles emphasized the "mobile striking power" of U.S. forces that need not and should not be easily pinned down at many points around the circumference of the communist world (U.S. Senate 1954: 13–14, 17).

While this is a plausible explanation for why the United States wanted to limit any ground commitment to SEATO, it is less compelling as an explanation for the lack of multilateralism in SEATO. At the same time that the United States was creating SEATO, it was also trying to limit its ground commitments and increase reliance on nuclear deterrence in Europe. In NATO, however, the United States attempted to do this multilaterally through the sharing of nuclear weapons within the alliance (Trachtenberg 1999: 147–215; Weber 1991: 48–69). Thus, limited ground commitments and a multilateral alliance structure could potentially have been as compatible in Asia as in Europe. The United States, however, did not try to make them compatible in Asia.

In sum, several universal or underdetermined explanations of the rise of multilateral and bilateral security institutions in Europe and Asia suffer from one of two weaknesses. They offer accounts that do not consider regional variations, or they identify constraints and opportunities for U.S. foreign policy that could have been satisfied by either bilateral or multilateral arrangements.

Eclectic explanations: power, threats, and identity

To account for the different policies pursued by the United States in building its alliances in Europe and Asia after World War II, realist analyses focus on the distribution of power among the United States and its putative allies and enemies, while liberal explanations focus on the relative efficiencies of different institutional forms. While both approaches offer some insight into NATO and SEATO origins, both rely, often implicitly, on nonrationalist arguments about identity to make their cases plausible. As Alastair Iain Johnston and David E. Spiro, among others, have argued in their eclectic rendering of a realist analysis, variables like power status and threats are social facts, whose significance, while anchored in material reality, cannot simply be read off material capabilities (Johnston 1995; Spiro 1999). Constructivist explanations that focus on identity alone are similarly incomplete. Divorced from the material and efficiency factors stressed by realists and liberals, constructivist arguments about the importance of identity risk being empirically too thin and analytically too malleable. Rather than seeking to establish the superiority of one approach over another, we develop eclectic explanations that offer compelling insights into a specific empirical puzzle.

Great power status

The relative weakness of the regional members of SEATO is a strong realist argument for why SEATO was not formed along NATO lines. The discrepancy between the power of the United States and the power of its Asian allies may have made the multilateral bargain an unattractive one for the United States. George Modelski, for example, argues that "in NATO the benefits and obligations are shared fairly equally. In SEATO the disparity between the great and small powers is greater. . . . Most of SEATO's concrete operations represent one-way traffic to help area states and not a two-way cooperative enterprise" (Modelski 1962: 39). If it is restricted to material capabilities only, however, this explanation encounters some problems. A huge disparity between the United States and its regional allies existed not only in Asia but also in war-destroyed Europe. Moreover, Japan was not invited to join SEATO even though as a modern industrialized state it potentially could have contributed many resources to the fledgling alliance. Similarly, other regional states with strong militaries, like South Korea and Taiwan, were not invited to join the alliance. Material capabilities alone do not offer a compelling answer for why the United States did not pursue this course.

Great power status, however, did matter. U.S. officials believed that, despite current disparities in capabilities due to the ravages World War II had inflicted on Europe, their European allies would soon rebuild their strength, while their Asian allies would remain permanently weak. While U.S. policy-makers may have acted condescendingly to their European partners in comparison to their Asian allies, it was condescension tempered by the expectation of Europe's revival. Indeed, much of U.S. policy toward Europe was driven by the perception of the European states as great powers. According to Steve Weber, President Eisenhower, one of the strongest proponents of multilateralism in NATO, "held strong views about the traditional place of Britain, France and even Germany as great powers in world politics." Their position as "secondary actors . . . was simply unnatural" (Weber 1991: 41). Most Southeast Asian states, by way of contrast, were in the late 1940s only at the threshold of shedding their colonial status and gaining national sovereignty for the first time.

In Asia, the United States really had only one potential great power ally— Japan (Duffield 2001: 77–80). However, an analysis focused solely on the material balance of power leaves important questions unanswered (Reiter 1996: 41–54). In Asia, why did the United States not ally with China against the Soviet Union? The Chinese revolution and Mao's victory in 1949 were of critical importance. A threat is rooted not solely in differential material capabilities but also in the view of the difference between self and other that shapes interpretations of actor intentions and interests. Although conceivable in terms of material balance of power, for ideological reasons communist China was not a plausible alliance partner for the United States after 1949. Eclectic theorizing enriches balance-of-power explanations.

Efficient responses to threat

A liberal explanation for why the United States failed to push multilateralism in Asia focuses on the different threats faced in Asia and Europe and the most institutionally efficient response to those threats. The military and civilian leadership in the United States was in general agreement that Southeast Asia was less important and less threatened than Europe (U.S. Department of State 1984: 3, 831). Furthermore, the threat in Asia, it could be argued, was one of national insurgencies rather than cross-border war. These differences suggest the appropriateness of different institutional countermeasures in the two regions.

In Europe, the military structure of NATO was designed to hold off a massive Soviet offensive. U.S. officials expected no large-scale offensive by either the Soviet Union or China in Asia. The primary problem for the United States in Asia was fighting communist insurgencies. Security arrangements designed to fend off a Soviet assault might not have been appropriate for dealing with national insurgencies. Indeed, they might have been counter-productive. The varied nature of the internal subversive threats faced by the different states might have made a "one-size-fits-all" multilateral defense arrangement like the one built in NATO inappropriate (U.S. Department of State 1984: 1023–4). In one of the few references to SEATO in his memoirs, Eisenhower approvingly quotes Churchill's belief that "Since sectors of the SEATO front were so varied in place and conditions, he [Churchill] felt it best to operate nationally where possible" (Eisenhower 1963: 368).

It is important to note, however, that different perceptions of threat were tied to questions of identity. As Dean Acheson saw it, the threat to which NATO responded was posed "not only to our country but also to the civiliza-tion in which we live." "To understand this threat," Acheson continued, one had to "go back more than 2000 years, to the very beginning of Western civilization" (Jackson 2001: 429–30). Or, as Undersecretary of State Robert Lovett put it, the "cement" of the treaty "was not the Soviet threat, but the common Western approach and that Western attachment to the worth of the individual" (Reid 1977: 133).

It is evident that different threat perceptions often frustrated U.S. officials throughout the SEATO negotiations. One U.S. State Department official com-plained that Asian states were "preoccupied" with internal problems and "distracted" by memories of colonialism. Thus, "the idea that Communist imperialism is the immediate and major threat has been slow in taking hold" (Murphy 1954: 516). Secretary Dulles bemoaned the fact that "the countries which had won or were winning their independence from Western colonial-ism or Japan were often more concerned with past dangers . . . than the threat of new peril" (Dulles 1954: 743). Historical enmities, colonial legacies, and newly won state sovereignties affected how Asian elites viewed the commun-ist threat in Asia. In contrast to the Manichean vision of U.S. decisionmakers, Asian elites confronted a welter of relevant social facts rooted in the perception of self and other.

A direct line from a certain type of threat (cross-border Soviet attack) to a particular institutional form (multilateralism) cannot be drawn in Europe. The European situation after World War II, similar to the situation in Asia, was also complicated. In the early days of NATO the United States neither expected nor feared a massive Soviet assault. U.S. officials saw the creation of NATO as a political move that bolstered the morale of European governments and thus helped them deal with their internal troubles, and as a means of reassuring other European states against any resurgence of a threat from Germany (Gheciu 2001).

Consider also the development of these two alliances over time. While the multilateral nature of NATO grew over time with the perceived probability of a potential Soviet attack in Europe, the increased salience of cross-border conflict in Asia failed to have the same impact on U.S. relations with its Pacific allies. The Korean War in particular intensified U.S. threat perception of the Soviet Union's role in Europe. NATO's military buildup and German rearmament became a political option only after the onset of military hostilities on the Korean peninsula. In Asia, by way of contrast, the Korean War failed to spur any move toward increased multilateralism. Indeed, the two states most at risk of a cross-border threat from China (South Korea and Taiwan) were explicitly kept outside of SEATO (U.S. Senate 1949: 56–9).

These different responses raise a difficult problem for those who see a direct relationship between a particular type of threat and a specific institutional response. Why does a conventional war (as the United States saw it) in Korea lead to a multilateral response in Europe, but not in Asia, the actual location of the fighting? Despite Soviet caution in Europe, a conventional war in Asia acts as a catalyst for the growth of multilateral security arrangements in Europe, but fails to have the same effect for U.S. alliance efforts in Asia. Similarly, when the United States in the 1960s interpreted the Vietnam War as a conventional cross-border attack, it, too, failed to spur the growth of multilateral alliance arrangements in Asia.

Had the threat of a massive Soviet assault on Europe never developed, and had the Soviet threat remained entirely one of internal subversion, NATO certainly would have remained a much weaker organization than the one that has developed. The question, however, is whether it is the nature of this cross-border threat that can explain the U.S. preference for multilateralism in Europe. Fortunately, there is no reason to rely purely on counterfactual speculation to answer this question. As the implementation of the Marshall Plan illustrates, the United States preferred to operate multilaterally in Europe even when the Soviet threat was seen as one of internal subversion rather than cross-border attack. In brief, whether the threat was one of internal subversion or cross-border assault, the United States preferred to operate multilaterally in Europe and bilaterally in Asia.

Following Stephen Walt's classic treatment, threat is frequently invoked in realist and liberal analyses (Walt 1987). Yet Walt's theory of threat is a major departure from neorealist theory and pushes beyond rationalist styles of analysis. Specifically, in his analysis Walt moves a large distance from material capabilities to ideational factors. In his analysis, ideology is a variable that competes with others for explanatory power. Ideology is a system of meaning that entails the distinction between self and other in the definition of threat. The cost calculations that states make when they weigh ideological solidarity against security interests are thus not exogenous to their ideological affinities. Hence the threat perception of enemies is an explanatory variable that does not offer a compelling answer as much as it invites further investigation (Katzenstein 1996a: 27–8).

Explanations stressing differences in the great power status of European and Asian states or efficient institutional responses to the nature of the communist threat in Europe and Asia share an emphasis on the causal importance of identity—as a certain kind of power and as a specific kind of enemy. The following section builds upon and fleshes out these related explanations to provide a fuller account of the way collective identity helped create regional configurations in Europe and Asia that, respectively, included and excluded the United States.

Regions, identification, and institutional form

A border, argued Georg Simmel, is not a geographic fact that has sociological consequences, but a sociological fact that takes geographic form (Gienow-Hecht 2000: 488). The same can be said of regions. Neither the North Atlantic nor Southeast Asia existed as geographical facts. Both were politically constructed (Lewis and Wigen 1997; Polelle 1999).

The policy of the United States regarding the organization of both regions is puzzling. From a realist perspective, the U.S. preference for multilateralism in Europe after World War II is quite surprising. As Steve Weber notes, a hegemon can maximize its bargaining leverage by forging a series of bilateral deals with its allies rather than tying its hands in a multilateral framework (Weber 1991: 5–9). Conversely, liberals would probably find the U.S. preference for bilateralism in Southeast Asia after World War II the greater puzzle. As Anne-Marie Burley notes, multilateralism is "the form to be expected from a set of international regimes established by a liberal state" (Burley 1993: 145). A satisfactory explanation must account for both U.S. choices.

The effects of collective identity are an important ingredient of any such explanation. The institutional forms the United States favored in Europe and Asia during the early Cold War were shaped by the different levels of identification that U.S. policymakers had with these newly constructed regions. Identification, as Martha Finnemore notes, "emphasizes the affective relationships between actors" and "is an ordinal concept, allowing for degrees of affect as well as changes in the focus of affect" (Finnemore 1996: 160). An argument about the importance of identification in driving U.S. policy in these two regions is consistent with what is perhaps the dominant psychological theory about group identity and its effects—social identity theory (Tajfel 1978; Tajfel and Turner 1986; Prentice and Miller 1999). Once people identify themselves as part of a particular group, studies of social identity have found, they treat members of that group very differently than those outside the group. For instance, when people distribute gains within a defined group, they tend to look more toward maximizing absolute gains; in dealing with outsiders they tend to focus more on relative gains and maximizing the differential between insiders and outsiders (Mercer 1995: 239–40). These findings have been consistent across studies even with the flimsiest and most arbitrarily defined groups. In short, identification is the mechanism that helps connect the construction of specific regional groupings in Europe and Asia to particular institutional features—multilateral or bilateral—of particular military alliances.

Looked at from the perspective of social identity theory, U.S. policies in both regions become less puzzling. Once the North Atlantic was constructed as a region that put the United States in a grouping of roughly equal states with which it identified, multilateral organizing principles followed closely. As Ernest Bevin, the British foreign minister, put it, bilateral relations imposed by the strongest power, similar to what the Soviets were doing in Eastern Europe, are "not in keeping with the spirit of Western civilisation, and if we are to have an organism in the West it must be a spiritual union . . . it must contain all the elements of freedom for which we all stand" (P. T. Jackson 2001: 428–9). U.S. policymakers agreed, believing that the Europeans could be trusted with the additional power a multilateral institution would give them and that the Europeans deserved this increased influence.

Lacking strong identification, the United States did not, however, apply the same liberal principles when it came to organizing the newly created Southeast Asian region. Once Southeast Asia, in the view of U.S. policymakers, was constructed as a region composed of alien and, in many ways, inferior actors, bilateralism followed closely. U.S. policymakers did not believe that the Southeast Asian states could be trusted with the increased influence a multilateral institution would offer, nor was there any sense that these states deserved such a multilateral structure.

What was the basis for the identification of the United States with Europe and the lack thereof in its relations with Asia? The available evidence is relatively sketchy and permits only cautious inferences. In their identification with Europe, U.S. officials typically refer to religion and democratic values as the bedrock of a North Atlantic community. A common race is mentioned, though less often, perhaps because Germany's genocidal policies in the 1940s had thoroughly delegitimated that concept in European political discourse (Horne 1999: 454–9; Hunt 1987: 161–2). Perceived affinities of various types reinforced the political trust rooted in common democratic political institutions, "we-feeling," and "mutual responsiveness" that Karl Deutsch and his associates have described as central ingredients of the emergence of a North Atlantic security community, defined by the existence of dependable expectations of peaceful change (Deutsch *et al.* 1957). In the case of Asia, these various affinities and trust were absent, religion and democratic values were shared only in a few cases, and race was invoked as a powerful force separating the United States from Asia. The U.S. preference for multilateral or bilateral security arrangements followed from these different constellations.

The origin of the North Atlantic community

The creation of the political concept of the North Atlantic community is an excellent example of the process of identification at work in U.S. politics as well as a demonstration of how issues of identity are entwined with material factors and instrumental political calculations. The emergence of a North Atlantic region followed a dramatic change in the prevalent image of the United States' place in the world that occurred during World War II. Before the war, Alan Henrikson argues, maps were typically drawn with the United States in the center surrounded by two oceans. However, the efforts to resupply Great Britain and to later transport large numbers of troops to Europe caused a change in that cartographic and cognitive image. During and after the war, more and more maps appeared that put the Atlantic in the center with the United States and Europe positioned on opposite sides. During World War II, the Atlantic association thus became more natural (Henrikson 1975). The shift to a "North" Atlantic focus was given a boost after 1945 when the Soviet Union pressured Norway to sign a defense pact. Had the Soviet Union established a zone of influence over Norway it would have gained a large window on the Atlantic and thus exposed Europe's northern flank (Henrikson 1980).

The creation of the new geographic category of "North Atlantic" also served clear political ends and was in some ways the product of calculated political agency. Martin Folly, for example, argues that "the idea of a North Atlantic system was a stroke of genius" on the part of Ernest Bevin (Folly 1988: 68). In the early 1940s, the British government embarked on a political strategy aiming to prevent a disengagement of the United States from Europe after the end of the war. Bevin recognized that the United States would hesitate to join a "European" alliance, but would feel much more comfortable talking about sea-lanes, access to bases, and a "North Atlantic" alliance. A North Atlantic focus meshed nicely with the U.S. military's concern with "stepping stones" across the Atlantic. Reliant on bases and stopping-off points for the transportation of troops and equipment across the Atlantic, the armed services' emphasis on the importance of Iceland, Greenland, and the Azores also put the Atlantic in the foreground (Lundestad 1980: 251; Henrikson 1975, 1980: 19). In U.S. domestic politics, the focus on a North Atlantic community had a twofold advantage. It promised to be an easier sell to an electorate and a Congress wary of European entanglements (Kaplan 1984: 2–3, 7–8, 10, 31, 41–2, 52, 70, 78, 115–17); furthermore, the concept of "community" established a basis for identification that transcended military–strategic considerations.

Terminological innovation also suited Canada. Seeking to minimize bilateral dealings with the United States, Canada opposed any sort of "dumb-bell"-shaped arrangement combining a North American and a European pole. A North Atlantic arrangement would allow Canada to use the European states as a balance against the United States. It would also allow the Canadian government to portray its concessions to the alliance as concessions to a North Atlantic group of states and not solely as concessions to the United States. In short, a North Atlantic community meant that Canada did not have to deal with the United States alone (Reid 1977: 102–10, 131–2).

It is important to note that this geographically defined category constrained but did not determine membership. If geography is destiny, the inclusion of Italy, "unwashed by Atlantic waters," in NATO was clearly an anomaly (Lundestad 1980: 242). So was the subsequent accession of Greece and Turkey. Even after George Kennan acquiesced in the creation of a North Atlantic treaty, he continued to oppose Italy's participation. Only by limiting the treaty to a strict geographic area, Kennan reasoned, could the United States avoid provoking the Soviet Union and offending other allies by their exclusion. As Kennan saw it, "the only sound standard for membership in the Atlantic Pact was indeed a geographic one" (Kennan 1967: 411–12). While the administration readily conceded that Italy was not in the North Atlantic, it continued to support Italy's inclusion because it was too important to Atlantic defenses to be left out (Acheson 1969: 279; Truman 1956: 238–50). Italy's inclusion among NATO's founding members, along with that of undemocratic Portugal (given the strategic importance of the Azores), underscores the importance of eclectic explanations that encompass both strategic calculations and regional identities. In these two cases, the geographically defined region and the sense of identification with fellow democracies proved less decisive than strategic calculations in determining membership. Italy's membership ended up being consequential, however, because even as it violated "the 'natural' geographic basis of the North Atlantic, it had the subtle effect of extending the Atlantic concept itself to eventually include both the Western and the Eastern Mediterranean" (Henrikson 1980: 19–20).

In 1948, official and public discourse regarding Europe saw a major and sudden change. Before March 1948, a possible transatlantic alliance was invariably discussed under the rubric of a European or a Western European alliance. After March 1948, however, the focus of official discourse, as reflected in the documents produced at the time, shifted radically to an Atlantic or North Atlantic treaty system and community. The public discourse, as indicated by the coverage of the *New York Times*, underwent a similar transformation in late 1948. For example, in the editorial cartoons offered in the "Week in Review" section, the graphical opponent of the Soviet Union changes from Europe, to Western Europe, to the West, and finally, by December 1948, to the North Atlantic and NATO. The relatively sudden emergence of this "North Atlantic" focus demonstrates that new regional identities can emerge quickly if suitable material and ideational raw materials are available.

Considering the rapidity of this shift to a North Atlantic focus, it is noteworthy that U.S. State Department officials insisted that the signatories of the treaty did not invent the North Atlantic region. They maintained instead that the treaty merely codified a political community that had been in existence for centuries and that provided the basis for mutual identification. In the words of Dean Acheson, NATO was "the product of at least three hundred and fifty years of history, perhaps more" (Acheson 1949: 385). Yet, for all the stress on the reality and long history of the region, prior to 1948, with the exception of a few references to the International Civil Aviation Organization, State Department officials never talked about a North Atlantic region. Like geography, history was not destiny.

The origins of Southeast Asia

Southeast Asia as a particularly defined region has also had a relatively brief history. Before World War II, the region had been known by a number of different names. Some divided the area into Chinese-influenced Indochina, the Spanish-influenced Philippines, and those areas strongly influenced by Indian culture. Among European and U.S. diplomats, the region was often seen as an extension of either China or India and referred to as "further India," "greater India," "Indo-China," or "the Far Eastern tropics." The popular term in Japan was "Nan-yo" (southern seas) and in China either Nan-Yang or Kun-Lun ("Little China" or "the lands of the Southern Ocean") (Sar Desai 1997: 3; Williams 1976: 3–5; Warshaw 1975: 1).

The rise to prominence of the term "Southeast Asia" came with Japan's occupation of the area during the Pacific War. The term emerged to designate the areas south of China that fell to Japanese occupation (Williams 1976: 3; Warshaw 1975: 1). The private correspondence between Roosevelt and Churchill during World War II reflects the gradual emergence of this regional designation. A first mention came in early 1941 when Roosevelt wrote about Japan's proposal to forgo any armed advance into the "Southeastern Asiatic" area, provided the United States made a similar pledge. Roosevelt further explained to Churchill that the U.S. response was to simply warn Japan against taking any military moves in "South-East Asia" (Kimball 1984, 1: 275–6).

After the United States entered the war and decided to concentrate first on the European theater, discussion of the region faded. When attention shifted back to the Asian theater, what to call this region remained undecided. Churchill wrote in June 1943 that it was time for the Allies to think more about "the South East Asia (or Japan) front," and he recommended the creation of a new command for that region. Later, Churchill reiterated this call, but now denoted the envisioned entity as "a new command for East Asia." Here, practical political calculations heavily influenced the naming process as Roosevelt rejected Churchill's call for a unified East Asian command, arguing that creating such a command would alienate Chiang Kai-shek, who controlled the China theater. To avoid such offense, Roosevelt moved the focus back to "South-East Asia." Churchill accepted Roosevelt's worries about offending China and agreed that "perhaps it would be desirable to give the new command the title of 'South-East Asia' instead of 'East Asia' " (Kimball 1984, 2: 248, 263, 275–7, 282). At the Quebec conference in August 1943, the United States and Great Britain agreed to create a Southeast Asian Command (SEAC). SEAC's area of responsibility corresponded roughly to what today is conventionally called Southeast Asia.

After the victory of communist forces in China, the hands-off policy the United States had adopted after the Pacific War shifted quickly. In Andrew Rotter's words, the Truman administration " 'discovered' Southeast Asia at the intersection of its policy toward China, Japan, Great Britain, and France" (Rotter 1987: 5). Bolstering pro-Western forces in the region could help contain China, restore Japan's economy, strengthen Britain, and halt the bleeding of France. U.S. policy became "regionalized." "American policy makers," writes Rotter, "no longer regarded Southeast Asia as a disparate jumble of unrelated states, but as a region that had to be tied to the most important independent nations of the Far East and Western Europe" (Rotter 1987: 16). SEATO, established in September of 1954, should be seen as an extension of this regionalization and the political attempt at tying the region to the rest of the world. Only two of SEATO's members, Thailand and the Philippines, were geographically part of Southeast Asia. The other six members (Australia, France, Great Britain, New Zealand, Pakistan, and the United States) came from outside the region.

The inclusion of France and Great Britain and, to a lesser extent, Australia and New Zealand in SEATO raises a number of interesting issues. In one sense, it shows the importance of a sense of identity in forming alliances. As the United States endeavored to construct alliances outside of Europe, it sought the cooperation of European states even as European colonialism was collapsing in Asia. With Great Britain and France in the alliance, however, why not work multilaterally with them as the United States did with NATO? The answer to this question points to the malleability of identity—a source of weakness for explanations that focus only on identity. Looking to the postwar world, Franklin Roosevelt initially had hoped to work with China rather than European colonial powers in bringing stability to Asia. When the victory of communist forces in China made that course impossible, the United States turned reluctantly to the European colonial powers as a distinctly second-best solution. Here is one area where the U.S. identification with its European allies broke down. The U.S. government was unwilling to identify itself too closely with the colonial practices of the European states in Asia; this limited the degree to which the United States wanted to work multilaterally with the European states in Asia. The pliability of this sense of identity—America is like the Europeans in Europe, but not like the Europeans in Asia—shows the limitations of explanations that focus only on collective identity and underlines the advantages of eclectic explanations.

NATO and SEATO

Based on civilizational, ethnic, racial, and religious ties as well as shared historical memories, identification with Europeans rather than with the peoples of Southeast Asia was considered to be quite natural. These different levels of mutual identification are an important cause of the different institutional forms that the United States favored for its alliances in Europe and Asia during the early Cold War.

One of the most striking aspects of the discussions surrounding the formation of NATO is the pervasive identification of the United States with Europe. This aspect is exemplified by the strident assertion that the North Atlantic already existed as a political community and that the treaty merely formalized this pre-existing community of shared ideals and interest (Hampton 1995). In political debates in the United States, one found constant references to a "common civilization," a "community," a shared "spirit," "like-minded peoples," and "common ideals" (U.S. Senate 1973: 87, 344; U.S. Senate 1949: 15, 197, 292). As W. Averell Harriman put it, "there is a spiritual emotion about this which is hard to emphasize . . . free men are standing shoulder to shoulder" (U.S. Senate 1949: 206). Even while criticizing the Truman administration's overall policies, the columnist Walter Lippman argued that the members of the "Atlantic Community" are "natural allies of the United States." The "nucleus" of this community, according to Lippman, is "distinct and unmistakable," based on geography, religion, and history (Jackson 2001: 320–1). The rhetoric of the United States' European allies similarly referred to a "spiritual confederation of the West," protecting "Western bastion[s]," "the virtues and values of our own civilization," and how the "North Atlantic Community is a real commonwealth of nations which share the same democratic and cultural traditions" (Jackson 2001: 427–8; Gheciu 2001: 3–5). This sentiment found ultimate expression in the preamble of the NATO treaty, which affirmed the determination of the members "to safeguard the freedom, common heritage and civilization of their peoples."

Identification had an undeniable racial component. For example, former U.S. Assistant Secretary of State Will Clayton hoped that NATO could be the first step in the formation of an Atlantic Federal Union. In his testimony in support of NATO, Clayton explicitly linked his support of closer U.S. and European relations to racial grounds in addition to cultural ones. He argued that "my idea would be that in the beginning the union would be composed of all countries that have our ideas and ideals of freedom and that are composed of the white race" (U.S. Senate 1949: 380).

In part because Americans identified strongly with Europeans, Europe was also judged to be a strong ally. Indeed, strong identification with Europe led the United States to consistently give very high and favorable estimates of the strength of its European allies (Urwin 1995: 14). Throughout the Cold War, U.S. officials distinguished their NATO partners from other alliance members. Europe was seen as a "center of world power" populated by a "vigorous" people who had been powerful in the past and would be again in the future (H. M. Jackson 1967: ix; U.S. Senate 1949: 192). Looking at what he called the "great industrial complex of Western Europe," President Eisenhower believed that America's Atlantic allies could not long remain intimidated by "190 million backward" Russians. Speaking specifically about the Eisenhower administration's plan to create a multilateral nuclear sharing arrangement within NATO, Dulles argued that a unilateral U.S. nuclear guarantee could not be "a sound basis for a major country's security" and that he simply could not "contemplate a situation in which there were first and second class powers in NATO" (Trachtenberg 1999: 147, 177, 194, 197, 210).

The United States' reaction to the formation of SEATO was very different. U.S. debates show hardly a trace of identification, and there are no equivalent statements of shared ideals or future visions of the Asian allies as great powers. Indeed, it is the differences, not the commonalties, in civilization, race, ethnicity, religion, and historical memories that lead to the articulation of strong doubts about the current and future strength of these nations as parts of an Asian alliance. Even as colonialism was ending, the colonial mindset remained strong. This outlook stemmed in large part from the personal backgrounds of the men who dominated the U.S. foreign policy machinery after World War II. Drawn from elite New England prep schools, Ivy League universities, and Wall Street businesses and law firms, the so-called "Eastern Establishment" was then in its heyday. These men, alternating between their private- and public-sector careers, switching positions "like lines in a hockey game changing on the fly," ventured into the post-World War II world with a European and even an Atlantic bias (Isaacson and Thomas 1986: 19–31, 128). Having "grown up and succeeded in a world marked by European power, Third World weakness, and nearly ubiquitous racial segregation," they could accept such distinctions between Europeans and others without question (Borstelmann 1999: 552). Interestingly, when these men attempted to explain what they saw as the more alien and difficult to understand behavior of the Soviet Union, they invariably stressed the "Asiatic" or "Oriental" nature of the regime (Borstelmann 1999: 552–3; Isaacson and Thomas 1986: 306, 320). As Senator James Eastland viewed the nascent Cold War, it was a struggle between "eastern and western civilization," a battle between "the Oriental hordes and a western civilization 2,000 years old" (Jackson 2001: 293).

A multilateral approach in Europe also allowed American politicians to evade the potentially delicate challenge posed by different ethnic voting blocs in the United States. With large numbers of Americans tracing their ancestry to different European countries, attempting to play favorites or to make distinctions among these states in American foreign policy would be a risky strategy for elected politicians if these distinctions upset significant ethnic voting blocs. By treating all European allies the same, multilateralism offered a solution to what could otherwise have been a tricky balancing act. Since Asian-American voting blocs were less important during the early stages of the Cold War, a similar electoral dilemma did not arise with regard to U.S. foreign policy in Asia (Cowhey 1993; DeConde 1992: 148–51, 194).

There were, of course, segments in U.S. society that had more interactions with and material interests in Asia than Europe. Represented mostly by the midwestern and Pacific wings of the Republican Party, these individuals called for an "Asia-first" strategy after Pearl Harbor and continued to criticize U.S. foreign policy into the Cold War for paying too little attention to Asia. Part of the attention they gave to Asia was driven by their desire to criticize the European-focused Eastern Establishment that dominated the Democratic Party, the presidency, and the foreign policy apparatus of the U.S. government. A large part of this attention, however, was also driven by the commercial links Western businesses had forged across the Pacific and the large number of American missionaries who had gone to Asia (Westerfield 1955: 240–68; Purifoy 1976: 49–73).

Why did the preferences of American elites looking to Europe prevail over those of the Asia-firsters? In keeping with our emphasis on the need for eclectic explanations, we find that the answer lies in a combination of identity and material factors. Identifying with Europe, the Eastern Establishment not only had a preference for cooperating with and focusing on Europe, it also controlled the institutional means of power within the United States to implement such a foreign policy. The Europe-first/ers had political clout as "the foreign policy center was owned by the Establishment . . . largely from the northeastern part of the United States" (Destler, Gelb and Lake 1988: 22). And the United States had "a tradition of selecting foreign service officers from the Ivy League, and secretaries of state and treasury from Wall Street" (Cumings 1990: 95). In addition, a large number of the foreign service officers that did specialize in Asian affairs were purged from the government as a result of the McCarthy Red Scare following the fall of China.

Although represented by powerful figures on the American political scene, like Senator Robert Taft of Ohio and publishing magnate Henry Luce, himself the son of Asian missionaries, Asia-firsters were never as influential as their Eastern Establishment rivals (Cohen 2000: 177–80). Furthermore, the opposition Republicans were split on the issue of a European versus an Asian focus, with the northeastern wing of the party solidly in the Europe-first/ers camp and the midwestern wing of the party torn on the issue. Indicative of this split is the well-noted conversion of Senator Arthur Vandenberg of Michigan to support of Truman's foreign policy, especially NATO. This conversion was, in part, a result of an administration strategy, as Paul Nitze put it, "to build up Senator Vandenberg, as opposed to Senator Taft, and create a split within the Republican Party, and to drive our policy in between these two poles" (Fordham 1998: 370). This strategy was favored, no doubt, by the growing international interests and the political influence of the auto industry centered in Detroit (Cumings 1990: 38, 92, 97). Eisenhower's victory over Taft in the Republican presidential primaries in 1952 indicated and solidified the triumph of the internationalist (and Europeanist) wing of the Republican party.

In explaining why one set of ideas triumphs over another, many analysts have pointed to the importance of the "fit" between any particular idea and the general ideological context, existing political institutions, and pressing political concerns. As Mark Laffey and Jutta Weldes note, however, fit does not simply exist; instead it is made by political actors (Laffey and Weldes 1997: 202–3). Indeed, the stridency with which proponents of NATO stressed a pre-existing community and common civilization can be seen as part of a deliberate construction of "fit," drawing on both identity and material factors. A European strategy proved an easier sell to a nation that saw itself as an offshoot of Europe and whose levers of power were in the hands of men who identified closely with Europeans. In addition, strong economic links between the United States and Europe provided ample material incentives.

Although the Europe- and Asia-first/ers disagreed over which region more deserved American attention and resources, it is important to stress that this disagreement did not involve a debate over the multilateral or bilateral forms of international cooperation that the United States should adopt in these regions. This is most clear when one examines how Asia-firsters thought about their preferred policy in Asia. Their commitment to Asia did not extend to a willingness to pursue a multilateral path in that region. Their interactions with Asians, especially as part of Christian missionary work, did not lead to the development of a sense of identity with Asian peoples that could serve as a basis for a multilateral institution. The exact opposite occurred. Part of what made dealing with Asians rather than Europeans attractive to Asia-firsters was the sense that backward Asians could still be saved under American tutelage (Cohen 2000: 179: Purifoy 1976: 51). Asians were viewed as "barbarian but obedient," and Asia was thought of as "a region of vast resources and opportunities, populated by dutiful and cringing peoples who followed white leadership." The goal was not multilateral cooperation among equals (or even semi-equals), but one of unilateral U.S. dominance (Cumings 1990: 97, 93, 79–97). The case of the Asia-firsters demonstrates the indeterminacy of arguments linking perceived interests and threats to particular institutional forms without consideration of collective identity. Even those Americans who saw U.S. interests as more tied to Asia than to Europe, and who believed that the Cold War would be fought and won in Asia, did not reach for a multilateral framework for cooperation in this region. The belief that Asians were not only foreign, but also inferior, helped push these individuals to support unilateral or bilateral, rather than multilateral, policies in Asia.

When issues of identification, trust, and power arose with regard to SEATO, they did so in the context of explaining why Asian allies could not have, and did not deserve, the same privileges that had been given to the European allies. After signing a bilateral treaty with Japan, John Foster Dulles explained that, in the absence of identification, there could be no Asian equivalent of NATO. At the same time, however, he included Japan and the Philippines on the list of nations with which the United States shared a common destiny (Dulles 1952: 183–4). This indicates both the diversity of sources and the varying strengths of U.S. post-World War II identifications. Even though Japan and the Philippines were situated outside of what Dulles saw as a Western "community of race, religion and political institutions," shared historical experiences (the war and subsequent occupation of Japan and the colonization of the Philippines) could provide some basis for identification with particular Asian states. Identification is a matter of degree, not an all-or-nothing proposition. If race, religion, and shared political institutions helped to put the United States' European allies in a class ahead of its Asian allies, shared historical experiences similarly helped put certain Asian allies ahead of others.

There is a strong note of condescension in many of the U.S. discussions of SEATO; this condescension did not exist with regard to NATO. Many American policymakers did not see Asians as ready or sufficiently sophisticated to enjoy the trust and the same degree of power that the United States had offered to European states. In one particularly vulgar example, in the context of possible economic aid to the Philippines, one U.S. State Department official explained that the United States had to closely supervise the use of such aid because, as he saw it, they "were only one generation out of the tree tops" (McMahon 1999: 58).

The denigration of the importance of Asia and the skill of Asians reached the highest levels in the U.S. State Department. While Dean Acheson was secretary of state he visited Europe at least eleven times, claiming at the same time to be too busy to make even a single visit to East Asia. With the outbreak of war on the Korean peninsula in June 1950, Acheson decided to actively support U.S. involvement in the war primarily to demonstrate American credibility to its new European allies. With regard to the later war in Vietnam, Walt Rostow attributed Acheson's eventual opposition to American involvement to the former secretary of state's calculation that it was "too much blood to spill for those little people just out of the trees" (Isaacson and Thomas 1986: 506–7, 648, 698). Later in his career, while reflecting on his overall approach to Asians, Acheson maintained that "I still cling to Bret Harte's aphorism, 'that for ways that are dark/And for tricks that are vain/The Heathen Chinese is peculiar.' But no more so than the heathen Japanese" (Horne 1999: 457). Acheson was hardly alone. An even blunter example of America's condescension toward its potential allies in Asia can be found in a State Department memo discussing the possibility of forming a general Pacific Pact:

> The plain fact is that any exclusive Western joint action in Asia must carry with it the clear implication that we do not take the Asians very seriously and in fact regard them as inferiors. We shall not be able to avoid this implication because that is indeed our attitude.
>
> (U.S. Department of State 1984: 262)

The difference in identification and the different U.S. policies followed in Asia and Europe after World War II were not an aberration. In many ways, they were a continuation of U.S. war-time attitudes that led to a "Europe first" strategy; the internment of Japanese-Americans; a greater degree of hatred regarding America's Asian enemies (the Japanese) than European opponents (usually the Nazis rather than the Germans); and the basic decision, even before the war in Europe was over, to use the atomic bomb against Japan first, not Germany (Dower 1986; Makhijani 1995; DeConde 1992: 118). Indeed, as Michael Hunt has argued, there is a long tradition in U.S. foreign policy of dividing the world into a racial hierarchy, with the United States and Great Britain at the top, followed by other European peoples, and with Asians, Latinos, and Africans further down the list (Hunt 1987: 46–91). While overtly racial categories became less prominent over time and have been replaced in U.S. rhetoric, in recent decades, with allusions to cultural and civilizational values, the basic hierarchy has remained the same. The men in charge of handling the United States' post-World War II foreign policy were no exceptions. Franklin Roosevelt likened "the brown people of the East" to "minor children . . . who need trustees." Similarly, Harry Truman's private writings often lavished great praise upon the British, while speaking dismissively of "Chinamen" and "Japs." President Eisenhower placed "the English-speaking peoples of the world" above all others. As one of his advisors put it, "the Western world has somewhat more experience with the operations of war, peace, and parliamentary procedure than the swirling mess of emotionally super-charged Africans and Asiatics and Arabs that outnumber us" (Hunt 1987: 162–4; Lauren 1988).

U.S. decisionmakers' ready identification with Europe and the perception of Europe as belonging to the same political community as the United States helped, together with material and instrumental factors, move the United States to favor multilateralism in Europe. The weakness of identification with Asia and the belief that the Asian countries belonged to a different and inferior political community led to a U.S. preference for bilateralism in Asia.

Conclusion

The origin of the North Atlantic and Southeast Asian regions, as well as their institutional forms, discloses a great deal about the shape and shaping of world politics. In this chapter, we have not explored all empirical and analytical aspects of this process. For example, we do not investigate fully the effects that the policies of the European and Asian states had on U.S. foreign policy or the relationship between institutional form and the success or failure of particular alliances. In addition, there remains a great deal of potentially valuable historical material that could shed further light on the development of these regions and the historical variation of the United States' level of identification with them beyond the snapshot focus of the post-World War II years discussed here.

Furthermore, analytical eclecticism leaves room for disagreement about the shape of particular causal arguments and the sequence in which variables interact. While instrumental rationality and identity as well as material and social factors are intertwined, the particular combination of these factors in various concrete situations need not be the same. In the aggregate, these "explanations are complementary rather than mutually exclusive, may be hard to distinguish empirically, and in some cases there might not even be any fact of the matter to distinguish at all" (Fearon and Wendt 2001: 29). The strident insistence on the existence of a North Atlantic community, for example, and the quickness with which that concept was embraced by U.S. policymakers, suggests that in Europe, the invocation of a North Atlantic collective identity probably played an instrumental role in a situation in which the building blocks for a multilateral security arrangement were more readily available than in Asia. Members of the executive branch and the United States' potential allies were after all trying to do everything to rally a skeptical public and Congress to the arduous task of a prolonged engagement in Europe. This is not to deny, however, that those building blocks included, besides material factors, ideational ones such as a sense of shared Western, European, white, or democratic cultures (Jackson 2001). Similar ideational raw materials did not exist in Asia, making any construction of a regional identity there far more difficult. References to civilizational and racial differences with Asia were offered and accepted as a matter of fact. This suggested that it was these ideational differences, not simply the material consequences of international anarchy, that must be taken into account in a compelling explanation of how and why U.S. decisionmakers defined the interests that informed their policy choices. NATO and SEATO thus were not natural objects reflected only in the material realities of geography. Political actors constructed them through the instrumental political objectives of potential member states (balancing U.S. preponderance in NATO in the case of Canada, for example, or tying the United States to Europe on a long-term basis in the case of Britain) and through the invocation of unquestioned ethnic or racial identities (in U.S. domestic debates).

The causal structure of eclectic arguments need not be uniform. Such arguments refuse to grant primacy to any one analytical construct or paradigmatic orientation. We argue for the treatment of culture as a focal point to solve the problem of indeterminacy in games of strategic interaction, culture as a source of information for sending and receiving signals, and culture as a source of symbolic resources to be deployed in domestic political battles. We go beyond these productive ways of thinking about culture by also focusing on culture's relevance to constitutive processes, that is, to the creation and re-creation of collective identities. Rationalist theories of culture that highlight focal points, information, and resources neglect the importance of constitutive processes. Many strands of constructivist theory make the opposite mistake. They elevate constitutive processes a priori above all other causal influences. In this chapter, we seek to develop a third, eclectic stance that grants constitutive processes causal relevance rather than assuming irrelevance or asserting primacy.

A preference for eclectic theorizing contradicts the insistence on paradigmatic purity that typifies important analytical controversies in the field of international relations. A problem- rather than approach-driven style of analysis fits the complexity of political processes that occur within specific contexts (Jervis 1997). And it is in full agreement with how theoretically informed research is conducted in other areas of political science and the social sciences more generally. Up to a point, abstract debates can be useful in elucidating ontological, epistemological, and methodological controversies. But it is the identification of empirical anomalies and the construction of disciplined, theoretically informed explanations with particular attention to the specification of causal mechanisms and multiple methods that pushes outward the boundaries of knowledge. One substantial advantage of a problem-driven approach is to sidestep often repetitive, occasionally bitter, and inherently inconclusive paradigmatic debates. While a problem-focused, eclectic style of analysis has many advantages, at this stage of our knowledge it does not, however, permit us to distinguish conclusively between different types of causal chains.

Cultural constructions of U.S. national identity have resisted profoundly all notions that the United States might be anything else "but the transplantation of a European civilization on the North American continent." Within a dominant Anglo-Saxon culture, Asian-Americans have been denied recognition as Americans. From this perspective, "the Pacific contrasts sharply with an Atlantic region. Ties across the Atlantic have derived their perceived cohesiveness ultimately from assumptions about a metahistorical cultural affinity between the United States and Europe. On the other side of the continent . . . the same cultural self-image rendered the Pacific an alien territory, peopled by alien cultures that must be overcome" (Dirlik 1993: 315–16; see also DeConde 1992: 10–26, 50–2, 158–9, 193–4; Skrentny n.d.: 78–87). Multilateralism in Europe and bilateralism in Asia flowed naturally from this construction of U.S. collective identity.

Explicitly considering the role collective identities play in world politics can help advance our theoretical and empirical understanding of international relations. Collective identities matter because they help shape the definition of the actors' interests. An eclectic stance suggests that rationalist theories are more compelling when they are combined with constructivist insights into the importance of norms and identities, as is true of explanations focusing on great power status and the presence or absence of threat. In the 1990s, for example, rationalist theories that are eclectic in seeking to incorporate central insights of constructivism speak of the advantages and disadvantages of strategies of "self-binding." Reflecting purposive political choices, self-binding may look advantageous from a liberal perspective. It prolongs U.S. hegemony by lessening the threat the United States poses to others and eliminating the balancing process against the United States by lesser states (Lake 1999: 262; Ikenberry 2001). In these explanations, however, the distinction between self and other remains undertheorized, and the effects of self-binding remain relatively weak. From a realist perspective it is inexplicable why a strong state would choose to pool its sovereignty in the interest of setting credible limits to the unilateral exercise of power, as Germany did in supporting economic and monetary union (Grieco 1993: 338). Strategies of self-binding cannot be fully understood without analyzing explicitly the content and change in collective identities.

Once a region is formed or once a particular institution is put in place, that construction then has effects on the future of regional and global politics. There is a great deal of path dependency at work. In Europe, Italy's inclusion in

NATO underlines the fact that a region that might not be snug and plausible at first may, over time, be regarded as perfectly natural and set an important precedent. It is difficult to conceive how a geographically limited "North" Atlantic community, excluding all the Mediterranean countries, could have been expanded as readily as NATO was in the 1990s (Schimmelfennig 2001). With expansion, however, comes a new danger to NATO's identity as a separate community. As Michael Brenner (1995: 233) argues, with the Soviet Union defunct, communism dead, liberal democracy on the march, and NATO expanding eastward, "what then distinguishes the Atlantic partners? What justifies their banding together—as allies, as a diplomatic formation, as a brotherhood?" Looking toward the further expansion of NATO, James Kurth has noted that one of the strongest arguments for allowing the Baltic States into the alliance is precisely that "these countries have represented the easternmost extension of Western civilization" (Kurth 2001: 15).

Debates about regional definitions and regional institutions are also occurring in Asia and are similarly influenced by the choices made in the aftermath of World War II. Currently, East Asia and Southeast Asia are beginning to merge, through debates and controversies, as Mie Oba and Susumu Yamakage note (Oba and Yamakage 1998: 31), and through diplomatic initiatives such as the Association of Southeast Asian Nations Plus Three process. And Southeast Asia and East Asia are nested in a more encompassing Asian or Asian-Pacific region. It is not clear what to call that larger region because there is no accepted definition of the Asia Pacific Region. Indeed, there exists not even a standard convention for writing it. Asian Pacific, Pacific Asia, Asia-Pacific, Asia/Pacific, Pacific Rim, and Asia and the Pacific are all used (Alagappa 2000: 20; Emmerson 1994: 435). A collective regional identity cast in a multilateral institutional form, however, has been slower to emerge in Asia than in Europe. Looking to explain this difference, many analysts have pointed to some of the obstacles to multilateralism that were also seen as key during the early Cold War, including cultural diversity, disparate economies, asymmetries in power, and historical animosities (Duffield 2001: 86–9; Nolt 1999: 96–100; Simon 1993: 257). To these factors we would also add the continuing lack of Asian-Pacific collective identity and the lack of institutional experiences that could have helped provide a sense of community. Undoubtedly spurred by the growing influence of Asian-Americans in the U.S. political process (Cohen 2000: 210), in recent years U.S. policymakers have been increasingly calling for the development of multilateral security communities in Asia. As yet, however, there have been few concrete moves by the United States. Instead of fully embracing multilateralism and a common Asian-Pacific identity, the United States has limited its actions to calls for increased multilateral cooperation among the states of Asia while the United States pursues what the U.S. ambassador to South Korea calls an "enriched bilateralism." While there is much talk of the common interests the United States has with other Asian states, the United States is still far from embracing an identity as a member of an Asian-Pacific community similar to its membership in the North Atlantic community that would be needed to sustain a multilateral commitment (Blair and Hanley 2001: 7–17).

As this discussion suggests, the United States' sense of identity continues to influence the direction of U.S. foreign policy, in combination, of course, with other factors. For example, recent debates over why the United States chose to intervene in Kosovo but not in Rwanda intimately involve questions of America's identity. When asked about intervening in the former Yugoslavia as opposed to halting genocide in Africa, George Kennan warned against overburdening the United States with commitments but also concluded that "Europe, naturally, is another matter." The United States, Kennan reasoned, had to go after Milosevic because his "undertakings strike at the roots of a European civilization of which we are still largely a part" (Ullman 1999: 8). Whether the growing demographic presence and resulting electoral power of Asian-Americans, Hispanic-Americans, and African-Americans will change this sense of a European-focused American identity or whether these groups will remain in some sense "perpetual foreigners" remains to be seen (Watanabe 2001: 613). As the arguments we advance in this article indicate, however, the answer to this question is likely to have a substantial impact on the future of U.S. foreign relations (Nau 2002; Smith 2000; Ikenberry 2001).

Note

1   For criticisms and suggestions on earlier drafts of this chapter, we would like to thank Tim Borstelmann, Steve Burgess, Allen Carlson, Jeffrey Checkel, Matthew Evangelista, Martha Finnemore, Judith Gentleman, Mary Hampton, Robert Keohane, Jonathan Kirshner, Masaru Kohno, Stephen Krasner, David Lai, Walter LaFeber, David Laitin, Kier Lieber, Rose McDermott, Matthew Rhodes, Thomas Risse, Jae-Jung Suh, and Chris Way. We also are grateful to the editors and reviewers of *IO* whose careful readings have greatly improved this chapter. The views expressed here are those of the authors alone and do not necessarily reflect the views of the Air War College or any other U.S. government department or agency.

References

Acharya, Amitav (2000) *The Quest for Identity: International Relations of Southeast Asia*, Oxford: Oxford University Press.

Acharya, Amitav (2001) *Constructing a Security Community in Southeast Asia: ASEAN and the Problem of Regional Order*, London: Routledge.

Acheson, Dean (1949) Statement on the North Atlantic Treaty, *The Department of State Bulletin*, 20, 508: 385.

Acheson, Dean (1969) *Present at the Creation: My Years in the State Department*, New York: W. W. Norton.

Adler, Emanuel and Barnett, Michael (eds) (1998) *Security Communities*, Cambridge: Cambridge University Press.

Alagappa, Muthia (2000) "Asia-Pacific Regional Security Order: Introduction and Analytical Framework," paper prepared for the Second Workshop, Security Order in the Asia-Pacific, Bali, Indonesia, May 29–June 2.

Bix, Hermann P. (2000) *Hirohito and the Making of Modern Japan*, New York: HarperCollins.

Blair, Dennis C. and Hanley, John T., Jr (2001) "From Wheels to Webs: Reconstructing Asia-Pacific Security Arrangements," *The Washington Quarterly*, 24, 1: 7–17.

Borstelmann, Thomas (1999) "Jim Crow's Coming Out: Race Relations and American Foreign Policy in the Truman Years," *Presidential Studies Quarterly*, 29, 3: 549–69.

Brenner, Michael (1995) "Conclusion," pp. 232–6 in Michael Brenner (ed.) *Multilateralism and Western Strategy*, New York: St Martin's Press.

Burley, Anne-Marie (1993) "Regulating the World: Multilateralism and the Projection of the New Deal Regulatory State," pp. 125–56 in John Gerard Ruggie (ed.) *Multilateralism Matters: The Theory and Praxis of an Institutional Form*, New York: Columbia University Press.

Cohen, Warren I. (2000) *America's Response to China: A History of Sino-American Relations*, 4th edn, New York: Columbia University Press.

Cowhey, Peter F. (1993) "Elect Locally—Order Globally: Domestic Politics and Multilateral Cooperation," pp. 157–200 in John Gerard Ruggie (ed.) *Multilateralism Matters: The Theory and Praxis of an Institutional Form*, New York: Columbia University Press.

Cumings, Bruce (1990) *The Origins of the Korean War*, Vol. 2, *The Roaring of the Cataract, 1947–1950*, Princeton, NJ: Princeton University Press.

DeConde, Alexander (1992) *Ethnicity, Race and American Foreign Policy*, Boston, Mass.: Northeastern University Press.

Destler, I. M., Gelb, Leslie H., and Lake, Anthony (1988) "Breakdown: The Impact of Domestic Politics on American Foreign Policy," pp. 17–29 in Charles W. Kegley and Eugene R. Wittkopf (eds) *The Domestic Sources of Foreign Policy: Insights and Evidence*, New York: St Martin's Press.

Deutsch, Karl W. *et al.* (1957) *Political Community and the North Atlantic Area*, Princeton, NJ: Princeton University Press.

Dirlik, Arif (1993) "The Asia-Pacific in Asian-American Perspective," pp. 305–29 in Arif Dirlik (ed.) *What Is in a Rim? Critical Perspectives on the Pacific Region Idea*, Boulder, Colo.: Westview Press.

Dower, John (1986) *War without Mercy: Race and Power in the Pacific War*, New York: Pantheon Books.

Duffield, John S. (1998) *World Power Forsaken: Political Culture, International Institutions, and German Security Policy after Unification*, Stanford, Calif.: Stanford University Press.

Duffield, John S. (2001) "Why Is There No APTO? Why Is There No OSCAP?: Asia-Pacific Security Institutions in Comparative Perspective," *Contemporary Security Policy*, 22, 2: 69–95.

Dulles, John Foster (1952) "Security in the Pacific," *Foreign Affairs*, 30, 2: 175–87.

Dulles, John Foster (1954) "The Issues at Geneva: Address by Secretary Dulles," *The Department of State Bulletin*, 30, 777: 739–44.

Eisenhower, Dwight D. (1963) *The White House Years: Mandate for Change: 1953–1965*, Vol. 1, New York: Doubleday.

Emmerson, Donald K. (1994) "Organizing the Rim: Asia Pacific Regionalism," *Current History*, 93, 587 (December): 435–9.

Fearon, James and Wendt, Alexander (2001) "Rationalism versus Constructivism: A Skeptical View," unpublished paper.

Finnemore, Martha (1996) "Constructing Norms of Humanitarian Intervention," pp. 153–85 in Peter J. Katzenstein (ed.) *The Culture of National Security: Norms and Identity in World Politics*, New York: Columbia University Press.

Folly, Martin H. (1988) "Breaking the Vicious Circle: Britain, the United States, and the Genesis of the North Atlantic Treaty," *Diplomatic History*, 12, 1: 59–77.

Fordham, Benjamin O. (1998) "Economic Interests, Party and Ideology in Early Cold War Era U.S. Foreign Policy," *International Organization*, 52, 2: 359–96.

Gheciu, Alexandra (2001) "NATO's History: The Politics of 'Securing the West' since 1949," PhD dissertation draft, Ithaca, NY: Cornell University.

Gienow-Hecht, Jessica C. E. (2000) "Shame on U.S.? Academics, Cultural Transfer, and the Cold War—a Critical Review," *Diplomatic History*, 24, 3: 465–94.

Grieco, Joseph M. (1993) "Understanding the Problem of Cooperation: The Limits of Neoliberal Institutionalism and the Future of Realist Theory," pp. 310–38 in David A. Baldwin (ed.) *Neorealism and Neoliberalism: The Contemporary Debate*, New York: Columbia University Press.

Haftendorn, Helga, Keohane, Robert O., and Wallander, Celeste A. (eds) (1999) *Imperfect Unions: Security Institutions over Time and Space*, Oxford: Oxford University Press.

Hampton, Mary (1995) "NATO at the Creation: U.S. Foreign Policy, West Germany, and the Wilsonian Impulse," *Security Studies*, 4, 3: 610–56.

Hampton, Mary (1998/9) "NATO, Germany and the United States: Creating Positive Identity in Trans-Atlantia," *Security Studies*, 8, 2 and 3: 235–69.

Henrikson, Alan K. (1975) "The Map as an Idea: The Role of Cartographic Imagery during the Second World War," *American Cartographer*, 2, 1: 19–53.

Henrikson, Alan K. (1980) "The Creation of the North Atlantic Alliance, 1948–1952," *Naval War College Review*, 33, 3: 4–39.

Hess, Gary R. (1990) "The American Search for Stability in Southeast Asia: The SEATO Structure of Containment," pp. 272–95 in Warren I. Cohen and Akira Iriye (eds) *The Great Powers in East Asia 1953–1960*, New York: Columbia University Press.

Horne, Gerald (1999) "Race from Power: U.S. Foreign Policy and the General Crisis of 'White Supremacy'," *Diplomatic History*, 23, 3: 437–61.

Hunt, Michael (1987) *Ideology and U.S. Foreign Policy*, New Haven, Conn.: Yale University Press.

Ikenberry, G. John (2001) *After Victory: Institutions, Strategic Restraint, and the Rebuilding of Order after Major Wars*, Princeton, NJ: Princeton University Press.

Isaacson, Walter and Thomas, Evan (1986) *The Wise Men: Six Friends and the World They Made*, New York: Touchstone.

Jackson, Henry M. (ed.) (1967) *The Atlantic Alliance: Jackson Subcommittee Hearings and Findings*, New York: Praeger.

Jackson, Patrick Thaddeus (2001) "Occidentalism: Rhetoric, Process, and Postwar German Reconstruction," PhD dissertation, New York: Columbia University.

Jervis, Robert (1997) *System Effects: Complexity in Political and Social Life*, Princeton, NJ: Princeton University Press.

Johnston, Alastair Iain (1995) *Cultural Realism: Strategic Culture and Grand Strategy in Chinese History*, Princeton, NJ: Princeton University Press.

Kaplan, Lawrence S. (1984) *The United States and NATO: The Formative Years*, Lexington, Ky: University Press of Kentucky.

Katzenstein, Peter J. (ed.) (1996a) *The Culture of National Security: Norms and Identity in World Politics*, New York: Columbia University Press.

Katzenstein, Peter J. (1996b) "Introduction: Alternative Perspectives on National Security," pp. 1–32 in Peter J. Katzenstein (ed.) *The Culture of National Security: Norms and Identity in World Politics*, New York: Columbia University Press.

Kennan, George F. (1967) *Memoirs, 1925–1950*, Boston, Mass.: Little, Brown.

Kim, B. Sang Joon (1965) "The United States and SEATO," PhD dissertation, New Haven, Conn.: Yale University.

Kimball, Warren F. (1984) *Churchill and Roosevelt: The Complete Correspondence*, 2 vols, Princeton, NJ: Princeton University Press.

Kohno, Masaru (1996) "Limits of Neoliberal Institutionalism: Learning from the Failure of Multilateral Institutions in East Asian Security," paper presented at the conference organized jointly by the Japan Association of International Studies and the International Studies Association, Makuhari, Japan (September).

Koremenos, Barbara, Lipson, Charles, and Snidal, Duncan (2001) "How Rational Are International Institutions? Findings, Extensions, Omissions," *International Organization*, (forthcoming) [here used: January 1999 typescript].

Kurth, James (2001) "The Next NATO: Building an American Commonwealth of Nations," *The National Interest*, 65: 5–16.

Laffey, Mark and Weldes, Jutta (1997) "Beyond Belief: Ideas and Symbolic Technologies in the Study of International Relations," *European Journal of International Relations*, 3, 2: 193–237.

Lake, David A. (1999) *Entangling Relations: American Foreign Policy in Its Century*, Princeton, NJ: Princeton University Press.

Lauren, Paul Gordon (1988) *Power and Prejudice: The Politics of Diplomacy and Racial Discrimination*, Boulder, Colo.: Westview Press.

Legro, Jeffrey W. (2000) "Whence American Internationalism," *International Organization*, 54, 2: 253–90.

Lewis, Martin W. and Wigen, Kären (1997) *The Myth of Continents: A Critique of Metageography*, Berkeley, Calif.: University of California Press.

Lundestad, Geir (1980) *America, Scandinavia, and the Cold War, 1945–1949*, New York: Columbia University Press.

Lundestad, Geir (1999) " 'Empire by Invitation' in the American Century," *Diplomatic History*, 23, 2: 189–217.

McMahon, Robert J. (1999) *The Limits of Empire: The United States and Southeast Asia since World War II*, New York: Columbia University Press.

Maier, Charles S. (1978) "The Politics of Productivity: Foundations of American International Economic Policy after World War II," pp. 23–49 in Peter J. Katzenstein (ed.) *Between Power and Plenty: Foreign Economic Policies of Advanced Industrial States*, Madison, Wis.: University of Wisconsin Press.

Makhijani, Arjun (1995) " 'Always' the Target?," *Bulletin of the Atomic Scientists*, 51, 3: 23–7.

Marks, Frederick W., III (1993) *Power and Peace: The Diplomacy of John Foster Dulles*, Westport, Conn.: Praeger.

Mercer, Jonathan (1995) "Anarchy and Identity," *International Organization*, 49, 2: 229–52.

Modelski, George (1962) "SEATO: Its Functions and Organization," pp. 1–45 in George Modelski (ed.) *SEATO: Six Studies*, Melbourne: F. W. Chesire.

Murphy, Robert D. (1954) "Japan's Progress and Prospects: Address Made before the Japan Society at New York," *The Department of State Bulletin*, 30, 771: 513–17.

Nau, Henry (2002) *At Home Abroad: Identity and Power in American Foreign Policy*, Ithaca, NY: Cornell University Press.

Neumann, Iver B. (1999) *Uses of the Other: "The East" in European Identity Formation*, Minneapolis, Minn.: University of Minnesota Press.

Nolt, James H. (1999) "Liberalizing Asia," *World Policy Journal*, 16, 2: 94–118.

Oba, Mie and Yamakage, Susumu (1998) "In Search for Regional Identity: A Tale of Two Liminal Nations in Asia and the Pacific," unpublished paper, University of Tokyo, Komaba campus.

Paasi, Anssi (1986) "The Institutionalization of Regions: A Theoretical Framework for Understanding the Emergence of Regions and the Constitution of Regional Identity," *Fennia*, 164, 1: 105–46.

Polelle, Mark (1999) *Raising Cartographic Consciousness: The Social and Foreign Policy Vision of Geopolitics in the Twentieth Century*, Lanham, Md.: Lexington Books.

Prentice, Deborah A. and Miller, Dale T. (eds) (1999) *Cultural Divides: Understanding and Overcoming Group Conflict*, New York: Russell Sage Foundation.

Purifoy, Lewis McCarroll (1976) *Harry Truman's China Policy: McCarthyism and the Diplomacy of Hysteria 1947–1951*, New York: Franklin Watts.

Reid, Escott (1977) *Time of Fear and Hope: The Making of the North Atlantic Treaty, 1947–1949*, Ontario: McClelland & Stewart.

Reiter, Dan (1996) *Crucible of Beliefs: Learning, Alliances, and World Wars*, Ithaca, NY: Cornell University Press.

Rotter, Andrew J. (1987) *The Path to Vietnam: Origins of the American Commitment to Southeast Asia*, Ithaca, NY: Cornell University Press.

Ruggie, John Gerard (1993) "Multilateralism: The Anatomy of an Institution," pp. 3–47 in John Gerard Ruggie (ed.) *Multilateralism Matters: The Theory and Praxis of an Institutional Form*, New York: Columbia University Press.

Ruggie, John Gerard (1994) "Third Try at World Order? America and Multilateralism after the Cold War," *Political Science Quarterly*, 109, 4: 553–70.

Ruggie, John Gerard (1997) "The Past as Prologue: Interests, Identity and American Foreign Policy," *International Security*, 21, 4: 89–125.

Ruggie, John Gerard (1998) *Constructing the World Polity: Essays on International Institutionalization*, London: Routledge.

Rusk, Dean and Thanat, Khomen (1962) "Joint Statement, Washington, March 6," *The Department of State Bulletin*, 46, 1187: 498–9.

Sar Desai, D. R. (1997) *Southeast Asia: Past and Present*, 4th edn, Boulder, Colo.: Westview Press.

Schimmelfennig, Frank (2001) "The Community Trap: Liberal Norms, Rhetorical Action, and the Eastern Enlargement of the European Union," *International Organization*, 55, 1: 47–80.

Simon, Sheldon W. (1993) "The Clinton Administration and Asian Security: Toward Multilateralism," *Australian Journal of International Affairs*, 47, 2: 250–62.

Skrentny, John D. (n.d.) "The Minority Rights Revolution," unpublished manuscript, San Diego, Calif.: University of California.

Smith, Tony (2000) *Foreign Attachments: The Power of Ethnic Groups in the Making of American Foreign Policy*, Cambridge, Mass.: Harvard University Press.

Spiro, David E. (1999) *The Hidden Hand of American Hegemony: Petrodollar Recycling and International Markets*, Ithaca, NY: Cornell University Press.

Tajfel, Henri (ed.) (1978) *Differentiation Between Social Groups: Studies in the Social Psychology of Intergroup Relations*, London: Academic Press.

Tajfel, Henri and Turner, John C. (1986) "The Social Identity Theory of Intergroup Behavior," pp. 7–24 in Stephen Worchel and William G. Austin (eds) *Psychology of Intergroup Relations*, 2nd edn, Chicago, Ill.: Nelson Hall.

Trachtenberg, Marc (1999) *A Constructed Peace: The Making of the European Settlement, 1945–1963*, Princeton, NJ: Princeton University Press.

Truman, Harry S. (1956) *Memoirs*, Vol. 2, *Years of Trial and Hope*, Garden City, NY: Doubleday.

Ullman, Richard (1999) "The U.S. and the World: An Interview with George Kennan," *The New York Review of Books*, 46, 13: 4–6.

United States Department of State (1984) *Foreign Relations of the United States: 1952–1954*, Vol. 12, *East Asia and the Pacific*, Part I, Washington, DC: Government Printing Office.

United States Senate (1949) *North Atlantic Treaty: Hearings before the Committee on Foreign Relations*, 81st Congress, 1st Session, Washington DC: Government Printing Office.

United States Senate (1954) *The Southeast Asia Collective Defense Treaty: Hearing before the Committee on Foreign Relations*, 83rd Congress, 2nd session, Washington, DC: Government Printing Office.

United States Senate (1973) *The Vandenberg Resolution and the North Atlantic Treaty: Hearings Held in Executive Session before the Committee on Foreign Relations*, 80th Congress, 2nd Session, Washington DC: Government Printing Office.

Urwin, Derek W. (1995) *The Community of Europe: A History of European Integration since 1945*, New York: Longman.

Wallander, Celeste A. (1999) *Mortal Friends, Best Enemies: German–Russian Cooperation after the Cold War*, Ithaca, NY: Cornell University Press.

Wallander, Celeste A. (2000) "Institutional Assets and Adaptability: NATO after the Cold War," *International Organization*, 54, 4: 705–35.

Walt, Stephen M. (1987) *The Origins of Alliances*, Ithaca, NY: Cornell University Press.

Warshaw, Steven (1975) *Southeast Asia Emerges: A Concise History of Southeast Asia from Its Origins to the Present*, Berkeley, Calif.: Diablo Press.

Watanabe, Paul Y. (2001) "Global Forces, Foreign Policy, and Asian Pacific Americans," *PS*, 34, 3: 639–44.

Webb, Leicester C. (1962) "Australia and SEATO," pp. 49–82 in George Modelski (ed.) *SEATO: Six Studies*, Melbourne: F. W. Chesire.

Weber, Steve (1991) *Multilateralism in NATO: Shaping the Postwar Balance of Power, 1945–1961*, Berkeley, Calif.: University of California at Berkeley.

Weber, Steve (1993) "Shaping the Postwar Balance of Power: Multilateralism in NATO," pp. 233–92 in John Gerard Ruggie (ed.) *Multilateralism Matters: The Theory and Praxis of an Institutional Form*, New York: Columbia University Press.

Wendt, Alexander (1999) *Social Theory of International Politics*, Cambridge: Cambridge University Press.

Westerfield, H. Bradford (1955) *Foreign Policy and Party Politics: Pearl Harbor to Korea*, New Haven, Conn.: Yale University Press.

Williams, Lee E. (1976) *Southeast Asia: A Short History*, New York: Oxford University Press.

9 Same war—different views: Germany, Japan, and counterterrorism

Peter J. Katzenstein (2003) [1]

Big events in world politics, Peter Gourevitch noted long ago (Gourevitch 1977: 281), provide students of international relations and comparative politics with the closest thing to a natural experiment. The terrorist attacks on the United States on September 11, 2001 are no exception. The al Qaeda terrorist organization, an extensive cross-border network of violence-prone groups and individuals, created with its attacks a second "day of infamy" reminiscent of the attack on Pearl Harbor. Those terrorists involved in the attacks held fervently religious beliefs, came from a wide variety of national backgrounds, were well educated, practiced secular lifestyles, and moved unobtrusively in liberal societies. Loosely linked through both a common vision and a few trusted emissaries, al Qaeda appears to form neither a clear network nor a clear hierarchy. Its organization thus differs from groups traditionally engaged in left- or right-wing violence in industrial societies (Katzenstein 1998).

Al Qaeda had learned from its bungled 1993 attempt to bring down the World Trade Center. In 2001, al Qaeda foreign agents, apparently acting alone, slipped into the country and did not survive their attacks, unlike 1993 when foreign residents associated with the mosques in the New York area made their escape after their attack. Al Qaeda also used a new weapon of mass murder—crashing fully fueled jetliners into heavily populated buildings (Mylroie 2001; Dwyer *et al.* 1994; Parachini 2000; Hershberg and Moore 2002; Booth and Dunne 2002; Correspondence 2002). This chapter argues that the attack on the World Trade Center and the Pentagon is like a strong beam of light that gets filtered by national lenses, of different self-conceptions and institutional practices, which create distinctive political responses that will test severely alliance cohesion in the years to come.

German and Japanese counterterrorism policies differ from those adopted by the United States as well as from one another. Defeated in war, occupied, and partially remade during the Cold War, Germany and Japan became clients of the United States first, then close allies. Both countries, which are of central importance in Europe's and Asia's regional orders, offer easy tests of the extent to which the United States can hope to fight the war against terrorism, as the United States fought the Cold War, supported by a broad coalition of like-minded states. On this central point the chapter's conclusions are not reassuring. In contrast to the Cold War, the relative importance of different self-conceptions and institutional practices appears to be larger and the systemic effects constraining national divergences smaller. Even among the closest allies of the United States, the early stages of the war against terrorism point to substantial strains. Over a prolonged period such strains are likely to affect profoundly long-standing patterns of alliance.

For the United States, the September 11 attack was an act of "war" that required and justified, foremost, a response by the U.S. military. After quickly defeating the Taliban government in Afghanistan, U.S. armed forces in 2003 led a determined campaign that brought down Iraqi leader Saddam Hussein, a central figure in what President George W. Bush has called the "axis of evil." While law enforcement efforts against terrorism have continued unabated both at home and in Afghanistan and Iraq, these efforts have played a subordinate role in how the United States has been fighting the war on terrorism—with its military strength politically backed often by the use of unilateral action.

The German government has cooperated actively and energetically with the United States in combating the "crime" of global terrorism. For the first time since 1945, it deployed German troops outside of North Atlantic Treaty Organization (NATO) territory in the Afghan War. Germany took this step against strong domestic opposition, because it conceived of itself as an integral part of an international coalition fighting a global network of terrorists. In German eyes, September 11 required intense international collaboration in multilateral institutions. Unilateral action was inappropriate and ineffective in the combating of horrific international crimes. The German government felt that war, however, was less suitable for defeating global terrorist networks than careful attention to the underlying social and economic causes of terrorism in failing states, patient police cooperation, intelligence sharing, and international legal proceedings. The opposition of the German government to the U.S. policy of broadening the war against terrorism to a war against Iraq was strong and was supported strongly by German public opinion.

For the Japanese government, September 11 was, foremost, a "crisis" event. It offered the government an opportunity of showing Japan's symbolic support of the U.S. war against terrorism. It provided another welcome opportunity for gradually expanding the regional scope of operation of Japan's Self-Defense Forces (SDF). It also afforded Japan a chance to improve slightly its previously inadequate preparation for situations of national emergency. Compared with Germany, the response of the Japanese government was less insistent and less fraught with risk.

These differences in interpretation—war, crime, and crisis—reflect past institutionalized practices and different conceptions of self and other. Although Japan had lived for two decades with a domestic cycle of terrorism culminating in the world's first-ever terrorist attack with weapons of mass destruction, the government responded with considerable caution after

September 11. Germany's multilateral and activist stance after September 11 was different. It evoked memories of Germany's counterterrorist campaign in the 1970s and 1980s, when Germany viewed terrorism as a crime against the state and pursued its defenses energetically both at home and abroad.

This chapter develops its analytical framework and expectations in the first section before investigating German and Japanese counterterrorist policies before and after September 11 in the second and third sections respectively. It concludes with a brief comparison between German and Japanese policies and those of the United States.

Analytical expectations

Counterterrorist policies raise new issues for theories of international relations. A neorealist analysis of material capabilities at the level of the international system (Waltz 1979; Mearsheimer 2001) would lead one to expect roughly similar responses from two similarly placed states in the international system, such as central U.S. allies Germany and Japan in Europe and East Asia, respectively. This chapter demonstrates that the causal factors do not operate at the systemic level. These factors are not materialist, and they do not lead to similar outcomes.

In a political analysis of terrorism and counterterrorism, what matters most are processes that shape how groups and governments conceive of the use of violence, how publics perceive and interpret insecurity, and how threats are constructed politically. Such conceptions, interpretations, and processes of threat construction occur primarily within polities rather than between them (Crenshaw 2002: 19).

This difference in analytical perspective is one important reason why the analysis of international terrorism had not been considered part of conventional scholarship on national or international security before September 11 (Leheny 2002). The leading U.S. journals specializing in security issues published only a handful of articles on terrorism and counterterrorism. Judging by the reading lists of courses dealing with national and international security at the leading U.S. universities, terrorism was typically not considered a germane topic in the training of graduate students. Analysis of this issue was left to a small handful of scholars working on the fringes of the field, and to a large number of applied policy analysts working for the government or government-sponsored think-tanks. One of the leading scholars of terrorism, Martha Crenshaw, has pointed to the almost total neglect of terrorism in a theoretically sophisticated and politically contentious literature on grand strategy that focused on primacy, selective engagement, and offshore balancing (Crenshaw 2002: 14; Brown *et al.* 2000). She added poignantly that analysts of grand strategy, while freely criticizing the U.S. government after September 11, do not "offer an explanation of why they ignored the threat of terrorism as well as the government's inertia before 9/11" (Crenshaw 2002: 19). Analyses that focus on raw military capabilities and that operate at the

level of the international system have inherent difficulties in capturing analytically terrorist and counterterrorist politics.

As a substantial deviation from the systemic and materialist assumptions
of neorealist theories of international relations, realist balance-of-threat theory offers more insights into the altered security landscape after September 11
(Walt 1987; Midford 2002). Terrorism is about the politics of threat magnifi-
cation. Al Qaeda illustrates this general point. Its main weapon is symbolic
violence that spreads psychological terror that is disproportionate to the
death and destruction its actions unleash. For example, in 1996, the cause of
death per 100,000 people was 33 times larger for meningitis, 822 times for
murder, 1,200 times for suicide, and 1,833 times for car accidents than for
international terrorism (Falkenrath 2001: 170). Such statistics underline the
political importance of processes that shape how groups and governments
conceive of the use of violence, how publics perceive and interpret insecurity,
and how threats are constructed politically.

Balance-of-threat theory offers a plausible situational analysis that focuses
on the different magnitudes and sources of threat. On September 11, the
United States suffered massive casualties in one day as the result of an act of
international terrorism. Germany and Japan experienced significantly smaller
casualties over a period of two decades. Because it was attacked from outside,
the United States responded with war; because Germany and Japan were
attacked from inside, they did not.

The distinction between domestic and international terrorist attacks is,
however, far from clear. Germany's and Japan's domestic counterterrorism
policy in the 1970s and 1980s had clear international components. In Japan,
for example, the police initially tried to solve the problem by pushing Japan's
terrorists abroad. If the terrorists caused havoc in other countries, that was not
Japan's problem. The international safe haven that East Germany provided to
West German terrorists was one, though not the only, reason for the relative
failure of the German policing strategy. September 11 illustrates similarly
blurred lines between domestic and international terrorism. When members
of Aum Shinrikyo (in 1993) and al Qaeda (in 2000 and 2001) were honing
their flying skills in Florida, should this activity be considered an international
or national source of terrorism, for attacks staged, respectively, in Japan and
the United States? And was the failed 1993 attack on the World Trade Center
an instance of domestic or international terrorism? The central protagonists,
although they resided in the United States, in that attack were not U.S. citizens
for the most part and had extensive international ties. Because terrorism is a
transnational phenomenon, counterterrorist policies are not easily classified
into neatly differentiated domestic or international components.

The intuitive plausibility of a balance-of-threat argument is reinforced by
the difference in Germany's and Japan's reaction to September 11. Germany's
role as a host of terrorist leader Mohammed Atta and his accomplices created
a greater security threat situation in Germany after September 11 than the
national security threat faced by Japan. Furthermore, because Germany is

mostly a landlocked country with a large foreign population—many of whom come from Turkey and other Muslim countries—it is exposed to greater threats of terrorist attack than is Japan, an island nation with a relatively small number of foreign residents, few of whom are from Muslim countries. Differences in the magnitude of threat that terrorism poses to Germany and Japan are thus linked to a German counterterrorist policy that is more activist at home and concerted abroad than Japan's.

This "situational" threat analysis tends to highlight differences in situations as a plausible explanation for observed differences in counterterrorism policy.[2] By itself, however, situational analysis is unsatisfactory. On close inspection it disintegrates into an intellectually incoherent list of analytically hetero-geneous factors, in this instance, political relations with the United States, geography, and social structure. Situational analysis does not offer a logic by which to rank the relative importance of these diverse factors. It also fails to contribute to existing research programs in international relations. At best, situational analysis offers a list, not an explanation. By its very nature situational analysis tends toward ad hoc reasoning.

One can strengthen a situational balance-of-threat analysis by linking it to a focus on institutionalized norms that express conceptions of "self" and "other." Actor identity is not inherent in the actors themselves but in the games they play over time. Conceptions of self and other define the standards of appropriate behavior that govern Germany's and Japan's counterterrorist policies. In the 1990s, the German and Japanese governments, for example, derived such standards for policy from classifying as the "other" Germany's and Japan's political regimes of the 1930s and 1940s rather than religious fanatics in the 1990s. As guides for how to respond to the September 11 attacks, Germany has relied on its relatively active counterterrorist policy and involvement in strong multilateral institutions, while Japan has relied on its relatively passive policy and predilection for bilateral deals. Institutionalized norms expressing conceptions of self and other and standards of appropriate behavior are thus a promising way of strengthening a situational threat analy-sis and exploring German and Japanese counterterrorism policies.

As Carl Schmitt noted long ago, conceptions of identity, of self versus other, are always part of threat perceptions (Schmitt 1976). The norms and identities that trigger different threat perceptions are not merely derivative of material capabilities. Nor are these norms and identities simply deployed for instrumental reasons by autonomous actors with unproblematic identities. The threat perceptions of groups and states are embedded instead in systems of meaning that affect what is and what is not defined as a threat: terrorism typically is a threat and suicide typically is not, in sharp contradiction of powerful statistical evidence. The cost calculations that the leaders of groups and states make when they weigh their options thus cannot be treated as exogenous to the systems of meaning that constitute threat perceptions. Although policies are often influenced by the logic of instrumental choice among alternatives subject to rules of maximization or satisficing, policies are

also shaped by habitual standards of appropriateness, social processes of interpretation, emotional arousal, and political visions (March and Olsen 1989:
51). Strategic behavior is embedded in a social environment that helps constitute the identity of actors: the "self" interests that they define, the threats that
they perceive in "others," and the reactions to harm inflicted by these outsiders. The depth of this embeddedness can vary from shallow to deep. At one
extreme, social environments are shallow, such as in arm's-length bargaining
in auction markets. At the other extreme, social environments are deep, such
as in the effects that traumatic historical events and memories have on subsequent behavior. Analytical perspectives, such as rationalism or constructivism, that specialize in one or the other context are not inherently right or
wrong. These perspectives are more or less useful depending on the empirical
context to which they are applied.

Germany's and Japan's counterterrorist policies provide strong evidence
for the depth of the social context in which they are formulated. Institutionalized norms shape actor interests. Different types of norms work differently.
Regulatory norms define standards of appropriate behavior that shape interests and help coordinate behavior. Constitutive norms express actor identities
and also define interests and affect behavior. Two explanatory factors in particular have shaped German and Japanese counterterrorism policy: norms
of appropriate behavior linked to conceptions of self and other on the one
hand and institutionalized practices on the other. It would be desirable
to disentangle these two factors analytically. In practice they are tightly
interwoven. Over time institutionalized practices both reinforce and alter
self-conceptions and thus the interests that shape policy.

On questions of security, Germany's and Japan's conceptions of self and
other differ greatly (Katzenstein 1996: 153–90). The domestic aspects of
German counterterrorist policy reveal a Hobbesian fear of violent attacks on
an inherently fragile domestic political order. Japan's policy, in sharp contrast, betrays a Grotian confidence in the solidity of the national community.
The international aspects of German and Japanese counterterrorist policies
show an inverse pattern. German policy betrays a Grotian sense of belonging
to a larger community of nations. Japanese policy, by way of contrast, operates in a Hobbesian international system. These differences in self-conception
lead one to expect different counterterrorist policies: relatively active for
Germany at home and seeking multilateral solutions abroad; relatively passive for Japan at home and eschewing multilateral solutions abroad.

These analytical categories are easily reified, and Amy Gurowitz has
developed analytical categories that specify further this distinction (Gurowitz
1999: 30–68). She identifies four different dimensions of a state's identity.
The first dimension is strength of commitment to the principle of multilateralism, as indicated by the international pursuit of national objectives and
the extent of involvement in international institutions and organizations.
The second dimension is the extent of activism or passivity in international
activities, as indicated by assumption of leadership roles in international

initiatives and participation in global problem-solving. The third dimension is the extent of self-identification in terms of material and cultural attributes with the core of a Western international society of states, as indicated by self-perceptions, and the perceptions of other states, of a position of centrality or marginality. The fourth dimension is the relationship with the dominant state in the global system, currently the United States, as indicated by the degree of amity, neutrality, or enmity. Germany and Japan vary along these dimensions quite consistently, with Germany leaning more toward the international and Japan more toward the national pole along each of the first three dimensions. The difference between a primarily national and a primarily international orientation is a matter of degree, however, not of kind. Collective identities are always nested in other identities, and they are always contested politically. For Japan, for example, internationalization was both a process experienced in the past two decades and the subject of a political debate fundamentally shaped by national purposes. For Germany, its Europeanization is intimately linked to the "Germanization" of Europe (Katzenstein 1997; Katzenstein and Shiraishi 1997). In sum, differences in self-conception lead one to expect different counterterrorist policies.

These differences have become institutionalized during the past three decades in interaction with states and violence-prone groups in Western Europe and East and Southeast Asia. These two regions offer very different contexts for the operation of terrorist groups, such as al Qaeda, and counterterrorist policies to defeat them. In Southeast Asia, Islamic extremist movements have been motivated largely by local concerns. Ethnic secession and the Islamization of politics have been typical political goals. Long-standing local issues, such as a specifically Muslim resentment of the economically more successful Chinese and Indian communities, appear to have been as important as reactions to the events of September 11 and the war on terrorism (Hedman 2002; Gershman 2002; Leheny 2005; Kurlantzick 2001; Tan 2000; Chalk 1998).

Because the initial mission of the Association of Southeast Asian Nations (ASEAN) was defeating domestic, not international, communism, for the past four decades the insistence on national sovereignty has been much more important in this region than cooperation in external or internal security affairs. In the first thirty-one years of its existence, ASEAN never saw reason to establish a high-level working group on terrorism (Kurlantzick 2001: 21). When, during the Peruvian hostage crisis, Prime Minister Ryutaro Hashimoto of Japan visited Southeast Asia in January 1997, he insisted on a process of information exchange and consultation among experts specializing on terrorism in the region. Such exchange has intensified since September 11 (Itabashi, Ogawara and Leheny 2002: 368; Kawano 1999: 40–1; Leheny 2005). How such policy initiatives translate into police practice is far from clear, however, in a region where Malaysia does not require visas for citizens from other Muslim states, where the Philippines is notoriously lax in its immigration controls, where Indonesia and the Philippines are not cooperating with international efforts to curb money-laundering, and where piracy has increased sharply in the 1990s (Gershman 2002: 68–9).

In sharp contrast to the terrorism policy in Southeast Asia, al Qaeda's 2001 attack was planned in an integrated Europe with a distinct policy field of internal security. European states have been gradually exchanging their diminishing capacities to control systematically their territorial borders for an increasingly proactive surveillance of certain sectors of their populations, primarily foreign residents and immigrants. September 11 both accelerated further the Europeanization of policing and illuminated the incompleteness of European counterterrorism policy. Under the leadership of the Portuguese European commissioner for justice and home affairs, Antonio Vitorino, European Union (EU) member states agreed in the first half year after September 11 on (1) a single European arrest warrant for crimes punishable by three or more years in prison; (2) a common list of about thirty Euro-crimes; and (3) a common definition of terrorist acts and organizations. Movement has been slow, however, in making Europol, an embryonic European police organization operating since 1999, more important in the sharing of intelligence. Although distressing to Europhobes, the more or less advanced process of Europeanizing law-and-order issues offers a striking contrast to the weakness of multilateral arrangements governing cross-border policing in Southeast and East Asia. On questions of counterterrorism, Germany's energetic multilateralism and Japan's cautious bilateralism have been practiced and institutionalized in different world regions.

Combining situational threat analysis with environmental conditions of norms and identities offers a more plausible and powerful way of understanding counterterrorism than treating either in isolation from the other. More generally this approach moves beyond the exclusive focus on linear effects that characterizes economic models. Combinatorial analysis focuses attention on the dynamics of nonlinear systems in which even an apparently trivial event can at times cause radical change (Masters 1993; Jervis 1997).[3] It makes intuitive sense to approach highly complex political phenomena, such as terrorism and counterterrorism, with an analytical perspective that aims at capturing the emergent properties of nonlinear effects rather than seeking to isolate a few key variables that reduce the statistical variance of linear effects.

German and Japanese counterterrorism policy before September 11

Institutional norms are shaped by experience. Hence a situational threat analysis should be informed by relevant historical context. Although Japan and Germany are comparatively peaceful countries, each experienced serious episodes of political terrorism in the 1970s and 1980s that had domestic roots and international ramifications. Rather than viewing national security through military lenses, on the basis of their historical experience—military catastrophe in the first half of the twentieth century with state success in trade in the second—Germany and Japan have come to view security in broader political and economic terms, with Germany favoring multilateralism more than Japan. A broad international police cooperation in the case of Germany and economic aid in the case of Japan have been their preferred weapons to combat terrorism. At home, Germany relied in the 1970s and 1980s on a formal, legal, and technology-intensive approach to counterterrorism. This was in sharp contrast to Japan, which tended to downplay both law and technology in its domestic policing strategy. In brief, Japan favored an informal, low-tech, and unilateral approach, while Germany favored a formal, high-tech, and multilateral one (Katzenstein 1996: 153–90).

Germany

In recent decades the number of deaths in Germany resulting from terrorist activities was four times greater than in Japan. Between 1970 and 1979, there were 649 attacks that killed 31 people and injured 97. In addition, 163 people were taken hostage. Between 1980 and 1985 the number of terrorist acts increased to 1,601 (Katzenstein 1996: 155; Katzenstein and Tsujinaka 1991: tables A1–A13). Virtually all of this terrorism was homegrown, the activities of various generations of the Red Army Faction (RAF), the Revolutionary Cells (RZ), and other groups. Foreign terrorist groups mattered much less. To be sure, in the 1980s and 1990s various factions within the Turkish and Kurdish populations, such as the Grey Wolves and the Kurdistan Workers Party (PKK), were engaged in bloody conflicts. The symbols of German state and society were unfortunate collateral damage for these groups, never the primary targets of foreign terrorist attacks. The German police never focused on foreign terrorists the way it focused on German, and especially left-wing, terrorism. On this point the difference with the United States and the September 11 attack is striking.

Germany's security policy has distinguished strictly between internal and external security. "National security" as the meeting ground for both has not existed. Counterterrorism policy has reflected two basic lessons of history that have shaped how policymakers and the public think about issues of state security. The Weimar Republic taught the first lesson: Germany's lawful state (*Rechtsstaat*) and its democratic system with teeth (*streitbare Demokratie*) should not permit the enemies of constitutional democracy to use the cover of the rule of law to attack the foundations of the polity. Nazi Germany taught a second lesson: the security forces of the state need to be under firm parliamentary control and the gathering of intelligence needs to be severely circumscribed. The peculiarity of the German approach to counterterrorism has rested in the inescapable contradictions between both lessons. In Europe, Germany has been known for its "strong state" approach to counterterrorism. At the same time Germany has had a relatively liberal asylum policy, has extended far-reaching freedoms to religious associations, has imposed strict limitations on the intelligence gathering of the police and other government agencies, and has opposed strongly the death penalty. These contradictions have not undermined the conviction of Germany's political class, police, and public that a durable foundation of the polity requires a secure system of norms that are legally guaranteed and firmly anchored in human rights.

Terrorist acts and violent demonstrations accounted for about 0.33 percent of all recorded criminal acts; yet 5–10 percent of the country's police resources were committed to defending state security (Katzenstein 1996: 155). As part of the Social Democratic reform program of the 1970s, terrorism and mass protest reinforced a modernization and expansion of police powers. In the interest of enhancing internal security, Germany's legal statutes were changed. Revised in 1976 and 1986, Article 129a gives state officials broad discretionary powers. The article forbids the "support" of and, until changes made in 2002, "advertisement" of terrorist organizations and, under certain conditions, permits the arrest of individuals even in the absence of criminal behavior. Mere suspicion that an individual is supporting a criminal organization can provide legal grounds for the issuing of search and arrest warrants. In brief, Article 129a subjects criminal intent rather than criminal behavior to legal prosecution.

This extension of the German government's coercive powers beyond criminal conduct has been an important part of proactive police practice in Germany. Rather than reacting to terrorism, proactive police work sought to prevent terrorist attacks, thus blurring the line that separates normalcy from emergency and weakening the tenets of liberal government. Improved methods of data collection, storage, retrieval, and use were considered the most promising avenue for police work. On questions of internal security, Germany went high-tech. The police developed novel methods of computer matching as part of its counterterrorist campaign (Katzenstein 1990: 43–8). Large amounts of statistical data were scanned into computers in the effort of identifying overlapping clusters of suspicious traits in particular population segments. For example, the police used the files of utility companies to identify customers who paid their bills in cash or through third parties. This group was narrowed down further by running data checks on lists of residence and automobile registrations as well as receipts of social security and child-care payments. The people that remained in this "drag-net" were potential suspects. They tended to be young, single, and unregistered; to own no automobiles; and to pay their utility bills in cash. If they lived in large apartment complexes with underground garages and unrestricted direct access to four-lane highways, even during rush hour, changed their locks as soon as they moved in, kept their curtains closed, and received little or no mail, they were put under direct police surveillance. As much as 5 percent of the West German adult population appear to have been covered by some form of police surveillance system in the 1980s. Computer systems for potential terrorists were, of course, much smaller. One such system, Apsis, reportedly contained the names of 33,000 individuals in the late 1980s (Katzenstein 1990: 18–20). It is not known how many other computer systems were developed for similar purposes. In brief, preventive or "intelligent" police work, conducted in the name of enhancing internal security, was informed by abstract social categories that the police had defined. It was not informed by any evidence that a targeted individual had engaged in criminal behavior.

The fact that Germany's police was preoccupied with homegrown terrorism in no way diminished the relevance of the international dimension. Terrorists, after all, have been helped greatly by having guaranteed access to territorial sanctuaries provided by abetting states from which they can operate with relative impunity. Germany's RAF had international links that were less consequential for its attacks than for the survival of some of its cadres after the organization's decline. In the 1970s, some RAF members received training in Palestine Liberation Organization (PLO) camps that operated under the auspices of the Syrian government in Lebanon's Bekaa Valley. The links between the PLO and RAF became an international drama in Mogadishu in 1976. Special police forces flown in from Germany stormed a Lufthansa jet that PLO terrorists had hijacked to force the release of the top RAF leadership from a high-security prison in Germany. After the successful seizure of the plane, the imprisoned RAF leaders committed suicide. Although lack of access to PLO camps would have impeded the RAF's operation, it would not have stopped the RAF from its bombing and kidnapping campaigns in Germany. More consequential and politically explosive was the fact that Germany's unification quickly led the German police to a number of "retired" members of the RAF. These members, hosted by the Stasi, the former East German secret police, had been living incognito in the German Democratic Republic (GDR). In the 1970s, the GDR appears to have been an important transit country for RAF members as they traveled abroad to elude the investigations of the West German police. To this day it remains unclear whether the Stasi looked at these erstwhile members of the RAF, and then good socialist citizens in the GDR, as comrades-in-arms deserving of support now that their dangerous mission had ended, or as potential weapons that could be redeployed in West Germany should the occasion warrant it. One thing is certain: without the support of the GDR state bureaucracy, RAF members would have had an exceedingly difficult time surviving in Germany or anywhere else in central Europe. The crumbling of the Berlin Wall and the disintegration of the GDR robbed RAF cadres of the protective cocoon the GDR had provided.

In line with its general approach to questions of national security, Germany's counterterrorism policy has been consistently international. Germany became a champion of a deepening and broadening of police cooperation in Europe and beyond. Persistent German pressure resulted in the creation of a European secretariat of Interpol in 1986. The primary locus for police cooperation was, however, the EU. It was again German pressure, over a period of twenty years, that led, in the Maastricht Treaty, to the creation of Europol. On questions of cross-border policing and counterterrorism, the German approach has consistently favored international over national approaches and institutionalization over informal arrangements (Katzenstein 2002: 9–12).

Japan

In Japan, left-wing popular protest, on a scale unknown in Europe or the United States in the 1950s and 1960s, gave way to smaller terrorist attacks staged by extremist groups of both the Left and the Right. Between 1969 and 1989, Japan recorded more than 200 domestic bombings; and between 1978 and 1990 there were about 700 domestic "guerilla" attacks, using arson and Molotov cocktails (Katzenstein and Tsujinaka 1991: table 2; Katzenstein 1996: 155–6). A 1995 sarin gas attack in Tokyo's subway killed twelve and injured 5,000. Internationally, too, Japanese terrorists have distinguished themselves, especially in the 1970s, with daring attacks and brutal murders.

Japan's counterterrorism policy has been linked closely to the concepts of peace and human rights that are central to its Peace Constitution. Japan's policy has been focused on the root causes of terrorism more than on the immediate actions that were required in a crisis; Japan has been risk-averse and has shrunk back from allowing any casualties in terrorist incidents; and it has shunned public debate (Miyasaka 2001: 72–5). Japan's distinctive, long-standing definition of comprehensive security views terrorism in conjunction with other social problems under the heading of "crisis management" (Leheny 2001a: 10). Despite the shock of the 1995 sarin attack and the policy initiatives taken since then, the Japanese police and system of government still suffer from serious limitations in their organizational and intelligence capabilities (Itabashi, Ogawara and Leheny 2002: 352–65; Kawano 1999; Higuchi 2001).

In contrast to Germany, Japan pursued a low-tech, reactive counterterrorism policy. Police power increased in ways that were reflected less in formal statute, as in Germany, and more in informal police practice. In the interest of creating a favorable public climate that permits continuous surveillance, Japan's police has relied primarily on maintaining and cultivating further its close ties with the public (Katzenstein 1996: 63–8). Policy innovations, such as massive searches of apartment complexes and the creation of police support organizations with memberships numbering in the tens of millions, have provided the police with rich sources of human intelligence. Privileged access to the private security industry and regular contacts with organized crime have added important tools in the police arsenal. The social presence of the police has been pervasive, unofficial, and low key.

After its initial successes in the early 1970s, the Japanese police has had, however, a difficult time in coping with the attacks of subsequent cohorts of terrorists operating inside Japan. The militant cadres of the most prominent left-wing organization, the Chukaku, for example, succeeded in staging daring and murderous attacks throughout the 1980s (Katzenstein and Tsujinaka

1991: 14–29). During the 1986 Tokyo summit, for example, members of that group launched an unsuccessful rocket attack on a palace residence in downtown Tokyo. Fired from a distance of three kilometers, the rocket overshot its target. The incident humiliated the police, who had searched 50,000 apartments within two kilometers of the conference site, had arrested 900 leftist activists without clear cause, sealed off downtown Tokyo within two kilometers of the conference and lodging sites of foreign dignitaries, mobilized about 30,000 policemen, and tested $40 million worth of new equipment acquired just for this occasion (Katzenstein and Tsujinka 1991: 145–6, 153).

In the late 1960s, Japanese police pressure on the forerunners of Japan's Red Army (JRA) was so intense that its leadership decided to relocate abroad to increase its odds of operating successfully (Katzenstein and Tsujinaka 1991: 21). Because of their strong international ideology, left-wing radicals moved to North Korea and the Middle East. From these foreign locations, the JRA staged daring operations, such as the attacks on the Tel-Aviv airport in 1972, on a Singapore oil refinery in 1974, on the French embassy in The Hague in 1974, and on the U.S. and Swedish embassies in Kuala Lumpur in 1975. In the 1980s, the JRA had about thirty core cadres operating abroad (Katzenstein and Tsujinaka 1991: 14–29; Farrell 1990). Japanese officials misjudged totally the political significance of Japanese terrorists' operating abroad. The attacks on the embassies in Kuala Lumpur in August 1975, for example, caught the Japanese government and security officials by surprise. The link between the Popular Front for the Liberation of Palestine (PFLP) and the JRA had escaped their attention completely (Katzenstein and Tsujinaka 1991: 157).

Compared with the United States, "Japan is more methodical, less willing to create alarm by preparing for crises, more sympathetic to the root causes of terrorism, and less willing to respond to terrorism as a global problem" (Japan Society *et al.* 2001: 20). When the JRA started hijacking planes and kidnapping passengers, the Japanese government's initial response was complacency. Having pushed terrorists out of Japan, the Japanese government no longer felt that the terrorists' nefarious activities were a pressing problem. Once the government recognized the untenability of this position, it sought to avoid loss of life at almost any cost. But a terrorist incident in September 1977 forced a change in policy. While the public was fully behind Prime Minister Takeo Fukuda's decision to pay a $6 million ransom, to release some JRA cadres from Japanese prisons and to issue blank passports, the Japanese Minister of Justice, Hajime Fukuda, resigned in protest. Subsequently Japanese policy aligned itself gradually with the "no concession" policy on which the industrial states agreed, starting with the Bonn summit in 1978. It is not yet totally clear whether Japanese policy in fact changed. According to persistent rumors that the government has resolutely denied, the kidnapping of four Japanese geologists in Uzbekistan in 1999 was resolved by the payment of a substantial ransom, either directly by the government or indirectly by a Japanese corporation.

The Japanese government's still emerging international commitment has not been fully shared by the Japanese public. It thus has remained uncertain which policy the government would actually adhere to if put to the test. In the course of the 1996–7 hostage crisis in Lima, for example, the Japanese government appeared to put a much higher value on the safety of the hostages and a peaceful resolution of the crisis than did Peruvian President Alberto Fujimori. Although the police had created special assault teams for use in terrorist incidents in 1995, none of Japan's political conservatives or defense hawks suggested a year later that such teams should be dispatched to Lima during the four-month hostage crisis to take part in a possible rescue mission (Leheny 2000: 11–12).

With the hope of creating long-term contacts in other national police organizations, Japanese officials have cultivated short-term professional police exchanges with other countries (Katzenstein 2002: 23–4; Itabashi, Ogawara and Leheny 2002: 346–53, 365–70; Katzenstein 1996: 92). Government policy has avoided bloodshed. Japan's preferred instruments of counterterrorist policy consist of the paying of ransoms; adhering cautiously to a still untested, internationally agreed on "no concession" policy; and the granting of economic aid.

The importance of the JRA and its international operations waned in the late 1980s. The Oslo Agreement of 1993 accelerated the JRA's withdrawal from the Middle East. The weakening of the PFLP and a change in Syrian policy in the mid-1990s left the JRA no choice but to withdraw completely. Within a few years, with the exception of seven JRA members believed to be living in Lebanon, all of the senior JRA cadres had been apprehended and were in jail. The status of the surviving members of the JRA in North Korea remains uncertain (Steinhoff n.d.). If the JRA were to return to Japan, they would face certain arrest. As a result of the Oslo peace process and the U.S. war on terrorism, the threat the JRA once posed has all but ended.

Hesitation and caution marked Japan's reaction to the first terrorist attack with weapons of mass destruction, the disastrous sarin gas attack in the Tokyo subway in 1995 carried out by Aum Shinrikyo, a religious sect with an apocalyptic vision. In 1995, Aum had assets in excess of $1 billion, operated more than thirty branches in six countries, and claimed 50,000 members worldwide (Sansoucy 1998: 19). At the time of the attack, Aum had stockpiled large amounts of chemical weapons, had plans to attack Tokyo's metropolitan police with laser weapons, and had sought to buy nuclear and conventional weapons from Russia, where some of Aum Shinrikyo's leadership traveled frequently.

It is also widely believed that Aum perpetrated more than one major crime. A report of Japanese law enforcement agencies lists numerous attacks between 1989 and 1995 to which Aum has been linked directly (Miyawaki 2001: 1). In addition, Aum Shinrikyo was linked, though not conclusively, to a number of murders, dozens of extortions, a shooting that the head of the National Police Agency (NPA), Takaji Kunimatsu, barely survived, and a letter bomb sent to Tokyo's governor (Sansoucy 1998: 3–4, 11–12). Aum's terrorist campaign was a massive intelligence failure steeped deeply in politics, as there was ample evidence that the Japanese police "studiously avoided investigating Aum" (Steinhoff 1996: 17). And once the government brought charges it chose to treat the attacks as individual murders and assaults rather than bringing charges under Articles 77 (carrying out civil war) and 78 (preparing for civil war) of the Japanese Constitution. The prosecution thus sidestepped investigating the group's extensive transnational links, especially with Russia (Miyawaki 2001: 2–3). Even though Aum's organization and political purpose were radically different from traditional right-wing organizations, the police chose the easy path of treating it as basically similar to many other right-wing groups that had traditionally enjoyed the patronage and protection of the Japanese state (Szymkowiak and Steinhoff 1995).

Aum was not simply a millenarian Japanese organization led by a charismatic crackpot. As Lisa Sansoucy amply illustrates, Aum had important transnational ties (Sansoucy 1998: 23–32). In various countries it set up front organizations for purchasing weapons, chemical and biological agents, and high-tech components. In Russia, Aum was particularly active at a time of state collapse. By 1995, Aum's branch in Russia was the largest in the world, with eighteen affiliated organizations and about 18,000 members, twice the number of its Japanese membership. The leadership of the Russian branch was in Japanese hands. Without the help of Russian scientists, it is highly improbable that Aum could have built its huge chemical factory in its Kamikuishiki village compound. At the time of the sarin gas attack, Aum remained very interested in acquiring gas laser weapons, space-launch rockets, tanks, and nuclear weapons. A great coup for Aum was the acquisition of a large Soviet MIL Mi-17 helicopter. "In order to fly the helicopter, several Aum members went to Florida where in late 1993 they received helicopter training at a private firm, Kimura International. It is a tribute to the dramatic changes that have taken place in the international security environment since the end of the Cold War," writes Lisa Sansoucy in 1998, "that Japanese terrorists can now receive American training to fly Russian military helicopters" (Sansoucy 1998: 27).

In a political climate highly conducive to enhancing the government's counterterrorism policy after the Aum attack, what was striking was the tepidness and slowness of the government's response. This slowness was in agreement with the Japanese public's complacency that regarded Aum as a bizarre religious cult with no clear political objectives and little likelihood of having enhanced the probability of future terrorist attacks with weapons of mass destruction (Japan Society *et al.* 2001: 21; Miyasaka 2001: 76). The Liberal Democratic Party (LDP) government sought to strengthen its counterterrorist capabilities but was unsuccessful in overcoming deep suspicion of the potential abuse of executive authority. Even after the sarin gas attack, the Japanese Federation of Bar Associations, human rights activists, and mass media were successful in stopping the attempt at outlawing Aum; it was permitted to survive as a religious organization (Mullins 1997; Miyasaka 2001: 69, 77; Pangi 2002: 40). Aum derives most of its income from the sale of personal computers and software systems and has acted as sub-subcontractor, among others, to the National Defense Agency and the National Police Agency (Miyasaka 2001: 69–70). A low-profile approach and patience have been the hallmark of Japan's approach to terrorism, with Japan's police content to wait up to fifteen years or longer before making the arrests of key individuals, either in Japan or, by luck, abroad.

When they fought domestic terrorism in the past, Japan and Germany waited patiently and were witness to, and capitalized on, international changes that they did not help bring about—the end of the Cold War and the disinte-gration of the GDR in the case of Germany, the Oslo Agreement and the Middle East peace process in the case of Japan. That patience resulted from failure, not success. For about two decades, the German police was unsuccess-ful in stopping domestic terrorism. Repeatedly the German police would declare victory in its campaign, only to be surprised again and again by the activities of new terrorist cells ready to carry on. In the end what mattered were not advances in police technology, but the passing of time, the end of the Cold War, and domestic "exit" programs or amnesties for those willing to break with terrorist groups. Despite its initial success in pushing the JRA out of the country, the Japanese police also failed in fighting domestic terrorist groups. Between 1969 and 1985, as a percentage of total arrests, security-related arrests have declined roughly tenfold. Yet urban terrorist and guerilla activities continued, with 144 incidents recorded between 1983 and 1989 (Katzenstein 1996: 96, 154).

Germany, Japan, and counterterrorist policies

September 11 had a larger effect on Germany than on Japan. Three of the four pilots of the planes attacking the World Trade Center and the Pentagon had previously been living in Hamburg. German solidarity with New York and the United States was overwhelmingly strong. In Berlin a quarter of a million people showed up at a demonstration for New York, the largest of scores of such demonstrations that occurred all over the country. Japan, by way of contrast, felt more removed from al Qaeda. It seized on September 11 as a political opportunity to show resolve and thus to escape the criticism of being a do-nothing power. Rather than prepare for new security threats, the gov-ernment adjusted incrementally its foreign security policy. As was true of the 1995 sarin gas attack, the Japanese government adhered to a low-key coun-terterrorist policy after September 11.

Germany

Of the members of the al Qaeda terrorist cell centrally involved in the September 11 attacks, three had lived in Hamburg. They had arrived from three different Muslim countries; two others were still at large in 2003. At least two other cells in Germany have also been linked to al Qaeda leader Osama bin Laden. With the deployment of German troops in the Kosovo war, Germany had more or less resolved the issue of the use of force in a multilateral operation, with the precise balance of United Nations, NATO, and European support to be decided on a case-by-case basis. After September 11 for the first time Germany assumed military responsibility in a worldwide context (Maull 2001). Although a minority in the Social Democratic Party, the Greens and the former Communists—the Party of Democratic Socialism (PDS)—were clearly unnerved. In his forceful Reichstag speech on October 11, 2001, Chancellor Gerhard Schröder declared Germany's "unrestricted solidarity" with the United States and committed Germany to military operations in defense of freedom and human rights, and for the restoration of stability and security. A month later, a small group of the Chancellor's opponents in the Social Democratic Party (SPD) and the Green Party were close to breaking up the coalition government by opposing the deployment of 3,900 German troops as part of the U.S.-led coalition fighting the Taliban in Afghanistan. In one of Germany's rare no-confidence votes, the government won by a mere ten votes. In November 2001, 37 percent of the Germans supported Germany's military participation in the war against the Taliban, twice the support given during the Gulf War and the war in Kosovo. But public support for the Afghan war was still in a minority. Germany has played a central role in the policing as well as the political and economic reconstruction of Afghanistan, and in the surveillance around the Horn of Africa, a division of military labor that suits the German and the U.S. governments.

The solidarity with the United States and the international orientation of Germany's counterterrorist policy was very evident in NATO as well. After the September 11 attack it took the Permanent Representatives at NATO only two meetings and thirty hours to invoke the mutual defense clause in Article 5, provided that it was proven that the September 11 attack had been launched from abroad (Tuschoff n.d.; Lansford 2002). This astonishingly quick action was made possible by the decisions taken at the Washington summit in April 1999, and the new strategic concept slowly implemented since then. Article 24 of the Washington summit communiqué had stated that, beyond an armed attack on the territory of allies, alliance security is also affected by other risks of a wider nature. It made specific reference to acts of terrorism and thus created a new trigger for invoking Article 5 and declared political solidarity without necessarily guaranteeing collective military action. While NATO documents had previously referred to terrorism as a criminal offense, the April 1999 declaration changed that. Terrorism was now conceived of as a threat to the alliance members' territorial integrity and equated with an armed attack. The 1999 declaration contained clear standards: "armed attack," "directed from abroad," and "within the geographic scope covered by the NATO treaty." Unambiguous standards made possible quick action after September 11. In the wake of September 11 and Russian President

Vladimir Putin's wholehearted support of the United States, the upgrading of Russia's role in NATO, a subject of prolonged discussion throughout the 1990s, followed easily.

Germany also took important counterterrorist measures at home that tilted the balance between liberty and security toward the latter without the Constitutional Court having to adjudicate irreconcilable conflicts, as had been true in the 1970s. Specifically, the German parliament passed two counterterrorism laws. The main provisions in both were not simply triggered by the September 11 attacks; many of them had been debated before (Lepsius 2002).

The first law withdrew the statutory provision, granted in 1964, that exempted religious groups from the law of associations because they were presumed to be law-abiding. As a consequence, legal rules prohibiting associations whose objectives or activities aimed at breaking criminal laws, undermining Germany's constitutional order, or opposing the concept of international understanding, apply now fully to religious associations. Religious associations can be banned under the same conditions as all other associations, including terrorist groups.[4] Shortly after the law took effect on December 8, 2001, the government moved against twenty religious associations and conducted more than 200 raids. The main target was the Cologne Caliphate whose leader, Metin Kaplan, had received in November 2000 a four-year sentence in connection with the murder of a rival in Berlin. He had also planned an airplane attack on the Ataturk mausoleum in 1998 and had close ties to al Qaeda. The first counterterrorism law also proposed insertion of a new Article 129b into Germany's criminal code, henceforth permitting the prosecution of individuals who supported terrorist acts committed in other countries. This was a highly contentious issue as the smaller coalition party of the SPD, as well as a faction of the SPD, objected strongly. The political log jam was broken only after the explosion of a truck outside of a Tunisian synagogue, the oldest in North Africa, on April 11, 2002 had killed nineteen tourists, twelve of whom were German. In Berlin, the political reaction was almost instantaneous. Parliament quickly passed Article 129b, complementing Article 129a that had been enacted in 1976. Membership in, and the assistance, beyond verbal support, of a terrorist organization operating abroad became a criminal offense. This was the legal instrument that allowed the German police to launch efforts to arrest foreign terrorists operating from Germany.

The second counterterrorism law adjusted more than 100 regulations in seventeen laws and five administrative decrees. The gist of the changes was to strengthen the government's preventive approach to terrorism. The law, which became effective on January 1, 2002, gave Germany's various security organizations the power to access the telephone, banking, employment, and university records of individuals. In addition to their original mandate of collecting general overview information on the activities and tendencies of radical groups intent on subverting Germany's constitutional order, the primary mission of Germany's security organizations has been redefined. It now includes the surveillance of the activities of individuals who are threatening to undermine the idea of international understanding and world peace. Identity papers of foreigners will soon include new biometric information such as fingerprints and face-recognition data, a provision that may soon be extended to the identification cards of all German citizens, once parliament specifies guarantees against possible abuses of new police powers. Further investigative powers have been granted to the two federal security organizations, the Federal Criminal Police and the Federal Border Police, and cooperation between local and regional police organizations has been improved.

Germany's immigration laws also have been rewritten to further enhance information on foreigners, including voice recordings of asylum seekers to be stored for a decade, and online access of the police to the data of the immigration and naturalization services. Because of the strong opposition of the smaller of the two parties forming the coalition government since 1998, some controversial measures, such as the expansion of the investigative powers of the three federal intelligence services, have a sunset clause of five years. Although Germany was a major base of operation for al Qaeda, German laws had previously prevented arrests without serious suspicion of illegal activities. By late April 2002, however, the German police was able to make numerous arrests, among them eleven members of the al-Tawhid movement, a little-known Palestinian group with links to al Qaeda, and eight members of a group apparently controlled by Abu Musaab Zarqawi, a top al Qaeda operative who was in hiding.

Police practice also changed. In the largest operation ever mounted by the federal police, 600 officers working in cooperation with the U.S. Federal Bureau of Investigation (FBI) investigated the September 11 attack. Within weeks of the attack, five of Germany's *Länder* reactivated the dragnet approach, fallen out of use after 1980. The statistical profile of potential suspects consisted of men aged twenty to thirty-five, from the Middle East, enrolled in engineering schools and without earlier criminal convictions. The operation turned out to be a flop; after several months not a single "sleeper" terrorist had been identified (Jansen 2001: 7–8). Published reports about the arrest of seven suspected members of a new cell in Hamburg did not fit the statistical profile. One member was fifty-one years old; another was a German citizen; and several had not been university students.

Why key al Qaeda terrorist cells were operating from Germany appears to be self-evident, at least in retrospect. Germany has had more foreign residents than any other society in Europe, including 3 million Muslims. The crackdown with which the French government had answered a spate of terrorist bombings in the 1990s dispersed some Algerian cells to surrounding countries, including Germany. Large numbers of asylum seekers also were admitted to Germany in the 1980s and 1990s, including many from countries whose governments waged war on religious fundamentalist movements. Compared with 10,400 far-right German extremists, twenty Islamic organizations with a total of 32,000 members were under observation by the Office for the Protection of the Constitution in 2001.[5] The German police also estimated that there were about 100 radicals living in Germany in 2001 who received training in al Qaeda camps in Afghanistan or Pakistan.

Germany's various security organizations were not totally unprepared for September 11, but they often felt powerless. The head of the Command Center of the SWAT-Team/Surveillance Unit of the Federal Criminal Investigation Office (Bundeskriminalamt) in Wiesbaden, Klaus Jansen, referred to Germany as a "place of rest" (*Ruheraum*) for terrorists (Jansen 2001: 3). The Federal Security Service (Bundesnachrichtendienst) and the Office for the Protection of the Constitution prepared a long study in 1997 that addressed the threat foreign extremist and terrorist groups posed for Germany. In 2000, after more than a year of investigation, the Federal Criminal Investigation Office submitted to the Office of the Federal Prosecutor a report detailing various connections between Osama bin Laden and Germany.

Such reports were not sufficiently alarming, however, to shake the liberal legacy of Germany's post-Nazi history. History and memory have a powerful effect on policy. The current generation of German political leaders have taken pride in learning the lessons of Germany's Nazi past: treat persecuted minorities liberally. Because terrorism was defined only with reference to attacks inside Germany, cooperation with foreign intelligence and police services necessarily was limited. Only two notable terrorist acts perpetrated by Muslims have occurred in Germany since 1949—the assassination of Israeli athletes by Palestinian gunmen during the Munich Olympic Games in 1972, and the bombing of a Berlin nightclub in 1986. The prominence of the anti-authoritarian 1968 generation in positions of political power in the 1990s probably weakened the standing of the security organizations of the state and strengthened the position of liberal defenders of political activism.

Japan

Prime Minister Junichiro Koizumi responded quickly and decisively to the 2001 attacks on the World Trade Center and the Pentagon. A seven-point emergency plan committed the Japanese military to support U.S. countermeasures in Afghanistan. In pictures that were broadcast around the globe, units of the Japanese navy accompanied the aircraft carrier USS *Kitty Hawk* and other ships as they left Japanese coastal waters for their destination in the Middle East on September 21, 2001. Specifically, Koizumi committed three destroyers and other ships to provide support for U.S. forces in the Indian Ocean. Although these were largely symbolic moves, they mattered politically. Koizumi wanted to pre-empt the criticism that had met Japan's tepid response after the Persian Gulf War a decade earlier. His stance assured the United States that the upgrading of U.S.–Japan security policies since the mid-1990s was honored in times of crisis.

For the first time since 1945, Japan played a regional security role in support of the United States. September 11 thus consolidated a redefinition in the U.S.–Japan security arrangements that had gradually taken shape during the 1990s, starting with the International Peace Cooperation Law of June 1992, the revision of the Guidelines for Japan-U.S. Defense Cooperation of September 1997, and the passage of legislation in May 1999 that enables the SDF to provide logistical support for the U.S. military to defend Japanese security in the event of regional crises. The net result of the various policy changes has been to regionalize more thoroughly the scope of the security arrangements to deal with issues of peace and security throughout Asia-Pacific. SDF operations will no longer focus solely on the defense of the Japanese home islands (Katzenstein and Okawara 2001; Okawara and Katzenstein 2001). In addition, the Japanese government agreed to provide refugee relief and other humanitarian assistance, to supply grant aid to frontline states, to share intelligence, to participate in international police cooperation, to work with other central and commercial banks to restrict funding for terrorist organizations, and to help establish a government in Afghanistan with a broad political base. These steps, Michael Armacost and Kenneth Pyle argue, "move Japan decisively toward some middle ground between the hypernationalism of World War II and what some have described as the 'toothless pacifism' of its post-war defense policy" (Armacost and Pyle 2001: 60). It is, however, far from clear whether Koizumi's and the Japanese Diet's initial reaction did much to enhance Japan's capacity to address terrorist threats. The new Bill to Support Counterterrorism, which passed on October 29, 2001, was no more than a marginal extension of existing legislation. This law, writes David Leheny, was basically "an initiative to help U.S. action in this specific instance" (Leheny 2001b: 5; Maeda 2002). The law did little to prepare either the government or the public for the eventuality that the government's counterterrorist campaign may spread to Southeast Asia.

The law balanced a potentially radical shift in policy permitting the dispatch of ground troops to foreign lands with extreme caution in sidestepping all accusations of supporting, as did NATO after September 11, the principle of collective self-defense. It accomplished this with legal ingenuity by stressing the compatibility between the collective security language of UN Resolution 1368 and the wording of the Preamble of the Japanese Constitution. In defense of international peace and security in general, the law permitted the dispatch of the SDF to the Indian Ocean and, significantly, its coastal states to support U.S. combat troops in Afghanistan with water and fuel supplies. It permitted the SDF to conduct surveillance and intelligence operations far away from Japan, as long as the SDF did not become part of the military force used by any country. It also authorized Japan's soldiers to use weapons not only in self-defense but also to defend people under their protection.

Furthermore, the Cabinet prepared and the Diet enacted legislation that has permitted Japan to ratify the Convention for the Suppression of Terrorist Bombings that the UN General Assembly had adopted in 1997 and that Japan had signed a year later. Yet many of the measures adopted were modest at best. The National Police Agency, for example, tightened airport security measures and decided to arm Japan's police forces with 1,000 automatic rifles. The Ministry of Foreign Affairs (MOFA) established a special unit within the Policy Coordination Division, staffed by about ten officials and headed by a division chief charged, among others, with assisting the newly created post of "ambassador in charge of terrorism." In brief, the new counter-terrorism legislation dealt with the fallout of September 11 in terms of the established political fault lines about what was and what was not permitted under Japan's Peace Constitution. The bill did not deal with counterterrorism as conventionally understood, for example in the United States. If the U.S. war on terrorism were to be fought in Japan and Southeast and East Asia, this legislation left Japan woefully unprepared. In the words of one of Japan's leading specialists on international relations, Akihiko Tanaka, "we have laws for when there is a crisis in the region, and now we will probably have a law when there is a crisis far overseas. But the laws for when Japan is attacked are inadequate" (*Financial Times*, October 17, 2001, 2).

In addition to the counterterrorism legislation, in spring 2002, the Cabinet approved a package of three bills for the eventuality of a direct attack on the Japanese home islands (Furukawa 2000).[6] At issue, politically, was not pre-paration for the most acute of Japan's security threats—from North Korean spy ships or from missile or terror attacks. The emergency legislation was instead designed to chip away at the government's traditional interpretation of Japan's Peace Constitution without engaging head-on with the politically volatile issue of reformulating Article 9. With many Japanese leaders quietly uneasy in the governing coalition and vociferously critical in the opposition, the opposition's boycotting of the Diet and an unrelated scandal involving the Defense Agency and the SDF led to the government's decision not to push the bills through the Diet in the session ending in July 2002. The bills were approved in June 2003.

Japan's security strategy after the end of the Cold War has seen no radical change. It remains "comprehensive." The office in the Ministry of Foreign Affairs is called, in English, "Anti-Terrorism Bureau," and in Japanese, "Office of Special Measures for Our Citizens Overseas." It is under the jurisdiction of the Consular and Migration Affairs Division of MOFA, whose chief responsibility is to protect Japanese citizens overseas, not apprehend terrorists (Leheny 2001b: 42). Japan's counterterrorism stance had not been shifted by two politically all-consuming terrorist episodes that the country had faced in the 1990s, the sarin gas attack by Aum Shinrikyo in Tokyo in 1995, and the takeover of the Japanese ambassador's residence by the Tupac Amaru move-ment in Lima in 1996. It comes as little surprise, then, that the policy response to September 11 has been muted as well.

The U.S. war on terrorism in comparative perspective

Together with a situational threat analysis, institutionalized norms express-ing different conceptions of self and other have been decisive for Germany's and Japan's counterterrorist policies. The net result of these policies was to export the problem of terrorism to others, as did Japan in the 1970s and Germany in the 1990s. There is not a shred of evidence that this was an act of cold-blooded calculation seeking to attain a "free ride" from the international community. Exporting the terrorist problem was instead the consequence of institutionalized norms and commonsense practice. In the 1980s and 1990s, Egypt and France, to name just two examples, behaved similarly. By ignoring and reducing terrorism in their polities, Germany and Japan inadvertently increased it for others.

This chapter's argument is germane to the policies of other participants in the U.S. war on terrorism, such as Saudi Arabia, another close ally of the United States. As with Germany and Japan, Saudi Arabian policies have shifted the costs of terrorism to other states. According to royal Saudi intelligence sources, since 1979 as many as 25,000 young Saudis received military training or experience abroad, most with the intent of waging an Islamic holy war. These Saudis were being prepared for this mission by militant clerics whose teachings the Saudi rulers tolerated, afraid of the backlash a crackdown would cause among the religious right, returnees from other wars, and the ranks of the unemployed. The Saudi government and police let these young radicals leave unhindered. From among them, terrorists were recruited for the wars in Afghanistan, Chechnya, Kosovo, and Bosnia as well as for the bombing of U.S. targets in Saudi Arabia, Kenya, Tanzania, and Yemen, killing hundreds of Americans and non-Americans. Only after the September 11 attack did the Saudi government cut its ties with the Taliban government in Afghanistan, and only after the U.S. forces attacked Afghanistan militarily on October 7, 2001 did Saudi authorities detain young men who wished to join the fight. According to Martin Indyk, an assistant secretary of state for Middle East policy during the administration of President Bill Clinton,

> the Saudis' policies made the world safer for Saudi Arabia and the Saudi regime. I don't think it was their intention to make it unsafe for the United States. But that was the actual, if unintended, consequence of buying off the opposition, and exporting both the trouble-makers and their extremist ideology.
>
> (*New York Times*, December 27, 2001, A1)

As is true of three of its closest allies, institutionalized norms expressing conceptions of self and other are also powerful in shaping the U.S. approach to the war on terrorism. War, for the United States, is a response that follows quite naturally from a national security policy that had been institutionalized over half a century, during the hot wars in Korea and Vietnam and the cold one with the Soviet Union. With a broad arsenal of sophisticated weapons systems, U.S. security policy had aimed for decades to prevent the recurrence of another surprise attack. Seeking to extend that policy, one of the most important political priorities of the Bush administration before September 11 was the construction of a costly and inadequately tested national missile defense system. The mountain of rubble in lower Manhattan and the charred Pentagon symbolize the shattering of the U.S. yearning for invulnerability (Heymann 2001).

As is true of Germany's and Japan's identity, the U.S. collective identity is both nested in a variety of other identities and deeply contested politically, thus preserving the element of political choice. Changing sectional alignments (Trubowitz 1998) and competing foreign policy traditions (Mead 2001), for example, fuel political conflicts about what the United States stands for and what policies it should follow. In those conflicts, the enormous material resources of the Department of Defense and its pervasive institutional presence throughout the U.S. system of government make it quite plausible and normal to define September 11 and its aftermath in terms of war, just as it was quite plausible and normal in Germany or Japan to define the same event in terms of crime or crisis.

A comparison of the U.S. counterterrorism response to Germany's and Japan's highlights a similarity in German and Japanese self-conceptions and a sharp difference to the United States on one aspect intimately tied to the resurgence of religious violence. Because of Germany's and Japan's experience with religious persecution and state religion in the 1930s and 1940s, both states after 1945 granted religious groups an unregulated space for operation, largely protected against unwanted state supervision, not to speak of state intervention. Strict observance of the political respect for religious freedom was for politicians and the police in both countries an important marker of a mature democracy that had learned its bitter lessons from history. It is a political axiom in two of the most secular polities existing today that the government should stay out of religious affairs.

The religiosity of U.S. public life, and specifically the rise of the Christian Right in the Republican Party, offers a striking contrast (Pew Global Attitudes Project 2002). The German state offered terrorist Atta and his accomplices a politically unrestricted space in the Hamburg suburbs for meticulously planning the September 11 attack. The Japanese government licensed Aum Shinrikyo and then turned away despite overwhelming evidence that the group posed an acute danger to Japan's security. In sharp contrast, after September 11, President Bush, claiming God to be an ally of America, repeatedly has invoked biblical language in the nation's pursuit of the war on terrorism both at home and abroad (Woodward 2002). The United States has been mobilizing on all fronts for war—military, diplomatic, juridical, economic, organizational, and psychological—and it has been doing so in support of "good" over "evil." When a serious conflict appears to divide "us" from "them" in the United States, national security becomes a potent symbol in U.S. politics, as Theodore Lowi argued persuasively during the Cold War (Lowi 1969: 157–88). This symbol is linked to a Manichean vision of world politics that is both culturally activated and strategically deployed. It is culturally activated by a highly ideological approach to foreign policy that dates back to the beginning of the Republic and that Hans Morgenthau decried at the outset of the Cold War (Morgenthau 1951). It is strategically deployed by democratically elected elites seeking to rally support for programs and policies that otherwise would encounter domestic opposition. Since September 11, national security has been expressed often in religious language.

This chapter holds some important lessons for the domestic and international aspects of the U.S. war on terrorism. Although Germany and Japan have what are widely considered to be effective policing strategies, their starkly different approaches to domestic counterterrorism have been remarkably unsuccessful. Patience and luck proved to be more important than the reliance on formal and high-tech approaches in Germany and informal and low-tech ones in Japan. Thus, one should be wary of putting too much trust in government promises that tilting the balance decisively against civil liberty will be rewarded with special gains in security. For U.S. Supreme Court Justice Sandra O'Connor was surely correct when she argued after September 11 that "we're likely to experience more restrictions on our personal freedom than has ever been the case in our country" (*New York Times*, September 29, 2001, B5).

Furthermore, despite their forceful approach to counterterrorism in the 1970s and 1980s, Germany and Japan are, by all accounts, more liberal polities today than they were in the 1970s. Thus, one should also be wary of arguments, advanced frequently by critics of German and Japanese policies in the 1970s, that view the restrictions of some civil liberties as heralding a thinly disguised return to fascism. Germany's and Japan's experience with counterterrorism suggests, furthermore, that the elimination of territorial sanctuaries of terrorist networks is essential for constricting the operational freedom of a terrorist group and for capturing eventually many or all of the group's main operatives. The war against the Taliban government that had offered sanctuary to al Qaeda was an important initial phase of the U.S. war on terrorism.

In fighting this war, perhaps for several decades, the United States will face great difficulties even with its closest allies. Fighting an enemy whose preferred staging area for planning operations is inside the polities of our allies in Europe and Asia, not to speak of our own, is a fiendishly difficult undertaking. These polities embody different judicial philosophies that institutionalize norms expressing different conceptions of self and other. The United States and the European states have found themselves at odds over numerous issues. Without exception all European countries have been deeply concerned about the indeterminate detention of an unknown number of enemy combatants at the U.S. military base in Guantanamo Bay, Cuba. The European states are legally bound, and politically committed, to refuse cooperation in judicial proceedings should suspected terrorists, if convicted, receive the death penalty; this poses a serious hurdle in the negotiations of an EU–U.S. extradition and judicial cooperation agreement commenced in spring 2002. Besides the thorny issue of extradition in cases involving the death penalty and trials by special tribunals, Germany has called also for strong guarantees to ensure stringent data protection.

More than the Cold War ever did, the U.S. war against terrorism will test different security ideologies and, thus, alliance cohesion. Even though the future sharing of intelligence will likely be high among governments threatened by terrorism, as has been true since September 11, such cooperation by necessity will remain largely unreported and unnoticed by mass publics. It thus will not help in the articulation and shaping of collective identities in democratic politics. The sense of clarity about "us" and "them" that followed the attack on September 11 among the closest allies of the United States was temporary and misleading. Although September 11 significantly changed the United States, the terrorist attacks did not change much of the world at large. The U.S. sense of urgency to engage in what it regards as a war of good against evil has not been widely shared abroad. The U.S. Manichean vision of international life will be tested, and tested severely, by a prolonged, complicated, messy, and contested series of counterterrorist campaigns. A nebulous threat environment makes deeply problematic the effort of the world's leading power to impose unilaterally its distinctive political logic even on its closest allies, not to speak of an increasingly plural world.

Notes

1   For their critical comments, I thank Martha Crenshaw, Matthew Evangelista, Albrecht Funk, H. Richard Friman, Peter Gourevitch, Bruce Jentleson, Arie M. Kacowicz, Mary F. Katzenstein, Robert O. Keohane, Jonathan D. Kirshner, Stephen D. Krasner, David Laitin, David Leheny, Roger Masters, Nobuo Okawara, Mark Selden, Henry Shue, and Leslie Vinjamurie. I also thank participants in seminars at Cornell, Dartmouth, Georgetown, Harvard, and the London School of Economics, and two anonymous readers and two editors of *International Organization* for their comments and criticisms, and the Russell Sage Foundation for its financial support. The usual disclaimers apply. A sharply condensed earlier version of this chapter was published under the same title in *Current History* 101 (659): 427–35.

2   Some call it "structural," but this is an unfortunate misnomer. Situational analysis lacks the theoretical sparseness of structural theories such as neorealism.

3   I would like to thank Roger Masters for drawing my attention to the relevance of this important general point for my specific argument.

4   I would like to thank Professor Ulrich Preuss of the Free University Berlin for clarifying these legal issues for me.

5   Of these, 27,500 were members of a radical Turkish organization, Milli Görüs; in addition, there were twelve Arab Islamic extremist organizations with 3,100 supporters, including the Muslim Brotherhood, Hamas, Hizbollah, and the Algerian groups FIS and GIA. *Der Spiegel*, September 24, 2001: 28–9; *Financial Times*, May 25, 2002: 2.

6   The most important of the three bills defines more precisely responses in the eventuality of a direct attack, although the concept of "direct attack" is given an ambiguous definition. The other two bills amend the Self-Defense Forces Law and the law governing the Security Council of Japan. Prime Minister Koizumi

thus appeared on the verge of a successful reform of Japan's security laws, an accomplishment that was denied to his father, Junichiro Koizumi, when he headed the Defense Agency in the 1960s.

References

Armacost, Michael H. and Pyle, Kenneth B. (2001) "Japan and the Engagement of China: Challenges for U.S. Policy Coordination," *NBR Analysis*, 12, 5: 5–62.

Booth, Ken and Dunne, Tim (eds) (2002) *Worlds in Collision: Terror and the Future of the Global Order*, New York: Palgrave Macmillan.

Brown, Michael E. *et al.* (eds) (2000) *America's Strategic Choices*, rev. edn, Cambridge, Mass.: MIT Press.

Chalk, Peter (1998) "Political Terrorism in South East Asia," *Terrorism and Political Violence*, 10, 2: 118–34.

Correspondence (2002) "The World Responds to September 11, 2002," *Correspondence: An International Review of Culture & Society*, 9: 1–39.

Crenshaw, Martha (2002) "Terrorism, Strategies, and Grand Strategies: Domestic or Structural Constraints?," paper presented at the 43rd Annual Convention of the International Studies Association, March, New Orleans, La.

Dwyer, Jim *et al.* (1994) *Two Seconds under the World: Terror Comes to America: The Conspiracy behind the World Trade Center Bombing*, New York: Crown.

Falkenrath, Richard (2001) "Analytic Models and Policy Prescription: Understanding Recent Innovation in U.S. Counterterrorism," *Studies in Conflict and Terrorism*, 4, 3: 159–81.

Farrell, William (1990) *Blood and Rage: The Story of the Japanese Red Army*, Lexington, Conn.: D. C. Heath, Lexington Books.

Furukawa, Shun'ichi (2000) "An Institutional Framework for Japanese Crisis Management," *Journal of Contingencies and Crisis Management*, 8, 1: 3–14.

Gershman, John (2002) "Is Southeast Asia the Second Front?," *Foreign Affairs*, 81, 4: 60–74.

Gourevitch, Peter (1977) "International-Trade, Domestic Coalitions and Liberty: Comparative Responses to Crisis of 1873–1896," *Journal of Interdisciplinary History*, 2: 281–313.

Gurowitz, Amy I. (1999) "Mobilizing International Norms: Domestic Actors, Immigrants, and the State (Germany, Japan, Canada, Malaysia)," unpublished manuscript, Cornell University, Ithaca, NY.

Hedman, Eva-Lotta (2002) "The Threat of 'Islamic Terrorism'? A View from Southeast Asia," *Harvard Asia Quarterly*, 6, 2: 38–43.

Hershberg, Eric and Moore, Kevin W. (eds) (2002) *Critical Views of September 11: Analyses from around the World*, New York: New Press.

Heymann, Philip B. (2001) "Dealing with Terrorism—An Overview," *International Security*, 6, 3: 24–38.

Higuchi, Tateshi (2001) "Inter-Agency Partnerships against Criminal Organizations," Occasional Paper 01–01, Program on U.S.–Japan Relations, Harvard University.

Itabashi, Isao, Ogawara, Masamichi, and Leheny, David (2002) "Constrained Reforms in Japan's Counterterrorism Policies," pp. 337–73 in Y. Alexander (ed.) *Combating Terrorism: Strategies for Ten Countries*, Ann Arbor, Mich.: University of Michigan Press.

Jansen, Klaus (2001) *Fighting Terror in Germany*, Washington, DC: American Institute for Contemporary German Studies. Available at <http://www.aicgs.org/strategic/publications.shtml> (accessed May 19, 2003).

Japan Society, the National Institute for Research Advancement (Tokyo), and the Research Institute for Peace and Security (Tokyo) (2001) "New Approaches to U.S. Japan Security Cooperation: Conference Report," pp. 11–37 in M. Green (ed.) *New Approaches to U.S.–Japan Security Cooperation: Terrorism Prevention and Preparedness*, New York: Japan Society.

Jervis, Robert (1997) *System Effects: Complexity in Political and Social Life*, Princeton, NJ: Princeton University Press.

Katzenstein, Peter J. (1990) "West Germany's Internal Security Policy: State and Violence in the 1970s and 1980s," Occasional Paper 28, Cornell Studies in International Affairs, Western Societies Program, Cornell University.

Katzenstein, Peter J. (1996) *Cultural Norms and National Security: Police and Military in Postwar Japan*, Ithaca, NY: Cornell University Press.

Katzenstein, Peter J. (ed.) (1997) *Tamed Power: Germany in Europe*, Ithaca, NY: Cornell University Press.

Katzenstein, Peter J. (1998) "Left-Wing Violence and State Response: United States, Germany, Italy, and Japan, 1960s–1990s," Working Paper 98.1, Institute for European Studies, Cornell University.

Katzenstein, Peter J. (2002) "Security," unpublished manuscript, Russell Sage Foundation, New York.

Katzenstein, Peter J. and Okawara, Nobuo (2001) "Japan, Asian-Pacific Security and the Case for Analytical Eclecticism," *International Security*, 6, 3: 153–85.

Katzenstein, Peter J. and Shiraishi, Takashi (eds) (1997) *Network Power: Japan and Asia*, Ithaca, NY: Cornell University Press.

Katzenstein, Peter J. and Tsujinaka, Yutaka (1991) *Defending the Japanese State: Structures, Norms, and the Political Responses to Terrorism and Violent Social Protest in the 1970s and 1980s*, Ithaca, NY: East Asia Program, Cornell University.

Kawano, Makoto (1999) "The Targets of U.S. and Japanese Intelligence after the Cold War," Occasional Paper 99–06, Program on U.S.–Japan Relations, Harvard University.

Kurlantzick, Joshua (2001) "Fear Moves East: Terror Targets the Pacific Rim," *Washington Quarterly*, 4, 1: 19–29.

Lansford, Tom (2002) *All for One: Terrorism, NATO and the United States*, Burlington, Vt.: Ashgate.

Leheny, David (2000) "Watch or Die!: Two Rocks and a Hard Place in Japan's Counterterrorism Policies," paper prepared for presentation at the Annual Meeting of the American Political Science Association, August–September, Washington, DC.

Leheny, David (2001a) "Symbols, Strategies, and Choices for Political Science after September 11," unpublished paper, University of Wisconsin, Madison.

Leheny, David (2001b) "Tokyo Confronts Terror," *Policy Review*, 10 (December/January): 37–47.

Leheny, David (2002) "Strategies, Symbols, and Choices for International Relations Scholarship after September 11," *Dialogue-IO* (April): 57–70. Available at <http://mitpress.mit.edu/journals/INOR/Dialogue_IO/leheny.pdf> (accessed May 19, 2003).

Leheny, David (2005) "The War on Terrorism in Asia and the Possibility of Secret

Regionalization," pp. 236–55 in T. J. Pempel (ed.) *Remapping East Asia: The Construction of a Region*, Ithaca, NY: Cornell University Press.

Lepsius, Oliver (2002) "Das Verhältnis von Sicherheit und Freiheitsrechten in der Bundesrepublik Deutschland nach dem 11 September 2001," unpublished paper.

Lowi, Theodore J. (1969) *The End of Liberalism: Ideology, Policy, and the Crisis of Public Authority*, New York: W. W. Norton.

Maeda, Tetsuo (2002) "Nichi-Bei anpo saiteigi kara yujihosei" [From redefinition of the Japan–U.S. security relationship to the comprehensive emergency measures law], trans. V. Koschmann, *Gunshuku* [Disarmament] 266 (December): 6–11. Available at <http://www.zmag.org/content/print_article.cfm?itemID.3037 &sectionID.44>.

March, James G. and Olsen, Johan P. (1989) *Rediscovering Institutions: The Organizational Basis of Politics*, New York: Free Press.

Masters, Roger D. (1993) *Beyond Relativism: Science and Human Values*, Hanover, NH: University Press of New England.

Maull, H. W. (2001) "Internationaler Terrorismus: Die deutsche Aussenpolitik auf dem Prufstand," *Internationale Politik*, 6, 12: 1–10.

Mead, Walter Russell (2001) *Special Providence: American Foreign Policy and How It Changed the World*, New York: Knopf.

Mearsheimer, John J. (2001) *The Tragedy of Great Power Politics*, New York: W. W. Norton.

Midford, Paul (2002) "The Logic of Reassurance and Japan's Grand Strategy," *Security Studies*, 11, 3: 1–43.

Miyasaka, Naofumi (2001) "Terrorism and Antiterrorism in Japan: Aum Shinrikyo and After," pp. 67–83 in M. Green (ed.) *Terrorism Prevention and Preparedness: New Approaches to U.S.–Japan Security Cooperation*, New York: Japan Society.

Miyawaki, Raisuke (2001) "Lessons in Fighting Terrorism: American and Japanese Perspective [sic]," remarks prepared for the Global Security Roundtable at the Japan Society, November 7, New York.

Morgenthau, Hans J. (1951) *In Defense of the National Interest: A Critical Examination of American Foreign Policy*, New York: Knopf.

Mullins, Mark R. (1997) "The Political and Legal Response to Aum-Related Violence in Japan: A Review Article," *The Japan Christian Review*, 63: 37–46.

Mylroie, Laurie (2001) *Study of Revenge*, 2nd edn, Washington, DC: American Enterprise Institute.

Okawara, Nobuo and Katzenstein, Peter J. (2001) "Japan and Asian-Pacific Security: Regionalization, Entrenched Bilateralism and Incipient Multilateralism," *The Pacific Review*, 4, 2: 165–94.

Pangi, Robyn (2002) "Consequence Management in the 1995 Sarin Attacks on the Japanese Subway System," BCSIA Discussion Paper 2002–4, John F. Kennedy School of Government, Harvard University.

Parachini, Jon V. (2000) "The World Trade Center Bombers (1993)," pp. 185–206 in J. B. Tucker (ed.) *Toxic Terror: Assessing Terrorist Use of Chemical and Biological Weapons*, Cambridge, Mass.: MIT Press.

Pew Global Attitudes Project (2002) "Among Wealthy Nations . . . U.S. Stands Alone in Its Embrace of Religion," news release, December 19.

Sansoucy, Lisa (1998) "Aum Shinrikyo and the Japanese State," unpublished manuscript, Cornell University, Ithaca, NY.

Schmitt, Carl (1976) *The Concept of the Political*, trans. George Schwab, New Brunswick, NJ: Rutgers University Press.

Steinhoff, Patricia G. (1996) "From Dangerous Thoughts to Dangerous Gas: A Frame Analysis of the Control of Social Movements in Japan," paper presented at the American Sociological Association Meetings, August, New York.

Steinhoff, Patricia G. (n.d.) "Who Really Kidnapped Those Japanese in North Korea?," unpublished paper, University of Hawaii, Honolulu.

Szymkowiak, Kenneth and Steinhoff, Patricia G. (1995) "Wrapping Up in Something Long: Intimidation and Violence by Right-Wing Groups in Postwar Japan," *Terrorism and Political Violence*, 1: 265–98.

Tan, Andrew (2000) *Armed Rebellion in the ASEAN States: Persistence and Implications*, CP135, Strategic and Defence Studies Centre, Australian National University, Canberra.

Trubowitz, Peter (1998) *Defining the National Interest: Conflict and Change in American Foreign Policy*, Chicago, Ill.: University of Chicago Press.

Tuschoff, Christian (n.d.) "The Ties That Bind: Institutions, Allied Commitments, and NATO after September 11," unpublished paper, Emory University, Atlanta, Ga.

Walt, Stephen M. (1987) *The Origins of Alliances*, Ithaca, NY: Cornell University Press.

Waltz, Kenneth N. (1979) *Theory of International Politics*, Reading, Mass.: Addison-Wesley.

Woodward, Bob (2002) *Bush at War*, New York: Simon & Schuster.

Part III

Analytical eclecticism and security

10 Rethinking Asian security: a case for analytical eclecticism

Peter J. Katzenstein and Rudra Sil (2004) [1]

Throughout the 1990s the conventional wisdom of international relations scholarship in the United States held that, with the end of the Cold War and an intensification of institutionalized cooperation in Europe, Asia was ready to explode into violent conflicts. Large-scale war and conflicts were thought to be increasingly likely as an unpredictable North Korean government was teetering at the edge of an economic abyss on a divided Korean peninsula; as an ascendant China was facing political succession in the midst of an enormous domestic transformation; as a more self-confident and nationalist Japan was bent on greater self-assertion in a time of increasing financial weakness; and as Southeast Asia remained deeply unsettled in the aftermath of the Asian financial crisis, with its largest country, a newly democratizing Indonesia, left in limbo following the débâcle of East Timor and the fall of Suharto. None of these political constellations appeared to bode well for an era of peace and stable cooperation. Facing perhaps the most significant problems of any world region in adjusting to the post-Cold War era, Asia appeared to be "ripe for rivalry" (Bracken 1999; Betts 1993/4; Friedberg 1993/4).

The policies of the George W. Bush administration tend to confirm this view. Carefully nurtured throughout the 1990s, the policy of engaging North Korea, for example, was put on ice after the November 2000 presidential election. Political relations with China worsened during the early months of the Bush presidency. Since September 11 the war on terrorism has further strengthened the Bush administration's perception of Asia as a volatile region in which a U.S. presence is necessary to prevent conflict. The war has deepened greatly U.S. involvement in Central Asia; produced a growing military presence in Southeast Asia, particularly the Philippines, which had previously drawn little attention from the United States; and helped improve U.S. relations with China while worsening those with North Korea.

Tensions on the Korean peninsula and over the Taiwan Strait and the war on terrorism notwithstanding, during much of the 1990s large-scale war was more evident in "peaceful" Europe than among Asian "rivals." More recently, it is in Europe that we witnessed the most vigorous challenges to the Bush administration's war in Iraq, raising new questions about the future coherence of NATO and transatlantic relations; by contrast, key Asian powers reacted with either official support for the United States (Japan and South Korea) or remarkable restraint (China and India). And North Korea's decision to restart its nuclear weapons program has so far been met by countries in the region with calls for dialogue rather than military intervention. This undercuts the conventional wisdom about Asian security and suggests that an alternative perspective deserves serious examination (Alagappa 2003; Ikenberry and Mastanduno 2003). Such a perspective takes a much broader view of what is meant by the term "security." Instead of referring to military security narrowly construed, it considers also the economic and social dimensions of security. Specifically, this perspective focuses on the regionwide consensus on the primacy of economic growth and its interconnectedness with social stability, societal security, and regional peace and stability. Spearheaded by Japan and the original six members of ASEAN, this view has spread, most importantly, to China and Vietnam and, hopefully, with a helping U.S. hand, also to the Korean peninsula. Previously dismissed by U.S. security specialists as abstruse scholarly rumination with no relationship to the tough problems of Asian security, these broader, multidimensional views on Asian security have taken center stage since September 11, thus giving the alternative perspective a credibility it sorely lacked before.

The arguments marshaled in support of this view differ, however. Some tend to credit the dominant role of the United States in world politics and in Asia as the advantages of engagement are increasingly viewed as outweighing the advantages of balancing (Kapstein 1999). Others see that dominance, especially in the unfolding war on terror, as a possible source of instability and the intensification of conflict as U.S. policy and al Qaeda are offering global frames for local grievances and conflicts (Gershman 2002; Hedman 2002). Still others have suggested that the historical experiences and normative discourses shaping states' perceptions of their regional environment make the security problems in parts of Asia less serious than is conventionally assumed (Acharya 2001, 2000; Kerr, Mack, and Evans 1995). In light of these fundamental differences in perspective and the data to which they point, whether Asia is "ripe for rivalry" or "plump for peace" remains an open question.

Political reality, we surmise, is more complex than any of these perspectives allows for. This is unavoidable for the simple reason that in different parts of Asia-Pacific we find actors embracing quite different definitions of security. In Tokyo that definition tends to be broad and encompasses not only the deployment of troops in battle, unimaginable at least for the time being, but also the giving of economic aid, something that Japan does a lot of. In Washington, that definition tends to be narrowly focused on the military, which is large and powerful and dwarfs those of the rest of the world, and excludes economic aid, where the United States is exceptionally niggardly even after the promise of a doubling of the aid budget by President Bush in 2002. And in Beijing narrow and broad conceptions of regional security remain deeply contested.

Beyond the varied security conceptions that actors hold, there are the varied lenses through which scholars analyze security. Different analytic lenses require different kinds of simplifications in how questions are posed, facts assembled, and explanations developed. Such differences, in turn, are shaped greatly by factors largely unrelated to issues of Asian security: metatheoretical considerations that define appropriate domains of inquiry, acceptable methods of analysis, and agreed-upon standards of evaluation. Although debates over such problems continue to shape research in other fields of political science and indeed the social sciences writ large (Hall 2003; Lichbach 2003; Shapiro 2002), the field of international relations in the United States has been especially affected by long-standing programmatic debates that divide "paradigms" or "research traditions" from one another. In the effort to make sense of the world, such paradigms or traditions invoke a particular vocabulary, adhere to a specific philosophical perspective, adopt a specific analytic framework, and develop a particular style of research. In noting fundamental incompatibilities between realist and Marxist theoretical perspectives, for example, Tony Smith (1994: 350) observes that "each paradigm is monotheistic, home to a jealous god." These different research traditions have become central to how we identify ourselves and others as scholars and how we train the next generation of scholars. And they provide an enduring foundation for widely noted basic debates in the study of international affairs.

The growing interest in the existence of, and competition between, contending research traditions has not been without benefits. Indeed, one premier journal, *International Security*, has made a truly exceptional effort to present all sides of the debates, with extensive commentaries promoting or critiquing such research traditions as realism, rationalism, neoliberal institutionalism, and constructivism.[2] Similar interparadigm debates are also appearing regularly in European journals, although the tone, depth of philosophical grounding, and prevalent conceptions of world politics tend to be quite different than what one finds in the United States (Wæver 1999). This widespread attention to competing research traditions has marked international relations as a diverse field of scholarship and has contributed to increasingly nuanced articulations of theories and hypotheses within traditions. This is the sort of progress that some cite in advocating scholarship bounded within discrete research traditions (Sanderson 1987) as these contend with "the models and foils" put forward by competing traditions (Lichbach 2003: 214). This does not, however, mean that international relations research has embraced the spirit of intellectual pluralism or generated better solutions to existing problems. This is because paradigm-bound research can get in the way of better understanding as it tends to ignore insights and problems that are not readily translated into a particular theoretical language (Hirschman 1970). At the cost of sacrificing the complexity that policymakers and other actors encounter in the real world, problems are frequently sliced into narrow puzzles to suit the agenda of a given research tradition. As a result, whatever progress might be claimed by proponents of particular research traditions, there is little consensus on what progress, if any, has been achieved by the field as a whole.

The recognition of the existence of, and possible complementarities between, multiple research traditions holds forth the prospect of translating the analytic languages and theoretical insights of each in the process of improving transparadigmatic knowledge on specific substantive problems. For example, seemingly incompatible strands of liberal, constructivist, and realist thought offer different insights in different languages that can be cautiously translated and productively combined in problem-focused research. Scholars who champion the "triangulation" of methods as a promising avenue to more reliable knowledge (Jick 1979; Tarrow 1995) point the way to a different way of learning that transcends specific research traditions (Makinda 2000). Theoretical triangulation is certainly more complicated than method-ological triangulation given the risk of intellectual incoherence across com-ponents of research traditions. Nevertheless, the risk is worth the potential payoffs of encouraging, in the interest of better understanding specific research problems, self-conscious efforts to selectively incorporate concepts and insights from varied research traditions.

A generation ago Anatol Rapoport (1960) pointed the way when he iden-tified fights, games, and debates as three modal situations requiring a mixture of conflict and cooperation. Research traditions in international relations have tended to encourage conflict but have done little to foster cooperation. Fortu-nately, a number of international relations scholars are beginning to shun metatheoretical battles, preferring instead to turn their attention to the iden-tification of politically important and analytically interesting problems that reflect the complexity of international life and require answers that no single research tradition is equipped to provide. In their synthetic treatment of different strands of institutional analysis, for example, John L. Campbell and Ove K. Pedersen (2001: 249) seek to "stimulate dialogue among paradigms in order to explore the possibilities for theoretical cross-fertilization, rap-prochement, and integration." Similarly, others have begun to transgress the boundaries between realism, liberalism, and constructivism for the purpose of developing more integrated perspectives on particular aspects of international politics (Hellman *et al.* 2003). Some have been exploring the sources of "prudence" in world politics by explicitly seeking a "sociological synthesis of realism and liberalism" (Hall and Paul 1999), while others have implicitly crossed the boundaries between research traditions in exploring how aspects of political economy can produce tendencies toward both war and peace (Wolfson 1998) or how issues of status and recognition intersect with security concerns to drive weapons proliferation or military industrialization (Kinsella and Chima 2001; Eyre and Suchman 1996). These are just a few examples of works that have moved away from interparadigm "fights" in order to develop more eclectic perspectives.

Borrowing from Albert Hirschman (1981), we only suggest that "trespass-ing" across the sharp boundaries separating different traditions allows for new combinations of problem recognition and explanations that may be less parsimonious but intellectually more interesting or policy relevant. This chapter is part of that intellectual movement. We argue for the usefulness of relying on multiple explanatory frameworks that are consciously eclectic in language and substance rather than being driven by the tenets guiding particular research traditions. Such frameworks are formulated on pragmatic assumptions that permit us to sidestep clashes between irreconcilable metatheoretical postulates, and to draw upon different research traditions and the concepts, observations, and methods they generate in relation to particular problems. We discuss, first, the pragmatic quality and problem-focused character of eclecticism in the study of international affairs. Next, we articulate the general problematique for research on Asian security that draws attention to multiple and intersecting processes that shape how Asian states understand and address their security concerns. Finally, we introduce and preview the substantive contributions that, read collectively, represent an effort to build eclectic explanatory sketches not easily subsumed within existing research traditions.

Research traditions and explanatory sketches in international relations

Most scholars of international relations think of the theoretical universe as divided between different schools of thought to which scholars commit themselves in the belief that they generate better explanations with greater policy relevance. What ultimately distinguishes these schools, however, are not the substantive claims they produce but the underlying cognitive structures upon which these claims are formulated. These structures shape what phenomena are considered important and explainable, how research questions about such phenomena are posed, what concepts and methods are employed in generating explanations of the phenomena, and what standards are reasonable for evaluating these explanations. Such abstract specifications reflect enduring ontological and epistemological, that is metatheoretical, assumptions shared by members of some research communities but not others. Hence, as is true of the history of science and social science more generally, as a field of scholarship international relations is characterized by the emergence of, competition between, and evolution or degeneration of, discrete cognitive structures within which specific models and narratives are constructed, communicated, and evaluated.

Following Thomas Kuhn (1962), some scholars of international relations have referred to these structures as "paradigms." Paradigms are concerted intellectual efforts to make sense of the world. When fully institutionalized, their weak links are no longer recognized, their foundational assumptions are no longer questioned, and their anomalies are consistently overlooked or considered beyond the purview of specific research questions.[3] Dissatisfied with the monism implied in a Kuhnian vision of normal science, or perhaps frustrated by the absence of criteria for comparing supposedly incommensurable paradigms, some international relations scholars have employed Kuhn's (1962) concept of "research programs" that are at least assumed to be comparable to each other in terms of how effectively the successive theories they produce deal with novel facts or anomalies over time. These scholars find Lakatosian research programs to be "intuitively appealing and attractive" (Elman and Elman 2003a, 2002: 253) in making sense of international relations scholarship because individual theories in the field have indeed come to be clustered around competing sets of "core" assumptions, and because debates among adherents of contending perspectives do frequently revolve around the question of whether one or the other perspective is "progressive" or "degenerative."[4]

Although Kuhn and Lakatos represent contending epistemological perspectives, both "paradigms" and "research programs" face limitations as units for organizing and assessing international relations research. The persistence of divisive debates among proponents of different approaches is difficult to square with the notion of either a single dominant paradigm or the staying power of any one research program relative to another. Furthermore, the overlapping of some assumptions across different approaches suggests that different schools of thought are not always mutually exclusive cognitive structures that can be evaluated according to any one standard. More importantly, although framed in different languages in different periods, the foundational divides reflected in international relations debates—for example, objectivism vs. subjectivism, agency vs. structure, material vs. ideal— represent recurrent rather than episodic problems (Sil 2000d: 9–12), suggesting that there is neither a clear sequence of normal and revolutionary science as Kuhn envisioned, nor any evidence that progressive research programs will be recognized as such by any but their own adherents. Indeed, even those who find Lakatosian research programs to be useful in assessing scholarly research differ in terms of which elements of Lakatos's metatheory are given priority, with some emphasizing the significance of sophisticated falsificationism for the resilience of conflicting theories and others focusing on the criteria for identifying progressive problem shifts (Elman and Elman 2003b). Andrew Moravcsik (2003), for example, relies on Lakatos to critique realism and advance the case for liberalism as a progressive research program, but also warns that Lakatosian thinking encourages a zero-sum competition among approaches and diverts attention from exploring the possibilities for synthesis. Even more problematic are some characteristic, often unacknowledged, weaknesses within approaches identified as research programs in international relations: proponents of research programs tend to value substantive or heuristic novelty as a measure of their scientific progress, offer multiple definitions of what constitutes novel facts, engage in misstatements and tenacious battles that undercut tolerance and the acknowledgment of programmatic failures, and provide insufficient information to allow us to distinguish consistently between different research programs or to assign proper weights to a program's "hard core," "positive heuristic," or "protective belt" (Elman and Elman 2002: 245–52).

Because of the limitations that attend the concepts of "paradigm" or "research program," we follow here Larry Laudan's (1996, 1990, 1984, 1977) more flexible notion of competing and evolving "research traditions." This concept captures how scholars opt to identify, pose, and resolve problems in international relations research, including the vexing issues of Asian security. Like Kuhnian paradigms and Lakatosian research programs, Laudan's conception of research traditions suggests long-enduring commitments that motivate and distinguish clusters of scientific research. Typically such traditions consist of two things:

(1) a set of beliefs about what sorts of entities and processes make up the domain of inquiry; and (2) a set of epistemic and methodological norms about how the domain is to be investigated, how theories are to be tested, how data are to be collected, and the like.

(Laudan 1996: 83)

Unlike Kuhn and Lakatos, however, Laudan offers no single model of how disciplines as a whole evolve or of how to measure their progress. He argues instead that we should focus on different research traditions as intrinsically diverse clusters of scholarship that can engender diverse theories, some more useful than others in solving particular problems. Moreover, unlike Kuhn and Lakatos, Laudan sees research traditions as potentially capable of encompassing very different types of research products involving different, at times even contradictory, explanatory propositions. This allows for the possibility that propositions drawn from different research traditions complement one another in the solution of common empirical problems, in spite of the foundational divides associated with these traditions. Since in the social sciences not all components of competing schools of thought represent elements of mutually exclusive cognitive structures, and since these competing schools differ over time in their defining features and their core points of contention, it makes more sense to speak of the field in terms of more fluid research traditions rather than more rigidly defined paradigms or research programs.[5] We address the merits and limits of Laudan's reliance on "problem-solving" below, but for now we turn to the main research traditions in international relations, particularly as the field has evolved in the United States.

Although preferred labels and particular bones of contention have varied, since its inception in the early twentieth century the field of international relations has been divided by a long list of competing "isms" that may be viewed as competing research traditions. Enduring debates have existed among proponents of realism and idealism, behaviorism and traditionalism, neoliberalism and neorealism, rationalism and constructivism, and a variety of different structuralisms and poststructuralisms. In some cases, debate has revolved primarily around substantive interpretations or normative orientations; in others, around ontological or epistemological issues. Among research communities within the United States, rationalism, in both its realist and liberal variants, set the terms of scholarly debate early on. Elsewhere, the importance of ideas and identities has long been taken for granted and debates over world politics have revolved around competing understandings of the nature of "ideas" and "identity." There are then many ways of framing competing approaches to international relations. For the purpose of defining and promoting eclectic approaches to Asian security, we rely here on the familiar triad of constructivism, liberalism, and realism as a usefully simplified way to address some foundational, conceptual, methodological, and substantive debates in contemporary international relations research. There exist variations within and across these three approaches, for example, in the extent to which a particular argument is founded on positivist assumptions or specific methodological injunctions. Nevertheless, for the limited purpose of defining and distinguishing eclectic analytic perspectives, these labels capture meaningful differences in the way scholars identify themselves and in the cognitive structures that shape how they recognize, pose, and approach the problems they seek to solve. Thus, we could view constructivism, liberalism, and realism as three sides of a triangle that take for granted the centrality of some core assumptions of international life, for example, in their respective focus on identity, efficiency, and power (see Figure 10.1). At the same time, however, some variants of these traditions converge (at the triangle's corners) with one or the other research tradition's ontology, epistemology, methodology, or normative orientations. The field of international relations thus encompasses both the practices of normal science working around shared core assumptions as well as the possibility of eclectic theorizing.

Constructivism is based on the fundamental view that ideational structures mediate how actors perceive, construct, and reproduce the institutional and material structures they inhabit as well as their own roles and identities

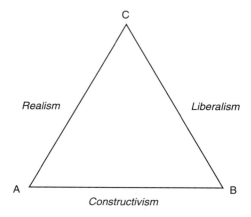

Figure 10.1 Research traditions and points of convergence

within them. Constructivism thus highlights the significance of transformative or generative processes such as deliberation, persuasion, and socialization that, for better or worse, can lead to the transformation of identities and preferences (Johnston 2001; Wendt 1999; Finnemore 1996). Assigning epistemological significance to such processes at the individual level requires "a conception of actors who are not only strategically but also discursively competent" (Ruggie 1998: 21), something that is precluded by the utilitarian assumptions held by most liberals and realists. In constructivist analyses of state behavior and the relations between states, ideational factors and processes are expected to be important for tracing whether collective actors are likely to construct or diffuse enmity or amity between self and other. And constructivist analyses pay attention to the reproduction and transformation of collective identities as they affect the prospects for social learning and also the diffusion of collective norms and individual beliefs. Constructivists do, however, exhibit important differences in their foundational assumptions: Some identify with a "naturalist" form of positivism predicated on a realist ontology (Dessler 1999; Wendt 1995), whereas others depart from a "pragmatist" conception of social knowledge (Haas and Haas 2002), and still others adopt a hermeneutic approach consistent with the relativistic epistemology of postmodernism (Walker 2000; Ashley 1995). The first two strands are more likely than the third to share some set of epistemological assumptions that overlap with those held by most realists or liberals (near corners A and B in Figure 10.1). The "soft rationalism" embraced by pragmatist constructivists is particularly conducive to engaging realist and liberal arguments over the character and formation of actors' material and ideal interests (Haas 2001). These differences suggest that constructivist research is rendered coherent and distinctive not by a comprehensive epistemological perspective or a unique normative orientation but rather by the ontological assumption of the social construction of world politics that requires endogenizing actors' identities and treating interests as variable and thus responsive to such ideational processes as social learning, norm diffusion, and socialization.

Contemporary liberalism in its various formulations focuses largely on how rational state actors seek to maximize efficiency in an interdependent world and how, even under conditions of anarchy, this intentionality can produce cooperative arrangements and a rational aggregation of social preferences. Because of their willingness to consider the independent effects of the environments in which actors operate, some versions of liberalism can converge with some types of constructivism (around the triangle's corner B) on the significance of ideas, values, and multilateral institutions in constraining actors and reshaping their preferences (Haas 2001). Moreover, many constructivists share with classical formulations of liberalism (near corner B) a normative concern for progress predicated on the idea that the relevant actors and their interests are not fixed but variable, embedded in a wider set of social relationships and amenable to the pressure of social norms and moral persuasion (Reus-Smit 2001). More concretely, both perspectives put much stock in the possibility that international organizations can engender shared values and reciprocal understandings that can sustain, even if they do not alter, actors' identities and preferences, and cooperative arrangements beyond the level one would predict solely from the strategic calculation of member states. This idea is evident, for example, in arguments about the significance of shared democratic values for the persistence of the U.S.–Japan alliance (Mochizuki and O'Hanlon 1998: 127) and the importance of shared discourses about North Korea in explaining the longevity of the U.S.–Korea alliance (Suh 2004).

At a more fundamental level, however, neoliberals are much closer to realists than constructivists in accepting utilitarian and rationalist assumptions in the identification of the relevant actors, interests, and structures in international politics (corner C). Thus, even when contemporary liberals take seriously the role of ideas and beliefs as focal points of common concern (Goldstein and Keohane 1993), they consider these as reflections of states' experiences in the international arena or new instruments for realizing the benefits of cooperation over the longer term. They do not view ideas and beliefs as forces capable of fundamentally altering the identities or core interests of actors. What distinguishes liberals from realists is not their ontology or epistemology but their designation of the central problems that need to be investigated. This, in turn, reflects competing assumptions about the preference-ordering of states (whether they seek absolute gains or relative gains) and the causal impact of international institutions (whether, in the interest of all member states, they introduce a greater degree of predictability, transparency, and reciprocity). Liberals allow for a wider range of conditions under which absolute gains motivate cooperative state behavior, and assign greater importance to international institutions as a basis for sustaining that behavior and mitigating the effects of anarchy. Institutions may be significant for constructivists as well, but mainly as reflections of social practice or as potential sources of unanticipated consequences and major shifts in actors' identities and perceptions of interest. Specifically for neoliberals, institutions represent equilibrium outcomes of strategic interaction, reducing transaction costs, providing information, making commitments more credible, and encouraging reciprocity (Keohane and Martin 1995).

In its current formulation, realist theory is concerned about outcomes at the systemic level (usually stability or conflict among states) or, in recent neoclassical variants, in the effects of actor preferences on state behavior in different environments (Finel 2001/2). Outcomes are assumed to be driven primarily by asymmetrical distributions in capabilities, measured largely in military terms or material resources, that are required to defend one's borders, inflict harm on other states, or prevail in domestic politics. Given the centrality and objective character of the material distribution of capabilities, realists diverge sharply from constructivism's emphasis on ideational factors. At the same time, contra liberalism, realists insist that states are inescapably operating in a self-help system in which their cooperation is constrained by the objective of maximizing relative gains in the distribution of capabilities. On questions of security, the unmitigating logic of *realpolitik* is independently articulated by the behavior of states. Under most conditions, "institutions have minimal influence on state behavior and thus hold little prospect for promoting stability" (Mearsheimer 1994/5: 7).

This difference in problem focus and substantive interpretation does not keep realists from sharing with important strands of liberalism the view that a state's interests, identities, and ability to identify opportunities and threats are all unproblematic. This similarity permits some convergence in substantive analysis (at corner C). This is evident, for example, in arguments about how the U.S. continued military and economic engagement in Asia serves the purpose of both guarding against potential regional hegemons and providing opportunities for increased cooperation and prosperity throughout the Asia-Pacific. By the same token, weak states participate actively in international institutions in the hope of diffusing security threats posed by stronger members of those institutions. This is one reason why ASEAN member states have sought wider fora, such as the ASEAN Regional Forum (ARF), to engage Japan, China, and the two Koreas, and why multilateralism holds some promise in the attempt to resolve the conflict between the two Koreas (Khong 1997a, 1997b; Kurata 1996). Furthermore, realist thought begins to converge with constructivist perspectives (at corner A) where realist behavior is viewed as a projection of particular ideas and beliefs held by state actors. This is evident, for example, in the "cultural realism" that drove Chinese grand strategy in various periods in Chinese history (Johnston 1995) and perhaps also in the symbolic significance of the Taiwan issue in the triangular relations between China, Japan, and the United States (Xu 2003; Christensen 1999).

This threefold characterization of contemporary international relations research is by no means the only way to classify research traditions. For example, the lack of deep epistemological disagreements between important variants of contemporary realism and liberalism have prompted some recent surveys of the field to refer to these schools as competing sets of claims about actors' preferences and behaviors *within* an overarching framework referred to variously as "rationalism" (Katzenstein, Keohane and Krasner 1999a) or "neo-utilitarianism" (Ruggie 1998). Alternatively, scholars may prefer to focus on analytic subdivisions that have emerged *within* research traditions. For example, those with intellectual sensibilities that are more "reflectivist" (Wæver 1996) than rationalist may prefer to apply the threefold characterization to disagreements among "natural" constructivists, critical constructivists, and postmodernists. Thus, no single set of metatheoretical differences distinguishes discrete research traditions in international relations; and, depending on the research community in question, the operative distinctions may range from deep differences over ontological issues (for example, in the debates between rationalist and constructivist conceptions of preferences) to differences over epistemological postures (for example, in the debates between

classical and structural realists or between conventional and postmodern constructivists). What matters more is that the questions and practices of
scholars lead them to identify with, promote, and communicate within separate groups—as has been the case with strands of realism and liberalism for
over two decades and is now turning out to be the case for constructivism
as well. So long as constructivists, liberals, and realists themselves see fit to
distinguish themselves from one another, and so long as the distinction produces repeated clashes over which problems are important, which variables
are assigned more causal weight, and which principles more consistently guide
the preference-ordering and behavior of actors, there are sufficient grounds for
treating them as competing research traditions.

Another potential problem is that the distinctions sometimes get blurred
when scholars deploy the rhetorical strategy of identifying their preferred
research tradition with the existence of a "reasonable mainstream" that supposedly enjoys almost universal assent, or of a "conventional wisdom" that
supposedly improves on and subsumes various "minority" positions. Some
realists, for example, claim that institutions only matter when they reinforce
preexisting common interests and thus regard neoliberal institutionalism as
simply realism by another name (Mearsheimer 1995). In response, neoliberals
retort that neoliberal institutionalist theory is flexible enough to subsume the
utilitarian and rationalist aspects of realism (Keohane and Martin 1995). A
while back, in the late 1980s, both realists and liberals could argue with some
justification that critics of the mainstream had failed to produce empirically
grounded research to back up their abstract claims. Over the last decade,
constructivists have responded to that charge. In doing so they have opened
themselves up to the opposite criticism. Some critical theorists and postmodernists have chided constructivists for having been mainstreamed by
positivism (Hopf 1998; Price and Reus-Smit 1998). Such rhetorical duels are
quite typical of social science debates. They cannot conceal, however, fundamental differences in a priori assumptions that guide analyses in different
research traditions. In fact, the existence of such rhetoric is itself indicative of
the vigor with which different research traditions attempt to establish dominance, with the paradoxical result that such efforts prevent the very monism
implied by a dominant paradigm and contribute to intensify competition
between the traditions (Sil 2000a).

Making the case for analytical eclecticism requires us to cut the link
between research traditions and the substantive interpretations and empirical
claims constructed within them. Research traditions cannot themselves be
evaluated against each other. Their ontological and epistemological foundations are often too incommensurable and too abstract to produce specific
methodological injunctions or substantive explanations and predictions. Nor
can they be synthesized into a single unified model of scientific research.
While the most doctrinaire proponents of any one research tradition will
reject the need for synthesis, "even coalitions of the willing may find the
going difficult as they discover the analytical boundaries beyond which their

respective approaches cannot be pushed" (Ruggie 1998: 37). But what can be tested, compared, and partially recombined are the "explanatory sketches" research traditions generate. We employ this term to sidestep the ambiguity and contestation often generated by the use of such terms as "theory" or "hypothesis," especially since these terms are often defined and qualified differently across competing research traditions. What passes for a "theory" is often little more than an empirical claim embedded in the metatheoretical structures associated with a particular school or approach. We define "explanatory sketches" broadly to refer to any interpretation of a set of observations that is intended to generate a causally significant understanding of specific empirical outcomes, whether these are specific historical events, patterns of similarity and dissimilarity in broad configurations, or variations across comparable events. As such, explanatory sketches are sufficiently open-ended to encompass a wide range of empirical claims. Such claims need not be limited to a single time- or space-bound context. And they should be formulated so as to permit, at least in principle, some form of validation or falsification through some empirical observation. Thus, a realist explanation for the conflict on the Korean peninsula, a narrative interpreting the sources and significance of Japan's culture of security in the postwar international context, or a choice-based model of security cooperation in Southeast Asia during the 1990s can all be regarded as explanatory sketches. All three impute causal significance to certain facts in relation to certain outcomes. And all three draw upon logics that can be adapted to an analysis of comparable contexts.

The relationship between explanatory sketches and research traditions is the point of departure for analytical eclecticism. For the most part, an explanatory sketch is likely to be "nested" within one or another research tradition, accepting as unproblematic the ontological, epistemological, and methodological assumptions characteristic of that tradition. Conversely, research traditions are highly significant for the purpose of identifying and classifying explanatory sketches in a given field of research. They indicate which explanatory sketches accept certain assumptions as uncontroversial background knowledge; which sketches conform to established conventions governing the collection of evidence and the testing of general statements; which sketches reinforce or undermine the intellectual coherence of a research tradition; which need to be altered because they introduce unanticipated problems; and which need to be excluded entirely from the tradition because of the insurmountable challenge they pose by violating foundational assumptions. Moreover, institutional factors—ranging from the venues for publication and funding patterns to faculty hiring and graduate training—strengthen the importance investigators themselves attach to presenting their projects and findings in the form of explanatory sketches that fit easily into a well-established research tradition. These factors account for why most research in international relations over the past century can be readily identified in terms of quite familiar labels such as realism, liberalism, behaviorism, or structuralism, each of which ultimately derives its coherence and significance from the kinds of beliefs and norms that Laudan identifies as the basis for a research tradition.

Although it is typically true that explanatory sketches are "nested" in particular research traditions, for two reasons this is not necessarily so. First, research traditions vary in terms of the significance they attribute to foundational assumptions, methodological orientations, and domains of inquiry. One research tradition may be identified primarily in terms of its ontological assumptions and theoretical language, allowing for a wide-ranging domain of inquiry and a large set of methodological tools. Another may be more recognizable through the application of common methodological tools to a well-specified domain of inquiry even if groups within that tradition differ on questions of epistemology. This is evident, for example, for much of constructivism, where we find empiricist and hermeneutic approaches both sharing the assumption of a socially constructed international world and both employing the language of "discourse" and "identity" in trying to offer insights about the world. Similarly, the underlying preference for methodological individualism is a central defining feature of neoliberal institutionalism, even though some of its adherents may be game theorists testing formal models and others empiricists in search of probabilistic hypotheses. Moreover, as research traditions suggest enduring commitments, it is also likely that they will have to evolve as particular assumptions or heuristic devices become more or less valuable or fashionable over time for different generations of scholars seeking to explain similar problems in new environments. While common foundational assumptions and methodological orientations are probably sufficient to produce similarities across explanatory sketches in adjacent generations of scholarship, as the number of generations increases, differences in the character of explanatory sketches may make them difficult to recognize as part of the same research tradition, as is true, for example, of work on security communities (Adler and Barnett 1998; Deutsch *et al.* 1957).

Second, the considerable differences *within* constructivist, liberal, and realist research traditions that we mentioned above generate significantly different explanatory sketches that can coexist as part of a single research tradition. Some may produce substantive claims that implicitly or explicitly challenge the "normal" expectations of their respective research traditions in spite of shared ontological and epistemological principles. And explanatory sketches constructed within different research traditions can converge in their wider implications and projections, despite fundamental disagreements over foundational or methodological issues and the characterization of specific problems. Thus, realism, regarded by some as a source of pessimistic scenarios for Asia (Friedberg 1993/4), can also provide the basis for theories suggesting lasting stability through, for example, the logic of nuclear deterrence (Goldstein 2001) or a regionally calibrated balance of power in which China's military strength is offset by regional alliances and by the United States as an "offshore balancer" (Mearsheimer 2001: 234–66; Layne 1997). Similarly, regarded by some as inherently optimistic about the prospects for peaceful change through norm diffusion and social learning, constructivism can be adapted to emphasize how enduring beliefs about sovereignty or resilient images of enmity can hinder the resolution of volatile issues such as Taiwan (Johnston 2004) or a divided Korea (Suh 2004; Moon and Chun 2003; Grinker 1998). A neoliberal institutionalist sketch might interpret the growth of such institutions as the Asian Development Bank as evidence of increasing multilateralism across regions in an ever more interdependent world, converging with constructivist sketches emphasizing the strength of shared norms and the socialization of particular groups of states in overcoming historical enmities and nurturing regional alliances, for example in the case of Southeast Asia (Acharya 2001; Johnston 1999; Khong 1997a, 1997b); at the same time, another neoliberal sketch might view regional institutions as evidence of a more sophisticated strategy conceived by Asian states to promote their economic interests in world markets, converging with realists who view Asia primarily as an arena of competition and conflict in the absence of a bipolar international system. And constructivist, neoliberal institutionalist, and neo-realist treatments of state behavior may proceed from quite different assumptions and identify quite different causal mechanisms while still agreeing on how China is likely to respond to new regional economic institutions or how Japan's changing role in such institutions indicates a reduced willingness to rely only on its bilateral relationship with the United States.

Research traditions are not rigid doctrines that produce uniform explanatory sketches employing similar logics. Explanatory sketches can be meaningfully grouped in terms of the implications of their substantive claims, in spite of significant differences in their philosophical or methodological foundations and their preferred causal mechanisms. It is thus possible to make adjustments to foundational or methodological principles to permit a more direct comparison, synthesis, or integration across explanatory sketches about similar phenomena even if these sketches are drawn from different traditions. This may pose problems for classifying all social science and international relations research in terms of distinct and competing research traditions (Ben-David 1978: 744–5). Yet it is precisely this flexibility in Laudan's understanding of research tradition that opens the door to thinking about the possibilities and merits of analytical eclecticism in relation to discrete problems in international relations.

Eclecticism and problem-solving

Analytical eclecticism detaches explanatory sketches from the competing metatheoretical systems in which they are embedded. It offers us an opportunity to draw upon clusters of empirical observations, causal logics, and interpretations spanning different research traditions. It thus permits us to take advantage of complementarities in the problems we address and the empirical claims we make. Ronald Jepperson (1998) has already alerted us to the combinatorial potential arising from several different types of complementarity.

Simple complementarity, he suggests, relies on the specialization of different perspectives in different empirical domains. Additive complementarity focuses on types of effects, now often called "mechanisms," such as aggregation (choice theoretic), selection (population ecology), or social construction (institutionalism). Modular complementarity either utilizes different approaches at different "stages" of a process, or it nests arguments constructed at one level of analysis within more general arguments constructed at a different level of analysis. Finally, complementarity in problem recognition combines some sketch that isolates and describes phenomena with a newly acquired significance, with another sketch that may be adept at providing explanations for these phenomena even though it may not have recognized them in the first place.

Although specialists from competing research traditions do not view their relationship to one another in these terms, in scholarly practice simple complementarity is not unknown in international relations. Explicit acknowledgment of this fact might help in taking advantage of other forms of complementarity, for example in the definition of problems or in the development of explanatory sketches. Problem recognition complementarity, for example, can lead us to view systemic outcomes and state behavior as part and parcel of the same problem in Asian affairs; thus, China's sensitivity on Taiwan, ASEAN members' interest in a continued U.S. role, and Japan's explorations in multilateralism could be viewed as interrelated trends tending toward regional stability or conflict. This could set the stage for explanatory sketches that rely on modular complementarity in complex arrangements where, for example, a constructivist account of identity formation may establish variation in threat perception across states that can then be employed to understand variations in the enthusiasm with which states pursue absolute gains through open regional institutions or relative gains through strategic alliances intended to offset the capabilities of a stronger regional power (Rousseau 2002).

Analytical eclecticism does not privilege any one type of combinatorial formula or seek to build a unified theory encompassing each and every variable identified in competing research traditions. Eclecticism is distinguished simply by the articulation of more complex problematiques that emphasize connections between outcomes stipulated in puzzles investigated in different research traditions, and by the construction of explanatory sketches that incorporate data, interpretations, and causal logics from at least two distinct traditions. That is, analytical eclecticism regards existing research traditions fluidly and is willing to borrow selectively from each to construct accounts that travel across the sides of the triangle representing constructivism, realism, and liberalism (Figure 10.2).

The basic logic of eclecticism is not limited to the triad of approaches we are discussing here. For example, in research communities outside the United States rationalist analysis has occupied a less central place in the study of international relations compared to identities and other ideational structures.

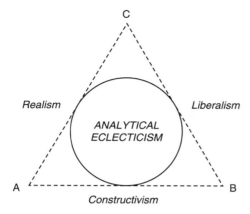

Figure 10.2 The possibilities of eclecticism

There the plea for analytical eclecticism might be tilted more toward integrating empiricist perspectives on international politics with postmodernist theoretical stances and text-based styles of analysis typical of the humanities. Alternatively, in a wider arena of research, eclecticism may take the form of identifying ways to bridge the gulf between the social and natural sciences, as is evident in recent creative advances in neuroscience, evolutionary biology, and the study of complexity. The point is that eclecticism is a relative construct, significant mainly as a strategy for coping with existing scholarly debate in a field in which competing perspectives may be reasonably identified as discrete research traditions. As an alternative to joining in such a debate on behalf of one or another perspective or dismissing it as proof of the fundamental incommensurability of theories, eclecticism explores new combinations of assumptions, concepts, interpretations, and methods embedded in explanatory sketches generated by competing research traditions. The potential value of engaging in such combinatorial exercises may be understood by way of analogy to two stories about watchmaking that exhibit what Arthur Koestler dubbed "holonic principles of architecture," the relation between the whole and its parts (Mathews 1996). For Herbert Simon (1981: 200–2) the social world consists of partly decomposable systems with tight causal linkages among specific sets of factors that, loosely linked to other clusters, form a weakly linked, broader ensemble. Simon tells a parable of two Swiss watchmakers that illustrates the advantage of eclectic reasoning. Tempus built his watch from separate parts. When he was disturbed and had to put an unfinished watch down on the table, it came apart, and Tempus had to start all over again. He built few watches. Horus built his watches by assembling the individual pieces into modules that he subsequently integrated to make a watch. When he was disturbed he put down the module he was working on and thus lost less time and labor. He built many watches. A second story comes from the more recent history of watchmaking. Seiko's watchmakers revolutionized miniaturization by splitting the motor into three components and inserting them into tiny spaces between the watch's gears. Rather than thinking, as did the Swiss, of motor and gear as natural components that help in the production of the watch, Seiko engineers thought of the total product and the purpose and role of each component in relation to the whole (Mathews 1996: 27–8). Horus and Tempus, the Swiss and Seiko proceed quite differently; but what made a difference in the productivity of Horus and Seiko was their recognition of the different ways the elements of a system could be assembled in different combinations of modules or subsystems. This, in turn, enabled them to ultimately solve problems that were not even recognized as such by Tempus or the Swiss.

Recognizing and solving problems, in fact, are at the heart of Laudan's view of scientific progress. Solved problems constitute scientific progress; unsolved problems chart areas for future exploration; and anomalous problems are those that a competing explanatory sketch may be able to solve. Research traditions and explanatory sketches vary in the kinds of problems they identify, the efficacy with which they solve these problems, and the extent to which they avoid anomalies (Laudan 1996: 79–81). The rationality and cumulation of scientific process ultimately depend less on the evolution, coherence, and status of different research traditions and more on their contribution to "problem-solving progress" (Laudan 1977: 109).

In principle, all explanatory sketches and research traditions contribute to problem solving and all have the "capacity to enable new observations of the world and thus even to generate entire new descriptive phenomenologies" (Jepperson 1998: 4). The quality of research still depends significantly on the kinds of information available and on the skills, intuition, and intellectual creativity of the researcher. Yet in contemporary international relations scholarship constructivist, liberal, and realist explanatory sketches differ greatly in terms of the kinds of insights they offer. Some sketches get much more purchase for understanding individual choices at the micro level, others for illuminating processes at the macro level; some sketches can make us understand problems of strategic interactions among actors, others the processes by which the actors acquire and alter their identities; some sketches are well suited for contexts in which material capabilities are decisive for explaining outcomes, others for contexts in which individual beliefs are of central importance, still others for those in which collective norms are of primary causal or constitutive importance. These differences do not merely represent competing empirical claims. They reveal also differences in problem focus and in the capacity to solve particular kinds of problems. Relying on sketches that draw on several research traditions, without being fully beholden to any one of them, is a virtue not a vice of a problem-focused eclectic approach. Its virtue lies in a pragmatism that avoids rigid commitments to working only within existing research traditions. For example, an eclectic approach alerts us to the possibility that balance-of-power arguments inspired by realist theory may have connections to security community arguments following a constructivist logic, enabling us to better articulate and understand such problems as the evolution of international relations in northern Europe (Katzenstein 1996). For Laudan, as for Chairman Deng, combining research traditions is a pragmatic move: it makes no difference whether the cat is black or white as long as it catches mice.

Attention to problem-solving is necessary but not sufficient for progress in international relations research. As Laudan himself recognizes, problem and tradition are after all intertwined: by their very nature research traditions are likely to channel attention toward particular empirical issues that appear to be more readily problematized using their preferred conceptual and method-ological apparatus. Moreover, there is the possibility that judgments about the problem-solving efficacy of specific research traditions may prompt some researchers to shift their tentative commitment prematurely from one trad-ition to another, even though such judgments presume that it is the same problem that is being explored in competing traditions and the same stand-ard that is being used in determining whether and how efficaciously the problem is solved. How should we think about problems that exist apart from traditions and sketches? How can we even communicate a problem in a language that will be intelligible to more than one research tradition? What is the status of unsolved problems that are potential rather than actual? And how do we form a consensus about the point at which a problem can be declared to have been solved? Realists, for example, are not likely to concern themselves with such problems as the rules governing entry into the WTO or the rate of diffusion of human rights norms across particular countries. Simi-larly, neither liberals nor constructivists are likely to expend much energy on problems of deterrence failure or the relative utility of offensive/defensive balances. Thus, claims that such problems have been solved are not likely to impress all students of international affairs, whether these claims are from proponents of specific research traditions or from scholars oriented toward eclecticism. In other words, research problems in international relations are not always like Chairman Deng's mice; in some cases, a cat may not even know that there is a mouse to be caught, and in other cases the white cat and black cat may have different rules for deciding if, when, and how quickly a mouse has been caught.

Ultimately, then, the case for analytical eclecticism is dependent not on its ability to solve specific problems already identified by one or another research tradition, but on the possibility of expanding the scope of research problems beyond that of each of the competing research traditions. Following Robert Cox (1981), we might say that in contrast to theory that aims to solve problems posed within a given perspective, eclecticism is closer in spirit to critical theorizing in transcending existing analytic subdivisions and research parameters to construct a larger picture of the prevailing order and its origins. In that way our questions may come to resemble less closely stylized facts, a favorite of approaches dedicated to analytic parsimony, while resembling more the messiness of actual problems encountered by actors in the real world. Conceptual frameworks developed by competing research traditions are designed to problematize only select aspects of international life that are interconnected. Such analytic accentuation can be fruitful and is sometimes necessary in light of practical research constraints. It also poses specific risks. One is that assumptions deemed valuable for solving the kinds of problems favored by a given research tradition will be hoisted upon the analysis of other kinds of problems for which these assumptions may not be well suited. For example, neorealist explanations aiming to show that central aspects of EU politics are best captured by relative-gains calculations have failed to generate a distinctive research tradition dealing with the EU (Grieco 1990). Another risk is that explanatory sketches nested within research traditions may only pay attention to certain aspects of problems and to certain preselected variables, ignoring a wide range of factors that are potentially relevant to recognizing and solving a more comprehensively defined problem. The total silence of a voluminous literature on U.S. grand strategy on the topic of terrorism is, after September 11, a shocking intellectual failure explainable largely in terms of an overly narrow conception of security and security-relevant actors (Crenshaw 2002).

This plea for analytical eclecticism is predicated not on the rejection of research traditions or on the futility of the research products they generate, but on the hunch that there are significant intellectual gains to be had from reversing the trade-offs faced by scholars working in one or another research tradition. Following Robert Alford (1998: 9), we do not seek to dissolve or reify the tensions between different traditions and sketches, but do believe that researchers who can theorize their problems within multiple traditions are in a better position to recognize previously hidden aspects of social reality. Since no one analytic perspective can confidently claim to offer all the insights we need, "the best case for progress in the understanding of social life lies in . . . the expanding fund of insights and understandings derived from a wide variety of theoretical inspirations" (Rule 1997: 18).

Eclecticism and Asian security: the shrinking of "natural expectations"

The relevance of different research traditions to different theoretical and empirical domains cannot conceal the fact that every research tradition generates its own unquestioned, that is "natural," worldview. This worldview contains within it templates that draw investigators to certain problems at the expense of other, related ones, to specify a priori the most relevant variables in understanding these problems, and, in the process, to identify some sources of behavior among actors while discounting others. Asian security offers ample illustrations for this proposition. The totally unanticipated end of the Cold War and collapse of the Soviet Union, for example, generated not reexamination of whether and why theories drawn from the major research traditions had proven inadequate. Instead, these events yielded another round of ad hoc explanations and bold predictions that essentially served to protect the natural worldviews embedded in each of the traditions. Getting trapped in unexamined premises is as easy for the adherents of all research traditions as it is for proponents of public policy. September 11 provides an illustration for how unexamined premises can generate striking simplifications, as does the stark distinction between "good" and "evil" as a rhetorical map for U.S. foreign policy in a strikingly complex international reality. This binary distinction is based on a cascading of mutually reinforcing images and the causal effects they imply: peaceful relations with prosperous, efficient states that are friends of America contrast with warlike relations with poor, inefficient states that are America's enemies. Explanatory sketches tend to be somewhat more subtle in the projection of worldviews, but the tendency toward undue simplification is still in evidence and is often debilitating to the endeavor of stating and resolving complex problems. Asian security is more complex than the unintended or deliberate cumulation of positive and negative images permits and than the natural expectations of any of the three research traditions accommodates.

For example, efforts to preserve and apply a realist worldview in the post-Cold War era initially led to overly pessimistic scenarios for Asia. Aaron Friedberg (1993/4: 7) thus argued that "in the long-run it is Asia (and not Europe) that seems far more likely to be the cockpit of great power conflict. The half millennium during which Europe was the world's primary generator of war (and economic growth) is coming to a close. For better and for worse, Europe's past could be Asia's future." We now know that the last decade has invalidated this prediction. To be sure, in the 1990s Asia had its share of military crises, and there remain numerous sources of lingering tensions that could easily lead to war. But it was Europe, not Asia, that was the scene of repeated episodes of ethnic cleansing and prolonged, bloody war. Our point is not that realist arguments must necessarily project pessimistic outcomes. Off-shore balancing (Mearsheimer 2001: 234–65) or nuclear deterrence (Goldstein 2001) may exert stabilizing if not pacifying effects. The initial application of realist concepts to Asian security dilemmas and national security strategies required simplification for the sake of consistency with a realist worldview. And these simplifications missed important parts of the story that had relevance for real-world outcomes even if that part of the story could not be told well in the theoretical language of realism. Although some neoclassical realists have sought to recast inexorable laws as tendencies that can be modified by the policy choices of rival states, notably the United States (Rose 1998: 171–2), in the end, such adjustments do not overcome the fundamental problem. An exclusive focus on realism, whether structural or neoclassical, privileges a particular set of problems and variables and arbitrarily precludes other lines of inquiry into potentially related domains.

Similarly unquestioned worldviews also mark liberal and constructivist styles of analysis. From a liberal perspective it seemed unquestionably true that Asia's economic miracle would continue, spurred on by the low transaction costs associated with close business–government relations, bringing another generation of prosperity. Yet the 1990s was the decade that showed Japan, Asia's largest economy, sinking into a structural economic crisis that has generated the highest unemployment and lowest growth rates the country has seen since 1945. Another example of a mistaken liberal analysis is the IMF's excessively optimistic assessment of the economic fortunes of Southeast Asia. A conference sponsored by the Bank of Indonesia and the IMF concluded in November 1996 that "ASEAN's economic success remains alive and well. . . . The region is poised to extend its success into the twenty-first century" (International Monetary Fund 1996: 378). In an April 25, 1997 press conference, IMF managing director Camdessus remarked that the global economic outlook warranted "rational exuberance" (International Monetary Fund 1997a). And at the spring 1997 meeting the Interim Committee of the Agreement committed itself to extend the IMF's jurisdiction to cover the movement of capital, thus completing the "unwritten chapter" of Bretton Woods, according to Camdessus (International Monetary Fund 1997b: 129). The rest, as the saying goes, is history. The Asian financial crisis began rumbling in Thailand in June 1997 and by the end of November massive speculation had forced very serious economic dislocations in Thailand, Indonesia, and South Korea and was soon to bring down the Suharto regime in Indonesia. In the following year, Brazil and Russia also fell as speculative attacks spread from Asia to the rest of the world. Now the contagion of liberal pessimism highlighted the disadvantages of the crony capitalism that marked the close relations between government and business, but also revealed the limitations of initial simplifications resulting from a liberal worldview.

Finally, constructivist analyses also make often far-reaching predictions based on unquestioned analytic premises. A theoretically innovative literature on ASEAN had extolled the emergence of a new collective identity in the early 1990s as ASEAN was moving toward an embryonic security community. ASEAN's ineffective response to the Asian financial crisis has forced some reassessment (Acharya 2003, 2001, 1999). So has the persistence of armed rebellion in Southeast Asia and the possible links of some of the resistance movements to global networks of terror (Katzenstein 2003; Tan 2000; Collier 1999). Constructivist scholars with a more pessimistic bent run the risk of making the opposite mistake. Thomas Berger (2000), for example, worries considerably about the force of ancient hatreds in an Asia in which race remains an acknowledged political force. Yet, compared to the early 1990s, there is no new evidence in Asian political or security affairs that gives more credence to this dark view. In both cases, a tendency to a priori privilege a particular type of identity led to simplified projections about the implications of that identity for cooperation or conflict.

None of the limitations exhibited by the application of natural worldviews, largely informed by the history of the European state system, to Asian security are especially surprising. The extension of realist insights from Europe to Asia, for example, cannot help but be incomplete. In contrast to Europe, the history of the Asian state system was shaped for many centuries by the principle of suzerainty. Furthermore, located at the European periphery, most Asian states were deeply affected by a colonial experience that was simply absent in the relations among the imperialist powers in the European core. Similarly, the nature of Asian political economies differs from that of Europe. It makes little sense to extrapolate from the political experience of the early industrializers with liberal market economies in Europe to the late industrializers with developmental states in Asia. Relatedly, in Asia the most important effect of international institutions, some of the case studies in this book suggest, is to maintain ambiguity about collective purpose while creating a sense of commonality, rather than to promote transparency of objectives while enhancing efficiency. Finally, the forming of supranational collective identities in Asia is affected deeply by national sovereignty having been acquired in the recent rather than distant past. And the nature of that collective identity may be affected substantially, in ways that contemporary theories of international relations have not yet begun to analyze, by the historical experiences and legacies of the Sinocentric world, which differ in many ways from the Greco-Roman world.

Natural expectations embedded in realist, liberal, and constructivist research traditions focus on the presumed likelihood of military conflict, economic prosperity, and variants of hyper- or supra-nationalism. Yet, in light of natural expectations that have remained unmet during the last decade, the complexities of Asian security invite further thought. This invitation extends not only to assessing questions of quantity, of more or less military conflict, economic growth, and collective identity. It also suggests that we inquire into the meanings of these concepts and the debates that surround them, that is, into the very factors that shape the world of beliefs and expectations that many of our explanatory sketches hope to comprehend. Far from applying a single logic ubiquitously or retreating to Orientalist or Occidentalist arguments about a supposedly unique "Asian" or "Western" way, stripping the political reality we seek to understand of its presumed "naturalness" is an important step to enabling intersubjective understanding. The analysis of discursive politics draws attention to the fact that, by definition, political reality is always contested and needs to be understood not only in general terms but also in relation to the specific political contexts in which it occurs and, as Weber reminds us, from the viewpoint of the actors involved. This requires a theoretical multilingualism predicated on the "denaturalization" of subjects and concepts as deployed in existing research traditions.

Thus, in the analysis of the security strategies of Asian states, an important task is to articulate a problematique that acknowledges the fluidity of the meanings attached to such terms as "Asia," "state," "strategy," and "security." Asia is not simply an objective geographic boundary that encompasses unambiguously several neighboring states. It is also an enduring set of social ties that have historically encompassed some sets of actors and relationships but not others, allowing for cases of both trust and mistrust, enmity and amity. Regions do not exist only as material objects. Although they have a behavioral dimension indicated, for example, by the flow of goods and the travel of people across physical space, they cannot be represented simply and succinctly by accurate cartographic depictions. They are also constructs that are imagined and thus can bend to the efforts of political entrepreneurs. Southeast Asia, as a category of geographic space, became a widely accepted term only in the 1940s and its persistence is closely associated with the history of the Cold War in that region. It remains to be seen whether this region will in a few decades acquire another designation such as "Maritime China" or "the extended Pacific Rim." And the very term "Asia" has been open to many and varied attempts at political interpretation. The "Asian values" discussion, for example, had perhaps the greatest impact among U.S. academics and in U.S. policy circles although it was mainly a belated 1990s export from Singapore which deployed the concept in the 1970s as it sought to unite its ethnically divided population (Katzenstein 2000).

The origins and character of "states" in Asia should also not be taken as unproblematic. Asian states are marked by suzerainty as a long-standing institutional legacy (Oksenberg 2001). The system of tributary trade relations organized around a central power not always interested in intervening directly in the affairs of lesser powers does not have a clear functional equivalent in the conventional interpretations of the Westphalian state system. We do not understand well how that legacy affects the worldviews and behavior of Asia's modern states. While most of Asia formally acceded to the Westphalian model of sovereignty that characterizes the globalization of the Western state system in the nineteenth and twentieth centuries, it would be very surprising indeed if such a legacy would have been superseded totally by the events of the recent past. We need to leave open the possibility that Asian states embrace somewhat different expectations about the boundaries that separate domestic from international affairs as well as about the motivations and behaviors of actors located in different spaces that connect both political domains.

Moreover, in understanding the "strategies" of states, it is important to appreciate that hegemony has material and nonmaterial components requiring that the hegemon's power in its various dimensions be recognized by less powerful actors who are expected to acquiesce to the hegemonic order (Mastanduno 2003). Asian states, and in particular China and its neighbors, define their individual, institutional, and national interests, incorporating beliefs about appropriate forms of governance, with special attention to the relevance of the existing regional and social context (Alagappa 2001: 63). For Asian security, Peter Van Ness (2002), David Kang (2003a, 2003b), and Jitsuo Tsuchiyama (2003) are all exploring the implications of a view that is predicated upon the assumption of hegemony as an important constitutive principle of international relations in Asia. This puts bandwagoning rather than balancing at the center of the analysis of Asian states' behavior. In their analyses they both draw on and undercut traditional theories of the balance of power, producing explanatory sketches that are not easily squared with the normal insights that any one of the major research traditions offers for our understanding of world politics.

Finally, compared to the notions shared widely among U.S. scholars and policy analysts, applied to Asia, the very idea of "security" needs to be understood in more comprehensive, historically contextualized terms, extending well beyond the military defense of territorial boundaries to encompass also a reasonable threshold of material welfare as well as collective understandings reflecting distinct ideational influences (Alagappa 1998a, 1998b). The latter encompass what Jennifer Mitzen (2002) refers to as "ontological security," a robust sense of collective identity embedded in a wider set of meaningful social relations. The military dimension of social life that is so central to U.S. politics is not absent in Asia. Far from it, as smoldering conflicts on the Korean peninsula, over Kashmir, and across the Taiwan Strait illustrate. But that dimension is embedded in the dramatic economic and social transformations that have reshaped much of Asia during the past half century and continue to do so today. In the understanding of many political actors it is that transformation and not Asia's distribution of military capabilities that is the politically defining aspect of the security landscape.

In light of these considerations, eclectic explorations with an open-ended understanding of the core subject: the "security" (broadly understood to encompass physical survival, material well-being, and existential security) "strategies" (reflecting different assumptions about actors' motivations and the character of power relationships) of "states" (which differ in historical experience and thus character from those in Europe) in the "Asian region" (as defined by the actors' own variable conceptions of the arena within which they have historically interacted with certain other actors). The "denaturalization" of the constructs that dominate perspectives on Asian security derived from existing research traditions is, however, only a first step. A second one is to open up possibilities for newly defined problems and causally significant interactions among variables normally privileged as part of distinct explanations embedded in competing traditions.

Before the mid-1990s, the theoretical discussion among scholars of international relations in the United States had concentrated almost exclusively on how to think about the relation between power and efficiency as realists dueled with neoliberals; only very recently has the crystallization of a constructivist research tradition prompted scholars of international relations to consider the intersection of issues of efficiency and identity or power and identity (Fearon and Wendt 2002; Katzenstein, Keohane and Krasner 1999b). In Europe, by way of contrast, liberal and constructivist scholars have been engaged in a long-standing theoretical debate about the relative significance of efficiency and identity, though sometimes at the expense of consideration of the continuing relevance of power. In the study of Asian international relations, an exclusive theoretical focus on either identity-driven state behavior, or regional institutions, or the distribution of military capabilities simply does not capture the complex political and analytic sensibilities triggered by different contexts. There exists considerable promise in combining the insights drawn from different explanatory sketches, seeking to understand the complex ways power, interests, and identities affect each other and combine to shape Asian states' behaviors and relationships.

Thus, for some of the authors, "institutions" are not only significant for minimizing transaction costs and enhancing efficiency among cooperating actors with separate interests (as liberals would stress); they are also constructions that reflect shared identities or the distribution of power among some sets of actors. Understood in this way, institutions produce shifts in actors' interests and identities, and can, in turn, be transformed by changing configurations of interest and identity. For other authors, power and wealth matter significantly, not as omnipresent and fixed determinants of behavior but as something mediated, constrained, and distorted by institutional structures and as something that is given meaning to and understood by actors in their social settings. Understood in this way, "power" may be significant not only as a means to defend borders or force others to cooperate, but also as a basis for formulas for decisionmaking within institutions or as a way of acquiring international prestige and diffusing "ontological security." For those concerned with ideational factors, norms and identities are significant not as ever-fleeting structures of meanings, but as something that is appropriated and denied by power and as something whose influence is facilitated and embodied by institutions that constitute actors and regulate their behavior. Understood in this way, "identity" becomes almost a statement about an actor's position relative to other actors, sometimes drawing attention to asymmetries of power, sometimes shaped by historical memories involving variable levels of institutionalized cooperation, and sometimes serving as a catalyst for cooperation or conflict. Were we to adhere strictly to any one of the three research traditions, these analytic possibilities would fall by the wayside or be viewed as epiphenomenal.

Conclusion

A problem-focused eclecticism is not cost free. In international relations research as well as in the social sciences writ large, the flexibility required of eclectic approaches may be too great to permit the formation of collaborations capable of mobilizing strong attachments and enduring professional ties, crucial ingredients in often not very subtle struggles for intellectual and other forms of primacy in the world of scholarship. Furthermore, the theoretical multilingualism that the expanded scope of problems and explanatory sketches requires may tax an individual researcher's stock of knowledge and array of skills while introducing also more "noise" into the established channels of communication, such as they are, within and across different research traditions. As a result, to those accustomed and committed to working within particular conceptual frameworks built on particular assumptions about social reality, the accommodation of eclectic perspectives may be dismissed as a waste of resources (Sanderson 1987) or merely undisciplined, "flabby" appeals for pluralism (Johnson 2002).

In light of the recurrent debates between, and inherent character of, research traditions, we are convinced that the advantages of eclecticism are well worth such costs. Without insisting that we have any prior knowledge of how best to construct different causal chains, we have gambled here on the intuition that analytical eclecticism can give us more purchase on interesting questions about Asian security than can analytic monism. The most significant advantage of eclecticism is that it facilitates intellectual exchanges that deepen and extend our understandings rather than producing the hard "truths" and "standards" of more parsimonious models addressing questions posed simply in the unidimensional space of only one research tradition. As Paul Diesing (1991: 364) notes, all explanations have to live with the fact that our truths will always be plural and contradictory. This does not mean that we need to give up the quest for explanation, and it does not mean that all analytic or empirical problems need to be considered from multiple analytic perspectives. What it does mean is that any *shared* sense of progress in the study of international affairs depends on a common recognition of the convergences, complementarities, and differences across substantive claims arrived at within different research traditions; and that this, in turn, requires a degree of methodological pluralism and analytic multilingualism that is more characteristic of self-consciously eclectic modes of inquiry than of approaches embedded in a particular research tradition.

The analytical eclecticism we embrace proceeds from a view of social scientific research as a collective endeavor, an ongoing practice built on inter-dependent relationships among individual researchers and research com-munities each with specific kinds of insights to offer in relation to particular questions cast at particular levels of generality (Sil 2000b). In this sense, analytical eclecticism has little in common with research traditions rigidly attached to core postulates, and more in common with calls for intellectual pluralism. Certainly, there are limits to how much integration can occur across approaches predicated on fundamentally incompatible foundational postulates and conceptual systems (Johnson 2002). Nevertheless, a principled refusal to "ontologize" analytic sketches offers something more disciplined paradigm-bound research cannot: it reinforces the dialogical character of international relations research and fights the tendency in scholarship to turn inward by preemptively establishing much stronger defenses of existing explanatory sketches than is warranted on intellectual grounds. For this reason, eclecticism is also principled in its opposition to the imposition of a uniform standard of scientific research practice, and, in line with current thinking among philosophers of science, it exploits the advantages and toler-ates the disadvantages of inquiring into multiple truths at different levels of abstraction. Considering the diversity of approaches and the different ways of establishing what is true, as revealed in current debates in the philosophy of science, insistence on any one standard, including that there be no standard at all, undercuts the social nature of scientific conversation. If the unit of evaluation is regarded as the community of social scientists as a whole rather than the individual researcher (Laitin 1995: 456), then creating more space for eclectic approaches is virtually a necessary condition for whatever progress may be possible in social scientific research if for no other reason than that it reveals connections, convergences, or complementarities between substantive insights usually presented in different theoretical languages within different research traditions.

The adoption of an eclectic stance tends to go hand in hand with a pragmatic, "post-positivist" epistemology that is open to explore conceptual and empirical connections between approaches located at different points on an "epistemological spectrum" (Sil 2000c) spanning absolute formulations of positivism and relativism. Such a pragmatism is predicated on the refusal "to accept as hard and fast the classic oppositions between understanding and explanation, between history and science, between objective and subjective" (Alford 1998: 123). Specifically, an eclecticism predicated on pragmatism involves viewing the social world as at least partially socially constructed; recognizing the difficulties this poses for defining social facts and analyzing actors' motivations; bracketing the investigator's own subjective perceptions and normative commitments; and accepting the uncertainty accompanying the analysis of a socially constructed world without giving up on either the systematic collection and interpretation of data or the task of seeking to persuade skeptical communities of scholars. Such a perspective also calls for attention to "middle-range" explanatory sketches that split the difference between nomothetic and ideographic research, negotiating between the formalism of parsimonious models and elaborate exercises in hermeneutics or phenomenology, and offering causal narratives that are transportable to a limited number of contexts, without being so far abstracted from these contexts that the operationalization of concepts for each case is open to vigorous contestation (Sil 2000b).[6] Research cast at such a level of abstraction will generate neither the most elegant models for investigating a problem nor the richest narrative about any one context, but it can enable simultaneous consideration of a wider range of analytic, interpretative, and observational statements drawn from varied social contexts and cast at different levels of abstraction.

In all these respects, eclectic modes of analysis contribute to what Thomas Fararo (1989) has referred to as a "spirit of unification," the diffuse intellectual state of mind required to enable consideration of combinatorial possibilities that have frequently produced unanticipated breakthroughs and common understandings of progress in the history of science.[7] Viewed in this light, a key benefit of analytical eclecticism is not to subsume, replace, or unify explanatory sketches from different research traditions, but to foster scientific dialogue and enable communication between the different communities that produce these sketches. The skill of listening and talking knowledgeably in the languages of more than one research tradition, although requiring a large investment in time and effort and a predilection for intellectual versatility, generates an analytic multilingualism that can foster new concepts and unexpected synapses, open up new avenues for research for all research communities and, last but not least, improve the tone of the collective discussions among scholars of international relations in general and national security in particular. The discourse culture of "taking no prisoners," so prominent not so long ago, may be on the wane. The sooner it disappears altogether the better for all of us. In the analysis of Asian security, and for the social sciences more generally, scientific dialogue is the best guarantee for progress, if progress is to be had, and the accommodation of analytical eclecticism offers the best hope for furthering scientific dialogue.

Notes

1   For critical comments and suggestions on prior drafts, we would like to thank Allen Carlson, Ron Jepperson, Alastair Iain Johnston, David Kinsella, Yuen Foong Khong, Audie Kotz, David Leheny, Nobuo Okawara, Karthika Sasikumar, John Schuessler, J. J. Suh, Alexander Wendt, participants of the PIPES seminar at the University of Chicago, participants of the research colloquium at the Free University Berlin, participants of the Cornell workshop on Asian Security, and the authors in J. J. Suh, Peter J. Katzenstein and Allen Carlson (eds) *Rethinking Security in East Asia: Identity, Power, and Efficiency*, Stanford, Calif.: Stanford University Press, 2004. The usual disclaimers obtain.

2   On neoliberalism, see the exchanges between Keohane and Martin (1995), Kupchan and Kupchan (1995), Ruggie (1995), and Mearsheimer (1995, 1994/5). On constructivism, see Duffield, Farrell, Price and Desch (1999), Desch (1998), Hopf (1998), and Wendt (1995). On rationalism, see the exchanges between Bueno de Mesquita and Morrow (1999), Martin (1999), Niou and Ordeshook (1999), Powell (1999), Walt (1999a, 1999b), and Zagare (1999). On realism, see Wendt (1995) and Mearsheimer (1994/5), and the exchanges between Feaver *et al.* (2000) and Legro and Moravcsik (1999).

3   Challenging Popper's gradualist theory of scientific progress as continuous and cumulative, Kuhn (1962) interpreted the history of science as a sequence of periods of normal science interspersed by shorter episodes of revolutionary science. Normal science is marked by the ascendance of a single paradigm that determines the central research questions, specifies the range of acceptable methods in approaching them, and provides criteria for assessing how well they have been answered. Revolutionary science occurs in those brief interludes when scientific communities, frustrated by increasing numbers of anomalies, begin to focus on new problems and take up new approaches that can address these anomalies. Once a new cluster of questions, assumptions, and approaches has acquired large numbers of supporters, this may pave the way for the emergence of a new and once again dominant paradigm. Significantly, paradigms are assumed to be incommensurable, with the standards and methods employed by supporters of one paradigm judged unacceptable by supporters of another.

4   Responding to Kuhn's rejection of objective markers of continuous progress, Lakatos (1970) introduced the concept of "research program." Thus, he captured more pluralistic scientific communities and left open the possibility for some limited comparisons of theories generated by competing research programs. For Lakatos, scholarship is marked by multiple research programs, some in

"progressive" phases, others in "degenerative" phases, depending on whether they are still capable of producing new theories that could explain new phenomena or surpass the explanatory power of past theories. At the same time, Lakatosian research programs have a number of features—a "hard core," a "protective belt" of auxiliary assumptions, and positive and negative "heuristics"—that essentially perform the same functions as Kuhn's paradigms.

5　See Walker (2003) for a more elaborate argument about why Laudan's understanding of research traditions is more useful than Lakatos's treatment of research programs for characterizing international relations scholarship and encouraging more cooperation than rivalry among proponents of different intellectual schools.

6　This strategy for negotiating the nomothetic–ideographic divide should be distinguished from the sort of integration attempted by proponents of "analytic narratives" (Bates *et al.* 1998). Analytic narratives proceed from a realist, not pragmatist, philosophy of science, and the principles of explanation in each narrative are ultimately embedded in a highly abstract model of strategic rationality the core logic of which remains unresponsive to the "thick" narrative. The thick narratives are constructed as interpretations that essentially reflect this logic but without reference to competing strands of historiography and without any possibility for generating alternative theoretical logics (Sil 2000a). A pragmatist approach to "middle-range" theorizing, by contrast, points to more modest generalizations within specified domains of inquiry, with a more dialectical understanding of the relationship between theoretical constructs and empirical interpretations.

7　Fararo (1989: 175–6) views "unification" as a series of recursive integrative episodes rather than the construction of a single theory supported by a heroic individual or a crusading group of researchers seeking to subsume everybody and everything. For example, Darwinian principles of natural selection first became integrated with the Mendelian hypothesis of inheritance through discrete genes, before a second integrative episode enabled this synthesis to incorporate principles of molecular biology. Both episodes required a diffuse state of mind that was open to consideration of facts and hypotheses from previously separate research traditions. It is this diffuse state of mind that Fararo refers to as the "spirit of unification."

References

Acharya, Amitav (1999) "Institutionalism and Balancing in the Asia Pacific Region: ASEAN, U.S. Strategic Frameworks, and the ASEAN Regional Forum," Toronto: Department of Political Science, York University/Singapore: Institute of Defense and Strategic Studies, Nanyang Technological University.

Acharya, Amitav (2000) *The Quest for Identity: International Relations of Southeast Asia*, Oxford: Oxford University Press.

Acharya, Amitav (2001) *Constructing a Security Community in Southeast Asia: ASEAN and the Problem of Regional Order*, New York: Routledge.

Acharya, Amitav (2003) "Regional Institutions and Asian Security Order: Norms, Power, and Prospects for Peaceful Change," pp. 210–40 in Muthia Alagappa (ed.) *Asian Security Order: Instrumental with Normative Contractual Features*, Stanford, Calif.: Stanford University Press.

Adler, Emanuel and Barnett, Michael (eds) (1998) *Security Communities*, New York: Cambridge University Press.

Alagappa, Muthiah (ed.) (1998a) *Asian Security Practice: Material and Ideational Influences*, Stanford, Calif.: Stanford University Press.

Alagappa, Muthiah (1998b) "Conceptualizing Security: Hierarchy and Conceptual Traveling," pp. 677–700 in Muthiah Alagappa (ed.) *Asian Security Practice: Material and Ideational Influences*, Stanford, Calif.: Stanford University Press.

Alagappa, Muthiah (2001) "Investigating and Explaining Change: An Analytical Framework," pp. 29–66 in Muthia Alagappa (ed.) *Coercion and Governance: The Declining Political Role of the Military in Asia*, Stanford, Calif.: Stanford University Press.

Alagappa, Muthiah (ed.) (2003) *Asian Security Order: Instrumental with Normative Contractual Features*, Stanford, Calif.: Stanford University Press.

Alford, Robert R. (1998) *The Craft of Inquiry: Theories, Methods, Evidence*, Oxford: Oxford University Press.

Ashley, Richard K. (1995) "The Powers of Anarchy: Theory, Sovereignty, and the Domestication of Global Life," pp. 94–128 in James Der Derian (ed.) *International Relations: Critical Investigations*, New York: New York University Press.

Bates, Robert *et al.* (1998) *Analytic Narratives*, Princeton, NJ: Princeton University Press.

Ben-David, Joseph (1978) "Progress and Its Problems: Toward a Theory of Scientific Growth," *American Journal of Sociology*, 84, 3 (November): 743–5.

Berger, Thomas (2000) "Set for Stability? Prospect for Conflict and Cooperation in East Asia," *Review of International Studies*, 26: 405–28.

Betts, Richard (1993/4) "Wealth, Power and Instability: East Asia and the United States after the Cold War," *International Security* 18, 3 (Winter): 34–77.

Bracken, Paul (1999) *Fire in the East*, New York: HarperCollins.

Bueno de Mesquita, Bruce and Morrow, James D. (1999) "Sorting through the Wealth of Notions," *International Security*, 24, 2 (Fall): 56–73.

Campbell, John L. and Pedersen, Ove K. (2001) "The Second Movement in Institutional Analysis," pp. 249–81 in John L. Campbell and Ove K. Pedersen (eds) *The Rise of Neoliberalism and Institutional Analysis*, Princeton, NJ: Princeton University Press.

Christensen, Thomas J. (1999) "China, the U.S.–Japan Alliance, and the Security Dilemma in East Asia," *International Security*, 23, 4 (Spring): 49–80.

Collier, Kit (1999) *The Armed Forces and Internal Security in Asia: Preventing the Abuse of Power*, Honolulu, East–West Center, Occasional Papers, Politics and Security Series, No. 2 (December).

Cox, Robert (1981) "Social Forces, States, and World Orders: Beyond International Relations Theory," *Millennium: Journal of International Studies*, 10, 2 (Summer): 126–55.

Crenshaw, Martha (2002) "Terrorism, Strategies, and Grand Strategies: Domestic or Structural Constraints?," paper prepared for presentation at the 43rd Annual Convention of the International Studies Association, March 24–7, New Orleans, La.

Desch, Michael C. (1998) "Culture Clash: Assessing the Importance of Ideas in Security Studies," *International Security*, 23, 1 (Summer): 141–70.

Dessler, David (1999) "Constructivism within a Positivist Social Science," *Review of International Studies*, 25 (January): 123–37.

Deutsch, Karl W. *et al.* (1957) *Political Community and the North Atlantic Area*, Princeton, NJ: Princeton University Press.

Diesing, Paul (1991) *How Does Social Science Work? Reflections on Practice*, Pittsburgh, Pa.: University of Pittsburgh Press.

Duffield, John S., Farrell, Theo, Price, Richard, and Desch, Michael C. (1999) "Correspondence: Isms and Schisms: Culturalism versus Realism in Security Studies," *International Security*, 24, 1 (Summer): 156–80.

Elman, Colin and Elman, Miriam Fendius (2002) "How Not to Be Lakatos Intolerant: Appraising Progress in IR Research," *International Studies Quarterly*, 46, 2 (June): 231–62.

Elman, Colin and Elman, Miriam Fendius (2003a) "Introduction: Appraising Progress in International Relations Theory," pp. 1–20 in C. Elman and M. F. Elman (eds) *Progress in International Relations Theory: Metrics and Methods of Scientific Change*, Cambridge, Mass.: MIT Press.

Elman, Colin and Elman, Miriam Fendius (2003b) "Lessons from Lakatos," pp. 21–68 in C. Elman and M. F. Elman (eds) *Progress in International Relations Theory: Metrics and Methods of Scientific Change*, Cambridge, Mass.: MIT Press.

Eyre, Dana P. and Suchman, Mark C. (1996) "Status, Norms, and the Proliferation of Conventional Weapons: An Institutional Theory Approach," pp. 79–113 in Peter J. Katzenstein (ed.) *The Culture of National Security: Norms and Identity in World Politics*, New York: Columbia University Press.

Fararo, Thomas J. (1989) "The Spirit of Unification in Sociological Theory," *Sociological Theory*, 7, 2 (Fall): 175–90.

Fearon, James and Wendt, Alexander (2002) "Rationalism and Constructivism in International Relations Theory," pp. 52–72 in Walter Carlsnaes, Thomas Risse, and Beth Simmons (eds) *Handbook of International Relations*, Beverly Hills, Calif.: Sage.

Feaver, Peter D. *et al.* (2000) "Correspondence: Brother, Can You Spare a Paradigm? (Or Was Anybody Ever a Realist?)," *International Security*, 25, 1 (Summer): 165–93.

Finel, Bernard I. (2001/2) "Black Box or Pandora's Box: State Level Variables and Progressivity in Realist Research Programs," *Security Studies*, 11, 2 (Winter): 187–227.

Finnemore, Martha (1996) *National Interests in International Society*, Ithaca, NY: Cornell University Press.

Friedberg, Aaron (1993/4) "Ripe for Rivalry: Prospects for Peace in a Multipolar Asia," *International Security*, 18, 3 (Winter): 5–33.

Gershman, John (2002) "Is Southeast Asia the Second Front?," *Foreign Affairs* (July/August): 60–74.

Goldstein, Avery (2001) *Deterrence and Security in the 21st Century: China, Britain, France, and the Enduring Legacy of the Nuclear Revolution*, Stanford, Calif.: Stanford University Press.

Goldstein, Judith, and Keohane, Robert (1993) "Ideas and Foreign Policy: An Analytic Framework," pp. 3–30 in Robert Keohane and Judith Goldstein (eds) *Ideas and Foreign Policy*, Ithaca, NY: Cornell University Press.

Grieco, Joseph M. (1990) *Cooperation among Nations; Europe, America, and Non-Tariff Barriers to Trade*, Ithaca, NY: Cornell University Press.

Grinker, Roy (1998) *Korea and Its Futures: Unification and the Unfinished War*, New York: St Martin's Press.

Haas, Ernst B. (2001) "Does Constructivism Subsume Neo-functionalism?," in Thomas Christiansen, Knud Erik Jørgensen, and Antje Wiener (eds) *The Social Construction of Europe*, London: Sage.

Haas, Peter M. and Haas, Ernst B. (2002) "Pragmatic Constructivism and the Study of International Institutions," *Millennium*, 31, 3: 573–601.

Hall, John A. and Paul, T. V. (1999) "Preconditions for Prudence: A Sociological Synthesis of Realism and Liberalism," pp. 67–77 in T. V. Paul and John A. Hall (eds) *International Order and the Future of World Politics*, Cambridge: Cambridge University Press.

Hall, Peter A. (2003) "Adapting Methodology to Ontology in Comparative Politics," pp. 373–404 in James Mahoney and Dietrich Rueschemeyer (eds) *Comparative Historical Analysis in the Social Sciences*, Cambridge: Cambridge University Press.

Hedman, Eva-Lotta (2002) "The Threat of 'Islamic Terrorism'? A View from Southeast Asia," *Harvard Asia Quarterly*, 6, 2 (Spring): 38–43.

Hellmann, Gunther *et al.* (2003) "Are Dialogue and Synthesis Possible in International Relations?," *International Studies Review*, 5, 1 (March): 123–53.

Hirschman, Albert O. (1970) "The Search for Paradigms as a Hindrance to Understanding," *World Politics*, 22, 2 (April): 329–43.

Hirschman, Albert O. (1981) *Essays in Trespassing*, New York: Cambridge University Press.

Hopf, Ted (1998) "The Promise of Constructivism in International Relations Theory," *International Security*, 23, 1 (Summer): 171–200.

Ikenberry, John G. and Mastanduno, Michael (eds) (2003) *International Relations Theory and the Asia Pacific*, New York: Columbia University Press.

International Monetary Fund (1996) "ASEAN's Sound Fundamentals Bode Well for Sustained Growth," *IMF Survey* (November 25): 377–8.

International Monetary Fund (1997a) "Good Governance: The IMF's Role," Washington, DC: The International Monetary Fund.

International Monetary Fund (1997b) "IMF Wins Mandate to Cover Capital Accounts, Debt Initiative Put in Motion," *IMF Survey* (May 12): 129–33.

Jepperson, Ronald L. (1998) "Relations among Different Theoretical Imageries," paper presented at the Annual Meeting of the American Sociological Association.

Jick, Todd D. (1979) "Mixing Qualitative and Quantitative Methods: Triangulation in Action," *Administrative Science Quarterly*, 24, 4: 602–11.

Johnson, James (2002) "How Conceptual Problems Migrate: Rational Choice, Interpretation and the Hazards of Pluralism," *Annual Review of Political Science*, 5: 223–48.

Johnston, Alastair Iain (1995) *Cultural Realism: Strategic Culture and Grand Strategy in Chinese History*, Princeton, NJ: Princeton University Press.

Johnston, Alastair Iain (1999) "The Myth of the ASEAN Way? Explaining the Evolution of the ASEAN Regional Forum," pp. 287–324 in H. Haftendorn, R. Keohane, and C. Wallander (eds) *Imperfect Unions: Security Institutions over Time and Space*, New York: Oxford University Press.

Johnston, Alastair Iain (2001) "Treating International Institutions as Social Environments," *International Studies Quarterly*, 45, 4: 487–501.

Johnston, Alastair Iain (2004) "Beijing's Security Behavior in the Asia-Pacific: Is China a Dissatisfied Power?," pp. 34–96 in J. J. Suh, Peter J. Katzenstein, and Allen Carlson (eds) *Rethinking Security in East Asia: Identity, Power, and Efficiency*, Stanford, Calif.: Stanford University Press.

Kang, David C. (2003a) "Getting Asia Wrong: The Need for New Analytic Frameworks," *International Security*, 27, 4 (Spring): 57–85.

Kang, David C. (2003b) "Hierarchy and Stability in Asian International Relations," pp. 163–89 in G. John Ikenberry and Michael Mastanduno (eds) *International Relations Theory and the Asia-Pacific*, New York: Columbia University Press.

Kapstein, Ethan B. (1999) "Does Unipolarity Have a Future?," pp. 464–90 in Ethan B. Kapstein and Michael Mastanduno (eds) *Unipolar Politics: Realism and State Strategies after the Cold War*, New York: Columbia University Press.

Katzenstein, Peter J. (1996) "Regionalism in Comparative Perspective," *Cooperation and Conflict*, 31, 2 (June): 123–59.

Katzenstein, Peter J. (2000) "Regionalism and Asia," *New Political Economy*, 5, 3: 353–68.

Katzenstein, Peter J. (2003) "Same War—Different Views: Germany, Japan, and Counter-Terrorism," *International Organization*, 57, 4 (Fall): 731–60.

Katzenstein, Peter J., Keohane, Robert O., and Krasner, Stephen D. (1999a) "*International Organization* and the Study of World Politics," pp. 5–46 in Peter J. Katzenstein, Robert O. Keohane and Stephen D. Krasner (eds) *International Organization at Fifty: Exploration and Contestation in the Study of International Politics*, Cambridge, Mass.: MIT Press.

Katzenstein, Peter J., Keohane, Robert O., and Krasner, Stephen D. (eds) (1999b) *International Organization at Fifty: Exploration and Contestation in the Study of International Politics*, Cambridge, Mass.: MIT Press.

Keohane, Robert O. and Martin, Lisa (1995) "The Promise of Institutionalist Theory," *International Security*, 20, 1 (Summer): 39–51.

Kerr, Pauline, Mack, Andrew, and Evans, Paul (1995) "The Evolving Security Discourse in the Asia-Pacific," pp. 233–55 in Andrew Mack and John Ravenhill (eds) *Pacific Cooperation: Building Economic and Security Regimes in the Asia-Pacific Region*, Boulder, Colo.: Westview.

Khong, Yuen Foong (1997a) "ASEAN and the Southeast Asian Security Complex," pp. 318–39 in David Lake and Patrick Morgan (eds) *Regional Orders: Building Society in a New World*, University Park, Pa.: Pennsylvania State University Press.

Khong, Yuen Foong (1997b) "Making Bricks without Straw in the Asia Pacific?," *Pacific Review*, 10, 2: 289–300.

Kinsella, David and Chima, Jugdep S. (2001) "Symbols of Statehood: Military Industrialization and Public Discourse in India," *Review of International Studies*, 27: 353–73.

Kuhn, Thomas (1962) *The Structure of Scientific Revolutions*, Chicago, Ill.: University of Chicago Press.

Kupchan, Charles A. and Kupchan, Clifford A. (1995) "The Promise of Collective Security," *International Security*, 20, 1 (Summer): 52–61.

Kurata, Hideya (1996) "Multilateralism and the Korean Problem with Respect to the Asia-Pacific Region," *Journal of Pacific Asia*, 3: 129–47.

Laitin, David (1995) "Disciplining Political Science," *American Political Science Review*, 89, 2 (June): 454–6.

Lakatos, Imre (1970) "Falsification, and the Methodology of Scientific Research Programmes," pp. 91–196 in Imre Lakatos and Alan Musgrave (eds) *Criticism and the Growth of Knowledge*, New York: Cambridge University Press.

Laudan, Larry (1977) *Progress and Its Problems: Toward a Theory of Scientific Growth*, Berkeley, Calif.: California Press.

Laudan, Larry (1984) *Science and Values*, Berkeley, Calif.: University of California Press.

Laudan, Larry (1990) *Science and Relativism: Some Key Controversies in the Philosophy of Science*, Chicago, Ill.: University of Chicago Press.

Laudan, Larry (1996) *Beyond Positivism and Relativism: Theory, Method, and Evidence*, Boulder, Colo.: Westview.

Layne, Christopher (1997) "From Preponderance to Offshore Balancing," *International Security*, 22, 1: 86–124.

Legro, Jeffrey W. and Moravcsik, Andrew (1999) "Is Anybody Still a Realist?," *International Security*, 24, 2 (Fall): 5–55.

Lichbach, Mark (2003) *Is Rational Choice Theory All of Social Science?*, Ann Arbor, Mich.: University of Michigan Press.

Makinda, Samuel M. (2000) "International Society and Eclecticism in International Relations Theory," *Cooperation and Conflict*, 35, 2: 205–16.

Martin, Lisa L. (1999) "The Contributions of Rational Choice: A Defense of Pluralism," *International Security*, 24, 2 (Fall): 74–83.

Mastanduno, Michael (2003) "Incomplete Hegemony: The United States and Security Order in Asia," pp. 141–70 in Muthia Alagappa (ed.) *Asian Security Order: Instrumental with Normative Contractual Features*, Stanford, Calif.: Stanford University Press.

Mathews, John (1996) "Holonic Organisational Architectures," *Human Systems Management*, 15: 27–54.

Mearsheimer, John (1994/5) "The False Promise of International Institutions," *International Security*, 19, 3 (Winter): 5–49.

Mearsheimer, John (1995) "A Realist Reply," *International Security*, 20, 1 (Summer): 82–93.

Mearsheimer, John (2001) *The Tragedy of Great Power Politics*, New York: W. W. Norton.

Mitzen, Jennifer (2002) "Dangerous Attachments: The Dilemma of Ontological Security," unpublished paper (August), University of Chicago.

Mochizuki, Mike M. and O'Hanlon, Michael (1998) "A Liberal Vision for the U.S.–Japan Alliance," *Survival*, 40, 2 (Summer): 127–34.

Moon, Chung-in and Chun, Chaesung (2003) "Sovereignty: Dominance of the Westphalian Concept and Implications for Regional Security," pp. 106–37 in Muthia Alagappa (ed.) *Asian Security Order: Instrumental with Normative Contractual Features*, Stanford, Calif.: Stanford University Press.

Moravcsik, Andrew (2003) "Liberal International Relations Theory: A Scientific Assessment," pp. 159–204 in C. Elman and M. F. Elman (eds) *Progress in International Relations Theory: Metrics and Methods of Scientific Change*, Cambridge, Mass.: MIT Press.

Niou, Emerson M. S. and Ordeshook, Peter C. (1999) "Return of the Luddites," *International Security*, 24, 2 (Fall): 84–96.

Oksenberg, Michael (2001) "The Issue of Sovereignty in the Asian Historical Context," pp. 83–104 in Stephen D. Krasner (ed.) *Problematic Sovereignty; Contested Rules and Political Possibilities*, New York: Columbia University Press.

Powell, Robert (1999) "The Modeling Enterprise and Security Studies," *International Security*, 24, 2 (Fall): 97–106.

Price, Richard M. and Reus-Smit, Christian (1998) "Critical International Theory and Constructivism," *European Journal of International Relations*, 4, 3: 259–94.

Rapoport, Anatol (1960) *Fights, Games, and Debates*, Ann Arbor, Mich.: University of Michigan Press.

Reus-Smit, Christian (2001) "The Strange Death of Liberal International Theory," *European Journal of International Law*, 12, 3: 573–93.

Rose, Gideon (1998) "Neoclassical Realism and Theories of Foreign Policy," *World Politics*, 51, 1: 144–72.

Rousseau, David (2002) "Constructing Identities and Threats in International Relations," unpublished manuscript (August 1).

Ruggie, John C. (1995) "The False Premise of Realism," *International Security*, 20, 1 (Summer): 62–70.

Ruggie, John C. (1998) *Constructing the World Polity: Essays on International Institutionalization*, New York: Routledge.

Rule, James B. (1997) *Theory and Progress in Social Science*, Cambridge: Cambridge University Press.

Sanderson, Stephen K. (1987) "Eclecticism and Its Alternatives," *Current Perspectives in Social Theory*, 8: 313–45.

Shapiro, Ian (2002) "Problems, Methods, and Theories in the Study of Politics, or What's Wrong with Political Science and What to Do about It?," *Political Theory*, 30, 4 (August): 588–611.

Sil, Rudra (2000a) "The Foundations of Eclecticism: The Epistemological Status of Agency, Culture, and Structure in Social Theory," *Journal of Theoretical Politics*, 12, 3: 353–87.

Sil, Rudra (2000b) "The Division of Labor in Social Science Research: Unified Methodology or 'Organic Solidarity' ," *Polity*, 32, 4 (Summer): 499–531.

Sil, Rudra (2000c) "Against Epistemological Absolutism: Towards a Pragmatic Center?," pp. 145–75 in Rudra Sil and Eileen Doherty (eds) *Beyond Boundaries? Disciplines, Paradigms and Theoretical Integration in International Studies*, Albany, NY: State University of New York Press.

Sil, Rudra (2000d) "The Questionable Status of Boundaries: The Need for Integration," pp. 1–27 in Rudra Sil and Eileen Doherty (eds) *Beyond Boundaries? Disciplines, Paradigms and Theoretical Integration in International Studies*, Albany, NY: State University of New York Press.

Simon, Herbert A. (1981) *The Sciences of the Artificial*, 2nd edn, Cambridge, Mass.: MIT Press.

Smith, Tony (1994) *America's Mission: The United States and the Worldwide Struggle for Democracy in the Twentieth Century*, Princeton, NJ: Princeton University Press.

Suh, J. J. (2004) "Bound to Last? The U.S.–Korea Alliance and Analytical Eclecticism," pp. 131–71 in J. J. Suh, Peter J. Katzenstein, and Allen Carlson (eds) *Rethinking Security in East Asia: Identity, Power, and Efficiency*, Stanford, Calif.: Stanford University Press.

Tan, Andrew (2000) *Armed Rebellion in the ASEAN States: Persistence and Implications*, Canberra: Strategic and Defence Studies Centre, Research School of Pacific and Asian Studies, The Australian National University.

Tarrow, Sidney (1995) "Bridging the Quantitative–Qualitative Divide in Political Science," *American Political Science Review* 89, 2 (June): 471–4.

Tsuchiyama, Jitsuo (2003) "From Balancing to Networking: Models of Regional Security in Asia," pp. 43–61 in G. John Ikenberry and Takashi Inoguchi (eds) *Reinventing the Alliance: U.S.–Japan Security Partnerships in an Era of Change*, New York: Palgrave Macmillan.

Van Ness, Peter (2002) "Hegemony, not Anarchy: Why China and Japan Are

Not Balancing U.S. Unipolar Power," *International Relations of the Asia-Pacific*, 2: 131–50.

Wæver, Ole (1996) "The Rise and Fall of the Interparadigm Debate," pp. 149–85 in Steve Smith, Ken Booth, and Marysia Zalewski (eds) *International Theory: Positivism and Beyond*, Cambridge: Cambridge University Press.

Wæver, Ole (1999) "The Sociology of a Not So International Discipline: American and European Developments in International Relations," pp. 47–87 in Peter J. Katzenstein, Robert O. Keohane, and Stephen D. Krasner (eds) *International Organization at Fifty: Exploration and Contestation in the Study of International Politics*, Cambridge, Mass.: MIT Press.

Walker, R. B. J. (2000) "Both Globalization and Sovereignty: Re-Imagining the Political," pp. 23–34 in Paul Wapner and Lester Edwin J. Ruiz (eds) *Principled World Politics: The Challenge of Normative International Relations*, Lanham, Md.: Rowman & Littlefield.

Walker, Stephen G. (2003) "Operational Code Analysis as a Scientific Research Program: A Cautionary Tale," pp. 245–76 in C. Elman and M. F. Elman (eds) *Progress in International Relations Theory: Metrics and Methods of Scientific Change*, Cambridge, Mass.: MIT Press.

Walt, Stephen M. (1999a) "Rigor or Rigor Mortis? Rational Choice and Security Studies," *International Security Studies*, 23, 4 (Spring): 5–48.

Walt, Stephen M. (1999b) "A Model Disagreement," *International Security*, 24, 2 (Fall): 115–30.

Wendt, Alexander (1995) "Constructing International Politics," *International Security*, 20, 1 (Summer): 71–81.

Wendt, Alexander (1999) *Social Theory of International Politics*, New York: Cambridge University Press.

Wolfson, Murray (ed.) (1998) *The Political Economy of War and Peace*, Boston, Mass.: Kluwer.

Xu, Xin (2003) "China and East Asia: Identity and Power in the Post-Cold War Era," PhD dissertation, Cornell University, Ithaca, New York.

Zagare, Frank C. (1999) "All Mortis, No Rigor," *International Security*, 24, 2 (Fall): 107–14.

Index